WILLING
TO LEARN

Mary Catherine Bateson

WILLING TO LEARN

Passages of Personal Discovery

STEERFORTH PRESS

HANOVER, NEW HAMPSHIRE

FOR CYRUS JAMES GRIFFIN

May you always be as curious as you are now.

〜

For information about permission to reproduce
selections from this book, write to:
Steerforth Press L.C., 25 Lebanon Street
Hanover, New Hampshire

Library of Congress Cataloging-in-Publication Data

Bateson, Mary Catherine.
  Willing to learn : passages of personal discovery / Mary Catherine Bateson. — 1st ed.
    p. cm.
  Includes bibliographical references and index.
  ISBN 1-58642-080-1 (alk. paper)
  1. Women's studies. 2. Sex role. 3. Self-realization. 4. Women — Social conditions. I. Title.
HQ1180.B38 2004
305.4'071 — DC22

2004013779

FIRST EDITION

CONTENTS

INTRODUCTION

Thinking Back

Although I no longer write poetry, I have chosen to begin this volume with a poem I wrote many years ago, which seems to express ideas that wind through the entire collection. Posed in the context of a particular genre and an earlier voice, it describes the discovery of worlds of difference and the vulnerable need to seek for pattern.

The Image

My life is a Chinese tray
Conforming to beauty,
A pattern of clear inked forms,
Too simple for truth.
The center is this cold lake
Where I sit,
Dipping slim fingers,
Watching reflections
Shimmering,
Distorted reality.
I sit there always,
Watching the grasses
Swaying, touching the lead lake,
Denting the Chinese tray
Painted with lilies.

And sometimes white birds,
Passing by,
Fly over my head,
Their reflections a troubling glimpse
Of a far off world.

Yet when they sometimes
Plummet
Down
Onto a silvery fish,
And splash,
Cleaving the waters,
Making my image shatter
Into strange fragments,
I have no meaning and I know fear.

The "I" of this poem, contained within the image of lake, shore, and sky, is living and wondering in a context highly stylized, a "Chinese tray" that permits only so much knowing but is open to the outside world. I grew up in New York City in the post-World War II era with highly cosmopolitan parents, so my use of "Chinese" refers to quite specific mental images, both familiar and exotic, seen in often visited households as well as in museums like the Metropolitan; it also echoes the experience of using brush and ink on rice paper, a medium that enforces an alternative vision. The birds may be read as intimations of sexuality, but they are also intimations of mortality, as well as glimpses of far-off worlds of possibility that are sometimes frightening but also liberating, liberating from a particular cultural way of construing the world. They suggest the task, as urgent for a fourteen-year-old as that of understanding sex, of defining and sustaining a sense of identity.

You do not even know that you "have" a culture until you encounter other ways of thinking and behaving. When I collected complaints and stories of misunderstanding between Americans and Iranians in the seventies, those were white birds I was pursuing. When I proposed "Thinking AIDS" as the title of a collaborative book, I was challenging readers to make meaning of a disruptive idea and of unfamiliar practices and alternative forms of sexuality, to change their habits of thought about life and love and biological vulnerability. Today we are challenged by other disruptive images: political events, such as terrorist attacks, and perturbations in the world's weather systems, to think more inclusively about other cultures and species, about the biosphere as a whole, to be unafraid as we make new meaning.

As I began the enterprise of looking back over essays and other short pieces I had written over the years, I was struck by a quality of unity that not only bridged differences of genre but affirmed those differences as a

source of insight, so I have included here pieces written in different styles
for publication in disparate settings, and put them newly side by side. I have
always been interested in the process of translation, the effort to frame the
same message in different ways, even as new meanings are created by a shift
in context. Courtesy requires very different behaviors in different countries,
but the visitor must adopt them to project a continuity of goodwill.
Familiar texts, reencountered in a new language, seem to me nearly unrec-
ognizable compared with English versions read earlier, yet moving back
and forth between them enriches the understanding. And the effort to
present an idea in the academic form appropriate to a scholarly journal may
show up hollow when explained in ordinary language, stripped of jargon
— or it may emerge from that cocoon as piercing insight.

I believe that all scholars should learn to explain their thinking to ten-
year-olds and then again to teenagers, as my parents took the trouble to
explain ideas to me — and also to share ideas through newspapers and television, from pulpits and from soapboxes. In this process of reshaping
they can discover much about what they are saying. Juxtaposing styles
produces oddities and is sometimes uncomfortable, but segregating them
produces distortion. In the same way, a division into conventional subject
areas is inappropriate. The lesson of whatever I have learned over time is
that looking carefully at anything — Arabic odes, for instance, or the
playful games of mother and infant — informs looking at everything.
Our task is to learn again to see things whole by respecting and treasuring
their "minute particulars."[1]

Habits of thought may be as distinctive as literary styles or even
handwriting. Of the many possible ways of thinking, my background
has led me to a lifelong search for pattern and its recurrence in different
contexts. In school I was drawn to math and the sciences on one hand
and to poetry on the other, interests that converged first in linguistics
and later in anthropology. This has meant a lifelong rhythm of intro-
spection, connecting personal experience to more distant phenomena,
exploring and testing metaphors and analogies to see what new insight
they might reveal. Sometimes the connection is visual, like Ezra
Pound's equation of the blank, pale quality of underground faces to
petals on a bough, sometimes abstract, like Ruth Benedict's comparisons of cultural patterns with individual personality types and psy-
chopathologies. Analogies are never perfect, so they can lead to error,
yet they are often surprising, opening doors of understanding from one

realm of experience to another. Beyond focused expertise, it is still possible to trace similarities between, say, the degradation of a forest biome and the decay of an urban neighborhood. Analogies from one person's experience to another's are often linked through the characteristics that all humans share: our bodies, our dependent beginnings, our growth through multiple stages, our learning and our dying.

My concern has been to look at these linkages and beyond them to larger contexts. All that we do can be seen as participation in larger systems that are not fully understood, and what we believe we know can be seen as an aspect of identity, constructed and urgently defended against the unknown. In 1968 I coined the phrase "each person is his own central metaphor."[2] The pronoun dates it, but the idea is still central to my thinking about empathy as a product of self-knowledge. Now, however, I think of persons as much less separate, in spite of the experience of limited understanding. As I wrote in *With a Daughter's Eye,* "More and more it has seemed to me that the idea of an individual, the idea that there is someone to be known, separate from the relationships, is simply an error . . . we create each other, bring each other into being by being part of the matrix in which the other exists."[3] The metaphor unfolds beyond the self into a sense of the life of this planet, not only as the mother that bears us but also as the future life to which we give birth, and which we must care for in ever closer patterns of interrelationship, as earth and air, flora and fauna, our kind and others play their complementary sustaining roles in the whole.

One of the questions I have come back to repeatedly over the last twenty years is how it is possible, even among human beings, to interact with others who do not share the same codes, whether of language or of values. Code sharing is always incomplete, but I have never seen this as a reason to give up trying to understand. In addition to the possibility of learning the codes of the other, there is the possibility of developing rules of coordination. This is the question that underlies my work on mother-infant communication — two persons with very different kinds of competence, developing harmonious and delightful patterns of interaction, playing without a shared set of rules of the game, and of course changing and learning in the process. This interest led me into work on ritual and the process whereby rituals are invented, and into work on problems of culture contact. In a larger sense the question of communication across disparate codes resonates with the questions of adaptation or coevolution or learning, is in fact the same as all questions of the coupling of systems which are unlike each other. I find myself exploring metaphors that liken the human relationship with the natural world to the continually tentative and changing relationships within marriage or between parent and child, relationships that always include a degree of uncertainty and strangeness, that thrive on complementarity.

I find myself often exploring the nature of the attention that makes such relationships possible. Some kinds of writing allow the expression of these background interests, while others do not. Fifteen years after writing "The Image" and a decade after struggling to translate H. N. Bialik's poem "The Pool," in which he finds in the reflective surface a "riddle of two worlds," I began to think about how parents gaze at new-borns, profoundly mysterious and yet deeply loved, in much the same way. I think that the best hope for our species lies in learning new patterns of attention to each other and to the biosphere, patterns that grow out of curiosity and respect and allow for wonder and learning. As I wrote in 1984, "Passionate attention to a lake, with its respiration, its maturation and aging, its dependence on interlocked forms of balance, its reflection of the self, is equally puzzling, equally revealing, equally the beginning of love."[4] So this is another theme that has run through my work, and connects to the relationship between attention and commitment.

It seems to me that in trying to develop an understanding of matters of this sort, one has to move back and forth between very abstract and very specific levels of focus, and indeed between types of discourse varying from poetry to formal analysis. I tell a lot of stories, mostly from my own life, and as I collect stories and weave them together, a few underlying themes keep surfacing, while any given story suggests new applications. I use examples from my own experience as a way of moving from the general to the specific, and also as a way of bridging, even confounding, different types of discourse, "a motion through concentric metaphors." The work I do "expresses a belief that multiple small spheres of personal experience both echo and enable events shared more widely, expressions of moment in a world in which we now recognize that no microcosm is completely separate, no tide pool, no forest, no family, no nation."[5] As I write about the lives of individuals, I hope to show how they both adapt to and create their environments so that they in turn are able to grow within them. Ultimately, I see this process as related to the question of how humankind is to make a home on this planet without soiling or incinerating its nest.

Most of the pieces included here were written after the deaths of my parents and after my husband and I returned from Iran at the time of the revolution and I had to rethink priorities and directions at midlife. The four parts into which this book has been divided correspond roughly to major themes developed over the long periods that produced my books, themes that began earlier and echoed later, ebbing and flowing and overlapping, but the newest pieces are reflected nowhere else in my published work. Most of the pieces were written for publication, usually in response to a request, but a few are based on transcribed talks, edited in a more informal style. I have selected these both because they reflect missing themes and because they reflect interesting contexts and applications — a talk given in South Africa, for instance, in 1991, dealing with culture change and social learning. Wherever it has seemed relevant, I have provided the personal context for the writings included here.

Part 1, "Family Memoirs," consists of writings about my parents and thoughts about autobiography and memoir. The word *memoir* is key, liberating the writer from the scholarly responsibility to be complete and to attempt objectivity, emphasizing the selective role of memory. Biographers attempt to be inclusive and systematic, even though they may understand that this is necessarily impossible. Memoirists, by contrast, write about what seems important to them. My memoir of my parents, *With a Daughter's Eye*, has sometimes been described as a biography of one or both of them. It is neither, for I tried to limit myself to those aspects of their lives that only I could write and, except for necessary continuity, to speak of my own life only in relation to them. Biographies of each of them have been published, and biographers continue to delve in their archives.

Working with personal narratives over the years, I have become increasingly interested in what I call "learning narratives," the narratives of people for whom learning is the warp of life, the through-line around which all other event unfolds. This collection then is in some sense an intellectual autobiography, a tracing of my own explorations, but beyond that I think it unlikely that I will ever write the full narrative of my own life. Instead, my life finds its way into print piecemeal. Stories from my experience are important building blocks in everything I write, and I have developed a pattern over the years of beginning every talk with an example — nearly always from my own life — so my life is spaced out through these pages. The tone remains rather personal, striving for disciplined subjectivity, the sustained examination of my own experiences and feelings rather than the pretense of being a fully neutral observer. Readers seeking a more explicit sequence can consult the chronology (page 412).

Thinking about my parents' lives reignited an early interest in the life cycle, so part 2, "The Shapes of Lives," traces my interest in age and gender with a series of pieces sequenced by the stages of the life cycle and reflecting the teaching I have done over the last decade, working with ethnographic and literary life histories, as well as two of my books. For many of these pieces, written about American women and men, looking at a life stage allows me to focus on change in my own society. The shapes of lives are determined by culture as well as by biology, and as culture changes so do the experiences of childhood and adolescence, marriage and work, aging and even death. Changes in the shapes of lives often take us by surprise, unplanned for and unstoried, so that learning to imagine and compose lives differently is a challenge to creativity.

Part 3, "Culture and Conviction," is the most anthropological portion of this volume, moving on from a focus on individuals to deal in rather different ways with questions of culture, belief, and change, primarily in the Islamic world. Belief systems, religious and political, are at the root of many contemporary conflicts, and although I have done no research on the Middle East since 1980, it seems important to share what I know. Several of these essays, previously unpublished, have been developed from reflections drafted long ago because the questions they pose seem relevant today.

Part 4, "Ways of Knowing," deals with issues of epistemology: how we understand the human place in the biosphere and the connection of culture and biology. These essays are inspired by the holistic character of anthropology, dealing with all aspects of human life and bridging the social sciences, the humanities, and biology. Several of these pieces draw on systems theory as a way of approaching complex wholes.

Issues of learning have been present in all my work, only gradually emerging as the central connecting theme. It is not possible to think of lives without watching unfolding learning or to think of knowledge and belief without questioning how they are acquired or altered, for learning is the basic adaptive strategy of the human species. At one stage I planned to put pieces dealing with learning into a separate section, but I finally realized that virtually all of my writings deal with learning in some sense or other.

Before each piece I have given some basic details of time and place. This form of introduction frees me to arrange the pieces thematically rather than chronologically, and challenges me in turn to seek relationships, contrast, and counterpoint, tracing the expression of slowly emerging ideas in different historical contexts. I have tried to make this a book that can be read front to back with some sense of continuity, but readers can and will pick and choose, taking it up and putting it down at different points, backwards and forwards. I have tried to avoid improving on history, resisting the temptation to alter published material except for typographical errors and occasional lack of clarity or grammatical roughness. The editing is heavier in transcribed talks, even if these were published in a partially edited form by sponsors, and heaviest in materials drafted but not published at the time of writing — but I have attempted even there to remain true to my earlier understanding. There were many possible ways to organize this book, so these were choices — but I recommend both the index and the bibliography of my published work, to be found in the back, for readers who like to move in different ways.

Styles change over time, usage varies, and different kinds of publications edit to different standards. In general these variations have been left standing. Some items, like spelling, have been corrected for consistency. Because most of the readers of this book will not be orientalists, spellings of Hebrew, Arabic, and Persian have been simplified. Arabic words are spelled as they would be in transliteration, and Persian words are spelled as pronounced, but in both cases diacritical marks have been omitted. Some pieces are fully referenced, some have only general references, and others are unreferenced except for quotations.

Like "a ring when it's rolling," in "The Riddle Song," this collection does not end but curves back on the beginning and proves to be all about learning. The underlying challenge has to do with becoming aware of the process that defines our humanness: we are not what we know but what we are willing to learn.

I

Family Memoirs

My transition to thinking of myself primarily as a writer came about after my parents' deaths, which also passed on to me the responsibility for their intellectual legacies and for keeping their work available. In the case of my mother, Margaret Mead, I was dealing with a well-known public figure who had played a key role in making Americans familiar with anthropology — so public that several colleagues found that using her name could get them into print and even that they could achieve fame for themselves by attacking her. In the case of my father, Gregory Bateson, I was dealing with a thinker who had been much less in the public eye, and whose highly abstract explorations were less accessible to the reading public but have become significant in a number of fields. In both cases there was work that needed to be done, even though the tasks involved were sometimes intrusive. I do them because the books and ideas remain important. I continue to feel that the concept of "culture," which Mead did so much to insert into the thinking of ordinary Americans, is indispensable in working for understanding across lines of difference. I continue to feel that Bateson's call for systemic thinking is key to developing nondestructive environmental policies.

The task my parents left to me is not purely custodial, for I find myself in a constant process of rediscovery. I published my memoir of them, *With a Daughter's Eye,* in 1984 and have written about them together and separately over the years. Some of the tasks involved have opened for me doors of intellectual understanding. Others have played a healing role in the emotional process of bringing parental and childhood memories into adult perspective. Sometimes I refer to them as Margaret and Gregory, sometimes as Mead and Bateson. When I first started writing about my parents, I had read almost nothing in the genres of memoir and biography, and I went about the task in my own way, but over the decades that followed the processes of remembering and reflection became critical to my thinking about learning. Now when I use life histories in teaching, I require that each student do some autobiographical writing and some interview-based biographical writing so that, having tasted the nature of the task, they can read more intelligently.

When audiences ask how I feel about having grown up as the daughter of Margaret Mead or Gregory Bateson, I have several ways of responding. Sometimes I say there is only one solution to having a famous parent and that is to have two — especially if they are different from each other in important ways, offering alternative styles of living and thinking rather than a single daunting exemplar. Sometimes I say that when things are going badly and I am feeling low, I am tempted to blame it on them — but when things are going well I find myself gladly acknowledging how much they taught me and how many doors they opened. Above all, I am grateful to them for their unceasing curiosity and effort to understand and share that understanding, even as they were approaching death. As a child, I knew that they listened with genuine interest to my ideas and questions. That caring attention has surely been the basis for my own continuing curiosity and desire to learn.

GHOSTS TO BELIEVE IN

A Writer's Companions

My parents both played important roles in my becoming a writer, above all by filling the house with their own writing projects and those of friends, so that writing books seemed to me to be the normal activity of adult life. I submitted this reminiscence to *The New York Times Book Review* after I completed *Angels Fear*, the book my father was working on at the time of his death, and published it as a joint project. The *Times* supplied the title to the piece (the original title is included here as a subtitle) and eventually ran it in 1987 face-to-face with the review of *Angels Fear* (my brief career as a "center-fold"), heading the review with my father's assertion "I do not believe in ghosts." But although Gregory did not believe in any supernatural beings, he knew that we are all haunted in various ways by the past, and that ideas, including hopes and memories, can in the living world be causes of behavior.

—MCB, 2004

⌐

The true exorcism of ghosts occurs when they are gradually absorbed into the lives of the living. All last year I was writing dialogues with my father, Gregory Bateson, who died in 1980, an ironic activity because he also wrote dialogues — called by him "metalogues" — between a father and daughter, dialogues that were largely but not entirely fictional. Because there seem always to be changing fashions in mediumship, I want to be quite clear that the reality of these séances is exclusively mental, a setting for clarifying ideas. Gregory is gone in an entropy of ash and ocean, but his ideas have an ongoing life.

Writing new metalogues has been a task of many layers — to frame and complement the chunks of manuscript left at his death, to claim and then transcend the fictional persona he gave me (I have been cousin to Alice and Christopher Robin), to capture his real speaking voice as well as his stylized written voice so that I can debate with him.

Still, I used to sit at my computer feeling as if I could actually hear the dialogue I was recording. This recalls yet another ghost, my mother, Margaret Mead, sitting at the typewriter and acting as my secretary so I could learn to write. She believed that all children should of course be expected to learn to read and write, but that the avenues of fantasy and self-expression should not be made dependent on the mastery of these skills. What a child six or seven or even twelve years old can read is only a shadow of the richness of the child's inner life, and nothing more effectively inhibits creativity than the need to take responsibility for spelling and punctuation when these and even the handling of a pencil are still difficult and awk-ward. Many people have argued that the best way to teach children to read is to read aloud to them; she took this a step further and argued that the best way to teach children to write is to take dictation from them.

My mother was a harum-scarum typist, self-taught, using a few fin-gers, and very fast. Her words raced onto the page, and during most of her life the revisions and editing were done by others. My own first dicta-tions, before I could write at all, were probably letters — thank-you let-ters for presents and then letters to my father in the Pacific. Even when I could write adequately, the long fanciful letters she took at dictation expressed my thoughts more directly than anything I would have put down on my own.

When I was about eight years old my efforts became more literary, and my mother used to sit at an old manual typewriter while I paced, dictating chants and songs I had composed to the first snow or a new kitten, or page after page of rumination about moonlight on the water. She supplied the punctuation from the rhythms of my voice, but she taught me how to para-graph and how to use parentheses. These skills recur in the logical structure of every page of notes or public speech I produce, as a lasting awareness of the logical structure of the train of thought. What fun, as a nine-year-old, to instruct "parenthesis!" and then, "close parenthesis!" and to experience the fluidity of speech and thought translated onto the written page. I find the evidence of lessons in different genres as well, as I learned to dictate plays, derived from dramatic improvisations with my friends, with conventional stage directions: "Enter messenger." Still, when the princess turns to the king and says, "Okay, well, I guess I might as well go to bed," you hear my voice between living room and bedroom.

Once the link is made between voice and written form, the day will surely come when the intermediary is no longer needed or wanted. By the time of adolescence the skills should be in place for journals and letters too secret to share. About the time I was twelve, my mother's typewriter disappears from my files and is replaced by my own handwriting, the texts already suffering from the assumption that written language should differ from spoken; words like "alas" or "eve" or "ere" appear. By then, Margaret was less available to act as secretary and school was demanding ever more written assignments. Even so I had no real doubt that what I heard, or almost heard, in my mind could be captured on paper. Sitting down to write for myself began to feel like taking dictation.

The written word, like all our uses of language, starts from dialogue. Indeed, as I found when I did research on mother-infant interactions long ago, the forms of conversation — echoing, interrupting, and taking turns — are learned before language. Nevertheless, the history of literacy is also the history of the gap between speech and writing created by mystification and mechanical difficulty. It's not easy to be fluent with a chisel, and the permanence and hieratic control of the written form seem everywhere to have suggested a preference for the formal and the archaic, a preference from which we are only just recovering. Today we value the written word that reads as if it were spoken, but the writer must still reshape actual speech in order to bridge the irreducible gap between speech and writing.

It took several generations for linguists and lexicographers to learn to treat the patterns of speech as primary, yet it is only rather recently that the conventions of translation of speech into writing that resembles speech have come to be studied in their own right. Tape recordings of speech, when directly transcribed, do not look natural, and the writing of colloquial language has its own set of conventions. What, then, of the idiom that echoes in my mind when I call up my parents' voices and try to capture them on the page? Gregory's speech was often implausibly close to writing, Margaret's too swift for the slower reception of the written word, and yet readers say they hear their voices in my writing. What writers write is not what they hear — or not what could be captured by a tape recorder.

It is tempting sometimes to believe that the spoken word has only to be captured and pinned to paper, but this idea recalls the many other contexts in which we can only write what we attribute to someone else. The role of amanuensis has for a long time been largely a female role, with many hours of full collaboration that is only acknowledged in a phrase or two. Mediums are commonly women as well. It is likely that a person who claims to be no more than a channel for some voice of greater authority is actually making no little contribution to the message; sometimes the entire message comes from her unconscious but is inhibited by conventional restrictions. (This is not, of course, entirely a matter of gender. Moses and Muhammad among others took dictation with distinction.) The claim of merely passing on what one hears has many layers.

So many ghosts to be entertained without belief. The ghost at the typewriter or the ghostly interlocutor fade, but they have played a crucial role in the formulation of thought and the transition to the page. They remain in that place in memory from which all of the honored dead speak to enrich our thought, so that even when we speak, we echo many voices.

CONTINUITIES IN INSIGHT AND INNOVATION

Toward a Biography of Margaret Mead

My mother died in 1978, while I was living in Iran. The annual meetings of the American Anthropological Association were in session, and an informal memorial was gathered on the evening she died, so colleagues could reminisce about the many years when she had been the best-known anthropologist in America and probably in the world, an unmistakable figure carrying a forked thumb stick and wearing a scarlet cape. This was only the first of many memorials, including a more formal session at the annual meetings in 1979, where I gave this paper, hoping to lay out a framework for work to come. By then I had made the decision not to write a full biography of my mother, but I had begun work on my memoir. I was already concerned about the converging pack of biographers and their tendency to pull pieces out of context instead of looking for overall pattern in her personal and professional life. At the 1979 session, I used the word *continuities* — a favorite word of hers that has become increasingly important in my own thinking about the threads that weave through lives and that sustain the fabric of life in times of change — to refer to such patterns.

This was written before the appearance of Derek Freeman's attack on my mother* in 1983, which stimulated a similar session of critiques of his scholarship and defenses of Mead's.

— MCB, 2004

∽

---

* See page 55.

When a child sits down to write about a parent, the personal side of the relationship takes primacy. After all, I knew Margaret Mead as my mother — someone who comforted me when I fell down, who read stories to me, and maintained a certain kind of home — long before I was aware of her as a professional person and a public figure. It was even longer before I became aware of anthropology and began to shift into the kinds of interests that allowed us to consider each other as colleagues. I became fascinated by linguistics as an undergraduate, with no sense at all that this was a related field — no sense indeed that a paperback book she gave me as I was leaving for college, which captured my imagination forever, had anything to do with her life or her work. The book was Edward Sapir's *Language* (1921). Only gradually did I become aware that a habit of looking for pattern that my father had conveyed through natural history and my mother had conveyed through folklore and poetry, and I first learned to apply in linguistics, was a basic habit of thought of cultural anthropology, and that I had been brought up to look and think like an anthropologist. (My mother once said, speaking of the time when she and Ruth Benedict set out to convey to Geoffrey Gorer what was distinctive about their way of looking, that there were two alternative ways of doing this quickly: linguistics and kinship. Kinship was the way they chose.)

Another permeating influence from anthropology was a profoundly pluralistic and self-conscious approach to experiences and relationships. My mother titled the last chapter of *Coming of Age in Samoa,* "Education for Choice,"[1] and, when I was sixteen, she let me choose to spend a year in Israel on my own. By that time the notion was also ingrained in me that customs and standards are different in different places, that the rules and values of each could be decoded, and that my own emotional reactions contained essential clues. This had been taught through a network of fictive kin, each of whose culturally diverse homes represented a chance to observe and to participate.

Thus, I received an upbringing that I now perceive as profoundly but implicitly anthropological. Inevitably then, I see the task of recording personal memories of Margaret Mead and of my father, Gregory Bateson, as an anthropological task. There will be journalists writing about her, and scholars from other fields as well, but here I wish to emphasize the need for anthropologically informed study of the way in which the personal and the professional were integrated in this particular life history.

Anthropology has always been a discipline with a special sense of the importance of looking carefully at individual lives. Ideally, even as anthropologists have sought to arrive at generalizations about whole societies, they have maintained an awareness of the uniqueness of each informant. Margaret Mead was fascinated by the relationship between the culturally patterned and the idiosyncratic, both in her methodological writings[2] and in her approach to her autobiography, and felt that the study of temperament was still waiting to be developed.[3] She expressed this concern in her emphasis on the "anthropological sample," and I will want to take this concept very much into account in trying to understand her particular life history.

The "anthropological sample" is usually not representative or random or clearly stratified — it is simply available and articulate. On the whole, anthropologists, concerned with wresting maximum insight from a period in the field, have not been willing to limit their inquisitiveness to matters that could be explored with members of a systematic sample. Instead, their work has often included long hours with individuals whose very aberrancy made them self-conscious and who were stimulated by it to find the communication of their traditions to the outsider useful or interesting for themselves. In order to use the statements and actions of such informants in the construction of a measured view of a whole culture, field-workers have had to look carefully at how each informant fits in to the whole, at the way in which informants' views might be expected to complement or counterpoint or indeed contradict — but never be simply irrelevant to — the views of other members of the community. They are not representative but are indicative.

There is a sense in which it is possible to look at my mother's life as indicative of twentieth-century American culture, even as one looks at her writings about American national character and at her popular articles dealing with topical issues on the basis of a background knowledge of national character. At the same time, there are clear contrasts. She was clearly an unusual individual, coming from an unusual home life and education and launched into a career that violated contemporary expectations of her sex and, at certain times, excited hostility and criticism, and in that sense aberrant. At the same time, it is clear that her idiosyncratic gifts fitted in with important trends in this culture, so that at the time of her death, in addition to the respect that she was given as a scientist, she was immensely popular. She pleased people, made them feel better about themselves as individuals and as members of society, told them, perhaps for the first time, things that they found helpful or that they would be coming to believe. The affection and warmth that she felt she received from her own society (she used to speak especially of people's solicitude when she traveled) far outbalanced the occasional flurries of hostility, and this combination of a sense of difference with a sense of affection was an essential component in her stance as a field-worker and as a social critic. She would have conceptualized both in terms of individual uniqueness within integrating patterns and interpersonal commitments, rather than in terms of marginality.[4]

The task of putting Margaret Mead's work into context will involve many of the same processes that are involved in using the "anthropological sample." It will be necessary, as in evaluating the work of social scientists in general, to sort out the strands of cultural assumption that have been intertwined with empirical observation. Some ideas will turn out to be derived from a cultural ethos, and others will turn out to be expressions of personality; of these, some will not stand the test of transferability across cultural lines that would mark them as scientifically valid. I am concerned here, however, not primarily with the erection of a set of filters for eliminating what will later be seen to have been locally or temporally limited, but with the special opportunity offered by this life of looking at the productive interplay of these different factors in facilitating both observation and the communication of innovative ideas.

In dealing with the lives of colleagues, anthropologists are concerned in a way that surpasses the interest of other disciplines in their intellectual ancestors. Physicists and biologists debate the relationship between personality and insight, but such debates have traditionally focused on the question of how a given idiosyncratic character enabled a scientist to see or to formulate something that, because generally true, would surely have been seen soon in any case. Only rather recently have historians of the other fields of science begun to wonder seriously about the relativity of their own brands of knowledge. Anthropologists, however, have long been acutely aware of the extent to which the characteristics of an individual field-worker, like those of a lens, influence the cultural image refracted through them.[5] Especially in the age of heroes, and heroines, when the number of field-workers was small and the urgency of salvage anthropology at the forefront of awareness, the writings of a single investigator might determine the whole knowledge of an ancient tradition, and biography is perhaps the central task of our historians of science.

In fact, the growing concern in anthropology about epistemological questions[6] raises for all of us the issue of self-knowledge. Any scientist needs to know the properties of the instruments used for observation. An astronomer must understand the telescope; an ethnomusicologist needs to pay attention to the capacities and distortions of given recording equipment — perhaps more than the astronomer, for, in the field, he or she will be responsible for maintenance. Similarly, Margaret Mead became increasingly interested in the nature of her own mental processes. This led her to take a number of projective tests (especially the Rorschach, which she took repeatedly over a period of years and had interpreted blind), and to experiments with handwriting analysis. She also encouraged the psychologist Jean Houston to "study her mind," recording extensive introspective material on her associations and imagery. She maintained records of such things as tests of her vision and hearing, so that she would be able to monitor even slight degrees of impairment. In recent years, this interest occasionally created opportunities for flattery and for being self-serving, but I believe that it derived from a genuine epistemological concern.

Because she was aware of the extent to which significant personal experiences and relations shaped her perceptions, she treated the records of these as valuable scientific data, so that, for instance, the mementos of my childhood have been carefully preserved; she once said, when my godmother suggested removing them from the office, "Cathy probably has the best documented childhood in the United States, and we've got to keep all these records together." Knowing that having a child would affect her response to childbearing and child-rearing in other cultures, she had movies taken systematically. Unfortunately, the photographer was a few minutes late for the delivery.

Central to her work, as it has been to my own,[7] is the clinician's notion of disciplined subjectivity. This has several aspects. For one thing, it means not striving for spurious objectivity when this would require deliberately suppressing or ignoring subjective response, but, instead, bringing the subjective response into consciousness so that it is part of the available data. To balance that, however, it is necessary to attempt a degree of detachment regarding events in one's personal life. We can dare to make feelings of indignation or empathy, disgust or delight, accessible to awareness in the field situation only because we have sorted through those feelings at home, watching our emotions and physical reactions. No one can do this fully, and the processes of disciplined subjectivity and purposeful empathy are not yet fully understood. Our understanding, incidentally, is still growing, and is enriched by the new perspective provided by several generations of women in fieldwork.[8] Clearly, this is one of the epistemological frontiers of anthropology. It is fitting, therefore, that, just as the objective record of fieldwork must be examined in detail, so also the personal aspect should be understood; and it is important that in the case of this one individual both sides are extraordinarily well documented. We will need to include the correspondence that gives a less determinedly optimistic version of her field experience along with that published so far.[9]

As anthropologists, we will gain from an increasing understanding of Margaret Mead as a person something more than an essential tool for evaluating her scientific work and mapping and distinguishing areas of idiosyncratic giftedness or bias and areas that may be useful to emulate. We will also find, in the concrete details of everyday decisions, expressions of her insights into the nature of culture and the possibilities of change. Not only did she publish many proposals for possible modifications in contemporary American folkways, of which perhaps the most famous and the most often distorted was the proposal for "two-stage marriage",[10] but she also implemented many of her ideas, making conscious innovations both in home life and in organizations she was involved with. Some of these were highly specific, others more general. For instance, she brought a great deal from her field experience to her practice of child-rearing. Breast feeding had almost disappeared from middle-class American child-rearing when she gave birth to me, but she found a young pediatrician named Benjamin Spock, who, though he had never seen a breast-fed baby, was willing to go along with the experiment.[11] She ended up with a view of self-demand feeding that combines her observation of primitive mothers with the potentials of technology, a view that does not come through in contemporary American understandings of "self-demand": the mother initially nurses the infant when he or she is hungry and records the time so that the infant gradually settles onto a personal schedule that is monitored by the clock but originates in the rhythms immanent in the infant's own organism. I have the notebook in which she recorded feeding times, and this was not an idea she had originally, for a number of days passed before she began recording, whereas in later years she recommended to young mothers that they start from the time the milk came in.

This, then, is the first of a series of innovations she made in child-rearing, some successful and others, no doubt, unsuccessful, influenced by her studies of early childhood and adolescence in other cultures. It now seems important to record what she did in raising me and also what she said to me about various issues as I grew up, as translations of her sense of the human potential. Many of her ideas are now part of American culture, but it is interesting that some innovations that are now fashionable never seemed right to her, against the background of cross-cultural comparison. The presence of fathers at deliveries, for instance, was a matter of considerable skepticism.

Another area that will repay study was her sense of communities and networks. She was always dubious of the nuclear family and went to considerable and self-conscious effort to create extended households and networks of ascribed kinship, supporting both her complex life and my childhood. She had quite subtle and not fully articulated notions about complexes of nonexclusive and noncompeting relationships, so that, for instance, during the years when my mothering was divided between her and Aunt Marie (Marie Eichelberger) and Aunt Mary (Mary H. Frank), there was an implicit etiquette about which of her proprietary rights she felt she had given to whom, and which were shared. Just as she tried not to assert exclusive rights, she was exasperated when people were possessive of her or competitive for her attention.

The kin and fictive-kin network constructed in New York City during the years when we had a joint household with the family of Lawrence K. Frank existed in a broader system of intellectual networks, for one of the most important of these also centered on the figure of L. K. Frank, starting with the Hanover conference in 1934. He is best remembered today as the founding father of the child-development movement in this country, but his biography has not yet been written, perhaps because the same percipience that allowed him to perceive key scientific and ethical issues far ahead of his generation has meant that many of his ideas have now been more fully explored by others, blurring their originality. He was, however, one of the outstanding intellectual entrepreneurs of this century, and created a network that included luminaries from fields as distinct as psychoanalysis and cybernetics, setting different currents of interdisciplinary effort in motion. Several of Mead's books record Mead's developing sense of how groups and networks function in cultural transmission, insight, and innovation, from the Paliau Movement in the Admiralties to the Columbia University Research in Contemporary Cultures project.[12] Significantly, her work was increasingly collaborative, and much of her contribution will turn out to be the way in which she stimulated and supported the work of others.

Such collaborations were never exclusively professional for her, but assumed personal depth. She was profoundly bored by the notion of encounter groups, simply because she was accustomed to being aware of the interpersonal dynamics of groups that were also wrestling with matters of substance, their insight and creativity sharpened as they fell in and out of love or replicated significant relationships of a lifetime.

One of the things that grieved her in the last two decades is that as her network spread around the globe it was less and less accessible to the appropriate cross-linkages and more and more centered on herself, becoming a long list of people who would recognize, if they did meet, ways in which the voice of each had been echoed in her relationships with the other. Her community could no longer meet to break bread or sing or delight in each other, so that the only sense of wholeness it could have was its personification in her, and her integration of its thought. This was an artifact of her greatly increased mobility, but she felt it as a fragmentation. Conceptually, it presented a problem analogous to the problem that the invention of methods for the "study of culture at a distance"[13] presented to anthropologists who had been accustomed to dealing with whole communities in which each individual could be seen in his or her relations with all the other members of the community, not simply in relation to the investigator. The members of Research in Contemporary Cultures created groups of investigators and especially gifted informants, usually with some members who were both, hoping thereby to construct a whole that would provide a microcosm of inaccessible communities in Germany or Russia or Eastern Europe. My mother, later in her life, traveled around constantly, weaving and reweaving ties between people who could not easily meet. She carried with her photographs of me and my daughter, Vanni, as if to assert that she too had a home and ties, although she might have appeared solitary and contextless, and she became godmother and honorary godmother to dozens of children, always trying to break out of the impersonal and limited dyad. This whole history needs to be looked at in the light of contemporary network theory.[14]

Among her papers are boxes and boxes of correspondence, arranged by organizations. It is to be hoped that these will be studied by someone on the lookout for structural innovations. For instance, when the Scientists' Institute for Public Information began to develop as a national movement, she proposed that it be highly decentralized and acephalous. It is not sufficient to chronicle a period of growing recognition or participation in a series of controversies. Much more important for all of us is the question of how her anthropological knowledge of how human groups create and sustain relationships and mobilize for action was expressed in practical organizational politics. In general, as a community, anthropologists seem rather rarely to bring cross-cultural perspective to their political and organizational lives, or indeed to their personal lives.

It is important, having advocated that anthropologists look at Margaret Mead's role as innovator, to emphasize her role as conserver as well. This is perhaps what I, as her daughter, must say most clearly, for there is a natural tendency to focus attention on things that have novelty value. I am convinced that one of the outstanding themes of her life was the feeling that the complex fabric of cultural tradition must be protected, that people must have continuity of ethical commitments and the rituals and symbols that bind together a lifetime. Thus she maintained contact with every kinsman she could find, and learned the stories of my father's family to tell to me in case I never heard them from him. We went together to the sesquicentennial celebration of the town of Winchester, Ohio, where our Ramsey ancestors had been early settlers. We made faithful pilgrimages first to Philadelphia, as long as her parents lived, and later to her sister's in Connecticut for Thanksgiving. On our Christmas tree hung ornaments going back to her childhood and to every major trip abroad over the years, and she was one of those who persuaded the Liturgical Commission of the Episcopal Church at least to preserve as optional some of the traditional language of the *Book of Common Prayer*. She wept easily at evocative phrases and symbols, and treasured the lifetime continuity of responsiveness that made this possible.

There is innovation within conservation as well. Within the discontinuities of her professional life, she would construct bits of detail that would provide tokens of continuity. She bought me a miniature tea set to serve tea to my English father when he came up from Washington for weekends during the war. I have often wondered, although I never asked her, whether her tradition, year after year, of giving silver juice cups, engraved with the child's name and her name and the birth date, to a series of newborn children of friends was a reference to Ruth Benedict's account of the Digger Indian who said that the clay cup of his people was broken.[15] She suggested that if I was not prepared to spend as much time cooking as my Armenian husband might expect, I could keep a pot of soup on the stove so that the smell of home cooking would greet him as he came through the door. For years she carried a small silk pillow that would convert into home the most uncomfortable pallet on the deck of a steamer. These different examples seem to me to form a family that deserves to be analyzed as such, with many other possible cases. From a semiotic point of view they vary, but all of them provided enduring bridges that she constructed across chasms of possible alienation.

In these points of conservation, I think we find clues to the optimism and openness with which she met the radical cultural and personal discontinuities of her lifetime, which made people feel she bridged generations. Correspondingly, one of the reasons that I feel obliged to put my various memories on record and to try to describe my evolving relationship with her is that so much of what she had to say about culture change was set in terms of cultural transmission, in terms of what people of different generations could expect to share with each other.[16]

Having emphasized the usefulness for anthropology of looking at Margaret Mead's personality and personal life, and the way in which she incorporated subjective experience into her research, it seems important to emphasize that, precisely because she knew she was doing so, she took a series of steps to transcend the importance in fieldwork of the single investigator's personality. First, after her field trip in Samoa, she did all her major fieldwork as a member of a team. Initially, the logic of this was that which has stimulated much anthropological teamwork — marriage — but later it was a deliberate policy. Second, she kept her notes and records in exemplary order, so that later generations of anthropologists would be able to examine the detailed observations that led to given conclusions and also to note the choices made in the field, such as her daily routine, that would tend to structure observation. Third, she gave her support to younger anthropologists wanting to go to areas where she had worked and gave them the materials and entrees that would allow them to consider her data genuinely in context. Fourth, although not herself a photographer, she was deeply committed to developing and using new methods of recording, and the intensive photographic work that went into *Balinese Character* was precisely designed to meet criticisms of subjectiveness.[17]

The plans for the disposition of her field materials that she made before she died fit in precisely with this scientific commitment to sharing data and making both cumulative knowledge and replication possible. Unlike her personal papers and the professional papers having to do with her complex interdisciplinary activity in the United States, which go to the Library of Congress, all of the records of her fieldwork, notes, diaries, letters from the field, projective tests, and so on, are to be preserved in an ethnographic archive where they will be joined by field materials of coworkers in the same field locations, such as my father, Gregory Bateson, archived and preserved in such a way that the work of different ethnographers and work in different media can be examined simultaneously.* Most of us will not be leaving general records of a public life to the Library of Congress, but all those who have done original ethnographic work could well consider the best way of preserving their notes, which are the bases for the claims that their work is science. At present the Institute for Intercultural Studies, which Margaret Mead founded, is attempting to implement her wishes and effect the appropriate transfer.

Conclusions

Papers such as those prepared for this issue [of the *American Anthropologist*] so relatively soon after Margaret Mead's death must of necessity be programmatic, for it will take years to evaluate her contribution. I am convinced that the study of her as an individual will significantly illuminate her scientific contribution. This is because of the richness of the available materials. We have available her original notes, which record to a truly exceptional degree the raw materials of her writing — what she actually saw and heard in the field. Corresponding to this and complementing it, as we try to discover the role of personality in shaping the concerns and insights of the ethnographer, is an exceptionally rich record of her personality, as she attempted to be self-aware, and a record of her innovations, expressing a vision of what is humanly and culturally possible.

It is in this context that I have decided to spend most of the next year or so recording my side of the story, from a very personal point of view, as daughter of both of my parents. Epistemology is by way of being a family

---

* When this was written, it was possible that the ethnographic archive would be deposited elsewhere. In the end, all of her papers were deposited at the Library of Congress. — MC3 2004

tradition, and in this case I believe that writing about my parents will contribute to our epistemological understanding of the concept "participant
observer," which turns out to involve layers of self-observation, active and
passive participation, and that special sense of participant observation that
we find in the artist, who, immersing self in what he or she "sees," creates
and shares a new and encompassing vision.

"DADDY, CAN A SCIENTIST BE WISE?"

This piece was written while both my parents were living, for a Festschrift to my father, called *About Bateson*, organized by John Brockman (my father's literary agent and later my own). I struggled with the context, not sure whether I was writing for my father or about or perhaps *at* him. I used the word *wise* in the title, but as I read it today I can feel my ambivalence coming through as I avoid asking my father if a scientist can love, for Gregory's attention to the people who loved him was a sometime thing. Yet the notion that wisdom and love might have to do with systems that go beyond individuals, of which the individual is only a part, turns up again and again in my writings, whether about environmentalism or fidelity or the communication between mothers and infants. An excerpt from one of my father's "metalogues," the fictional dialogues described in "Ghosts to Believe In," appears at the beginning, and the title echoes the opening questions of the various metalogues, but it was not until several years later that I had the courage to commandeer the form Gregory had created to write new metalogues for *Angels Fear,* conserving the fluidity of his uncompleted thought. Reading this today, it occurs to me that I should have said more clearly that the death of parts of a system or dissolution of their linkages is a necessary part of his thought.

—MCB, 2004

29

Daughter: What does "objective" mean?

Father: Well, it means that you look very hard at those things which you choose to look at.

D: That sounds right. But how do the objective people choose which things they will be objective about? . . . Which things do they leave out? . . . I mean — subjective experience shows them which things it is easy to be objective about. So, they go and study those things. But which things does their experience show are difficult? So that they avoid those things. Which are the things they avoid? . . .

F: Well, you mentioned earlier something called "practice." That's a difficult thing to be objective about. And there are other things that are difficult in the same sort of way. *Play,* for example. And *exploration.* It's difficult to be objective about whether a rat is really exploring or really playing. So they don't investigate those things. And then there's love. And, of course, hate.[1]

Here, then, is a list of things that the "objective people," who are essentially those who try to understand the communicational phenomena of the biological or social world (for which Gregory has used Jung's term *Creatura*) with linear models borrowed from the sciences that focus on the physical world, the *Pleroma,* avoid thinking about. The list starts with *practice,* which is difficult to think about in the rather flattened out manner of the "objective people" because it depends on a complex structure of contexts, several logical types deep. Then we have *play* and *exploration,* which present the same sort of problem, so that the rat could perform the same, visible, physical action, and only an understanding of the entire pattern of layers of context in its behavior and relationships could sort out whether its activity was play or exploration or practice. "And then there's love. And, of course, hate." Quite true still; nonetheless, Father has definitely shifted logical types on Daughter. But after all, he is both exploring and playing.

Now it might be tempting to think that love and hate and humor (the latter is mentioned shortly thereafter), although certainly ill-understood by most psychologists, are not rigorously included in the argument that underlies the metalogue. One might think that these references appear as a sort of "throwaway line," as theater people would say. The etiquette of the well-trained reader would treat them here as almost rhetorical, but it seems appropriate to the persona my father created for Daughter in the metalogues, like the one quoted here, to see what happens if they are taken as scientific terms, and what implications this has for the nature of the argument. I'm not sure whether this is mischief or filial piety, but at any rate, I see that *love* is indexed, which suggests that it is intended not as an ornament to the argument but as a landmark in it, as are many other concepts that might be thought to be used rhetorically and turn out to have rather precise meanings, like wisdom. (Indeed, for connoisseurs of indexes, *Steps* and *Our Own Metaphor* are two of the most satisfactory books I've ever seen. Where else are Galileo, Game theory, Garden of Eden, and *Gemütlichkeit* bedfellows? Or where do Sacrament, St. John's College, Cambridge, and Salk, Jonas, lead to Schismogenesis? In *Our Own Metaphor* we find such sequences as: *Alice,* altruism, analog coding, anthropology, Apocalypse; or homeostasis, horse training, humanness, humility, hydrogen atom.) We need to know what kind of landmarks *love* and *wisdom* are, to find our way through such diversity. Clearly, this is the "stuff as dreams are made on" and much of the problem lies in understanding the operators that relate references such as these to each other, before we can perform complex mapping activities from one type of discourse to another, and to our other worlds of thought and feeling.

Gregory himself has written about the relationships of some of these sorts of things and how they interact in the development of science. In the introduction to *Steps* he describes a diagram he once used in teaching, to try to dramatize to his students the nature of scientific thought and the shape of certain common errors. The diagram consists of three columns. In the first column, unanalyzed observations of various sorts are listed *(data)*; in the second column, common types of explanatory notions in the social sciences are listed, for instance *ego, anxiety, instinct,* or *maturity*. In the third column are listed what he calls "fundamentals": truisms (like mathematics) and general scientific laws (like the Conservation Laws, or the Laws of Thermodynamics). Within this diagram, " 'Explanation' is the mapping of data onto fundamentals, but the ultimate goal of science is the increase of fundamental knowledge."[2] In the inductive methodology of much of social science, however, a different movement is involved where new "heuristic" concepts (the second column) are developed by a study of the data. These are accumulated as "working hypotheses" and retained without being built into any sort of general or cumulative structure.

Now one of the striking things about Gregory's diagram is that the items in column three are propositions of various kinds, while the items in column two are single concepts. Whereas explanation, in relation to column three, involves mapping an observation (an event) onto a proposition, explanation as pursued through column two involves identifying some kind of causal factor. In the essay, Gregory considers the possibility that "the heuristic concepts will be corrected and improved until at last they are worthy of a place in the list of fundamentals. . . . But alas [in fifty years of work] scarcely a single principle worthy of a place in the list of fundamentals [has been produced.]"[3] All of the concepts in column two are the kind of thing which Gregory discusses elsewhere as false reifications. To be worthy of a place in the list of fundamentals concerned with scientific understanding of the Creatura, they would at least have to be embedded in propositions and deal with process and relationship.

Where, in such a diagram, would words like *wisdom* or *love, sacred* or *play* fit? Grammatically, they look like the items in column two. Social scientists often do take words of the language and, by modifying their definitions, insert them in column two. If we assume that these words are not being used ornamentally, we have to consider the possibility that they are being used heuristically, and that Gregory simply prefers to use the strong, old, resonating words for whatever concepts he has reached by induction. I think one would have to be of two minds about this. It is always good to read prose that sounds like English, and such words at least seem to deal with things that really matter. On the other hand, if social scientists must constantly cook up new causal principles inductively from the data, it might be better that they use terms that are recognizably jargon. Jargon allows our thinking a certain defense. Some terms are too awful to circulate freely or, when they do circulate, at least remind us of their doubtful origins. It might be a good thing if new concepts were labeled as such for a generation or so.

Another possibility, which some might regard as equivalent to the idea that such words are ornamental, would be that they enter the discussion as comments on relationship. Once when Gregory was talking to a group of specialists on cetacea (whales and dolphins), he commented, embedding that comment to his hearers in the scientific interchange, that in all our scientific discussion, because we are mammals and such things are important to us, we are discussing relationships.[4] Don't think it is possible, he warned, for us warm-blooded creatures to be simply objective and limited to conscious intellectuality. At the same time he is talking *about* whales and dolphins, who are absent, he is talking *with* the marine biologists. I don't think there is any question that when Gregory uses a word like *wisdom* he is at one level talking with the readers, asking us to take sides, to declare allegiances. This is part of a broader invitation that is carried by these words, to engage the emotions in the discourse. Such words as *play, love,* and *hate* refer to subjects about which it is difficult to be objective, which are nevertheless important to study and understand. Such words as *wisdom* and *sacred* remind us that we are in areas where concern and commitment are appropriate, where the deepest kind of truth is being discussed.

My own suspicion is that when Gregory uses such words, or when he intersperses poetry in the discussion, he is deliberately reaching for a double involvement of primary process and conscious thought. After all, Gregory argues that the emotions, those things that we are accustomed to regard as rather amorphous and unintellectual — indeed, as interfering with the effective pursuit of intellect — are the partial perceptions in consciousness of highly precise and patterned forms of computation. The unconscious mind *thinks,* computes, and "the heart has its reasons which the reason does not at all perceive." Emotions that enter consciousness seemingly imprecise and blurred are no more than the "outward signs of precise and complex algorithms."[5] Words like *love* and *wisdom* move us. Gregory is deliberately bringing our emotions and relationships into the discussion: Perhaps we will not be confused by them, distracted from the effort to be objective, but rather will think better. Religion and art are suggested again and again in his writing as modalities which bridge the divisions of primary process and conscious thought. Seemingly in using words like *love* and *wisdom* he is engaging our emotion in the discussion and creating something like a new column to the diagram. He is inviting us to map the meaning of these profoundly significant terms — words of a special sort that have become, through art and religion, landmarks of cross-reference between primary process and conscious thought — onto the fundamentals in the formal language of cybernetics.

Before going further in examining what occurs when such words are used, and what the scientific value of that process might be, it will be useful to examine exactly what Gregory means by the two technical terms, *love* and *wisdom.*

Love

Feelings of love, emotions, are the consciously experienced aspect of precise but unconscious computations about patterns of relationship. The nearest to a definition that I can find in Gregory's words comes in *Our Own Metaphor:*

> You could say that love is a rather difficult-to-define concept, related to things we have been discussing — systems. At least a part of what we mean by the word could be covered by saying that "I love X" would be spelled out as "I regard myself as a system, whatever that might mean, and I accept with positive valuation the fact that I am one, preferring to be one rather than fall to pieces and die; and I regard the person whom I love as systemic; and I regard my system and his or her system as together constituting a larger system with some degree of conformability within itself. . . . I'm very willing to love animals, ships, and all sorts of quite inappropriate objects. Even, I suppose, a computer, if I had the care of one, because care and maintenance are in this picture too."[6]

When Gregory produced this definition at the Burg Wartenstein Conference, he was operating on at least two levels. He was acting, at the end of a period of stress and conflict in the conference, as a peacemaker, persuading those present to work together. Thus, he was using it in an exemplary way, inviting us to unite in a thinking system, as a conference: "Little children, love one another." He was giving us, as he said, something to work toward rather than simply fanning our respective rages about the sickness of the world. He spoke with audible emotion — slowly and painfully, with brow tense, at some length. He was also inviting us to agree on a meaning for the word. If we agreed to use the word *love* in his way, we would be entering into an agreement to accept a whole epistemology, to think in terms of systems and indeed of the hierarchical ordering of systems within systems.

The philosophical ramifications of this definition are very wide. Each of us in this view is a composite made of dynamically related parts, and as we love we potentially enter into another composite, becoming part of something larger, which is in turn part of a still larger entity, in level on level of systemic organization. Thus, from the formal point of view, my heart and my lungs love; right and left ventricle love; the members of a family love; the Browns and the Smiths, carpooling and borrowing a lawn mower back and forth, love and are members of a larger system which, to the extent that it can live at peace, loves other societies. A man and the pruning shears he holds in his hand, and indeed the tree he prunes, are parts of a system, each having parts, and together involved in the orchard and a complex symbiosis of humans and trees (and birds and insects).

All of this, however, omits the event in consciousness. There is another and contrasting meaning of love, which cuts through the hierarchies of systems and places absolute value on one particular level, the level of the individual. In that view, persons love each other and only persons are lovable. Just as the linguists have been engaged in a discovery of the sentence as virtually an ultimate unit, so Western philosophy has been involved, particularly since the Renaissance, in discovering the person, the individual, as the key level in this hierarchy of organization, the ultimate locus of value, because the person is the locus of consciousness and conscious purpose. Then in the system of man and fruit tree the fruit tree is valued for its contribution to his life, not he for his contribution to it; the parts of his body are valued for sustaining his life but could be replaced by the transplanted parts of someone else's body or by plastic; and the society is an invention for bringing about sufficient conformability between persons so that as many individual purposes can be reached as possible: the "greatest good of the greatest number" (of separate individuals). Within such an epistemology, my love and I, gazing into each other's eyes or exploring each other's bodies, find above all that our own individual personhood and identity is enhanced thereby. I am confirmed and strengthened by recognition given and also by the process of giving, but we remain fundamentally separate.

Love in the cybernetic sense has profoundly different implications from love understood in this individualistic sense. Logically, within the individualistic way of thinking, if the personhood of one is constrained or exploited in a relationship, the relationship can be discarded: The relationship has no value in itself, only the persons have value. A man and a woman, each far more than the sum of his or her parts, are themselves not a part of something which has intrinsic value: A marriage is a sort of container for their individual values, easy to dissolve, with no life of its own. Even a woman with child, living through the most profound symbiosis in the human life cycle, is not valued as a single system, what the Bible called "one flesh." We debate for legal purposes whether there are two persons (each with a soul) involved or one person (conscious and with a conscious set of priorities), and one "product of conception." If the infant is carried to term, he or she will be the concern of a pediatrician while the mother (and her breasts and milk supply) is separately defined and cared for by the obstetrician. No one will care for the system.

At Burg Wartenstein, it became clear that Gregory was using the term *mind* in much the same systemic way that he uses *love,* cutting across the person as the locus of consciousness, and focusing on complexities above and below. I wrote:

> One might almost go back over the discussions and try substituting the word "mind" for the word "system" wherever either occurred. Then "mind" becomes a property not just of single organisms, but of relations between them, including systems consisting of man and man, or a man and a horse, a man and a garden, or a beetle and a plant. Some mind-like properties seem very simple when they occur by themselves, but together they suggest a way of thinking which neither reduces mind to a model of billiard balls, nor sets it off in contrast to matter, but allows for a search through all orders of material complexity for forms of organization comparable to our own. This is perhaps a basis for a new kind of respect for the structures of the world in which we live.[7]

Thus, the immanence of mind is closely related to this matter of love. Still letting the word *love* resonate, with all its literary, personal, and religious associations, it may be useful to look at the rest of that discussion of the properties of mind.

Mind

"Mind is immanent where there are a number of parts, moving and mutually constrained." This is of course a different way of saying that the word *mind* can be substituted for the word *system,* but it still brings out a few key issues: the issue of a dynamic relationship, of movement; the issue of constraint; the issue of mutuality. A man with a scythe is constrained by the form of the scythe; indeed his own body motion is informed by the curves of his tool, a concrete proposition about the interlocked movement of man and tool through deep growing fields across the generations; as time passes, his own musculature will become a record of the scythe's teaching, first in stiffness, then in emerging grace and skill. We need time to understand this system, to get beyond seeing it as simply instrumental.

"Mind is immanent where there are a number of parts . . . forming a system which is self-corrective, maintaining constants about the relations between the parts and relations to the environment." Certainly this is something which can be seen in families, how the entire family system adjusts to keep certain relations constant, even at very great cost to individuals within the family. That is, families in their ongoing life, both healthy families and families whose interlocking patterns of mutual exploitation force individual members into schizophrenia or alcoholism, evolve their own systemic patterns and stabilities. Families (not individuals within families but patterns of relationship) may fiercely constrain the individuals within them. Thus, perhaps the family, as well as the individuals within it, must be seen as a locus of value. Any such system may be engaged in maintaining not the constants of homeostasis but constants of continuous change, potentially destroying the parts that make it up or the larger system of which it is itself a part.

"Mind is immanent where energy is stored so that the system can be responsive to abstract cues." Here we meet our problem between man and scythe; since the scythe cannot store energy, its physical path is a direct result of the way the man wields it, albeit translated by its form. The particular scythe, unlike the peasant who wields it, cannot be thought of as a system in which mind is immanent, but mind is immanent in the system man plus scythe. He wields his scythe more swiftly as storm clouds gather or as, using the strength from his breakfast, he imagines his dinner ahead. Picking up the scythe, he becomes a part of a system. Mounting a tractor makes him part of a more complex system, complete with a gas tank.

Curiously, it is the failure to recognize the immanence of mind, to recognize for instance that the system of the man and his fields has mind, that leads to all sorts of personifications or anthropomorphizations of tools, plants, and animals, or of the very fertility of the fields. All of these so-called projections are derived from the intuitive observation that in our involvements with the non-persons we encounter in the environment, we are not alone, we are not subject and these others object, but somehow we are involved in a dialogue. Mind is present, immanent in the situation, and we have the choice between seeing ourselves as parts of a thinking system greater than either, or attributing mind to the other, often setting the other mind up as a rival and feeling bullied by the form of the scythe or sabotaged by the weather or the population cycles of "pests." It is easier to say either the tree has an indwelling spirit or it does not, either the tool has personality or it does not, either the fetus has a soul or it does not, than it is to say that all of these are terms for something which resides not in the person and (possibly) in whatever portion of his environment he is interacting with, but in the interaction. For modern man, dismissing the idea of the indwelling spirit of the tree or the soul in the unborn fetus is a way of largely dismissing them as valuable.

An odd sequence has taken place as between primary process and consciousness: Primary process has proposed the indwelling spirit as a metaphor for what is felt as real kinship between human and tree. After all, a tree is more like a woman than it is like a telephone pole, and it may be more accurate to say there is a demon in a bottle of rum than to focus on the isolated alcoholic separate from a pattern of relationship. The unconscious, in the language of art or religion, can also propose love as a proper relationship to the other. The conscious mind, however, has a strategy for this; it suggests an either-or which is quite unintelligible to the unconscious, so only a blurred intuition protests that the argument has shifted to false ground: *Either* the tree is a dryad or it is not and is not lovable, *either* the fetus has a soul or it does not — and if not, then we will not attribute value, that is, personhood, civil rights, and so on [the values associated with individuals] to it, and above all, we will not regard ourselves as involved in a real relationship of love. We speak of personification and the pathetic fallacy when in poetry we find ourselves forced to attribute richer being to other parts of the biosphere than our unwise conscious minds will allow. We attribute to them a similarity to ourselves partly in order to be able to love them, as part of our perception of their beauty.

Gregory's definition of *love* or of *mind* invites us to generate whole new orders of being to be valued or loved, as we perceive ourselves entering into various kinds of relationship, and thereby being changed. It suggests a sort of theogony, a new animation of the landscape of awareness.

Wisdom

As with the word *love,* to use the word *wisdom* with Gregory takes us right into the center of his epistemology. "Wisdom I take to be the knowledge of the larger interactive system — that system which, if disturbed, is likely to generate exponential curves of change."[8] "Love can survive only if wisdom (i.e. a sense of recognition of the fact of circuitry) has an effective voice" since "unaided consciousness must always tend toward hate."[9] The circuitry of systems is concerned with maintaining constancies of various kinds, so wisdom is essentially conservative.

From the definitions this is clear: Love entails a readiness to relate in the way that wisdom recognizes as the basic structure of the Creatura. Special experiences of self-loss, of readiness to give one's being for the beloved, of wishing it were possible to merge into a single body — these experiences are based on an accurate perception of the systemic nature of particular relationships, and yet we do not acknowledge this as the nature of all relationship. We can desire to become a part of something larger than ourselves because we know, in spite of the illusions of consciousness and the package of skin in which we move, that there is a sense in which this is how things really are. In love we encounter this as emotion; wisdom argues further — this is not the special experience of passion or dedication or self-sacrifice, this is how the world is made. Wisdom argues for love by acknowledging the kind of world in which that kind of love is the most basic experience.

Wisdom, however, differs from love in that in love our computations of relationship can remain unconscious, resonating into consciousness only as emotions. Wisdom demands not only a recognition of the fact of circuitry, but a conscious recognition, rooted in both intellectual and emotional experience, synthesizing the two. Thus, "I am not sure that wisdom can be got [via drugs]. What is required is not simply a relaxation of consciousness to let the unconscious material gush out."[10]

The paths that Gregory has discussed as leading to the growth of wisdom include love (and love of animals or natural systems as well as people), the arts, and religion, and these work in different ways and to different degrees. After all, contemporary society includes many highly institutionalized ways of functioning as a part person — of denying primary process, separating the body from the mind, emotion from reason, production from consumption, and Sunday from the rest of the week.

Because our instructional systems emphasize only parts, they both strengthen those parts and also convey the meta-message that such divisions are appropriate. There is a sense in which any experience that breaches these boundaries brings us closer to wisdom, in which any opening to the irrational may help to complete us — whether it's an LSD trip or a fleeting experience of compassion in a boardroom, meditation or trying to carry on a conversation with a four-year-old. Many people discard the rational, trying to reject conscious thought, and remain unwise and incomplete in a new way. Others, however, are striving to breach the separations. A few go further and are working at synthesis, either by spiritual self-disciplines or through the disciplines of the arts or, occasionally, in science. Wisdom is not simply an experience, but neither is it the sort of thing that can effectively be passed on in the language of scientific papers and monographs unless these are such as to evoke a visceral as well as an intellectual response. Wisdom is the conclusion to a many-layered process of cognition at all levels of mind, and this is why the traditional spiritual paths are marked so often by paradox, the experience of dissonance between levels, which must be transcended.

Wisdom, curiously, as a recognition of the nature of the system created by participation, is equivalent to systemic self-consciousness. When human beings, participating in larger systems of mind that do not stop at the boundaries of skin and sense receptors, know themselves as a part of mind rather than as individuals, they have arrived at wisdom, whatever language they may use for that recognition. Equally, however, one might say that the system of which they are a part has arrived at wisdom: Human consciousness is potentially the organ of self-knowledge for the entire ecosystem.

Love, mind, wisdom . . . although it is not apparent every time Gregory uses them, these are nevertheless precisely defined terms in his epistemology. At the same time, however, they have an evocative impact that goes beyond our grasp of the meanings of his definitions. The use of a word like *wisdom* or *love* in an essay on the conditions of human survival invokes a whole spectrum of artistic and religious traditions, summoning to our intellectual discussions Jesus, Pythagoras, and Buddha. Thus, we are approaching the area of the sacred, which is also a technical matter in Gregory's writing, and indeed the sacramental as well.

Basically, these words, like the Old Testament name of God, Yahweh, are words of power. Rabbinical scholars knew that some things cannot be talked *about,* for the name of God partakes of His very being. Similarly, we feel that words such as these should only be used by one who — in some measure — has experienced them: Let only lovers speak of love, and let psychologists speak of object cathexis. There is a potential of both ritual and poetry in such words, and thus they are sacred words (or words for thinking about the sacred) in Gregory's sense: "It is my suspicion that the richest use of the word 'sacred' is that use which will say that what matters is the combination of [conscious thought and primary process], getting the two together. And that any fracturing of the two is, shall we say, anti-sacred. In which case, the Roman Catholics and the Protestants of the fifteenth century were equally anti-sacred in their battles [about the nature of the Eucharist]. The bread both is and stands for the body."[11] This is actually a part of the technical definition of a sacrament by the Council of Trent: "A sacrament *effects* what it *signifies.*"[12] If I am right about the way such words resonate at different levels of our minds, using them is either a terrible presumption — a blasphemy — or it is an essentially hieratic act. But after all, Gregory is trying to effect what his words signify, is trying to produce wisdom and the possibility of love.

There is at present in Western civilization a new kind of emphasis on the disparity between primary process and conscious thought. At first, with the hippies and the early drug culture, there seemed to be a sort of replay of the Romantic Movement, with its revulsion against science and the effort of objectivity. However, many new elements have been added, especially the discussion of differences between the two sides of the brain. Science tends to look like an exclusively "left brain" activity, and yet any consideration of scientists as people shows that the best of them rely heavily on intuition. There is merely a formal convention in the modern publication of scientific results that filters out all that is not cut and dried, replicable and objective. In school we learn about Newton the physicist, not about Newton the religious mystic, about the experiments which confirm hypotheses rather than about the leap of questioning or perception from which they are born.

This arises from the fact that most people have models of scientific activity which are based on physics, the study of the Pleroma "in which events are caused by forces and impacts,"[13] and in which all that we are trying to understand is radically different from us and from our way of perceiving and understanding it, in that there are no *differences* in the Pleroma, for differences are all that we can respond to (see, measure, record, weave together as scientific knowledge). Physical science is predicated on conceptualizing what is being observed as totally separate.

I remember once talking to my father about the difference between the studies of dolphins done by people who came into the field from marine biology and those he hoped to do. The marine biologists came from the study of organisms sufficiently simple so that scientists could have little direct empathy with them. What he hoped to do, coming in from anthropology, from trying to think scientifically about the Balinese in the 1930s or the schizophrenic patient in the VA with whom he spent hundreds of hours in the 1950s, was to use empathy in a scientific way. "They fall in love," he said of his colleagues, "they get seduced by the dolphins and they can't think straight." There are, of course, the "objective people," thinking about dolphins or Balinese or schizophrenic patients in a flattened way that avoids, among other things, awareness that there are at least two levels to be studied all the time, dolphin events, relationships, and meanings, and events, relationships, and meanings involving scientist and dolphin. The methodology combining these in the social sciences is called "participant observation" and requires what Margaret Mead was probably first to speak of as a "disciplined subjectivity" rather than a pretense of objectivity.[14] The problem is not to resist falling in love. The problem is to fall in love and be the wiser thereby (yes, *wiser,* in Gregory's strictly technical cybernetic definition), although anyone trained, as Gregory was, in a classic tradition of Western science treads this path a little gingerly. Nonetheless, he has premised years of study of precise but unconscious patterning on the notion that primary process is, precisely, thought. Science, if it is to make headway in thinking about the Creatura, should have the benefit of primary process computation. "Oh dear," said Daughter in the metalogue on instinct, "those poor people. They try to study animals. And they specialize in those things that they can study objectively. And they can only be objective about those things in which they themselves are least like animals. It must be difficult for them."[15] Difficult indeed! It's a depressing thought that we depend so much on scientists who, if we are to believe the split-brain people, spend their time desperately trying to use only half their brains (and in fact only succeed in using a fraction of that). One would as soon depend for one's decisions on oracles and prophecies produced in trance, carrying only the other kind of knowledge. Not, in either case, wisdom.

I think we are a very long way from an understanding of the kind of

scientific activity that will lead to wisdom, but a keystone of Gregory's use
of cybernetics is that among the translations and analogical mappings it
makes possible is a restatement of the lucid computations of the heart.
Thus, it is essential that *love* and *wisdom* and *sacred* have cybernetic meanings. At the same time, Gregory writing or speaking is never only talking
about these issues. He is also using these evocative words to mobilize in his
listeners that reasoning of the heart that the reason does not perceive. He
is inviting one kind of synthesis and at the same time activating our intuitions to engage them in the scientific process. In using cybernetic definitions of love and wisdom, he is mapping what we at least partly know at
the primary process level onto the scientific fundamentals, which is a way
of confirming science in wisdom. A scientist, after all, like a sacrament or
a poem, "should not mean but be."[16]

THE WISDOM OF RECOGNITION

Activism and Aesthetics

My parents worked together very productively, but their different styles eventually drove them apart. I sometimes think I learned social engagement from my mother and abstraction from my father. In this paper I was trying to disentangle some of the differences and underlying similarities between them. Both my parents played important roles in the early development of cybernetics, participating for over a decade in the search for ways of thinking about the behavior of systems, their formal similarities and interactions, that could connect biology and the social sciences and inform various kinds of engineering and design, just as geometry is a way of thinking about the formal relationships between abstract shapes that can be applied to a wide range of objects. The word comes from the Greek for "helmsman," the one who steers the ship, and turns up in the English *govern* as well: the way an organism adjusts to circumstances has similarities to the way a "smart" missile stays on course, so by the time of my parents' deaths the term had largely been usurped by engineering and computer science and had become associated in popular usage with mechanical, inhuman constructions. Cybernetics, as my parents understood it, as a way of thinking about the living world, has never made its way into popular understanding, even under the more contemporary name of systems theory: How does an organism or a family or a business stay on course — or learn — or stay alive? How does it take in and deal with the information it needs in order to do so?

Almost alone among groups dealing with cybernetics and systems theory, the American Society for

> Cybernetics has preserved the early interdisciplinarity of the field and the goal of an integrative way of thinking that would be both beautiful and enlightening. This paper is based on the transcript of an address I gave at their annual meeting in Vancouver as part of a program titled "Remaining Human." It was published in abridged form in the *Journal of Cybernetics & Human Knowing,* which maintains the same holistic emphasis.
>
> — MCB, 2004

∽

It has been two decades since the deaths of my parents. One of the things that fascinates me about getting older is the process of revisiting things that I thought I understood. It is fascinating to realize that I'm still in the process of getting to know my parents, twenty years after their deaths, because after all, when they were sixty, I was a lot younger. I didn't know how it felt to be sixty. Now I do, so I can understand them better. When I think of Margaret and Gregory now, one of the things that is most striking to me is the contrast between them on issues of action or activism, for both understood the ways in which piecemeal change could disrupt systems and both were involved, as pioneers in the cybernetics movement, in seeking ways of thinking about whole systems that might allow for less disruptive human impacts on the living world. But so much has changed since they died that I have to push further behind the specifics of what they said and did to find the underlying patterns. It has struck me that a possible resolution to this contrast might lie in the way both of them valued the arts. Productive science often requires a narrowing of focus, but both of them rejected that limitation, crossing boundaries between disciplines and spheres of activity, seeking and attempting to communicate integrative visions.

We are drowning in disconnected information today. In spite of the tighter and tighter interlinking of the world by trade and communication, our understanding is ever more fragmented by specialization. In order to act with sensitivity in the world we need a unified vision, a capacity to understand the coupling of human societies with each other and with ecosystems and the biosphere. This is what cybernetics could offer. To me, cybernetics is a way of looking that cuts across the disciplines, that is necessarily both scientific and aesthetic. Years ago I wrote that "cybernetics . . . makes poets of us,"[1] it does this by providing a rigorous discipline of metaphor. It links art and science by allowing us to move from a single organism to an ecosystem, a lake, a forest, a university, a school, a corporation, and to see the essential recurrent patterns that provide the basis for using one to understand the other.

One of the surprising things Margaret and Gregory had in common is that both of them grew up regarding the arts as higher and more demanding than the sciences. This is not a common position nowadays, yet the arts are often a challenge to broader perception. This respect for the arts was most explicit in Gregory's case.

Gregory's father was a distinguished biologist, the person who coined the word *Genetics,* and who played a key role in introducing Gregor Mendel's work to the biological community in England. He named his youngest Gregory, and it was assumed that all three sons would be biologists. They spent their childhood and adolescence outdoors collecting beetles and butterflies, doing natural history. (Very few biologists today, only the small communities of ecologists and ethologists, spend much time outdoors or looking at whole organisms. The majority specialize on minute pieces of organisms. Physicians don't look at whole human beings much nowadays either.) So when the two older boys went off to boarding school, they adopted a younger boy to carry the collecting boxes, and that was Evelyn Hutchinson, who became one of the most distinguished ecologists of the twentieth century, an expert on the ecology of lakes. Yet the house was full of extraordinary art. William Bateson collected old master drawings, Japanese watercolors, and the watercolors of William Blake. Poetry was read aloud, and so was the Bible (so they would not be "empty-headed atheists"). When William Bateson wrote to Gregory to comfort him after the suicide of Martin, his artistic brother who had already defected from biology, he wrote that the arts were the highest calling, and only for the truly great, but that it was possible for ordinary people like the Batesons to make a contribution in the sciences.[2]

Margaret too was exposed to the arts in childhood. Some of her drawings survive, and as a young woman she published a number of poems. However, when she became the college roommate of Léonie Adams, later a distinguished poet, the realization that she was in touch with a great artist convinced Margaret that her gift was not of that order and that she should put her efforts into anthropology rather than poetry.[3]

The sense of humility as scientists in relation to the arts lasted right through both my parents' lives, and both of them continued to enjoy the arts and to have deep and appreciative friendships with artists. In Bali, the site of their most intense collaboration, their focus was on child rearing in relation to the adult culture, which was pervaded by an extraordinarily rich tradition of dance, music, and painting.

Yet they held opposing views on social action. I believe that much of the difference in their attitudes came out of World War II. Margaret and Gregory were both deeply committed to the importance of Allied victory. I find that sometimes it's very hard for people younger than I to empathize with intellectuals closely collaborating with government in order to help win a war. But when we think of the ideological positions on the Axis side, I believe you can see that my parents had a coherent and almost inevitable commitment. Both of them struggled to have their professional skills used in the war effort, but figuring out the best use for anthropologists was a new challenge, and in the event their skills were used in very different ways.

Margaret ended up working during most of the war to make cooperation and the utilization of resources more efficient. At one stage she was trying to answer the question "How should we talk to people about food and rationing so that they get optimal nutrition from what is available?" To do that you have to study eating habits and traditional ways of talking about food. Then she wrote about the kinds of information the American people would feel they had to have in order to do their best. Later, she toured in the United Kingdom, speaking about the cultural differences between the English and the Americans that needed to be understood to make cooperation efficient.

Coming out of that experience, she remained an activist, willing to deal with the press and the general public, and a strong supporter of applied anthropology. She was an advocate, as many anthropologists are, of progressive change in American society. She saw that the increase in intercultural contact created an obligation for anthropologists to get involved and to make their findings available to the broader public, so she worked toward the new phrasings of relativity and disciplined subjectivity needed to support active and self-reflective engagement by members of the profession. When there was a point of conflict or difficulty, she would say, "We need to make a new social invention!" Looking at cultures as complex patterns, she saw purposive change in terms of a process of design.

Gregory, by contrast, was sent to the Office of Strategic Services, where he was involved in psychological warfare and disinformation — in the disruption of pattern. Gregory came out of the war deeply skeptical of the possibilities for deliberate social change. After the war, when he did research in a variety of psychiatric contexts, first with alcoholics, then with schizophrenics, and then with families, you couldn't *get* him to make a therapeutic intervention with a patient. He thought it might help if he sat and listened, but he became very skeptical as therapists who were convinced by his theorizing began to develop specific strategies for acting in the therapeutic context.

In effect, Margaret's war work used her professional training and her aesthetic values to strengthen and increase understanding, while Gregory's used his training to create dissonance and disrupt understanding, violating his values in ways he was only beginning to recognize. Thus, although I think there was a temperamental difference as well, it was no accident that Margaret came out of the war deeply committed to using anthropology to improve society. The year 2001 was the centennial of Margaret Mead's birth (Gregory was several years younger, born in 1904). The slogan used for the Mead centennial was "Never doubt that a small group of thoughtful, committed citizens can change the world." She believed that you could change the world and do a good job of it. In contrast, it was twenty years after the war before Gregory was prepared to be an actor in society. Margaret was immediately involved in applied anthropology, in solving problems. I think one of the things that led to their divorce was the totally different states of mind in which the two of them came out of the war years following that long separation. Margaret was very much stimulated, solving problems and telling people how to cope, designing interventions and giving advice of various sorts. And Gregory was kind of depressed and looking at her work very much askance. Both of them understood change in systemic terms, but this understanding led Gregory to a hands-off philosophy and Margaret to advocate rapid systemwide change and careful planning. Both realized over time that no stance toward change could assume the continuing existence of harmonious ancient systems, for change was everywhere: boys from the New Guinea interior drafted to serve on plantations, old world grasses taking over meadows right across North America, and insecticide molecules in Antarctica.

Issues of the relationship between art and science, the formal analysis of systems, and activism and concern about the world were part of the early conversations in cybernetics, and they continue to echo in the structure and meetings of the American Society for Cybernetics, but they have tended to be lost in most activities that bear the label "cybernetics." Cybernetics, like anthropology, has become a victim of specialization and is less and less holistic (in the original meaning of that term, before it was co-opted by alternative medicine), less and less able to consider wholes.

Margaret and Gregory shared an interest in whole systems, coherent human communities. The concept was that every human group has developed a unique adaptive pattern — skills, myths, social structure — passed on from generation to generation. Not replaceable. And all these different aspects of life are interconnected and should be studied together. In those days, they used the term "salvage anthropology" to emphasize the urgency — which I keep thinking of when I hear about the danger today of the extinction of species of plants and animals — of avoiding the loss of cultural traditions. When cultures, which are alternative ways of being human, are destroyed, the understanding of what it is to be human is reduced for all human beings. The challenge was that if you went into a village that had never been studied (they met in New Guinea, where there are some seven hundred languages, lots of diversity to work with), you didn't say, "I am here to study the political structure of this village." You went and studied everything, because you might be the last person with the opportunity to see it whole and make a record. You'd write a grammar, you'd compile a dictionary, you'd make a census and collect genealogies and myths, along with trying to understand the political structure. All the details were interesting, but it was the design of the whole that they pursued. Of course you knew you wouldn't be able to get everything, there would necessarily be rough spots and omissions and errors, but you got as much as you possibly could. Other disciplines divide their research up; political scientists look at government and linguists look at the language and another group at house building, and so on. But it wasn't like that then in anthropology.

Gregory eventually drifted away from what his colleagues recognized as anthropology. The way he thought was grounded in biology learned as natural history, and he moved to cultural anthropology without abandoning the biological elements that were still closely connected in those days. So he thought in terms of organisms and evolution, and this approach led directly into cybernetic thinking about systems and formal analogies. He went from studying Balinese to studying alcoholics and the families of schizophrenics, and then to dolphins, and octopuses, and philosophical issues related to ecology. To some observers it looked as if he were flitting from one interest to another, and of course people held it against him. I think there are still quite a few of us who want to use sensitivity to certain kinds of patterns to allow them to move from one example to another, and our colleagues think that's probably rather frivolous and irresponsible! You have to specialize, right? It was certainly held against Gregory. It was said of him, "He just doesn't stick to any one subject." It really was not until the years right before the publication of *Steps to an Ecology of Mind*, I believe, that it became fully clear to him that he had not been merely blundering from field to field but had been struggling to develop a way of thinking that would be transferable, systematically, from one subject matter to another, so that what looked like a group of random essays was recognizable as steps — to a holistic way of thinking that he called an ecology of mind.

Margaret got into trouble for crossing boundaries in two different ways. One was for crossing professional boundaries to talk to ordinary people. (She did write technical monographs, but I have noticed that most of her professional colleagues don't read them; they read the popular books.) She wrote for the intelligent general public, which was deplorable behavior in the eyes of academics. She wrote a column for *Redbook* magazine. Many of her readers in those days, housewives staying at home with their children, probably had only a high school education, but they were trying to understand their world. Well, she'd been studying ordinary people, after all, in societies where the essence of being an adult, usually by the age of sexual maturity or a little after, was that you understood the culture, not as a scholar but as a competent participant. There would be a few people with secret esoteric knowledge or skills higher than others, but nevertheless there was a sense that to be a member of the society was to have the whole picture, something none of us have today. So a high school graduate homemaker probably comes as close as any of us to having that common knowledge base because our subsequent education and experience have been so divergent. There is something very shocking about anthropologists writing about ordinary people in ways which only specialists can understand, and being hopelessly snobbish about it.

Margaret also crossed boundaries in the sense that she drew parallels from every society she studied to issues in Western society related to education, gender, community, and so on, and she wanted to share those with people. She had opinions about everything under the sun — but that's what anthropologists do, they look at everything under the sun of whatever community they are in.

Margaret argued that "a culture is all of a piece."[4] A child grows up, and the lullaby the mother sings, the classes in school and the games that are played, the trades that are learned and the way marriages are negotiated, are all interlocked and mutually reinforced. Although this is less true of complex industrial societies with huge groups of immigrants from different regions, it's a place to start in thinking about how the parts of a cultural tradition fit together and reinforce one another. There were really two approaches to the unity of cultural systems, which one might think of as theories of ethnographic holism. One was "functionalism," associated with Bronislaw Malinowski, which emphasized the causal interconnections between different aspects of culture, and this was a model that the cyberneticists found compatible. The second, associated with Ruth Benedict, emphasized the stylistic congruence of different aspects of culture, so they added up to a single ethos, and this was very much an aesthetic concept. Both of these approaches fit with the argument that you can neither understand a culture nor act on it effectively in terms of little pieces, which was what Margaret argued in thinking about change.

In 1968 Gregory convened the Conference on Conscious Purpose and Human Adaption in Gloggnitz, Austria.[5] The theme was that the purposes humans formulate and pursue often have maladaptive results, because only a fragment of the implications of a particular action come into consciousness. He had arrived at an understanding of why efforts for change so often produce anti-aesthetic results — ugliness. Conscious purpose, he believed, failed all too often in holistic understanding. By that time he was deeply worried about environmental degradation. It was as interdisciplinary a group as you could have, including some from the original Macy Conferences on cybernetics, so the discussions moved from discipline to discipline: the pollution of Lake Erie, cargo cults among Pacific Peoples, dysfunctional families, back and forth through examples of systems going awry, unintended consequences, and paradoxical effects, especially in the environment. Again and again a member of the group would propose action and Gregory would dig in his heels and say, in effect, "We don't understand it well enough yet to feel that we can act without making things worse." At the end of the weeklong conference, he proposed that we have another conference the following year that would deal specifically with "the moral and aesthetic structure of human adaptation." Gregory prepared a theme paper[6] within weeks, and Wenner-Gren supported the conference, but the gathering did not really jell and the proceedings were never published.

Gregory was calling for a theory of action that would at least be moral in the sense of action that would "do no harm." The issue was what actions can be undertaken by humankind without damaging the larger system of which our species is a part. Gregory had a suspicion that, even though you might not be able to have a complete description and understanding of the state of a system and the implications of a particular action, some people might have something like a "green thumb."[7] You know? Like people who know how to look after plants. They say that medicine is as much art as it is science, and some doctors simply have a sense of how to care for a patient. Gregory proposed that somehow this ability to act without being able to say exactly why was analogous to aesthetic judgment. Just as a painter or a composer or a poet produces a work of art without a complete and detailed theory of what she is doing but recognizes the aesthetic value, so we, some of us, recognize it in work produced by others. Similarly, the intervention of an intuitive, skilled psychotherapist is based not on a detailed argument of what to say when and why but on a "feel" for what's needed. We write the theory afterward. By this understanding, health and healing become aesthetic matters, not strictly scientific ones.

"Is it the first virtue of art," Gregory asked, "to force the player and the listener, the painter and the viewer, and so on, to surrender to that necessity which marks the boundary between conscious self-correction and unconscious obedience to inner calibration?"[8] That inner calibration corresponds to one of the many meanings of Gregory's most famous phrase, "the pattern which connects." Not only do all living systems have certain characteristics in common but this similarity can be a basis for relationship, so some individuals might approach living systems on the basis of an internal template or calibration. "Like the tree," we might learn to say, "I am alive; therefore I treat the tree gently." Not knowing fully in consciousness what it is to be alive, not able to understand the tree, I rely on something beyond what I'm able to make explicit. So some people have the capacity to recognize aesthetic characteristics in organisms and organizations of other kinds and to act on them in aesthetic harmony, to act with wisdom. Just as there is artistry in composing lives, there is social and ecological artistry as well.

Gregory often spoke of Coleridge's "Rime of the Ancient Mariner," in which the mariner, who has created an ecological disaster by killing an albatross, suddenly recognizes the beauty of the tropical water snakes around the becalmed ship laden with the bodies of those that have died of thirst and thus returns to harmony with the world.[9]

O happy living things! no tongue
Their beauty might declare:
A spring of love gushed from my heart,
And I blessed them unaware:

"O happy living things! . . . I blessed them unaware." This blessing is not a purposive decision but a response of recognition. So we ask, Who is this mariner, to recognize the beauty of the snakes? And what are we saying about ourselves when we judge something beautiful? This is what Gregory is dealing with here. The judgment may reveal something we do not know about ourselves, bringing it into decision making. We discover that our bodies are in possession of an aesthetic sense or feeling that enables us to orient ourselves to another life.

Interestingly, Kant's third critique, the Critique of Judgment, which Gregory quoted in other contexts, makes the same kind of connection between the purposive and the aesthetic.[10] Kant uses examples from design and from science, a sense of the aesthetic structure of a theorem, say, to discuss this response. He also gives examples of moral actions as having this aesthetic quality. It is almost as if an awareness of adaptive fit might enable a greeting, as the ancient mariner greets the water snakes, as if there were something like a template within the self that makes possible the recognition of aesthetic order in the other, so we can ask what we say about ourselves by judging something to be beautiful. Gregory argued that an aesthetic sense, which we do not understand but can bring into decision making, might enable us to orient ourselves to other living beings.

Groups, like organisms, are systemic. Their lives, their harmonies and disharmonies, may be more accessible to awareness than our own systemic characteristics. Interestingly, both Margaret and Gregory saw the potential of groups for wiser decision making. At the Gloggnitz Conference we finally felt that our best wisdom came out of the diversity of the members of the group and the mingling of thought and emotion in their interaction, so that together they constituted a kind of thinking organism that might be able to look responsibly at complex problems and model a kind of wisdom.[11] Margaret had been convening groups to do just that, starting during World War II with carefully designed working groups of various sorts. From her point of view, the original cybernetics group was just such a living system.[12] Undoubtedly the actual Macy Conferences were important in both my parents' lives, but the love Margaret and Gregory shared for small conferences was grounded in a sense of the way they can take on a life of their own and spin that vitality into sensitivity. When Gregory decided to reengage with social action, his preferred form was designing conferences.

Since my parents' time, anthropology has been divided into a whole mess of little specialties that don't talk to one another, so the discipline that could try to understand what it means to be human in a holistic sense has deconstructed itself. The same thing has happened with cybernetics, so increasingly we think of cybernetics not as a unifying way of seeing the world but as a tool, to be applied for narrow and specific purposes. Even more serious, the excitement about the Human Genome Project has made us newly infatuated with simple causal models, direct determination by isolated manipulable factors. Humberto Maturana commented in a lecture the day before this talk that we are not determined by our genes: We are not determined by *any* single thing. This is surely right. We develop as we do within a pattern of complex interactions.

We repeatedly slip back into the same kinds of reification and oversimplification. We say we are interested in facts instead of responding to patterns. We do things in terms of numbers. Just within the last half decade, I see a whole new wave of simplistic biological determinism coming along, not only as a form of explanation but also as a model for intervention. What do we do when someone seems to be suffering from mental illness or when a child misbehaves in school? Increasingly we write a prescription. But the situation of the individual involves both biochemistry and social context, each of which is affecting the other. We are taking all sorts of complexly determined — sometimes adaptive, at least in the short term — behaviors, and saying they must be caused by particular genes. This kind of attitude was reflected in *The Bell Curve,* which implied that success might be determined genetically by race rather than by the social differential created by the construction of race.[13] To the extent that you believe in a single line of causation, you don't attend to the whole organism, the whole person, the whole social context. You don't make schools places where children grow up in more creative ways. You don't support psychotherapy that will allow people to work toward self-understanding and learn to deal with their problems.

It is my task at the moment to deal responsibly with a double intellectual heritage and to encourage people to use it to address some of these issues. What I see all too often is that little pieces of my parents' work come into focus, pulled out of context, without a unifying understanding. The greatest damage done by the attacks on Mead by opportunists such as Derek Freeman[14] was to lead everyone to focus on a tiny corner of her work, *Coming of Age in Samoa*, the first book she published, rather than on the unfolding of her thinking over time. My colleagues in anthropology have skillfully refuted his attacks on her Samoan ethnography, but they have not restored the focus to her visionary thinking about how human beings around the planet can learn from one another. And there are anthropologists and psychologists and environmentalists today who would advise dividing Gregory's work into categories so they can conveniently read only the pieces that serve their specialties.

Responsibility for this heritage is not mine alone, of course. It needs to be reaffirmed and embodied in communities of thought and action, in poets and grade school teachers and diplomats as well as engineers. It is a matter not simply of more effective manipulation or smarter machines but of building bridges between our many skilled and insightful ways of thinking. In the American Society for Cybernetics there is a significant reservoir of shared understanding of a way of being in the world which is created not by our genes but by our having participated in overlapping conversations across several generations. The connections need to be made with skill, and discipline, and precision so we can begin to act on the wisdom of recognition.

SIX DAYS OF DYING

When you grow up in an anthropological household, you have the opportunity to become a reflective observer and to use that process to respond to painful and emotional events as well as to encounters with cultural difference. This step-by-step account of my father's death in 1980 was written less than a month later, the best way I knew to work through the emotions and intensity of those days and learn from them, a way I had learned since childhood. In fact, both of my parents spoke during their final illnesses of writing about what they were going through and the ways in which illness and death are treated in our society, for they had observed mortality in many settings and continued to be actively curious until the end. Since this first intimate contact with the process of dying, I have never lost the sense that even dying can be a learning experience, that there is a maturation in death that begins long before with early learning and casual encounters but that is often blocked by denial. This awareness has continued to shape my response to other illnesses and deaths, so that I see death as a necessary part of the life cycle.

— MCB, 2004

Just as the intimacies of childbirth and early mothering have gradually been restored, first with natural childbirth and rooming in and most recently with childbirth in the home, so there is a growing effort to meet death more intimately and simply. The logical end of this development is that people die at home or in an environment as close to home as possible.

The depressions which used to afflict mothers after childbirth are probably related to interruptions in the early intimacy between mother and child, which plays a biological role in the establishment of parental love and care. Similarly, the shadows of guilt and anger which so often complicate grief may also be related to interruptions in the process of caring, and they may be lightened by the experience of tending someone we love with our own hands, so that much that seems externally repellent and painful is transmuted by tenderness.

Death is surely more variable than birth. Where experiences are difficult to predict or compare, the specific is more useful than vague generalization. This is an account of the period from the second to the seventh of July of 1980, the period in which I experienced the death of my father, Gregory Bateson. I can only describe events as I perceived them; other members of the family or close friends may find my perceptions bizarrely at odds with their own. Nevertheless, I think all of us agreed that the fact that we were with my father at the guesthouse of San Francisco Zen Center, where he spent his last days and was laid out after death, gave us the privilege of a rare and blessed participation. We felt that we gained a new understanding of some of the things that my father taught, and also of the teachings of Zen Buddhism. Trying to make experience explicit in words is not typical of Zen, but it was something my father cared about. Lois Bateson, his wife, commented that Gregory had been a teacher all his life and that he continued to teach in the manner of his death. The privilege we experienced can only partly be shared. Still, the attempt at description may be helpful, for it is at moments of birth and death that it is easy to become timid and to be cowed into an acceptance of standard institutional forms.

My father's final illness began in mid-spring and I came to California to be near him in June, arriving one day before he was hospitalized. While he was in the hospital I had to be away for about a week, to keep a previous commitment, and I returned to San Francisco on July 2 to find that he was out of the hospital and being cared for at Zen Center, where I too went to stay. Two days before I had left, we had been talking, with some sense of realism, about where he might be able to convalesce, but even as I departed that had come to seem unrealistic. Lois felt the gradual change in the quality of the nurses' care as, with implicit triage, they shifted from the effort of healing to courtesy to the dying. Towards the end of the week, Lois made the decision to discontinue intravenous feeding — he was eating and drinking a little, and was receiving no medication through the IV — and then to bring him to Zen Center and nurse him there, knowing that he would probably die there.

Gregory had entered the hospital on June 10 because of a respiratory crisis that proved to be pneumonia and an unexplained pain in his side. Everyone assumed that the pain was related to the lung cancer he had had in 1978, which was expected to be terminal and then went into remission. He himself felt that the pain might be a local nervous disorder related to his earlier surgery, and went back to a term used by his old friend the neurophysiologist and systems theorist Warren McCulloch, who had described how a group of nerves, regenerating after surgery, might get into a self-reinforcing cycle of resonating pain, but McCulloch's term, *causalgia,* proved to be unacceptable in current parlance and was treated as fantasy in the context of the cancer. The pain had driven him to his bed in late May, where pneumonia had followed in lungs long handicapped by emphysema and the cancer episode. He had been living at Esalen Institute in Big Sur since the cancer, and friends there came and went with counsels spun from different epistemologies, the multiple holisms of an unfocused new age. He had dutifully done a session of imaging and was told that perhaps indeed he did not want to live. He had by his bedside an array of megadoses of various vitamins and microdoses of homeopathic medicines, wheat grass juice available in any quantities he would accept it, and at the same time he was told that he was too preoccupied with the physical and should be concerned with the spiritual, this being available in various traditional and syncretic forms.

When we left Esalen, heading for San Francisco in a VW van with a supply of emergency oxygen, we had two possible destinations, either UC Hospital or Zen Center. I do not believe Gregory was making a choice between "holistic" and "establishment" medicine, but a choice between multiplicity and integrity. He maintained a profound skepticism towards both the premises of the medical profession and the Buddhist epistemology, but certainty is scarce and there is a kind of relief to be found in a system that expresses the disciplined working out of a set of premises, whatever these may be. Furthermore, he wanted to be in a place where he could have more information about what was happening and where his own curiosity would be allowed to play a role, his own vitality nurtured by knowledge rather than by hope.

When we arrived at UC Hospital and got the diagnosis of pneumonia, everyone concurred that pneumonia was something that establishment medicine knew how to handle and that it made sense to stay there. Gregory was deeply tired and in need of an impersonal, matter-of-fact environment, and for several days he wanted few visitors and as much new information about his condition as non-intrusive diagnostic procedures would provide. X-rays showed no growth or spread of cancer and provided no explanation for the pain. At that point, after working carefully on the details of a will, Gregory and his doctor decided that relief from pain was what he needed most, and he had several days of relatively frequent and large doses of morphine. When Lois demanded a recess in which he could be fully conscious and able to discuss other treatment possibilities after these days, he remained somewhat blurred and disoriented, and the pain was a dull ache rather than an agonizing burning sensation. He was terribly weakened, partly by vomiting caused by some of his medication. He spoke of going home and came lurching out of the bed in the middle of the night, asking for scissors to cut the IV and oxygen tubes. Much of his talk was metaphorical and so discounted by nurses, who made cheerful and soothing noises, but he remained very much himself, relating in clearly different ways to different people, compliant but skeptical. Our initial optimism in this period was a response to the decrease in pain and the improvement in the pneumonia, but it was premised on a recovery of strength and will to live which did not occur.

During the last week in the hospital, there was a recurrence of the pneumonia, necessitating another round of antibiotics, and finally an explanation of the pain, when an eruption around his side provided the identification of *Herpes zoster* (shingles). This form of herpes is a virus which attacks the nervous system, causing acute unilateral pain, especially in the elderly, and eventually a skin eruption. It is almost impossible to diagnose before the rash, and in Gregory's case the location of the pain on one side of his body was all too easy to connect with the cancer. No one dies of shingles, but the pain may continue indefinitely; it does seem reasonable to say that Gregory died by withdrawal from unexplained pain, and that the explanation came too late to save him.

The six days of the title are the three days from my return to the moment when his breathing ceased, approximately at noon on July 4, followed by the three days until his cremation. Thus, not all of the punctuation comes from the natural process of death, but it serves to frame a period instead of focusing on a single moment. During those six days we were at San Francisco Zen Center, with most of the family and a few close friends sharing in the nursing and the Zen community providing practical help and a context of coherent tranquility.

On the morning of July 2, Gregory asked his son to kill him. The asking was not a fully conscious request for practical steps — he suggested getting a stick and hitting him over the head with it, as if by brutal over-statement to achieve the opposite of euphemism — but it was a demanding paternal honesty. When I arrived, Lois suggested that John and her son, Eric, and I meet with Michael, Gregory's friend and physician, hoping that we could accept as a group what she had already accepted in the decision to leave the hospital. Michael talked about the fact that there were various aggressive forms of treatment that could be taken to keep Gregory alive, and about his sense, having observed Gregory during the earlier crisis and in the intervening period, that Gregory had been turning towards death and that such interventions would be inappropriate and ultimately futile. All of us felt that mentally at least Gregory's withdrawal was probably irreversible, whatever the mechanism involved, and that his wishes should be respected as far as they could be. What this meant was giving up the pressure on him to suffer those things that might prolong his life — sitting up for a few minutes, respiratory therapy or an oxygen tube at his nostrils, another spoonful of custard, another sip of broth — while making each of these available if in any way he seemed to want them, or doing anything else we could to make him more comfortable. The more deeply one rejects the separation of mind and body, the more difficult it is to treat the processes of disease and death as mechanical and alien to the self. Even as one gives up the image of an external enemy, of death personified as the Grim Reaper or reified in the name of a killing disease, the problem which lives in most people's unconscious becomes conscious, the feeling that the death of those we love is a betrayal. We tend to feel that someone who is dying has an implicit obligation to stay alive: to accept treatment, to make an unflagging effort, and indeed to think thoughts that would support the effort at life rather than the drift towards death, not because to do so is comforting but because it may be a real factor in what happens.

We went back into the room where a hospital bed had been brought for Gregory, and we shared some sherry and stilton cheese. Gregory accepted a mouthful of each. We sat in a half-circle open towards the bed, and a student and friend of Gregory's, Steve, played the violin, while Lois

accompanied him with chords on the tambur and those who could har-
monized their voices, weaving a wandering chant in the darkening room
for what seemed a very long time. During the music Gregory, half dozing,
brushed the tube that was supplying oxygen away from his nostrils, and
each of us, I supposed, struggled with the impulse to get up and replace it.
Some of us were crying quietly. The music was gentle mourning, uniting
the various terms to which each of us had come in the acceptance of his
death into a single covenant. When the music ended we sat for a while,
listening to his labored, drowning breathing. After a time, lights were lit,
Gregory stirred himself to eat and drink a little more, a few mouthfuls,
the night watches were shared out, and one of the Zen students entering
the room restored the oxygen tube. After that it was put back or offered
several times, but eventually each time he rejected it.

Within the rhythm of our day, one of a small group was always with
him: Lois, or Kathleen, a friend and nurse who had come with the family
from Esalen, or I, or John and Eric, or Robert, the Zen priest who manages the guesthouse. Each evening different Zen students, some of them
friends and others unnamed, would come and sit in the room also, erect
and immobile unless they were needed, for Baker Roshi, in touch every
day by telephone from across the country, wanted the students to
approach the suchness of dying and to give their quiet support to Gregory
and to us. He instructed them to deepen their empathy by breathing in
unison with Gregory, supporting and sharing. Those of us staying in the
house slept at different hours and slipped out briefly to join the medita-
tions in the Zendo or to chant or join in the Eucharist at a convent around
the corner. Others came and went. We felt that for Gregory the process of
dying proceeded gradually but without even a clear distinction between
sleeping and waking.

On July 3 Gregory spoke occasionally, making gestures of affection and
recognition, but much of what he said was blurred and unintelligible. He
also spoke to others he seemed to see around the bed and once or twice
asked whether a particular person was indeed present or only a dream. It
was often necessary to move his big, ungainly body, for he had become
almost completely incontinent. This more than anything was reminiscent
of the care of an infant, but moving him to clean or change pads or to guard
against bed sores became especially difficult on that day because although
he was not able to help at all, there was a sort of recalcitrance in his body
against these indignities. He gave an impression of deep concentration.

Jerry Brown came in on the evening of the third and Gregory recognized him and stretched out his hand to greet him, calling him by name. As Jerry left and we settled down for the night, Gregory's labored breathing had slowed to the point where sometimes the interval between breaths left room for a momentary doubt of whether another breath would follow. We shared the certainty that less than a day remained. Gregory was dying as people die in books, gradually sinking towards death in a self-reinforcing process. Intravenous feeding and continuous oxygen could drag that process out, interfering with the choice of mind and body not to sustain life, and another counterattack might have been possible on the pneumonia which we could hear in Gregory's breathing. But pneumonia has long been called the "old man's friend." I never thought of my father as an old man until he was dying.

During the late night and the morning hours of the Fourth of July, each of us had time alone with him. He still smiled and responded to a handclasp, or would draw a hand to his lips. Touching seemed important, and the hospital bed enforced an isolation that had to be bridged. I found I wanted to give him the sound of a voice, so I read aloud the final chapters of the Book of Job. I held up a flower from one of the vases, not as something sweet and pretty but as a symbol of the order of truth to which he had been most true, the grace and intricacy of mental phenomena underlying the patterns of the biological world, and wondered whether a flower could still evoke that allegiance as, for someone else, a lifted cross could evoke a whole life lived in the Christian context. He would have been able to call the flower by name.

By mid-morning he was unable to drink, and we put tiny amounts of water in his dry mouth to give some moisture, afraid that he would choke on any more, unable to swallow. His breathing was laborious and slow. Lois noticed a pattern of blotches on his chest which at first we thought was a further eruption of the *Herpes* and then realized was a result of a change in circulation. A short time later, Roger, a friend from Esalen, saw the pupils of his eyes dilate as his mind encountered the dark. So we gathered around the bed, some six of us who had been caring for him most closely, hardly breathing ourselves as we waited from breath to breath, the time stretching, the time stretching beyond the possible, and yet again and again followed by a gasping reflexive inhalation, and then again the lengthening pause. I kept praying that he would be free from each next compulsive effort, let go, rest, and when after a time no further breath followed, we still stood, slowly relaxing with the faintest sighs, barely able to return to a flow of time not shaped by that breathing. Lois reached forward, after her office, and gently closed his eyes.

We did not at that time pause to mourn but slowly found our way into the expression of continuing care. After Lois, in my turn, I reached out and began to straighten his arms, then folding his hands. Someone lowered the bed to the flat and dropped the sides. I thought briefly of those cultures in which the bodies of loved ones are transmuted at the moment of death into something impure, polluting those who touch them. During my lifetime few Americans have tended their dead, just as few have tended their dying, and we had to grope our way, following clues from other times or other cultures. For Lois the available model was the Balinese one, in which the bodies of men are washed by men, and those of women by women, but for me the model was the Western one where women have received the newly born and the newly dead into their care. In the end we all worked together, removing the soiled pads, cleaning away the final traces of excrement, lifting and turning and washing each limb, shifting from side to side this beloved body from which all tension and recalcitrance were drained so that he suffered our care with a curious innocence. The blotches on his skin had faded.

Roshi had instructed that all traces of the sick room be removed, and Gregory was lifted and carried to the double bed at the other side of the room, dressed in a bathrobe and covered with the sheet and spread. He was still a little too long for any bed. With half a dozen Zen folk joining in, the hospital bed and table were dismantled and carried out, the linens and the cloths and basin we had used to wash him were removed. Consulting each other in muted voices, we bound a kerchief around his chin, experimenting with the angle until we were able to close his mouth, collecting and composing ourselves even as Gregory's body and the room were made serene in composure. As the work was completed, Robert surveyed the scene and then went and straightened the folds of the bed cover so they fell in sculptured order to the floor. Then he set up a small altar, a table with an incense burner at the foot of the bed, and said that now he would show us how to offer incense to Gregory: bow (the bow whose name is "asking"), touch a few grains of incense to the third eye in the center of the forehead, place them on the burning charcoal, add a few more grains, bow. It seemed to me well to perform an act which was both alien and completely formal, combining affection and courtesy with total estrangement. From that time, incense burned constantly in the room, and two or more of the Zen folk sat and watched. Gregory was not a Buddhist, but Zen mindfulness and decorum were for him an affirmation of the intricate order of mind. We sat for a while, and soon I went and slept in another room of the guesthouse.

When I woke up and returned to my father's bedside it was late afternoon. His body was cold now when I touched his hands, and the tracery of red blood vessels in his cheeks drained of color. Someone had removed the kerchief and combed his hair. As his body had settled gradually into the rigor of death, his face assumed a gentle, just slightly mischievous smile, and with the wisdom of mothers who refuse to believe that their infants' first smiles are caused by gas, we felt we could recognize the carrying over of irony into peace. As he had weakened and had been able to express less and less, the final attribute distilled from the others was sweetness, so this was the natural form into which his features settled, unfalsified by cosmetics and the skillful artifices of morticians who teach the dead to lie to the living about what they meet at journey's end.

Downstairs we drank sherry and ate the stilton cheese that Gregory loved with other members of the immediate circle who had not been present at noon, in undefined shared sacrament. Through the next two nights and days, a new pattern developed, an echo of the rhythm of Gregory's last days. The Zen students came and went, keeping their vigil, and we also took turns being by Gregory's side, watching the continuing changes as death increasingly and more deeply asserted itself. The window was kept open to the cool San Francisco weather, and in the morning he seemed to me a thousand miles more distant, his skin pale as wax, his hand still and very cold. As a child I believed that the dead became such strangers immediately, not realizing that there is a maturation in death. Having offered incense once, I found I preferred to enter the room informally and sit close by his side, touching his hand in greeting and farewell.

Our Buddhist guides told of their belief that the soul lingers near the body for up to three days before it finally departs, so that cremation should not occur for three days and the body should be attended, especially during the first two days, and they encouraged us and other visitors to read out loud or to address Gregory. At the same time, all of us had limited experience and we were shy of the physical complications of keeping a body for too long a period of time, so the decision was made to send the body to the crematorium on the 6th. That morning the Zen students withdrew, leaving the watch with Gregory to the family. My sister Nora and I went in together, sitting for a time on either side of the big bed as she explored the quality of death, feeling his hands, asking about the mechanism of rigor, wondering at the absence of the familiar bulk. Reb, one of the Zen teachers, spoke of him as being like a beached whale, but at the end he was strangely diminished. Then the Neptune Society van came, and Gregory was wrapped in a sheet that someone had carefully ironed that morning, strapped to a stretcher, and finally his face was covered with a dark green wrapper. The Zen Guest House is an old and gracious building, with stairs wide enough for one to make a final departure on a stretcher or in a coffin, and probably Gregory was not the first person to leave it so.

Baker Roshi's advice was to stay as close to the process as possible, following Gregory step by step through the concrete reality, so on the 7th the family went to the crematorium with a small group of Zen monks who had also been close to Gregory. We took various things to send with him into the fire: a volume of Blake's poetry, flowers and sweet smelling herbs, individual roses. We gave him a small crab that Eric and John had gone out with a flashlight to capture the night before, in memory of the way he had taught each of us to study tide pools and of the way he had taken a crab with him year after year to his opening classes at the San Francisco Art Institute, to open his students' eyes to the "fearful symmetries" of organic life. Nora brought a bagel because he had once quipped at Esalen that the hole in a bagel would be reincarnated in a doughnut. There were incense and the ashes of incense from Zen Center.

We went into the backstage of the crematorium, where the great ovens are, a disheveled and unkempt region of noisy machinery. His body was on a plank on a wheeled stretcher, and when the covering was turned back we could see that rigor had passed and his mouth had fallen open, his head fallen sideways. His body seemed gray and abandoned as if finally life had fully receded. We piled our gifts within the shroud and offered incense, and as the Zen folk chanted in Sanskrit we each whispered whatever other prayers we felt the moment needed. Reb, the Zen priest officiating, whispered in his ear before the oven door was closed. None of us felt any longer the need or desire to touch him.

Reb showed Lois the button to press to start the oven, as in another age she would have set the flame to a pyre of fragrant woods. And then he suggested that we go outside to where the smoke of the crematorium was escaping into the bright sky.

COMPOSING A LIFE STORY

This essay is the edited and retitled transcript of a talk on my book *Composing a Life* given at a Common Boundary Conference in the early 1990s, later published as a book on the "power of stories to transform and heal." This piece reflects on the uses of memoir and how telling one's story plays a role in composing a life, for future possibilities are always understood in relation to an interpretation of the past. I have included it here as a bridge connecting what I have written about my parents to what I have written more generally about the shapes of lives and how they can be studied.

—MCB, 2004

There are three meanings that "composing a life," as a phrase, has to me. Two of those meanings compare living to different arts, in that I see the way people live their lives as, in itself, an artistic process. An artist takes ingredients that may seem incompatible, and organizes them into a whole that is not only workable, but finally pleasing and true, even beautiful. As you get up in the morning, as you make decisions, as you spend money, make friends, make commitments, you are creating a piece of art called your life. The word *compose* helps me look at two aspects of that process.

Very often in the visual arts, you put together components to find a way that they fit together and balance each other in space. You make a visual composition of form and color. One thing that you do in composing a life is to put together disparate elements that need to be in some kind of balance, like a still life with tools, fruit, and musical instruments. This sense of balance is something that women have been especially aware of in recent years because they cannot solve the problem of composing the different elements of their lives simply by making them separate, as men have.

Of course, less and less are men able to compartmentalize their lives. For a long time it was possible for men to think in terms of a line between the public and the private. A man would go to the workplace, and then, at a certain point, he would switch that part of the day off and go home to a world where the atmosphere was different. He could switch gears from one aspect of his life to the other.

But it hasn't been possible for women to separate their commitments in quite the same way. It is one thing in the traditional nuclear family for the husband to go to the office and stop thinking about his family during the day because he has left his wife in charge. It is quite a different thing for both parents to go off and feel that they can completely forget what is happening with the family. Many women have the sense that the combining of different areas in their lives is a problem that is with them all the time.

What this has meant is that women have lived their lives experiencing multiple simultaneous demands from multiple directions. Increasingly men are also living that way. So thinking about how people manage this is becoming more and more important. One way to approach the situation is to think of how a painter composes a painting: by synchronously putting elements together and finding a pattern in how they fit.

But of course *compose* has another meaning in music. Music is an art in which you create something that happens *over time,* that goes through various transitions. Examining your life in this way, you have to look at the change that occurs within a lifetime — discontinuities, transitions, and growth of various sorts — and the artistic unity, like that of a symphony with very different movements, that can characterize a life.

In addition to these two meanings of composing a life — one that relates to the visual arts and the other that relates to music — I want to emphasize a third meaning, one that has to do with the ways in which you compose your own *versions* of your life. I'm referring to the stories you make about your life, the stories you tell first to yourself and then to other people, the stories you use as lenses for interpreting experience as it comes along. What I want to say is that you can play with, compose, multiple versions of a life.

There are advantages in having access to multiple versions of your life story. I am not referring to a true version versus a false version, or to one that works in a given therapeutic context as opposed to others, or to one that will sell to *People* magazine as opposed to ones that won't. I am referring to the freedom that comes not only from owning your memory and your life story but also from knowing that you make creative choices in how you look at your life.

In the postmodern environment in which we live, it is easy to say that no version is fixed, no version is completely true. I want to push beyond that awareness and encourage you to think about the creative responsibility involved in the fact that there are different ways to tell your stories. It's not that one is true and another is not true. It's a matter of emphasis and context. For example, one of the things that people do at meetings is to introduce themselves. I was at a conference recently where, in the course of two days, I introduced myself three times in different breakout groups. One person who had been there all three times came up to me and said, "You know, you said something completely different every time." Of course I did. The contexts were different.

Imagine the choices you have in saying things about yourself and about other people. These are real choices, but they are made in the presence of a set of conventions. Think of a self-introduction as a literary genre. There are things you include and things you don't. Those decisions are related to who you're talking to and where you are, as well as who you're talking about.

You can do the same with versions of your life history. For instance, most people can tell a version that emphasizes the continuities in their lives to make a single story that goes in a clear direction. But the same people can also tell their life stories as if they were following on this statement: "After lots of surprises and choices, or interruptions and disappointments, I have arrived someplace I could never have anticipated." Every one of us has a preference for one of these versions, but if we try, we can produce both. My guess is that there are a lot of people reading this who think of themselves as growing and developing and moving on smoothly. That's part of the intellectual context many of us are in. But some of us experience our lives as discontinuous, interrupted processes.

For example, one version of my life story goes like this: I already thought of myself as a writer when I was in high school, and there hasn't been a year since college that I haven't published something. Now I spend half the year writing full-time and half the year writing and teaching. Many of my students are future writers.

That's one version of me. The other version goes like this: I planned in high school to be a poet. But I gave up writing poetry in college. The only writing I did for years was academic publish-or-perish writing. When I became unemployed because of the Iranian revolution, shortly after my mother died, I dealt with unemployment by starting to write a memoir. I suddenly found that I could write nonfiction. Now I'm considering switching again and writing a novel.

Both of these are true stories. But they are very different stories.

One person told me there had been so much discontinuity in her life that it wasn't hard to think of a discontinuous version, but it was painful to tell it. I think that's a problem many people have. Because our society has preferred continuous versions of stories, discontinuities seem to indicate that something is wrong with you. A discontinuous story becomes a very difficult story to claim.

I would say that the most important effect of my recent book *Composing a Life* has been to give people who feel that they've been bumped from one thing to another, with no thread of continuity, a way of positively interpreting their experience. You might be uncomfortable with your life if it has been like *The Perils of Pauline,* yet many of us have lives like that. One strategy for working with that kind of life is to make a story that *interprets change as continuity.* One of my favorites was someone who said, "My life is like surfing, with one wave coming after another." He unified his whole life with that single simile.

The choice you make affects what you can do next. Often people use the choice of emphasizing either continuity or discontinuity as a way of preparing for the next step. They interpret the present in a way that helps them construct a particular future.

One of the most striking examples here is the way people talk about divorce. Some people approach a divorce by emphasizing what was wrong with the marriage all along: "Finally we got a divorce. But it's been awful for twenty years." I think some of the anger that develops in divorce situations comes from a need to re-create a continuity. But then there are some who don't need to create continuity by tracing the problem back. They emphasize the discontinuity and view the problem as absolutely new. Perhaps they would tend to focus on loss in that situation rather than anger.

When I started *Composing a Life,* the issue I wanted to explore was discontinuity. Part of my interest was based on two events in my own life. One was that I had just gone through the experience of losing, in a rather painful way, a job I cared about. I had been forced to change jobs before, because of my husband changing jobs, and I had had to adapt to that situation. So what I set out to do was to look at a group of women who had been through a lot of transitions and who were able to cope with the changes. I was asking the question "How on earth does one survive this kind of interruption?"

The other circumstance that made me focus on the issue of discontinuity had to do with my experiences in Iran. At the time of the Iranian revolution, my husband and I had been living and working there for seven years. We, and a great many of our friends, had to make fresh starts; many Iranians became refugees. The way they interpreted their situation was absolutely critical to their adjustment. I could see very clearly, among them, that there were those who came into the refugee situation with a sense that they had skills and adaptive patterns they could transfer to the new situation. They were emphasizing continuity. Other people came into the refugee situation feeling that their lives had ended and they had to start from zero. You could see that the choices people made about how to interpret the continuities and discontinuities in their lives had great implications for the way they approached the future.

Much of coping with discontinuity has to do with discovering threads of continuity. You cannot adjust to change unless you can recognize some analogy between your old situation and your new situation. Without that analogy you cannot transfer learning. You cannot apply skills. If you can recognize a problem that you've solved before, in however different a guise, you have a much greater chance of solving that problem in the new situation. That recognition is critical to the transfer of learning.

It can be very difficult to recognize the ways in which one situation or event in your life is linked to others. When I was working on my memoir of my parents, *With a Daughter's Eye,* I found an example of this in my father's life. Some of you may know my father, Gregory Bateson, as a great anthropologist, a great thinker. But in the middle of his life, he went through a difficult period that lasted for some time. From year to year he didn't know whether he would have a salary, whether there would be anything to live on.

His career at that time must have seemed totally discontinuous. First he was a biologist. Then he got interested in anthropology and went to New Guinea. He made a couple of field trips that he never wrote up. Then to Bali. During World War II he wrote an analysis of propaganda films and worked in psychological warfare. Then he did a study of communication in psychotherapy. Then he worked on alcoholism and schizophrenia, and then on dolphins and octopuses. Somehow he turned into a philosopher.

One of the things that I realized while I was putting together the memoir is that only when he drew together a group of his articles — all written in very different contexts for very different audiences, with apparently different subject matter — to put them into the book called *Steps to an Ecology of Mind,* did it become clear to him that he had been working on the same kind of question all his life: The continuous thread through all of his work was an interest in the relationships between ideas.

The interruptions that forced him to change his research focus were absolutely critical to pushing him up the ladder of logical types, so that ultimately he could see continuity at a very abstract level. His insight, his understanding of what he had been working on all his life, was a result of a sometimes desperate search for a continuity beyond the discontinuities. So even when I was working on the memoir, I was picking at this question of continuity and discontinuity, and examining the incredible gains that can come from reconstruing a life history by combining both interpretations.

Of course, in composing any life story, there is a considerable weight of cultural pressure. Narratives have canonical forms. One of the stories that we, as a culture, respond to is the story in which the hero's or heroine's end is contained in the beginning. For example, there is a film about Henry Ford that I happened to watch recently on television. In one scene, he sees his first horseless carriage as a little boy and falls in love with it. In other words, you have an episode in childhood that prefigures all that is to come. Think about how many biographies you have read in which the baby who grew up to be a great violinist loved lullabies, or loved listening to the radio: stories about talent that was visible from the very beginning.

One of my favorite examples is a story from the life of St. Teresa of Avila, a Counter-Reformation saint. When she was a child, part of Spain was still controlled by the Moors: part of the country was Catholic, and part was Muslim. When she was ten or so, she set out, with her younger brother, for the territory controlled by the Moors in order to be martyred and go to heaven. This becomes an appropriate story to prefigure a life of self-sacrifice and dedication to God. Many biographies and autobiographies have this pattern.

Another popular form is one that we can think of as the conversion narrative. It's a simple plot. Lives that in reality have a lot of zigzags in them get reconstrued into before-and-after narratives with one major discontinuity. One very interesting example is the *Confessions of St. Augustine,* which tells the story of his life before and after his conversion to Christianity. The narrative structure requires that he depict himself before conversion as a terrible sinner, that he devalue all he did before he was converted, and that he dredge up sins to talk about so he can describe a total turnaround.

As I read this book today, what strikes me is that St. Augustine after his conversion to Christianity was not that different from St. Augustine before his conversion to Christianity. He pursued a reasonable, intellectual life. He was a seeker. He experimented with different things. After his conversion, it is true, he disowned his mistress, who had borne him a son, an act that is construed, in this story, as a sign of virtue. But he continued to be, as he is throughout the narrative, profoundly self-centered. The universe was apparently organized around bringing him to God, and other people were very peripheral. In that sense, you can follow the same story throughout the book.

A more complicated conversion story is *The Autobiography of Malcolm X.* Much of the book tells of how Malcolm X, who had been a small-time crook, was converted in prison to the Nation of Islam, Elijah Muhammad's American Black Muslim movement. About two-thirds of the book is written as a conventional conversion narrative: "I was deep in sin and then I was saved by Elijah Muhammad."

But then another big discontinuity occurs. Malcolm X becomes disillusioned with the corruption within the Nation of Islam and isolated by the politics around Elijah Muhammad. He separates from them, making a pilgrimage to Mecca and converting to orthodox Islam, and starts his own Muslim organization in the United States. So in this book you have the image of somebody who developed an interpretation of his life to support the validity of one particular message of salvation and then had to flip over into another one. It's an extraordinarily interesting and unusual story because the conversion happens not once but twice.

One very common example of the uses of the conversion story shows up in Twelve-Step programs. Twelve-Step programs essentially convey the message that if you can construe your life in such a way as to support a turnaround, we will help you construct a new life. But you have to define yourself, as St. Augustine had to define himself, as a sinner, or as Malcolm X had to define himself for his second conversion, as having been duped. An emphasis on a turnaround becomes the condition for moving on to the next stage.

The conversion narrative can be a very empowering way of telling your story, because it allows you to make a fresh start. The more continuous story, in which the end is prefigured in the beginning, is powerful in different ways. But what I want to emphasize are the advantages of choosing a particular interpretation at a particular time, and the even greater advantage of using *multiple* interpretations.

The availability of multiple interpretations of a life story is particularly important in how the generations communicate with each other. When we, as parents, talk to our children about our lives, there is a great temptation to edit out the discontinuities, to reshape our histories so that they look more coherent than they are. But when we tell stories to our children with the zigzags edited out, it causes problems for many of those children. A lot of young people have great difficulty committing themselves to a relationship or to a career because of the feeling that once they do, they're trapped for a long, long time. They feel they've got to get on the right "track" because, after all, this is a long and terrifying commitment. I think it is very liberating for college students when an older person says to them, "Your first job after college need not be the beginning of an ascending curve that's going to take you through your life. It can be a zigzag. You might be doing something different in five years." That's something young people need to hear: that the continuous story, where the whole of a person's life is prefigured very early on, is often a cultural creation, not a reflection of life as it is really lived.

The ways in which we interpret our life stories have a great effect on how our children come to define their own identities. An example of this occurred in my own life when my daughter was about to become a teenager. She said to me, "Gee, Mom, it must be awfully hard on you and Daddy that I'm not interested in any of the things you're interested in." I said, "What do you mean?" She said, "Well, you're professors. You write books about social science. I'm an actress. I care about theater." I said a secret prayer because it was clearly a very tricky moment. Maybe she needed to believe in that discontinuity. Maybe it was worrying her and she needed to get away from that discontinuity.

But what I said to her was "Well, to be a social scientist, to be an anthropologist, you have to be a good observer of human behavior. You have to try and understand how people think and why they behave as they do. It strikes me that that's pretty important for a good actor." She has been telling that story ever since because it gave her permission to pursue what she deeply wanted to pursue without feeling she was betraying me and her father. But it also gave her permission to use anything she might pick up from us by giving her a way of construing the cross-generational relationship as a continuity.

As parents, we also need to be flexible in how we construe our children's lives. Recently, I was in Israel visiting on several kibbutzim. Many of the older people on the kibbutzim are in distress about the fact that their children do not want to "follow in their footsteps." Their children want to travel. They want to live in the city. They want to go to the university. Some of them even want to leave Israel, to emigrate.

I started having a series of conversations with the older people in which I would say, "Tell me about your parents. Were they farmers? Did they live on a kibbutz?" People would say things like "Oh no. My father was a tailor in Poland. He lived in the city." Then I would ask how their parents felt when they became socialists and Zionists and came to Israel. In many cases the answer was "They were appalled." Sometimes the answer was "They were thrilled that I was doing something they never could have done."

What the parents I was talking to did not realize was that their children were indeed following in their footsteps. Their children were doing exactly as they had done: leaving the location, lifestyle, and convictions of their parents and going out to do something new in a new place.

The continuity and the discontinuity are at different logical levels in each of these examples. If you can be aware of those different levels simultaneously, you can have an advantage in coping with your life. Otherwise, it may happen that when you are trying to achieve continuity, you actually create the opposite effect. You may be looking for continuity in the wrong place.

If you create continuity by freezing some superficial variable, the result, very often, is to create deep change. This is something my father used to talk about in relation to evolutionary theory. He used the example of a tightrope walker. The tightrope walker is walking along a high wire, carrying a very light bamboo rod. To keep his balance, he continually moves the rod. He keeps changing the angle of the rod to maintain a constancy, his balance in space. If you froze the rod, what would happen to him? He would fall off. In other words, the superficial variation has the function of maintaining the deeper continuity. In evolution, the deeper continuity is survival. For the tightrope walker, it's staying on the high wire.

I found an interesting example recently of a group of people who were able to maintain a deep continuity in their lives through many superficial changes. They were members of an order of Catholic nuns between the ages of fifty-five and sixty-five whom I was invited to address at a convention. They had all joined the order before the reforms of Vatican II. When they joined, nuns lived in convents. They wore black habits and white headdresses. They never had friendships. They were told what to do in every way.

Then came the reform of the religious orders. It is well known that at that time many nuns left their orders. Some of them left because they felt there was too much change; others, because they felt there wasn't enough. But the interesting thing to me was the question of who stayed.

Among the people I talked to, it was clear to me that those who stayed were those who were able to ride the changes and to adapt. At some fundamental level, they were able to bridge all the superficial changes and to say, "My commitment is the same commitment that brought me here in the first place." They were people with an extraordinary capacity to *translate*. The people who were fixated on the habit or the details of ritual couldn't stay when they lost those things.

It's worth giving some thought to what kinds of things deserve to be held steady and what kinds of things it's most adaptive to vary. I think you can argue that one way of looking at addiction is that the addict is trying to keep something steady, a certain level of intoxication, that is, in fact, producing profound and worsening change. An addiction is a constancy of the wrong kind.

When you are able to see multiple levels of change and consistency, you are empowered to make your own decisions. I think this is true of diversity in general. I want to offer one final example from my own life. People who have one famous, successful parent are often locked into the problem of whether or not they succeed in living up to the model of that person. One of the things I gained by having two famous and very different parents is the freedom to be myself.

For a long time, I thought that my interests had nothing to do with theirs. When I went to college, I was fascinated with linguistics. I read the work of Edward Sapir and Benjamin Whorf and decided that linguistics was going to be my life's work. Nobody had told me that linguistics as done by Whorf and Sapir is a branch of anthropology. So I walked, as a total innocent, into the family business. But I opened up a branch in a new neighborhood.

~ II ~

The Shapes of Lives

Age and Gender

Human lives develop according to a biological ground plan that offers the potential for a great deal of learning over a life span within which formal schooling is a transient episode. What we learn, when we learn, and from whom vary from place to place and epoch to epoch. The more you look at individual lives, especially lives lived in times of change, the more you realize that no life is either fully free or fully determined, fully representative of a given culture or fully unique. And that every life is subject to change and further learning, up to and including the process of dying.

The pieces gathered in part 2 focus in turn on different stages of development and on the ways in which development varies with gender, always with a sense of the overall pattern of the life cycle underlying discussions of infancy or marriage, work or aging. As one moves on through life, however, earlier stages continue to be present, so I have included two long studies of individuals toward the end.

Lives, the ways they overlap and the ways they are changing, have turned out to be a central theme of my work. I avoided the social sciences as a college student, but the one anthropology course I did take to meet Harvard's distribution requirement reintroduced me to ideas from psychology and anthropology that had been debated around the dinner table during my childhood. It was then I first read Erik Erikson on the human life cycle, as well as other family friends like Ruth Benedict. In 1965, finding that teaching Arabic did not allow me enough depth of interaction with students, I joined a number of other Harvard faculty members in volunteering for the teaching staff of Erikson's course.

Erikson had gone to Vienna as a young artist and been analyzed by Anna Freud. Because his work grew out of the psychoanalytic tradition, it shared the insights as well as some of the weaknesses of that tradition, particularly its masculine focus. What remains most important to me about Erikson's work, however, is that his emphasis was not on pathology but on the distinctive strengths developed by the individual at each stage of development up through old age. This general approach of looking for strength rather than weakness stayed with me and has influenced my way of looking at cultural differences.

Erik Erikson and his wife, Joan, continued to play an important part in my thinking. I invited them to preview my memoir, *With a Daughter's Eye*, so they could critique it from the point of view of members of my parents' generation. Then in the eighties, a renewed interest in issues around gender was triggered for me by the need to function at a college moving ambivalently into coeducation, still mired in habits of discrimination and exploitation. Realizing that there was no traditional model for living in the present, I began thinking of life as an integrative work of artistic improvisation, the basic concept that I explored in *Composing a Life* (and developed further in *Full Circles, Overlapping Lives*). Joan Erikson was one of the women I interviewed and wrote about, the oldest member of the group, who had gradually become a full colleague to her husband. It is change that necessitates so much improvisation and adult learning in working out contemporary versions of the underlying pattern shared by all human beings. Taken together, age and sex constitute much of the diversity within families that provides a basis for adapting to difference and change in the wider society.

There is no such thing as the perfect childhood or the perfect marriage, just as there is no such thing as a complete education or work without tedium or fatigue. Every life includes deficits, hurt, and finally death. Everyone must sometimes act in ignorance. But these are all challenges to creative adaptation and may be the necessary preludes to wisdom.

YOU WILL KNOW THE FUTURE
WHEN YOU GET THERE

This piece is included here to serve as an informal introduction to many of the changes in the shapes of lives that
come up separately in the subsequent pieces. It is based
on a talk I gave in 1996 to an alumnae conference at the
Santa Catalina School in Monterey, California, a private
girls' school, similar in important ways to the Brearley
School, which I attended growing up in New York.
Because males and females mature at different rates at
different ages, it is hard not to put either girls or boys at
a disadvantage in certain grades, building resentments
and bad habits. This piece stands as a kind of salute to
the continuing value of separate education for girls and
the role that schools and colleges can play in the lifelong
development of their graduates.

When I began to read about the life cycle, the focus
was on the lives of men. But now that the shapes of lives
have changed for both males and females, the implications of change are especially apparent for women,
whose lives have been radically reshaped by the possibility of controlling conception and the other new free-
doms it has offered. As a result, women have taken the
lead in understanding changes in the life cycle that affect
men as well and define the meaning of lifelong learning
for all our futures. I often find myself explaining that I
write about women not because women are a special case
and therefore need separate study, but because women
are today the pioneers of the new territory that both men
and women will inhabit.

Every stage of development affects men and women
differently, but we share the increased demand for

learning of our era. Both men and women have a wider
range of choice than ever before, at virtually every stage,
so that choosing gets steadily harder. All of our learning,
whether the earliest skills of recognizing another
human being, or the skills of building and maintaining
relationships, or even the ability to encounter death, are
embedded in interaction and mutual recognition.

— MCB, 2004

So much of Santa Catalina School's history has had to do with physical
growth, adding to the property and adding buildings. One of the things
you discover when you build on a room to a house, or remodel a basement
or attic, is that the verb *add* is deceptive, because when a house has a new
space — even a passageway, an entrance, or a window that wasn't there
before — it has a pervasive effect on the living in the house. It affects
where people sit and have which kind of conversations, where they leave
their sneakers and the tennis rackets they haven't put away properly,
where the dust tends to gather, which bathroom — if there is more than
one — they go to in what part of the day. And other changes may be
caused by the disruptions during the building process, like students living
in trailers as they once did at Santa Catalina. In other words, it is deceptive to think of "adding" because what happens is a change in the entire
configuration. The whole character of an institution is modified as it goes
through the experience of growth. This kind of disruption and reconfig-
uration is what has happened to women's lives in our time, and I don't
believe we have completely absorbed the changes yet.

Why not? The Bible says life expectancy is "three score and ten."
That was by no means an average; that was an aspiration. But today the
average life expectancy for American women has in fact passed that three
score and ten. We have not fully taken in the fact that, for many of us, *half*
of our adult lives will occur after menopause. If you add in changes in
childbearing patterns, it turns out that, for most of us, the years in which
we are heavily engaged in caring for young children end up at less than a
quarter of our adult lives.

By way of comparison, consider hunting-gathering peoples such as
the Bushmen of the Kalahari.[1] Traditionally, they had no domesticated

animals, no bottled milk, and not much in the way of grain that could be made into a soft infant cereal, so they tended to nurse each child for about four years. If you nurse a child constantly — often several times in an hour — you generally don't ovulate and you don't conceive again. The average number of live births per woman was about five, half of them dying before puberty. Among such peoples, the basic experience of being a woman is carrying an infant all day long and nursing that infant on demand. Menstruation is a rare experience, because if you stop nursing, you become pregnant again soon after. So lactation — not childbirth, not menstruation — is the fundamental condition of womanhood for these women, and loss is a corollary. That picture shakes up our assumptions in profound ways and makes us question the basic physical facts of being female. It makes it easier to imagine lives having quite a different shape.

We're coming out of a period when most stories about women ended in marriage. The prince married the princess and they lived happily ever after. We all know it isn't that simple, but there are still vast numbers of romance novels being churned out that end with marriage: no suspense, no drama, no story after that.

I encourage women to tell themselves multiple versions of their own stories, because we get locked into a single version. "We met, we fell in love, it was wonderful." "He left me, he ruined my life, what a bastard." Then maybe after a while we say, "Well, it was good while it lasted." In other words, we don't have to be locked into the same interpretations of experience. Try out different versions. Then try telling yourselves multiple stories about the future as well. We are, beyond a certain age, singularly unimaginative about our futures. We've got to have some new stories.

We're also getting rid of the non-story that says to women, "You're over the hill at thirty-five — or thirty. By the time you reach menopause, you're uninteresting, unattractive, and you've lost your biological function." In this country, not many women any longer bear infant after infant and then die in childbirth — although there are places where they still do — so that isn't the accepted story either. The tremendous numbers of women writing novels and memoirs and making films about every stage of the life cycle are repairing this story deficit, and now the feminist pioneers of the 1960s and 1970s are writing books about menopause, and they'll probably go on to write about moving to nursing homes! There are other tasks that we have to take on, however. The subliminal messages about the life cycle — that there's no more suspense after you get married, or that childhood is when you get educated, or that your biological function is over after menopause — affect the way we perceive things.

We are still relearning who we are as women. I believe that even though child care is necessarily going to take up fewer years — and fewer hours in a day in those years — and although many women for one reason or another will decide not to have children, as many women who went into convents or joined religious orders have in the past, nonetheless, what we have to do is draw on the experiences of women's lives in the past to find the metaphors that will allow us to think about where our society — our institutions and our communities — is going. I know that this is not always a politically correct or popular point of view, but I believe that the experience of caring for a child is importantly paradigmatic. It provides a model, a metaphor for what needs to happen in our society and a way of thinking long term.

The women's movement was actually blindsided by the discovery of how much of adult life there would be after the childbearing years and how much it would have to change. Women worked out how to compose their lives so they could have a career and care for their children. Their children grew up, and because they had become productive in other ways they weren't suffering from the "empty-nest syndrome," but this does not mean that caring became irrelevant. Few of them foresaw the aging of their own parents, for as we live longer, of course our parents live longer, too. I have a friend who retired at sixty-five to look after her mother. Most grandparents' lives used to end while the grandchildren were still very young. There's a very satisfying human rhythm there. My sister-in-law went into labor at the family meal after the death of our common father-in-law. Death and birth were simultaneous then, but they aren't any longer.

I would like to suggest that we've got to get more juice out of older people for a longer time. The current concept of retirement — which goes with the notion that work is a bad thing — is terribly dysfunctional. Traditionally human societies have productive activities for older people that change as their capabilities change. We simply cannot afford a society in which people who live until a hundred start sitting in front of a television set at sixty-five. Just such a simple thing as sitting and looking out the window (instead of looking at the tube), being a neighborhood gossip and watching what's going on, was valuable and made the streets safer. That was one of the big functions of older people that's been lost.

We've got to value the contributions older people make, and we have to involve older people with children. I think every child needs more than one parent. I think every child needs more than two parents. In a wider sense, yes, it does "take a village to raise a child." Every person in her or his seventies or eighties or nineties needs young people to be involved with, and young people need older people, too.

We will need to think further about providing care through an institutionalized and monetized system, but that will not be enough, there will still be a need to provide for cherishing. We're going to have to make a lot of inventions to do that. Several of my women friends are facing the fact that they're likely to be widowed, likely to be single as they get older, and they're making the decision to set up housekeeping with two or three other women and look after each other, pooling funds for the kinds of caretaking that can be contracted out, and also offering each other cherishing companionship. I deeply believe that we need to get the institutions in place, but I don't think institutions can solve the entire problem.

The last thing I would say is that the great moral and ethical issue of the life cycle, which we're going to have to solve in the next ten or twenty years, is the willingness to die. People in the past saw the death of their parents in old age that came early, in their forties and fifties. They did everything they could for them, but there wasn't much they could do. Today we sometimes do too much. We have to be willing to talk to our parents and our children about death, to discuss living wills, to think about dying ourselves, to include dying as a part of life. I think one reason we have such difficulty with older people in this society is because they remind us of something most Americans would rather forget. I don't think you can afford to forget the fact that death is a reality and a part of life — a necessary part of life.

Biologists used to talk about the fact that human beings are what is called neotenous, which is to say that we never grow up. Thank heaven for that! If you look at a baby chimp, it's almost identical to an infant human being, but it's smarter and it develops and learns faster. But at a certain point, the chimp grows up and becomes less responsive. The shape of the skull changes, and the adult chimp is less like a human being, although very smart in many ways, less willing to learn, less willing to develop trusting relationships. Human babies are born extraordinarily immature and dependent, and our whole system of adaptation and survival as a species depends on the fact that we are cared for intensively over a long period of time. It is because of this that we can have an adaptation based on so much learning and we've been able to move over the entire surface of the planet, learning new adaptations — inventing science and technology and things of that sort — instead of following built-in instinctive programs.

What I believe is happening today, because of the speed of change, is that the demands we all face of learning to cope with new challenges and giving up familiar assumptions are escalating. Learning is now a lifelong process. You can't afford to freeze up, you can't afford to lock into a particular moment of cultural development. No school can say any longer, "Okay, kids, you're educated, you're prepared for life. Now, go live." It's a little more accurate to say: "A good school like Santa Catalina is a first step, like a really good kindergarten experience; it prepares you to go and learn constantly."

One of the ways I dramatize the possibility of lifelong learning is with the example of immigrants. Many people today warn that immigrants are difficult to absorb. Immigrants have trouble with the language and trouble making a living. And they don't have the same values. My friends, every human family is a mechanism for the absorption of immigrants. Children arrive, and they might as well be from outer space, but we turn them into members of the culture. Furthermore, if you stop and think, every one of you in this room today is an immigrant in the sense that you do not live in the country you were born in. It changed on you. You've got the same passport, you might even have the same address, but you live in a different world. The main difference, of course, between you and a new arrival from overseas is that you've been able to adapt piecemeal.

I grew up being told that if I didn't wait for an hour after a meal before I went swimming I would drown. Now they tell us that's not true. I learned to cook believing that if I burned myself I should quickly apply some butter. We don't do that anymore; we put the burn under cold water or get an ice cube. These are trivial examples compared with some of the more fundamental changes we deal with. But they're reminders that things you were taught as gospel when you were a child can get changed on you.

Anyone who's been taught to use a VCR or a computer by a son or daughter knows that our children are born and grow up in a different country from the one we grew up in. My daughter, who is twenty-six, is a great help to me in learning my way around the present. To regard her as having been born in a different country means not to take for granted that her values or her aspirations or her style of communication are going to be the same as mine. I say this to her and she says, "Mom, I look at the teenagers now, and *they're* born in a foreign country." We all live as immigrants. We are strangers in a strange land. We're going to be strangers for the rest of our lives, not just when we decide to travel or go out on the Internet. I think it's really important to notice that parents need to learn as much from children as children do from parents, that human infants are born with the capacity to educate their parents — not always successfully, but without that we'd be in deep trouble.

When you have the experience, as anthropologists do, of immersing yourself in a strange culture, one of the things you expect is a great deal of stress, changing things you've taken for granted. This learning and relearning involves a different kind of attention and a lot of anxiety about doing the wrong thing. You're just plain more tired at the end of the day when you have to deal with change.

This suggests the need to rethink the relationship between caregiving and learning. One of the things we know about the human capacity to keep on learning, to remain young at heart and willing to learn, is that it needs to be supported by cherishing. We needed to be cherished as infants, and as adults we need to cherish our children. But if we want to have a society of people willing and open and ready to learn, it has to be a kinder, gentler society, because we need a lot of mutual support to face change, to give up things we've always believed.

So our model of work has to change also, to give proper value to caring. The domestic work of women is treated as if it doesn't exist. It's not part of the gross domestic product; there's no value added. It's something that people just take for granted. It's a freebie, like the air, except that the air isn't free anymore, either, since now we have to pay attention to making sure that it's breathable. The difference in earning capacity between men and women is related to the notion that any kind of work modeled on caregiving is probably worth less than other kinds. We're going to have to change that. When we talk about a service economy, what we are talking about is the externalization and monetization of a great many activities that used to be done in the home, that are still looked down on as if they weren't essential. Care supports learning. Together they keep us human.

The whole recognition of lifelong learning connects to a personal slogan I sometimes use: "We are not what we know but what we are willing to learn." Take that another step and it suggests a new way of thinking about authority. I defer to authorities not only on the basis of coercion but because I trust their competence, not just what they already know or the degrees they have but also because I observe that they continue to be willing to learn. It's a mistake to pin one's trust or obedience on someone who's not willing to learn.

If things are changing in the world, you can't be prepared once and for all for life. You have to be learning and relearning and reinterpreting as you go along, not to be stuck with ways of thinking and understanding. I've had conversations with a lot of you at Santa Catalina School about what it means to be involved as alumnae, and what I've heard again and again is that Santa Catalina was not just a place where you learned key things as girls. You are finding your involvement with each other now, today, a learning experience. And so it should be. I would like to see all schools and universities converted into "learning maintenance organizations." Education is not a process that is ever finished.

Some of us return to the classroom now at every age, but most learning takes place outside the classroom. Take the old saying "Experience is the best teacher." We say it, but we don't often spell out what it means to learn from experience. To learn from experience, you must reflect on it, maybe record it in a journal, and then be ready to reinterpret it. This may mean spiraling back past something that you learned or experienced, perhaps long ago, and wondering, "If I rethink that now, is there something new to be learned from it?" It is useful to have time to read books, take a class, go to a museum. But I think the real issue is reflective time. You hear something about a friend, hear something on the news, read something in the paper, and to convert that experience into wisdom, you have to reflect on it.

We're being told all the time what we're supposed to want: It's a new car, it's wall-to-wall carpet. It's a pair of running shoes. Your accountant says you're not paying enough on your mortgage, it's messing up your taxes, so you had better buy a bigger house. And when you do, you work twice as hard because you have to make the payments.

We don't put a very high priority on time for reflection. I like to imagine a future in which we can say learning is more fun than consumption. Little kids know that; they get high on learning. Then we send them to school and teach them that learning should be unpleasant. We must recover, as a society, that joy that goes with being a neotenous human being, where discovery is more fun than anything else and where we organize our consumption patterns and make our decisions in life to fit that priority. We have to learn to say, "I don't want a bigger house, I want time to look out the window and reflect." Getting that time is up to you, and it's extremely difficult.

Let's go back to the image I started with, of building a new room onto a house, or the development of this campus and its land and buildings. It is a characteristic of institutions to want to build buildings. I've spent a lot of time in Boston and Washington, and both of those cities are built on swamp. They're not built on rock. And you in California are building on shifting tectonic plates. In such places, you can't conceptualize building as starting with rock, and on top of that a firm foundation, and on top of that a building that will last forever. In Boston, buildings are designed to float. In California, I guess, they're designed to shimmy. For both, the notions of solidity give way. This is also a characteristic of what we need to do with our lives and our institutions, involving continuous learning. We have to sort of float and shimmy and be a little childlike — and take care of each other because it's not easy to live like that.

I don't know how many of you are familiar with the Gaia hypothesis. It's the hypothesis that this planet has the systemic characteristics — both strengths and vulnerabilities — of a living organism. James Lovelock, who formulated the hypothesis, gave it the name Gaia hypothesis because Gaia (the same root that appears in the word *geography*) was the goddess of Earth. I've spent a lot of time thinking about that hypothesis. It's a huge improvement, instead of saying that I have my feet on solid ground, to say that I'm living on the surface of a living being. But if the earth we live on is a living being, it's as much like a child as like a parent. Of course the earth is very old, older than our species, but it is younger than the youngest child because it must endure longer. When you care for a child, there's so much you don't know about what life will bring, long after you are gone, but your responsibility is to learn from children and with them, to cherish them and to free them for an unknown future.

We need to find some different metaphors, different ways of thinking about work and caring and the meaning of home. We don't have to spend our whole lives caring for children any longer. I'm not saying that all women should stay home and be full-time mothers. What I am saying is that we should be full-time *homemakers*, working to make our institutions, our workplaces, our cities, our neighborhoods — our planet — livable homes.

What do I mean by a home? I don't mean a place where you go to relax, the opposite of work. Home has never meant that to women. (You may be a lawyer in a law office and work hard all day, and when you come home in the evening, you start working again. You cross the threshold and start the second shift. So the antithesis between home and work is not something we know as women.) What I would like to suggest by the concept of "home" is this: A home is a place where it is possible to learn and grow. That's something we need to create for our children, if we have them, and for our partners. God willing, they understand that we need it, too. It is something we would like to have in the workplace.

One of the things that has been pointed out about the move of women into the workforce is that they have brought with them a willingness to listen to other people and a concern that work should not be only menial activity. It should bring with it a sense that even when you make the same bed for the 364th time in the year, you're doing something valuable and meaningful.

Personally, I don't believe that childbearing is a punishment. Work is not punishment, either. Our concept of work is built onto the Genesis myth and based on the particular situation of early agriculture: The earth is full of thistles and weeds, and work means the sweat of the brow. It's a bad model, and every labor negotiation in this country is based on the notion that work is dreadful. Only women — who have for centuries worked for free and now want the additional kind of learning experience and development and contribution of having jobs — know that work is a privilege, not just an exaction, and that the workplace can be a place of growth and development.

It is critical to find metaphors that do not subvert what we are trying to say. Lyndon Johnson was the Great Society president who declared a war on poverty. We have all been told that the War on Poverty failed. The policies put in place didn't fail: Head Start is useful, along with a whole series of other programs. In fact, the War on Poverty improved the lives of vast numbers of people. It wasn't until about four years ago that the progressive unraveling of those programs allowed the number of people — particularly children — living in poverty to get back up to where it was when Lyndon Johnson started trying to do something about it.

But, of course, the War on Poverty could be said to have failed because the metaphor is such a bad one. Poverty is not something you can defeat finally and forever. The War on Poverty did not eliminate poverty. In the same way, you cannot win a war against pollution, ill health, or ignorance, because they keep coming back, just as nobody who has ever cared for a house makes the mistake of thinking you can declare a war on dirt and mess — and win it, once and for all. Every time I hear the war metaphor — that includes the "War on Drugs" and the "War on Cancer" — used by a politician, I cringe, because it's a bad metaphor. The most important dimension of work and caregiving and cherishing is maintenance. The most important tasks all of us have are tasks that will never end.

I suggested as a title for this talk "You Will Know the Future When You Get There" because we can't know what the future will be like, but we can know that if we try to keep things the way they are, if we stop learning, if we say, "This is the way it is going to be," instead of listening and looking and doing our homemaking for the future, the future's going to be pretty dreadful. The future is like a child — unknown, waiting to be born, waiting out there to teach you, not something that you can control. We can mess it up, but we can't decide exactly how it's going to be. What has to happen in this "learning maintenance organization" is a very clear realization that Santa Catalina too will change, the students will be different and look to different futures, but your involvement with Santa Catalina can refresh your spirit. We need to be willing to accept very dramatic changes in our lives over time.

Commitment is important. People ask me all the time, "Aren't there some things that don't change? Aren't there basic truths and commitments that never change?" They're usually talking about religion, but I asked myself more generally about the basic commitments of my own life. From the day my daughter was born, she has been the most fundamental commitment I have had. But she changes every day. This is not a commitment to something specified, something fully formed. This is a floating commitment, a moving target. My marriage is like that, too, and so I suspect are most long-lasting marriages. I've been married for thirty-six years to someone with the same surname and the same shoe size, but he has kept becoming a different person. And I have kept becoming a different person for him to deal with.

Yes, there are commitments, but I believe our commitments, like buildings on the San Andreas Fault, have to have a huge amount of flex and willingness to learn in them. This includes relationships, commitment to work, to democracy, to religious faith, to institutions — all have to have flexibility. This is something we experience on the most intimate levels of our lives — where we cannot build on rock.

"THE EPIGENESIS OF CONVERSATIONAL INTERACTION"

A Personal Account of Research Development

Like much of my work, this paper was written as a favor for a friend. In 1969–72, beginning when I was pregnant with my daughter, Sevanne, and continuing until we went to Iran when she was two, I worked part-time with Margaret Bullowa at MIT on a research project on precursors of language in infants. Several years later she asked me to write a personal essay about the development of that work, which had been presented at conferences and published as scientific papers in 1971 and 1975. It is the later, retrospective paper, published in 1979, that I have included here: the story of how my attention was shaped and the connections I made to my other interests.

The title is fairly daunting. The concept of "epigenesis" came to me from Erik Erikson, who borrowed it from embryology to describe the earliest stage of development of some later trait. For me this paper represented the epigenesis of my thinking about the relationship between the personal and the professional. It also exemplifies a characteristic play of analogies in referring to two other bodies of work not represented in this volume, my writings on Arabic poetry and on ritual. In both areas I had begun to think in terms of participation in shared performances as prior to competence, and I was moving toward considering the possibilities of communication across disparate codes. Looking at exchanges between mothers and infants that resembled conversations, I saw them as joint constructions, something mother and infant do together. The mother uses language: "Are you my good boy?" The infant coos. She speaks again and they take turns. My argument here deals with the differences in learning at different stages, where the fact that an infant is oblivious to certain kinds of detail allows him or her to learn a contextual structure into which later learning will fit. In schools, material is presented in carefully designed sequences; life is not so orderly, but the infant's stage of development can act as a kind of filter for still unmanageable complexity.

—MCB, 2004

∽

Background

The journals present us with dozens of highly specific research projects, described with only the most modest statement of the broader intellectual path that led to them, and the most restrained projections of the implications spreading from that narrow research activity. Since in this paper I will be discussing a piece of research that has already been fully described according to the conventions of scientific reporting, I propose to approach it here in a different way: to describe the miscellany of curiosities and interests that led to that research and to reflect on its broader implications. An awareness of these double shadows cast by any piece of reported research can enrich the process of research and clarify the way in which differences of theoretical orientation and personal experience inform it, especially in a field like the study of infant communication and language acquisition that tends to be populated by researchers of distinct and diverse orthodoxies.

In 1969–72 I did a relatively limited study of mother–child communication, concerned with the epigenesis of conversational interaction. When it first appeared, this study took a very different approach from most other studies then being done by psychologists and linguists, an approach that was related to work being done by some anthropologists and psychiatrists but not extensively applied to questions related to language learning. In a sense it was an accident that I applied that approach to mother–child communication, an accident that occurred through meeting Margaret Bullowa and being about to produce a child myself so that I was looking for a way of applying whatever heightened sensitivity this might bring to my work. The research I did on mother–child communication was from one point of view "time out" for me — a brief foray into a new field. From another point of view, it was in direct continuity with most of the work I had done before, research dealing with the structure of events and with communicational contexts.

During the preceding decade I had been pursuing a set of interests that were closely related at an abstract level and yet very different in terms of specific subject matter. In effect, I had concerned myself with the structure of mutually sustained performances ranging from neocharismatic prayer meetings to psychiatric interviews through the work of Scheflen and Birdwhistell[1] to the Arabic odes that I studied for my dissertation. I had also been involved in various ways with language learning and teaching and had come increasingly to think of the learner's problem as learning how to participate in and sustain joint performances, in spite of differences in competence from native speakers, and had come to focus on participation as providing contexts for the development of this competence. A psychiatric interview uses joint participation to bring about change, and so in a different way does a prayer meeting which is concerned with episodes of religious healing and conversion.

Thus, by the time I began to read the literature on child language learning, as a postdoctoral fellow at Brandeis in 1968–69, I had a set of rather special biases. One was towards the study of performances as events, events with several participants, communication in several modalities and a contextual structure, rather than the study of a single competence like language in the abstract spheres of Mind. Another was towards an emphasis on the phatic function of communication of any kind, for language cannot be used for any other purpose unless some agreement is established that one is "in touch." I was also concerned that much of anthropological and linguistic theory seemed to suggest such highly interlocked and interdependent structures that change was unimaginable. Even the successive grammars that some linguists had written about their own children presented the same problem: how did one get from grammar to grammar?

My interests in the problems of change were sharpened by my own experiences, as I became convinced of the biological bases of learning to be a mother, after the birth of my own child. I became convinced that the ethologists, whose work had first interested me when I was trying to understand the nature of ritual, had a great deal to offer to our investigation of human learning.

The Research

Shortly after I gave birth, I began working with the films and tapes Margaret Bullowa had collected of babies, from birth on, taken in their homes. Within a few weeks, I had selected for study a type of episode that occurred in the films. I selected five filmed and taped interactions between a mother and her infant (between the ages of 49 and 105 days) for intensive analysis, including analysis of the temporal and sequential relationship between maternal and infant vocalization. Each was very brief, so the total time of analyzed interactions was less than ten minutes. They occurred spontaneously in longer filmed sessions. In selecting brief sections for intensive study, I was partly building on the model of previous research in kinesics.[2]

A study of these sequences established that the mother and infant were collaborating in a pattern of more or less alternating, non-overlapping vocalization, the mother speaking brief sentences and the infant responding with coos and murmurs, together producing a brief joint performance similar to conversation, which I called "proto-conversation." The study of timing and sequencing showed that certainly the mother and probably the infant, in addition to conforming in general to a regular pattern, were acting to sustain it or to restore it when it faltered, waiting for the expected vocalization from the other and then after a pause resuming vocalization, as if to elicit a response that had not been forthcoming. These interactions were characterized by a sort of delighted, ritualized courtesy and more or less sustained attention and mutual gaze. Many of the vocalizations were of types not described in the acoustic literature on infancy, since they were very brief and faint, and yet were crucial parts of the jointly sustained performances.

The details of that research, including the instrumentation and the statistical and acoustic analysis, have already been published.[3] That description primarily emphasized parallels between these prelinguistic interactions and adult conversation. Here we will presume on that description and go further afield, examining such sequences of interaction as contexts for learning and for whatever they may suggest about the contextualization of learning in infancy. We will be looking at ways in which both parent and child are prepared for engagements of this sort, and ways in which the patterning of these interactions itself facilitates further learning, by providing contexts of variation and heightened attention, structured by the behavior of both participants. The development of the capacity for participation in complex sequenced behavior must lay the groundwork for participation in games and for the development of playful patterns of imitation, and so the study of such performances can shed light on a variety of types of learning, including language acquisition. Thus, having found in the proto-conversations contexts suitable for a certain type of accelerated learning, I shall consider a range of evidence on whether they really have that function and what its biological basis might be, which should suggest further research.

Contexts for Learning

The ethologists have been able to demonstrate a considerable range of innate species-specific mechanisms for learning. One example, which highlights some of the theoretical issues involved, is that very rapid type of learning called "imprinting" which takes place in genotypically highly specified contexts, best described for various birds.[4] In fact, imprinting can be regarded as working by the genetic specification of a context for learning.

Imprinting is similar to the instructions sometimes given for finding one's way: "When you get to a big square with a sort of little park in the middle, ask again," or, alternatively, "I don't know which turn you should take, but it will be the one with buses running along it." Thus, a duckling coming out of the egg, already able to walk, needs to learn to recognize its mother, an individual whose idiosyncratic and accidental features could not economically have been specified for recognition at the genetic level. So it emerges from the egg with a structured pattern of attention, knowing *when and how to learn* what its mother looks like.

The specification of a crucial period for imprinting is extremely efficient, for even where survival does not require speed, the setting up of specified periods for learning to take place seems to accompany learning of extraordinary rapidity and intensity — one brief exposure producing accurate and almost inextinguishable learning, with structured attention excluding irrelevant material.

The possibility of innate patterns that prepare human beings to learn, rapidly and efficiently, what needs to be learned at a specific stage of development, raises interesting and important questions for the study of language learning. Since Chomsky refuted the possibility of learning language according to the behaviorist model in his famous review of Skinner[5] and since Chomsky's argument[6] that linguistic performances in the child's environment are so muddled and incomplete that they would not allow language learning by imitation, we are aware that only an organism with rather specific characteristics would be able to develop complex linguistic competence. One approach is to regard some important part of linguistic competence as innate. A great deal of the response to this proposal depends on how fundamental a particular theorist considers the differences between languages to be. Human behavioral and adaptive diversity provide the prime argument against innate knowledge, unless we can express that knowledge as an innate, perhaps highly specific, ability to learn. In fact, imprinting and other such innate learning and teaching mechanisms are what we should expect to find in human learning, because imprinting is precisely a way of taking advantage of the economies of genotypic programming in species whose patterns of adaptation require flexibility and variation. The instructions for finding one's way from the great square are likely to take that form just because the square is the sort of place from which many possible different paths diverge. In situations of this sort, rigid pre-formulated instructions may not be useful, but alerting the traveler to how and when to discover the appropriate path is. The capacity to learn always depends on a biological given, so the ant hatches knowing what to do, and the duckling hatches knowing how to find out what to do, and the human being is born knowing . . . how to find out how to find out what to do? . . . over a very long period of time.[7]

The duration of human childhood allows for massive, gradual and variegated learning, whereas the duckling must learn to follow its mother immediately because a fox may appear at any moment. However, it is reasonable to expect variations in the learning texture, where special contexts may be genotypically defined as appropriate for intensified learning — where, so to speak, the stage for rapid learning is set. Cultural definitions of contexts or models for learning could be expected to build on those that are genotypically defined. Thus, e.g., the acceptance of parents as appropriate models for imitation is certainly based on biological patterns, and then the culture elaborates on that by inventing school teachers and psychoanalysts. We do indeed know that human learning, cognitive and affective, takes place according to certain schedules, and that certain types of learning, if not achieved at the appropriate period, never will be achieved.

We need, however, to discover a great deal more about how contexts for learning are structured during development. We know that development is gradual and discontinuous, but little has been done to define the variations in texture and the way in which, in any stage of development, certain moments may be moments of especially intense or focussed learning. An understanding of the early contextualization of human learning is essential in order to understand the cultural elaboration of this contextualization, and the kinds of interactions that develop and sustain it.

To sum up, I am suggesting that many of the dilemmas that face the description of human language acquisition may be resolved if we ask whether the infant has a rather highly specific *readiness* to learn language — or, to put this in other words, to take the appropriate steps, in the appropriate sequence, that will lead to a knowledge of language. Since the task is a massive one, we should expect to find contexts of very high mobilization (such as in imprinting) simply for the sake of economy, as well as structured patterns of attention and inattention, and sequences where what is learned at one stage keys in to what is learned at the next stage.

When we consider the form that might be taken by such sequences, certain intellectual strategies suggest themselves, some of which are already very much a part of the discussion of how infants learn language. Thus, there has been considerable discussion of when a child is able to perceive differences between various types of stimuli. It is clear that such abilities may be a precondition for some learning — but *lack* of such abilities may also facilitate learning at a previous stage, giving priority or selective attention to something that needs to be learned first, blocking out confusing distraction. In the case of proto-conversations, where sentences spoken by the mother are structurally equivalent (in terms of the rules of alternation) to monosyllabic murmurs by the infant, learning to participate in the give and take may depend on perceiving the mother's vocalizations as unitary. Similarly, using one part of experience to parse another part may depend on innate patterns, in terms of selecting what experience, in what modality, gives a handle on something else. After all, even the capacity to be reinforced depends on knowing how to relate two events.[8] Again, we need to consider the possibility that out of the continuum of experience certain intervals are marked for especially intense learning. In whatever internal analysis is taking place, the experiences of those intervals would have very high preference, just as certain models take precedence for imitation.

Thus, we are looking for cases where patterned materials provided by the environment meet a patterned receptivity. This receptivity can be innate and species specific, but it need not be an elementary linguistic competence — rather it needs to be a way of arriving at linguistic competence. However, considering the economies of genetic programming, where we continually learn that more and more is provided by the environment, we must expect the patterned receptivity of each stage to have been built up incorporating components learned in the previous stage. This drives us inexorably back to the very earliest experiences.

Readiness for Proto-conversation

In what follows, I will consider, from the point of view of a structured readiness to learn and the provision of patterned stimuli by the environment, some of the background of those brief moments when mothers (and perhaps other caretakers) and infants "converse" with one another. It is not reasonable to suppose that the infant is "programmed" to learn in an especially intense way from such interactions unless their occurrence is also provided for, perhaps in some "programming" of the mother, presumably with cultural variations. This may also serve to underline the propriety and relevance of ethological analogies.

First to review a few familiar and general ideas. Human infants, unlike ducklings, cannot walk away, are in fact extraordinarily helpless. Therefore, the immediate biological task is not to teach the infant to recognize the mother but to teach the mother to recognize, acknowledge, and care for the infant — to mobilize a set of maternal behaviors or, alternatively, to set the stage so that she will learn these very fast. She must meet both the infant's physical needs and his emotional and communicational needs, thus structuring the environment so that the infant can learn. Thus, in addition to asking how the mother is triggered to nurture the infant and protect him (documented by a whole library of material on how nursing is established), we must ask how she is triggered to provide those stimuli that will allow the infant to learn according to his internal schedule. One of the simplest examples of this would be the establishment of mutual gazing, if it can be shown that once a pattern of mutual gazing is established, the mother tends to behave in a given way within mutual gaze episodes. This would seem to be the case with proto-conversations:

mutual gazing sets the stage for maternal vocalization, which sets up the possibility of an unfolding process of learning, probably strengthened by selective attention. I would assume that my rapid focus of interest on the proto-conversations was also a case of such triggering carried over from my own post-partum state and transferred to research.

Most of the genotypically given guidelines for mother and child in this early adaptation are apparently extremely evanescent — rapidly replaced or modified by new learning — for instance, the sucking reflex, which is shaped so rapidly by experience to adapt to breast or bottle. The period immediately after delivery when such patterns might be visible has, until very recently, been so drastically tampered with for most Western births that we have been almost completely ignorant of the normal pattern of development of mother–child communication. Since the mother is the one who should be initially highly programmed for learning appropriate maternal behaviors, post-partum depressions may be due to this disruption. This is also perhaps the real function of the extreme suggestibility or influencibility of women in the early post-partum period — an adaptively useful biological readiness to learn how to be a mother, to grasp on every clue offered by the environment or by the infant. It seems possible that many cognitively very important experiences of order in the caretaking environment occur because of the mother's willingness to learn from the infant and respond to his patterns — again, a matter of selectively intensified attention. Thus, the mother's observation of regular rhythms in the child's hunger, which become reflected in her readiness to nurse, may instruct the infant on the nature of order sooner than the arbitrary order built into a nursing schedule.

Even the process of learning to recognize one's own infant, the basis for the pleasures of mutual gazing and recognition, probably has a biological basis. In 1966 I had a premature delivery of a boy who died after five hours, whom I saw for only a few seconds. Many women who have had such experiences describe how the image of the infant was etched on their memory, recurring with perfect ineradicable detail in dreams and in waking hours for months and even years afterwards. Surely here we have an example of imprinting, and instead of dismissing it by saying that the emotional stress of the moment and the significance of the event were bound to leave a sharp and vivid memory, we should search reports of other such vividly etched memories for comparative study, to evaluate them as learning and consider their possible adaptive significance. This vividly etched image of the newborn is surely, under normal circumstances, immediately overlaid with multiple images, but must provide a basic foundation for the developing relationship.

Another element in the readiness of mother and child for protoconversation concerns rhythm. Movement, sound, and rhythm make up much of the common experience infant and parent bring to their meeting — patterns of synchrony and potential patterns of counterpoint and syncopation. Just as we don't recognize the dog's behavior as instinctive when we see him digging in the forest, the ways in which mothers tap and jiggle their infants to soothe them (and hold them with their heads against their hearts) seem self-evidently reasonable and effective and are only recently being intensively studied. However, when the dog begins to paw at the living-room rug, we begin to wonder about the basis for the behavior. I was fascinated after the more felicitous birth of my daughter in 1969 to find that for about thirty-six hours after birth, if I was not holding my daughter but could see or hear her, I was likely to start tapping and jiggling anything I held, a book, or my own knee.

This is only an example of a range of patterns that can be understood as ways in which the mother is activated to care for the infant, ways in which nursing is initiated and regulated, and so on — all areas where very rudimentary and quickly extinguished or developed patterns provide a starting place for rapid mutual learning, where maternal commitment and infant need must be orchestrated very rapidly in trustworthy common events in time. My purpose here is to discuss the way in which they also provide the framing and internal structure for contexts of further learning. Thus we can integrate them into the more general topic of what order of pattern must already be present in order for learning to take place and, when the two interactants are so very different, what order of commonality must exist in that pattern?

The Establishment of Conversational Patterns

The proto-conversations I studied reached, by forty-nine days after birth, a length and complexity that made it possible to use statistical methods to study sequencing and temporal spacing of vocalizations. However, on the tapes much briefer examples could be found, when the infant was slightly less than one month old, and it was when she was approximately one month old that I became aware of such sequences in my interactions with my own daughter. I say "aware" because I know that before that period I certainly talked to her and gazed into her eyes and found the process meaningful, but only when she was about one month old did I begin to have the sense of complex sequenced joint participation in interaction in two or more modalities. Bullowa describes such sequences beginning within a few hours after birth: "It seems to be a spontaneous behavior of mothers in our culture* to initiate such behavior and for the infants when awake and in the appropriate position vis-à-vis the adult to gaze at the mother's face and vocalize softly. Such exchanges are usually brief."[9]

Infant gazing behavior — and infant fascination with even simplified models of the human face — has been extensively studied. Jaffe *et al.* argue that infant gazing should be seen as a precursor to later gazing patterns rather than to verbal conversational patterns.[10] This is obvious but somewhat misses the point. Conversation, whether for adults or for parent–child pairs, is a highly complex activity, involving communication in many (or all) modalities, according to varying rhythms. Speech is characterized by very short signals, with the communicationally useful characteristics of discreteness and rapid fading.[11] Kinesic behavior (communicative body motion) contains a great many sustained signals which provide transfixes to the staccato of speech: a gaze, a cocked eyebrow, a tension in one shoulder modifying and unifying a long stream of speech.[12] These signals would not be communicative if they were not varied and terminable. The essence of conversation is in fact the possibility, provided in ordinary conversation by kinesic behavior and paralanguage, of organization into units larger than the syntactic sentence, so that both participants are included in an ongoing pattern. Infant gazing is indeed a precursor of adult gazing, infant gesticulation a precursor of adult gesticulation, and infant vocalization a precursor of adult vocalization. But would learning in each of these types of signalling occur if they were not juxtaposed and their communicative functions were not complementary? Maternal imprinting to an individual infant's face and the infant's genetically given liking for faces bring them

*Bullowa rightly emphasizes the culture (mainly American and British) in which the observation has been made; although we don't know that such interactions do not occur in other cultures, we do know that in one case at least, that of Japan, they are statistically less frequent at later stages of childhood — mothers and infants simply vocalize less. (William Caudill, "Tiny Dramas: Vocal Communication between Mother and Infant in Japanese and American Families," in *Mental Health Research in Asia and the Pacific*, vol. 2, *Transcultural Research in Mental Health*, ed. W. P. Labra [Honolulu: University Press of Hawaii, 1973]).

into mutual gazing; mutual gazing provides the *framing* for a context of learning and perhaps also triggers or is connected to an intensification of attention and readiness to learn.

Neonates are "old hands" at sound and rhythm, which form part of their environment before birth, although in a very global kinesthetic way. Mothers are skilled at the sounds and rhythms of speech, and some at least are equipped with translations of the cadences of their lullabies and endearments into the same whole-body experiences of sound and rhythm that preceded birth, tapping and jiggling. Can we think of the tapping and jiggling, intelligible and satisfying to the infant in terms of earlier experience, as a sort of carrier wave that gives him more access to the new types of sounds and rhythms of song or speech? Both mothers and infants seem to move rapidly into patterns of mutual gaze of varying intensity and duration. Following the carrier-wave metaphor, these periods of mutual gaze may provide contexts in which vocalization becomes increasingly meaningful. Such contexts would serve as frames of attention within which pattern can be discerned in otherwise fragmented and inchoate material, and the translation from perceptions of the frame to perceptions of internal structure may be facilitated by experiences of interlocking rhythm.[13] When I was looking for additional examples of "proto-conversation" to study in my research, I located them by scanning through stretches of film at accelerated speed, looking for mutual gaze, and then checking with the sound to see if I found alternating vocalization. That may be, in a sense, what both infant and mother do — take the mutual gaze as the signal that identifies the nature of the framed material, and identifies the period as a valuable period of intensified attention.

My interest in this has in part been focussed by a striking phenomenon in patterns of child care I have observed in Iran, with older but still preverbal children. Iranians act as if they believed that children, when *not* in interaction with adults, are in a sort of neutral gear, a sort of suspension, doing nothing. Although, as a cultural perception of childhood, this seems to miss a great deal that goes on in the child's mind *out* of interaction with adults, it lays a very great stress on the significance of episodes of intense interaction. This may be a cultural prolongation of the perception of an infant condition in which attention is swamped by physical events most of the time but there are brief periods of high attention.[14] One of the things that creates or contextualizes those periods is interaction with an adult, as in proto-conversations. For a Westerner, used to thinking about the child's mental activity outside of interaction, it is a useful reminder of the greater potential significance of the interactional sequences.

Another way in which we can find interesting evidence of the high learning significance of the proto-conversations of infancy is by looking at the most closely equivalent events of later childhood. Proto-conversations tend to take place after feeding, caretaking, bathing, dressing — at a moment when the bustle is over and physical needs are met and sleep is not yet urgent. These are the moments that in many households in our culture are kept almost ritualized for the most intimate converse of parent and child. Perhaps prayers are said, perhaps the day is reviewed and the morrow planned and concerns of the day put into perspective, perhaps sudden questions of God or love, death or sex are trusted to speech as at no other hour of the day: conversation, which occurs framed and with a sustained commitment of attention, represented in earliest childhood by mutual gaze.

Conversation and Ritual

From the very beginning of my research on child communication, I was aware of a convergence of key ideas in this research with a different strand of interest in ritual, approached through a study of neo-Pentecostal or "charismatic" prayer groups.[15] Initially I was primarily interested in glossolalia, or "speaking in tongues," as a form of "regression in the service of the ego" such as crops up in relation to many different kinds of religious and mystical experience, harking back to meaningful experiences of vocalization combined with communion in pre-verbal infancy — much the kind of experience provided by a proto-conversation. (All studies which I have seen depict glossolalia as non-meaningful phonation, sometimes highly repetitive and simple in structure, sometimes more varied, corresponding generally to the phonology of the tongues-speaker's native language and the rhythms of speech, without the grammatical structure).[16]

From this point of view, the connection of non-semantic vocalization and a sense of religious communion, the study of glossolalia provides supporting evidence for the apparent pleasure of proto-conversation in infancy. But there is still another connection, and this is through the notion of ritual contexts as contexts for learning. The study of charismatic prayer meetings presents a number of analogies with proto-conversations. These, too, are performances framed in time, with several participants interacting in various modalities and using various different codes. In the prayer groups, vocalizations vary from glossolalia to memorized prayers through spontaneous prayers of various degrees of stereotypy. Whereas proto-conversations present the theoretical problem of how two persons with disparate codes can orchestrate their behavior in a common performance, the prayer groups provide examples of a group of persons each of whom is capable of performing in several different codes, orchestrating those codes within a joint performance — that is, code switching is not tied to individual participants. Each case raises the question of *codes governing performance,*[17] and the further question of whether performance codes might not provide frameworks for changes in competence. I have described changes of this sort occurring in the prayer group context as aspects of the process of *ritualization* — that is, the meaning and structure of certain types of vocal and other behavior are progressively altered by their performance in ritual contexts. In ritual, sequences of behavior become fused so that they are no longer generated anew each time, nor do they any longer mean what an analysis of their components and structure would suggest. Our question here is whether the contexts provided by proto-conversations are not contexts for the opposite process, a process of fission — that is, contexts in which the infant can participate in terms of large, fused chunks of behavior (treating the complex utterances of the mother as single counters in an exchange), while at the same time allowing for a progressive analysis and potential recombination of smaller elements.

Conclusions

The original research on which this paper is based focussed intensively on five interactions between a single mother–infant pair, totalling no more than 10 minutes. The striking thing about these brief interactions was that mother and child, in spite of the vast differences between them, were able to participate jointly in performances that seemed to give great pleasure to both. Infant and mother may enter into such interactions because previous experience combined with phylogenetic characteristics prepares them to do so. The particular kind of preparation, as well as a comparison with other kinds of contexts in which rapid and intense learning takes place, suggests that interactions of this sort have a very high potential not only for pleasure but also for learning. This is highly suggestive. The inadequacy of linguistic performances in a child's environment for the learning of language has been a major issue in attempts to evaluate the level of innate knowledge needed for language learning. However, the evidence from animal ethology strongly suggests the need for study of specific ways in which the young organism is equipped to *select* from among environmental stimuli and to match them selectively with phylogenetically given patterns. A concept of structured receptivity or readiness to learn, as we are able to define it, casts a totally different light on the value and usefulness of environmental input. Specifically, in this case, we are suggesting that mother and child, long before speech, have the potential for developing joint vocal performances (although these will clearly take different forms in different cultures), which function as contexts for learning.

Further we are suggesting that in addition to the advantages for learning given by intense attention and pleasure, the infant's participation sets the stage for learning: once he knows the "rules of the game" and can anticipate patterns, he can also deliberately and playfully vary them and he has a "handle" on what he is trying to understand. Here at the prelinguistic level we can see the child playing a "grammatical" game. This should cast new light on our data on games playing, imitation, and mother–child interaction at later stages of development. Indeed, it provides an analogy for understanding a wide variety of interactions in which change or learning takes place, from psychotherapy to religious ritual to the ordinary pleasures of conversation, and the general phenomenon of active participatory learning.

For purposes of this volume [Margaret Bullowa's retrospective on the research I participated in], it seems important to emphasize the way the special interests and personal experience of the researcher influenced the research. Vast as is the range of human adult behavior, it all grows from potentials for development that infants, in general, have in common, and we can expect contributions to our understanding from scholars with all sorts of specialized interests in the human sciences. At the same time, the researcher's skills in observing behavior are also closely akin to the capacities he or she has needed to mature as an individual human being, and this too can contribute to our expanding knowledge.

HOLDING UP THE SKY TOGETHER

This piece was written in response to a request from *Civilization* magazine, a short-lived venture into popular publishing by the Library of Congress, for an article on the future of feminism. It went back and forth to and from editing for a year, finally appearing in 1995, and still does not read quite like my own voice, but it does reflect my conviction that discussions of feminism are often as lopsided as the androcentric traditions they challenge. The social construction of gender has been both wasteful and unjust, but we cannot correct it unless we make sure that the full spectrum of human needs continues to be met, even as the burdens are reduced and the rewards are more equally distributed.

—MCB, 2004

The familiar slogan says that women hold up half the sky. Imagine a long line of caryatids suddenly heading off in different directions, turning their hands to new challenges and new pleasures. The roof is likely to fall in.

The transition in human society today is even greater. The sky may indeed be falling. The piecemeal changes that are allowing women access to the privileges once reserved for men, making them more equal and more similar to men than ever before, are altering the very structure of society. This process of pervasive change would ideally lead toward a society in which all members can develop and contribute, and in which human needs are met and aspirations fully engaged. At the very least, this real progress will involve rethinking the life cycle and the way we work and care for each other and for our families. I believe it will also involve a move toward a more sustainable society, which means small families and moderated consumption. These are feminist issues, but they go beyond the divisive contemporary debates over theories and priorities to a reshaping of society that can only come about through common action.

The extended dependency of human infants is central to humanness, linked to the development of upright stature, large brains, continuing family ties and an adaptation based on learning and teaching. Human survival once depended on many births and sustained breast-feeding, so that throughout the world women have been assigned tasks — as cooks or nurses, for example — that were compatible with or analogous to the care of young children.

In our time, the division of labor is no longer tied to breast-feeding, and rearing offspring no longer fully defines adulthood for women — or men. It is not only that women want to participate fully in society but that the traditional division of labor no longer makes sense.

In the future, many couples will avoid parenthood, while others will improvise new ways of arranging their lives. Devoting a portion of the life cycle to staying at home with children — five or six years perhaps — or working part-time for a longer period should be possible and legally protected for those who choose to do so, but these domestic commitments absorb only part of a life. Our foremothers commonly raised a dozen children (many of whom died), gardened, wove cloth and made candles, and died some twenty years younger than we do. Theirs was a valuable and challenging career. But this model of *lifetime* motherhood is no longer as fulfilling or necessary as it once was. It can of course still be simulated in America today by having large numbers of children (almost all of whom will live into adulthood), schooling them at home, and making an art form of domesticity.

This raises a touchy political issue. Feminists have often been chided for disparaging full-time homemakers. While housework and childcare represent valuable work, they are no longer satisfying *lifelong* careers for most women. Of course, many women who call themselves full-time homemakers are engaged in other kinds of work as well, supporting their husbands' careers or sustaining community institutions. And some men and women, when resources allow, thrive on lives of relative idleness, or else find their meaning in consumerism. But most people are probably happiest when they have a sense of doing productive work, of making a contribution to society.

Since the industrial revolution, productive tasks have moved steadily out of the household, and more and more women have worked for pay. At the end of World War II, however, women who had been working in factories, like Rosie the Riveter, were sent home to make their jobs available for returning veterans. These jobs gave the returning soldiers a sense of dignity and paid a "family wage," supposedly sufficient to support wives and children. The pressures on women to remain at home were equaled by the pressures on men to provide for them. The reduction in traditionally female homemaking tasks went hand in hand with the invention of various forms of "make-work" such as daily vacuuming and repeated redecoration, the domestic equivalent of featherbedding.

Housework and childcare have rarely been counted as productive work by economists and statisticians, so we are only slowly recognizing the contributions women have made. By now, however, the "family wage" has eroded, and the inflated standard of living of a contemporary household cannot easily be met by a single wage earner. Women are still paid less than men and often come home after work not to relax but to begin a second shift, which, because it does not bring in cash, is undervalued. Programs to support or help poor mothers and children are under attack because the women "don't work" (meaning they don't have a paid job), but there has been significant resistance to providing the childcare that would allow these women to join the work force. Oddly, although we are told that we should value the homemaking activities of middle-class women without jobs, supporting these activities for poor women is seen as waste. Paid work is still the yardstick of value and dignity, while much essential work is unpaid. It may be that in the future all forms of full-time caregiving should be remunerated, either publicly or privately.

At present we live in a society that does not provide enough paid jobs to shape the days and give a sense of achievement to all its members. Because we use jobs to distribute resources, some people inevitably go without the essentials of food and shelter, or obtain them in ways that further deplete their dignity. We also use jobs to distribute many other social benefits, including social security and medical care, even for dependents. All these add-ons to a basic salary shrink the availability of jobs as employers attempt to limit the number of individuals they are responsible for. If the costs of health care were spread evenly across society and work were regarded as a right, we could move toward instituting more jobs with shorter hours that reduce the work burden for every member of society, and toward job sharing, part-time work with benefits, a higher minimum wage, and lower wages at the top. Many of these jobs would involve caregiving.

We are also suffering a lack of committed and effective care, ranging from a friendly greeting and a cup of tea at the end of the day to family support at home during illness. The solution proposed by some religious groups is a return to the "family values" of the 1950s, sending women back to the home. But although there is undoubtedly a need for care, there is no longer any reason to assume it will be provided primarily by women, or in nuclear families, but possibly in cooperative relationships between families or in new businesses and institutions. Indeed, many studies show that children can benefit from half a dozen involved caregivers of both sexes: As the African proverb says, "It takes a village to raise a child."

The biology that will continue to shape the "destiny" of human society is not sex — the relative differences in height and strength between men and women, the debatable differences in cognitive ability, or even differences in endocrine systems and genitalia — but the human need for care, which both males and females can give. Infants can drink formula based on cow's milk (or even mother's milk, expressed and saved), but raising human beings still requires a vast investment of care and commitment, in spite of technological advances. And our needs do not stop with adulthood. Normal adults, having been dependent on their parents for so long, continue to yearn for support throughout their lives. Even many "dink" couples (dual income, no kids) operate at the edge of burnout, both husband and wife in need of cherishing. Meanwhile, medical advances have allowed more and more people to live on with chronic illnesses.

We all face the question of who will care for us. Care is as basic a need as clean air, and just as we have been learning that clean air is not a free good but a resource to be valued and protected, so caregiving needs to be supported and recognized as essential, a national priority like agriculture and education. This could be accomplished with public or private funds, or a combination of the two.

Advances in technology are gradually decreasing the human role in producing goods and thus threatening the viability of the blue-collar middle class. Meanwhile, the service sector, which continues to grow, looks suspiciously like a way to take caregiving outside the home and make it a paying job. Many traditionally domestic tasks are being channeled through the GNP in various industries: health care, day care, ready-to-serve foods, psychotherapy, even escort services. This may add jobs, but it increases inequality at the very basic level of comfort, since these services are available only to those who can pay.

As we have seen, caregiving is no longer a necessary extension of the roles of childbearing women. Is caregiving then intrinsically feminine? And, if so, will caregivers remain underpaid, insecure, and often undertrained? If work just "comes naturally," what is the appropriate recompense for it? How different are women from men anyhow? Are they uniquely caring? We simply don't know, which is why the futile debate rages on. Every adult today has grown up in the context of socially constructed and polarized gender roles. The successful career woman and ardent feminist still bears the mark of her exposure to traditional female roles. The man most sympathetic to feminist goals remains affected by cultural ideas of masculinity. Gays and lesbians, who have rejected much of this stereotyping, are still influenced by it. We cannot know what women or men would be like if they were not molded by the social constructions of gender, but one might reasonably expect their differences to be less pronounced — that we would all prove to be made of sugar and spice as well as snips and snails and puppy dogs' tails, in individual proportions.

Many differences between the sexes will prove to be not the simple result of either nature or nurture but of complex relationships between the two, for the history of human evolution is the history of a gradually increased reliance on culture and learning. When a woman gives birth, her bonding with the newborn is biologically supported — learning made easy by biology. In many societies men have minimal contact with infants and children, but men who are involved in infant care do bond, particularly those who have assisted at deliveries. And both men and women are capable of care and commitment to adopted children. Biology helps, but it is only the beginning of the human story. One day perhaps we shall recognize that men are suited to caregiving and should take equal responsibility for it. They will reveal a range of talents and preferences, just as women have when new options have opened up. Freedom works both ways. Similarly, women belong at all levels of what were once considered the male provinces of decision making — enriching the process with different experience and equal talent.

Reducing the importance of reproduction is only one of the changes in the life cycle that are inevitably going to affect ideas about gender. Full social and economic adulthood is increasingly deferred beyond physical maturity, so that adolescence and youth become part of childhood, while active maturity extends longer and longer after the reproductive years. We need to move beyond the idealization of sexual differences as they appear in the early years of puberty, to create conceptions of beauty and strength that can develop and last a lifetime. Adolescence is hardly the place to find our ideals. This is the time when many girls lose confidence and cave in to traditional expectations; it is also the period when many boys assert themselves by driving too fast, drinking too much, or even carrying guns and joining gangs. Early decisions, constrained by gender stereotypes, tragically preempt later development in a society that has extended the period of dependency needed to secure satisfying careers. At the same time, current ideas about femininity subject women to especially damaging forms of ageism. But men and women may become more similar as they age, finding time to choose new careers and move beyond stereotypes.

The old system of stereotyped gender roles for men and women is not only unfair, it is also toxic; Playboy bunnies and gangsters make lousy models. There is too much aggression in traditional stereotypes of masculinity. Too many women are still being told that glamour followed by childbearing is the single route to honorable adulthood, that marriage leads to living "happily ever after."

The disarray among feminists today may be a sign that it is time to shift from the specific concerns of women to broader social issues. You cannot change only half the structure of society. The current "values crisis" cannot be solved by turning back or by tinkering — it requires a new understanding that women are not a "special interest." It is time to make it possible for everyone to do work that is valued, by sharing out the productive jobs and treating care as the right and obligation of every member of society. Holding up the sky is going to have to be a joint project.

CARING FOR CHILDREN, CARING FOR THE EARTH

This brief piece began life as a sermon at New York's Cathedral of St. John the Divine in 1979, which explains the occasional references to biblical texts and hymns. A sermon is a different genre from a speech or a lecture, which makes it an interesting assignment. I believe that it is useful to be able to switch from one genre to another and to build in contextual references that will strengthen any message for its particular audience. This piece is a little longer than a sermon would be because when it was cleaned up for publication in the cathedral newsletter and later in the journal *Christianity and Crisis*, I edited in answers from the question-and-answer session that took place outside the sanctuary after the service. I enjoy Q and A's not only as opportunities to root out possible misunderstandings but as ways of transforming the rather authoritarian format of most forms of public speaking, including preaching, into dialogue.

Anthropologists have long been interested in the different ways of organizing family and kinship. What is not always made explicit is that family structures and patterns of age and sex roles, which are so basic to any tradition and so hard to change, can be seen as a kind of key to other systems of ideas — about the organization of political life, or God, or the cosmos.

—MCB, 2004

Several years ago I heard an address by a Tibetan abbot on a meditation called "The Recognition of the Mother." This meditation is supposed to lead people to the discovery of compassion. One reflects that the world has existed from all eternity through countless cycles of reincarnation; therefore, it follows that all other sentient beings have — in some incarnation, at some point in infinite time — been one's mother. Reflecting on that, one discovers compassion for them.

The good abbot paused with a puzzled frown, while the translator caught up with him. Then he said, "You know, that just doesn't seem to speak to Americans. They may not feel quite the same way about their mothers. So I tell Americans, 'Try to meditate on the recognition of the best friend.'"

One of the things my anecdote illustrates, of course, is that people acquire their ability to receive and to give love from their early family experiences. And that, in most cultures, the metaphors and thought patterns that are used to teach the ethical treatment of persons outside the family are derived from the particular culture's system of kinship. Thus, we hear in the Gospel that the peacemakers are the sons of God. We speak of ourselves as children of God, and hope that this will help us deal more gently with one another.

The anecdote also reminds us, however, that kinship patterns differ from culture to culture, and that they change with time. Part of the point I hope to make here is that when we choose metaphors in order to speak vividly and powerfully to issues such as war and peace or the preservation of the environment we must be careful that the images we use convey the meaning we intend to the audience we reach. All of us today are becoming aware, for example, that the patrilineal imagery that has been so important in our culture no longer fits our lives, any more than would the totemic imagery that guided the aboriginal Australians in their relationships to one another and to their ecosystem, or the matrilineal systems that have existed in different times and places.

Consider the poster that most of us have seen with a striking photo of the earth, taken from space, and below it the line "Love Your Mother." That is an effort to use the immediate, universal experience of intimacy and, through the use of metaphor, to extend our experience to a broader understanding of our relationship with nature and one another. And yet, given the present state of civilization, this may be a most unfortunate image now. For people leave their mothers. Mothers (and fathers, for that matter) get worn out and are put on the shelf. Instead of reminding us of intimacy and mutual tenderness, the image may recall that spaceships are launched, casting off umbilical ties to the planet; we may be encouraged in our resignation to the wearing out and using up of the earth's wealth.

People also need images derived from kinship to think about time; that is to say, in addition to providing a model for relationships to people in the present — strangers, new people — kinship provides models for relationships to the past and future. Here again we are in crisis. We seem to be at a point where we are profoundly unable to place what we do in relation to the past and the future. We live with the extraordinary probability that within one or two generations we will exhaust resources that required millennia to come into being: energy resources, oil especially.

We are using up the past. And this is almost symmetrically reflected in the way in which we are now likely to preempt — to use up — the future before it can arrive. Just as the substances created through past time will be exhausted, in turn we are creating substances, such as radioactive wastes, excess carbon dioxide, fluorocarbons, that may be with the planet equal millennia into the future, endangering all life.

Fostering the Future

Thus we are in urgent need of new ways of thinking about time and about relationships. Metaphors of kinship remain the best place to start, but we need to enrich the form in which we use these metaphors. We can go on speaking, with St. Francis, of our Brother Sun, Sister Moon, Earth our Mother, above all God our Father. But we need to incorporate our changing sense of family and relationships so that the metaphors will not do more harm than good, and consider how our metaphors apply to the future. This is not only a matter of words and images; we need also to refresh our experience of the persons and relationships behind our choices of language.

Let me therefore suggest another meditation, the meditation of "The Adoption of the Child," through which we can discover both compassion and responsibility through a sense of a share in parenting. I believe each person trying to decide in this period of history how to live, what action to take — where to set the thermostat, how often to drive the automobiles, what party or candidate to vote for, what to do with Coca-Cola bottles —

all of us who in making such decisions want to be responsible to the future need to be sure we have a relationship with at least one real, flesh and blood child.

Many of us lack this. There are an increasing number of adults who do not plan to have children; there are a great many others whose children have grown up and moved away, who do not have relationships with children built into their lives. I think we also must expect an increasing number of people who will want to push the children they already have out of their lives, to repudiate contact with children — even to raise the question whether parents should not be able to decide, later on, that dealing with children they chose to give birth to is a burden they don't want to continue to bear.

One reason, I am convinced, that many people are deciding not only not to bear children but not to have children in their lives is that we are today living at the expense of children. What we use and what we waste will not be there for them; the pollution we create will be. In these circumstances it is not surprising that people feel that their style of life is lived at the expense of the future, and that they do not want reminders of the future around them.

I know there are risks in what I am saying. I could be taken to be urging people to have children without regard for the population crisis. But I am not saying that every couple must *have* children in order to preserve our link with the future; I am talking, rather, about our need as adults to be in relationship with children, to share in parenting and to give children the support of many caring adults. People need not give birth to children to be in touch with them. When they decide they are not going to have children, or when their children are grown, they ought not to cut themselves off from children altogether.

There are many different ways of relating to children, and they are different for different people. My husband and I didn't have any children until I was thirty, and when I was about twenty-six I found myself beginning to be shy with children, almost avoiding them, because I had lost the habit of being with children. At that point I purposefully began cultivating the children of my friends — for instance, inviting their twelve-year-old daughter to come to dinner or to stay overnight, without her parents. I did different things with children of different ages; taking a younger child, for example, to the circus.

There are also many children in institutions who need contact with loving adults, and there are opportunities for volunteers in such institutions. There are civic programs like the Police Athletic League and the Big Brother Big Sister program through which adults can work with somewhat older children in problem situations. Or one can find means of helping families where there has been child abuse. Abuse sometimes happens because the father and mother are bearing great burdens and feeling great anxiety that finds expression against the child and is less likely to happen when there are uncles and aunts and grandparents, or other loving adults, to relieve the pressures. This is true at every economic level: All children need contact with a range of adults. When families move, for example, parents could go out of their way to find people of different ages to relate to their own children. It would be nice to have an adopt-a-grandparent program, places for willing grandparents to find honorary grandchildren.

I have shifted here from the needs of adults and of civilization to the needs of the child, but we have all been children. The fact is that when we were small there were people, including our parents, who loved us and kept us from dying, and what they did then enables us now to relate to others. It is an error of the age that we think children are raised only by parents. It is an error that leads to our becoming possessive and protective, and thereby depriving them of experience they must have. No two people can raise a child; much less, one and a half people, or two halves.

A Living Network

Particularly now, in this time of great and fundamental change in family structure, in kin relations, indeed in the very notion of family, we must begin to think of child rearing as we think about the growth of organisms, including the realization of how complexly structured are the nutrients they must have; how much pattern there must be in the environment to make life and growth possible; how much diversity and stimulation and love from many people a child needs to mature.

What we are realizing is essentially that the environment a child needs to grow in is one of the great and complex miracles. If we meditate on the future of an individual child, we must gradually embrace the whole human community and the whole biosphere of our planet, as sharing in providing the environment for that child's growth. This environment is a vast collaboration, a dance of co-parenting by air and water and sun and moon; by bacteria and plants and other living creatures; by other people.

Even, in the end, by other nations. Something my mother said often and often was that in this nuclear age, as nice as the Russians are to their children, their children live because we don't blow them up. We are the only people who can look after the children in Russia. And vice versa. When we talk about co-parenting, about being jointly responsible and careful for children, we are talking about an issue that is worldwide, that concerns all families, all neighborhoods, all countries, not only our own.

And yet, broad as this is, we have to start from our own bodies and our own families as our metaphor for understanding our need for others. The trick is not to stop there, not to cut off the process of interaction or let it become static. We must be able to move from our own bodies, our own families, to include our society and our country, the sun, the earth, the soil, the world. We must constantly explore the new meanings, new metaphors, and new possibilities suggested by the evolution in our kinship patterns. And our images must be fresh, we must root them in and compare them with immediate experience.

This is why I do not ultimately believe that it is old-fashioned to think about parenting and kinship and concern for children as among the central ethical issues. In our culture, we constantly risk pursuing individual goals — we work, we pursue careers, we acquire money, we become involved with self-realization — while losing our sense that all this must be grounded in a responsibility, almost a biological one, for the present and the future. If we do not remain related somehow to the fundamental biological orientation to the future through reproduction we run the risk that our other choices will become more concerned with gratification and exploitation and comfort than with responsibility. This possibility becomes more nearly a probability now when there is such a risk that abortion, contraception, and technological advances related to the bearing of children may be skewed by social forces and individual choices away from an ethic of responsibility and caring.

The needs of children and the needs of adults are, then, reciprocal. One reason we need to involve ourselves with the life of at least one child is so that this one child will not be isolated, restrained, and overburdened; so that children generally will have as many adults concerned about them as possible. The other reason is so that we, looking at the child, can reflect on the vast network needed to give that child a future, so that we can build up in our imagination the sense of all the other human beings and all the natural forces interlocked in support of and care for the child.

It is not enough that we look at one another and say, We are brothers and sisters. That is a way of saying we come from a common past, that we have a shared origin and a certain similarity that binds us to one another. But we must also look at one another, at the planet, at the natural forces around us and say, Together we will be parents. We will become kin to one another and treat one another with love, because out of our differences comes the future. We will knit ourselves to one another by metaphors of kinship, in common nurturance of the ongoing life of this planet. And as we realize how many must be engaged with us in that parenthood, how broad is the communion and interrelationship that makes all life possible, then we will find that we are indeed encompassed about by a host of witnesses. And it is this that makes faith possible.

"A SPADE WITH WHICH TO DIG"

Valuing Human Occupations

In the 1990s a group of occupational therapists proposed a rethinking of their profession with the new name "occupational science." All too often, their field has been trivialized as "harmless activities to keep patients busy." The new emphasis was on looking at all of the meaningful ways in which individuals spend time and on promoting their ability to do so in spite of chronic illness or disability — so *occupation* might refer to paid work but might as easily refer to child care or study, prayer or gardening. For the professionals in the field, the change of name was a claim for respect for themselves as well as for the clients with whom they worked.

The issue I was addressing in this talk, given in Nova Scotia, is broader than the issues of disability that engage the professionals, for an understanding of the interconnection of the different kinds of activity that occupy our days is central to composing lives. Dividing life's activities into separate categories leads to assigning higher value to some and lesser value to others, including activities that are indispensable. We need to understand how all our occupations fit together and are enfolded one within the other, especially in the work done by women, how they balance each other, so that human capacity requires both cherishing and being cherished, and how choices are made, priorities set, and values assigned.

—MCB, 2004

120

I am going to start with an example from the Jewish tradition that shakes
up the categories of occupations in a way that I think may be helpful. This
is an example from the culture of Eastern European Jewry that was essentially destroyed by the Holocaust, the culture of the *shtetl,* although rem-
nants of it can be found today in Israel and elsewhere. The most valued of
activities was the study of sacred texts — the study of Torah, the study of
Talmud — study, and restudy, and debate of those texts. Men made a lifetime of learning, but they were instructed that it was not appropriate to
make of the Torah — the first five books of the Old Testament, the
teaching or law — to 'make of the Torah a spade with which to dig."
Scholars were supported by the community but they were not paid for
their work as scholars. Indeed, traditionally rabbis were paid for various
administrative tasks, but not for teaching and studying law. Of course, a
Talmudic scholar was the ideal son-in-law and rich men aspired to have
their daughters marry scholars who would spend their lives learning in
this most valued of occupations, unremunerated but fully supported. It
was understood, and this is an interesting point here, that the care and
feeding of a scholar was more demanding than that of a husband doing
some other kind of work. A scholar was engaged in an extremely
"macho" task. He was expected to need better food and to be more interested in sex than men who merely worked with their muscles. Whereas a
truck driver might want to sleep with his wife once a week, a scholar
might want to every day because of this heroic effort.

Now, I offer this model of scholarship to shake up what we mean by
work, what we mean by occupation, what we mean by productivity. You
have probably all been exposed to the notion that academics do not really
work and that intellectuals are enervated. They don't produce any material good and maybe their masculinity is a bit in question (or indeed their
femininity). But the Jewish tradition offers a different point of view that
says that the highest work of mankind (and it really is just *man*kind in the
shtetl!) is learning. Doing that through a lifetime has no end to it, but
somehow it is fundamental to the life of the entire community.
Interestingly, the Hebrew word for work is also a word for worship, just
as in the Christian monastic tradition the *opus dei,* the work of God, was
the work of prayer. The monks might do some farming or even make
liqueurs or something like that to support the community. But the real

work, the work that was important, was the life of prayer, which produced no material good nor was it remunerated. It was possible, for many centuries and in different traditions, to sustain the sense of something valuable without measuring it by material production.

Now that I have combined three different categories, learning, work, and worship, let me add play. It is sometimes said that play is the work of childhood. You could also say learning is the work of childhood. But it is not clear either that there is an end to play or that play is somehow useful and important in childhood and then becomes frivolous at a later stage — or that there is an end to learning: in fact there is something very odd about that idea.

If play is the work of childhood, if playing is the central developmental task, then there is something wrong with the familiar meaning of work. We live in a tradition developed from the Garden of Eden story in the Book of Genesis, right up to the industrial revolution, that suggests that work is by definition onerous, burdensome, difficult, a curse on humankind, comparable in awfulness to having babies. That is a terrible idea, actually, that work is a curse. It is also a terrible idea that having babies is a curse. This idea about work has shadowed human experience. Incidentally, I think it has fed into the notion that if something is good for you it has to be unpleasant, which has had such a negative effect on education. For some of us who are very lucky, work is the play of adulthood just as play is the work of childhood. Work and play and learning are all involved in growth and development, and are really necessary to living a satisfying life. If work or learning is turned into a torment, we're doing something terribly wrong.

What I want to do today is to add another category to these categories of occupation that I've mentioned that seem to me far more similar than we usually allow. That's the category of caregiving or cherishing. The occupation, or activity, of cherishing someone else or even oneself needs to be compared with learning, worshipping, various kinds of work and study and even play. Through history, caregiving has mostly been delegated to women, and over the centuries the unremunerated work that women have done as caregivers has not been counted. It is not included in the Gross National Product and there are almost no statistics on it. I am old enough to have grown up before women learned that there was something wrong with saying "Oh, I don't work, I'm just a housewife"; "I don't do anything, I'm just at home." For some reason, what women did in the home was not taken seriously as work *or* as play, as worship *or* as learning. Yet if you spend your life caring for the needs of other human beings you necessarily are learning from them. Caregiving is not like repairing shoes. Women's work was a free good, because theoretically women did it instinctively. They didn't have to be taught. They would just follow their nature and were not paid for it.

Nowadays, of course, we realize we have to make provision for a lot of things that have been taken for granted. Women's work is in that category. We have to make provision for breathable air because unless we pay attention the air will be polluted. We have to make provision for drinkable water because unless we make provision the water will be polluted. At one time the volume of human waste was small enough so that it would self-purify in running water, but that's no longer true.

I am in complete sympathy with women who want the options and the training to do things other than homemaking, women who want the fulfillment and the autonomy of diverse careers. Absolutely. But because society has been so profoundly unaware of the value of the work done by women, we have not yet faced the need for rethinking the provision of care and cherishing that this entails. I believe we are at a time of unacknowledged crisis.

One of the things I hear very often from women is "I need a wife." Many women are doing two jobs, only one of which is called a job, while the other is supposed to be a free good, something she does when nobody's looking. Well, when you come home from the office at six o'clock that can be extremely difficult. The much vaunted switch to service industries is partly a monetization of caregiving, a way of outsourcing work that at one time women did for free, work that needs to be done for both men and women. Whether it be the dry cleaners or the fast food restaurants or the psychotherapists we turn to, we need to be cared for. We need to be listened to, to have someone focus her or his concern on us, and listen, even if only for fifty minutes a week. It used to be that men could count on getting that attention, but no longer, and now their wives need it too.

There is a very widespread deficit in society of caregiving, or cherishing. We are addressing this by inventing more and more categories of service jobs that are gradually being recognized as requiring high-level skills and proper pay. Yet we are still stuck on this idea that only production is valuable. All this service stuff, as well as entrepreneurship and management, all these occupations are in some sense seen as parasitical or second-rate especially when done by women. Caregiving is still under-paid. People will not pay someone who cares for their child nearly as much as they will the mechanic who fixes their car.

So we are moving in the direction of turning caregiving into a spade with which to dig, in more and more different ways, necessarily so, as we realize that care is not a free good. It is something that has to be planned for, provided for, supported, trained. We are also going to be dividing it up in new ways, like the division of other kinds of labor.

There is another destructive idea around, that if you need to be taken care of, it means there is something wrong with you. You are an infant and incompetent, or sick, or handicapped, or elderly, or whatever. We believe that normal healthy adult human beings do not need to be taken care of. I want to examine that notion. Human beings have the longest period of dependent childhood, of needing adult care in order to survive, of any mammal. A colt or a calf can stand up in a tottery sort of way within a matter of hours after birth on its own four feet. Right? Now, why is it that we say to human beings, "Stand on your own two feet," when in fact one of the most distinctive things about human beings is that they spend much of their lives unable to do just that. Would it not have been a logical direction of evolution to become more and more independent? But that is not how our evolution went; our evolution went in the direction of increasing dependence and interdependence. When you read the books on child development, one of the main things that is emphasized is independence training: how to take this dependent, needy, helpless infant and get her or him to stand on her or his own two feet; to take responsibility for self. This is almost perverse if you think of the millennia of evolution it took to arrive at our extended dependency, because that extended dependency correlates directly with the importance of learning in human adaptation. The calf or the colt is born literally knowing how to walk. It is preprogrammed: the information is already there. But in general, human beings are born without a set of procedures and behaviors with which they can survive. They have to learn and be taught, and this of course is why human beings have been able to adapt to every climate on the planet and over time to develop more and more elaborate systems of behavior. What I want to point out is the direct connection between learning as a human activity and the need for care, the correlation between teaching and the giving of care. We need to rethink how these activities run through the life cycle and how they constitute essential occupations in society.

You know, we do terrible things to babies. A lot of people have the idea that if you can afford it you need to have the baby's own room and the baby's own crib. You want to take a little helpless newborn creature and put her in a bed all by herself in a room all by herself. That is so familiar as a Western middle-class norm that it is not easy to realize that as a piece of human behavior it is absolutely extraordinary. Most human beings through history have gone through life always sleeping beside other people. If you ask foreign students, "Have you ever lived alone? Have you slept in a bed by yourself?" they will tell you that, at home, they shared at least a room, probably a bed, with brothers, sisters, grandparents, parents. Sharing is far more common than isolation. It is interesting to see the beginning of independence training expressed as isolation, virtually immediately after birth.

One of the things that we know is that infants and children learn better when they are cherished. I recently heard a term I had never heard before, infant massage. As it happened, I was getting a massage. I felt a need for a little cherishing and there was nobody to give me one at home. The massage practitioner was talking to me about what was going on in the field and described someone who was giving a course in infant massage. There have been studies in places like orphanages or with infants that were not sent right home from the hospital for one reason or another, employing someone simply to hold and rock and stroke them for an hour a day. It turns out that that stroking makes a significant difference in their ability to thrive and learn and respond to what's going on around them. We need stroking too. I interpret infant massage as more and better stroking, professional stroking, stroking for pay. Some people are inhibited in their ability to express emotion, to be sensuous with an infant. Even as amateurs they may feel better about cuddling an infant if they have taken a course in it. That is part of this feeling that what we enjoy is probably frivolous and maybe immoral. There are also techniques being taught today for systematically rocking infants even before birth.

One of the great ironies is that we have evolved not just to be dependent during a period of learning, but to be greedy for learning. Infants and children love learning. They have, in fact, a built-in motivation, until they get to school and get taught that learning is not fun. Those who talk about the evolution of our species and how we are different from our primate cousins and the great apes emphasize that in some ways we are not so much "naked apes" as "infant apes." There have been experiments with baby chimps or baby gorillas lovingly raised in human families. At first they seem to be so much more responsive, to learn so much more, and so much faster than human infants do, and then they slow down. One of the peculiar characteristics of human beings is that we do have the capacity to go on learning throughout the life cycle.

Sometimes I get kind of discouraged about the capacity of adults to learn. You look at the time it has taken in the United States, for example, to get from knowing the dangers of cigarette smoking to actually reducing how many people do it. Or how long it took for people to start using seat belts, or eating less fat. Somehow, they do not seem to be ready to learn. It turns out that the lead time in the United States for people to modify behavior in a way that will preserve their health is about fifteen years. Then, of course, you have new people coming into the population and you have to keep on with the message, so I guess human adults can learn but are slower at it than infants and children. You may have noticed that yourselves.

Here's what I think we have to consider. We have to consider the fact that the demand for new learning over the course of the life cycle is steadily increasing. We live longer, technology is changing, and society is changing in many ways. Whether I have to learn how to change a halogen lightbulb, which I learned to do only a couple of years ago, or whether I have to learn to recycle, or to use the Internet, or to maintain friendly relationships with the next-door neighbor who happens to be from Cambodia, or Iran, or Zimbabwe, I am being challenged to new learning. What I want to suggest is that learning is stressful, and that lifelong learning increases the need for cherishing. When you say to someone, "Stand on your own two feet, nobody's going to look after you," you may be decreasing the capacity to learn. Those who have no one to cherish them may stand on their own two feet, they may cope and survive. But a little loving care will increase their resilience, their flexibility, and their ability to learn new and appropriate patterns of adaptation. These are all arguments for the fact that cherishing is something we steadily need more of. Alas, it is not a free good, not something we can count on having without making provision for it.

Today, we live in an increasingly stressful environment and we need more massages. We need someone to say: "How was your day?" "Would you like a cup of tea?" We all need it, men and women and children. The day has passed when that kind of caregiving was just there, to be taken for granted. The statistics suggest that when in midlife a woman finds herself alone, divorced, or widowed, or whatever, she may, after a period of mourning, have an increased sense of well-being. Women friends often care for each other. Many men, when they find themselves in that position, are less happy — for all they have talked about the glories of bachelorhood — and less healthy, living shorter lives, because nobody is saying: "Would you like a cup of tea?" Some of the needed care can be bought — they can send the laundry out — and some of it cannot. Some of it can only be exchanged for care offered in return.

Many of our habits of consumption probably reflect other deficits: a lack of cherishing, a loss of the joy of learning, an inability to play. In this sense, we all need occupational therapy. Not everything can be monetized. We are going to want to move toward a society where what we consume — when we say, "Ah, now I can have what I've been longing for" — will not be running shoes, or a new car, or a bigger house. Instead of more and more things, we will embrace occupations: a chance to join a French class or to hear a lot of symphonies or play in a string quartet or get a massage. All of these activities depend on human interactions in one way or another, and many require interaction. I might decide that I want to go out and dance every Saturday night, or that I want to join a chorus and sing. I want to learn to meditate or read plays and poetry with my friends. And in doing all of this we will develop new kinds of communities and networks of mutual caring and support.

The one thing that we simply cannot afford in a world of diminishing material resources is to say that the only human activities that are really respected are those that involve material production. It is the other way around. We are going to have to find ways so that, if the society depends on money, the people that provide the care will have access to that money. Otherwise it is not going to work. We need a society where the two most valued activities in the society are learning and cherishing, and we do them for each other: giving and receiving care, teaching and learning. No economic system is going to be viable unless it moves us in that direction.

THE UNENDING THRESHOLD

Learning and the Life Cycle

By 2000, my efforts to understand how people adapt to
cultural change had drawn me to an exploration of the
difference between education and learning in the new
century, and the way in which making learning a lifelong activity would reshape experience and the basis of
authority. One of the projects I undertook during a
research year at the Radcliffe Institute was trying to put
this new understanding in context.

— MCB, 2004

ↄ

Once upon a time, education, logically set early in the life cycle, could be
regarded as preparation or prologue for the responsibilities and challenges
of adulthood. We currently need to rethink this relationship for all adults.

In many preliterate societies the transition from preparation to full
participation was marked by initiation rites that defined social maturity
in some rough relationship to physical maturity or puberty, usually
acknowledged differently for males and females. Often such rites
included substantial periods of instruction, as well as elements of ritual
or ordeal, combining new learning with new affirmations of commitment.[1] In complex societies, this preparation has become increasingly
specialized, and institutions — schools and universities, filled with
young people who must pass through them before moving on to full participation in society — have been created to support it. Institutions (and
their personnel, whether shamans or professors) have their own priorities, of course, and much has been taught that was not likely to be particularly useful thereafter, while much that is essential was omitted.
Learning, primarily through experience, has always continued through
adulthood, with a great deal of individual variation. Societies have recog-

nized the special wisdom of elders created by years of experience and reflection. Indeed, we recognize as wisdom only the kind of learning that is integrated with what came before, often involving extended reconsideration, and transferable to new situations.

Learning is a term used to describe a process that occurs throughout the life course and across the animal world. The fish in an aquarium learn when and where their food will be dropped in. But birds and mammals can also be observed teaching their young, often at specific developmental stages. *Education* is a term largely reserved for human beings, yet what we see in birds and mammals might easily be equated, if we read *education* literally as the "drawing forth" of innate potentials like flight. We use the word *education* more broadly, however, to include both such a drawing forth or evocation and the transmission of a complex accumulated tradition, primarily when these occur in an institutional framework. Anthropologists sometimes use a different term, *enculturation,* which emphasizes the process of acquiring a distinctive culture and language, specific to a particular human community. Sociologists use an overlapping term, *socialization,* which emphasizes the learning involved in moving into each new social role, at whatever stage of the life cycle: we are socialized into kindergarten and into parenthood, into new jobs and into senior citizenhood. *Schooling* is a handy word for remembering that what takes place in kindergarten through twelfth grade is narrower and more specific than any of these. The processes overlap: children learn far more in school than their schooling intends them to.

None of these terms fits well with the range of other processes that depend on learning: the acquisition of basic character traits and habits of mind and the ways in which these are sometimes modified by experiences of trauma or therapy or conversion,[2] or the process of deutero-learning,[3] learning to learn in a particular context or to function as if all of life matched that context. Every one of these processes needs to be newly examined, as do the attitudes toward age and authority that are derived from them. Alas, conversations about learning often run downhill into discussions of education, and these in turn often devolve into discussions of schooling: instead of asking how to become a learning society, we end up focusing on school-leaving examinations. In fact, the distinction between learning and education continues to erode because it has become useful and profitable to consider more and more ways of institutionalizing or supporting learning at later stages of the life cycle.

Once upon a time, it was possible for the president of a great university to welcome the new graduates to "the fellowship of educated men." This is no longer an appropriate greeting, not only because it harks back to the time, before the middle of the nineteenth century, when women were excluded from higher education. Its obsolescence is related to the increasing presence and participation of women in more complex ways, for women have been the pioneers of the most recent relocation of both education and learning in the life cycle.[4] Easy enough then, to amend the greeting to "the fellowship of educated men and women" (oddly, *fellowship* is a term that has not been rejected as sexist). It is the adjective, however, *educated,* that needs to be revised. The claim that "we" (the teachers and professors) have (transitively) "educated" someone and finished the job is no longer tenable. Welcome, then, to the fellowship of lifelong learners. And welcome to a world in which the life cycle is no longer structured in terms of a separation between preparation and participation. Learning is no longer *before,* but *whenever.* There has been a broad social recognition that learning requires a variety of new kinds of institutional support. Women have played an important role in this reconceptualization, and their experience needs to be studied, both to understand the place of learning up to the end of life and to understand the institutional changes that lie ahead.

It is fashionable today to experiment with new rituals in the hope that adolescents will have a more reliable sense of transition from childhood to adulthood or that men and women will take as more serious and more binding the transition to the married state. These discussions tend to emphasize the factors of ordeal or solemnity rather than the actual instruction that characterizes rites of passage around the world, for we already have plenty of instruction going on, partially stripped of its ritual elements. We do not tattoo or subincise our young men — but Parris Island and other kinds of boot camp do indeed involve ordeals. Instead, schooling, which like most initiation rites begins with a degree of separation from the home, is for many a long ordeal of anxiety or boredom that has gradually been stripped of a sense of awe.

In classic initiation rites, as these were first described by Arnold van Gennep,[5] a sudden separation from the childhood setting (frequently acted out as a ritual kidnapping, just as marriage is sometimes acted out as a ritual abduction) is eventually followed by reintegration into the community with a new status. The period in between has been characterized as a period of liminality — literally of being on the threshold.[6]

The honeymoon, for instance, is a liminal period between single and married life, and postpartum segregation of new mothers postpones social participation as a parent. The boy or girl going through initiation is during that time neither a child nor an adult but on a threshold between one and the other. The depth and solemnity of the rite depends in part on the disorientation of being in a no-one's-land where nothing is familiar, so the initiate is dependent and suggestible, amenable to highly intensified learning. It may be important to explore whether, in a society of lifelong learning, this sense of being "out of place," or "betwixt and between," with its associated stress and suggestibility, becomes a lifelong experience. Certainly the awareness of incompetence is intensified in societies with a very high division of labor — which is why engineers hang on the words of their physicians, and dentists are bullied by auto mechanics. Perhaps all members of contemporary society share some of the blurring of identity and vulnerability of the liminal state.

Many factors have converged to change the place of learning in the life cycle, and the implications of this convergence are still not fully explored. It has always been the case that some institutions have provided lifelong sanctuaries within which an elite few pursued perennial learning, often phrased as scholarship or research. Within these contexts, learning has been thought of as a *vocation* — a calling — and indeed it can be argued that learning is a form of spiritual practice.[7] The medieval universities only gradually evolved from monastic institutions, dedicated exclusively to the study of sacred texts, into transit stations for preparation and certification that provided credentials to be used elsewhere. Higher education still builds on a congruence between the continuing research and scholarship of the faculty and the short-term preparation of the young. Rituals, including those rituals that are repeated week after week, often contain large components of indoctrination. Studying sacred texts has been the act of continuing learning most often acknowledged and celebrated in different traditions, often pursued in a curious kind of separation from full adult roles, in cloistered and celibate communities, free from family responsibilities.

The phrase "lifelong learning" has become a mantra in our time because parents and educators can know less and less of what life will demand ten or thirty or sixty years ahead. Women have pioneered the latest forms of lifelong learning by returning as adults to the classroom, because the lives they lead today are so different from the lives for which they were prepared. Every life encounters unexpected elements, and some degree of unimagined learning has always occurred at every stage of the life cycle short of advanced dementia.

There is a sense in which real achievement has always been impossible to prepare for. Much of American culture is organized around the difference between what sociologists refer to as ascribed and achieved status. Royalty carries an ascribed status, already set at birth, like the expectation that a little girl will become a mother. A prince may not become king for many years or may die before ascending to the throne, but the possibility is part of his birthright and can, in part, be prepared for (though one can only hope for a modicum of good sense). But an elective office, such as president of the United States, is achieved, and we are made uneasy when we see signs of dynastic patterns. Wealth, position, and influence are sometimes achieved — we would like to think of ourselves as a meritocracy — but often depend on birth, including race and sex. Clearly, the possibility of achieving an unanticipated role implies the need for a new order of socialization at whatever stage in life it occurs. How do the nouveau riche learn "good taste"? How does the frontiersman who goes to Washington learn congressional courtesies and foreign affairs? And how is the learning process facilitated by a new position's rituals of initiation and swearing in? American culture has generated a vast range of tools to reeducate adults for new roles. This process in turn produces the anomaly of persons close to the top of any hierarchy who are rank beginners or, indeed, amateurs. It also has created repeated clashes between educating a child for his or her expected place in life and educating him or her to "be all you can be," as exemplified in the contrasting approaches of George Washington Carver and W. E. B. DuBois — and experience does not necessarily match slogans.

Added on is the importance of immigration. Every year thousands of adults enter America who have been enculturated in childhood into societies that are very different. They have grown up speaking different languages, seeking different relationships, and recounting different legends. They arrive with the skills of a Vietnamese peasant farmer or a Somali herder or a Soviet apparatchik. They face as adults the task of becoming effective and competent participants in a new society, at least to the point of earning a living, and the greatest part of their learning comes from the surrounding community and from their own children. Local government and ethnic organizations have both been involved in resocializing immigrants — and both have held views about how far that process should go and what kind of commitment it should imply.[8] In general, however, the resocialization of immigrants has been carried out in separate remedial settings, while the resocialization of women for new roles has increasingly led them into classrooms full of much younger students, opening these classrooms in turn to older males.

In the twentieth century, several new and powerful kinds of technological, demographic, and ethical change accelerated the demand for life-long learning. Trends can creep up on the observer, with many small shifts building to a cascade that makes life suddenly bewildering. They interact in unexpected ways. Dealing with the interactions and the needed reintegration is what places the greatest demand on the individual — not just acquiring a fact or a skill but newly exploring what it all means.

Technology has always required that those who use it learn new skills, whether adding them to specialized professional knowledge or building them into everyday life. But in the past new technologies must have become available one at a time, whereas today there is suddenly an explosion of new skills needed, each one in turn giving way to others. "Learning to use the computer" is now an ongoing rather than a single task, as software mutates and multiplies; technical competence is not something that can be achieved once and for all but must be built into ongoing activities. This means that those at the top of any hierarchy are now expected to be learners and that the aura of weakness and vulnerability that has sometimes clung to the student role (and made reentering the student role easier for women who already carried that burden) is diminishing. It is no longer embarrassing to acknowledge in public that one is still learning. Globalization is technology driven, with information available instantaneously. Economic restructuring has shifted expectations about who should be competent in using the new technologies — increasingly we demand steadily updated skills from the entire work-force. Many licensed professions now require time invested in receiving instruction every year. Some technologies also require changes in basic patterns of thought, as the automobile demanded a new way of thinking about distance and place. These changes are learned without being explicitly taught, yet in effect we are demanding new ways of thinking and seeing the world, and we should expect shifts in commitment as well.

Demographic changes have been brought about partly by technology, but the problems they pose to learning do not involve mastering the biomedical technologies themselves so much as living with their effects: more human beings worldwide, fewer deaths in childhood and midlife, increased longevity, and control over conception. Together these provoke changes in family structure and attitudes. Even as technology moves more rapidly, demanding accelerated learning to keep up, we live longer, so that individual lives span eras of greater disparity. The return of women to the classroom at midlife was directly driven by demographic change, as child-bearing came to occupy a smaller portion of the life span and as years of health and energy increased.[9] Within a brief period, demographic changes have radically affected the shapes of women's lives, and the associated rights movement has entailed increased participation in learning at every level. Demographic changes also demand a basic rethinking of institutions such as marriage, which evolved when it was unlikely that both partners would live more than twenty years beyond their wedding day, for if two individuals are learning, they may be learning separate paths and may need to learn new ways of thinking about each other. Another institution that is changing is grandparenthood — we have a lot more grandparents around than we used to — some children have six or seven — but their aging is no longer timed for the transmission of their lore to children, for they are not settling back into rocking chairs until a decade or two too late, and quite likely in a different part of the country.

Ethical changes have driven much of the emphasis on lifelong learning. Just as one of the first reactions to the emancipation of slaves had to be the creation of schools for the newly free, the breakdown of the old colonial empires might have inspired — though often it did not — massive educational investments for students of every age group, mixing children and young adults. Each time we have newly understood that some social group had the right to full participation, innovations in education have been needed to make that transition possible. The community college movement was a major expression of the push for equality in the "Great Society."[10] Special education for children with learning disabilities has spread across the country. In the past, whenever some dominant group has wanted to prolong hegemony over another, they have found it convenient to limit learning. Authoritarian societies struggle with the tension between the need to prepare technically competent populations and the risk that this preparation will encourage independent thought. Several privileged women's colleges, like Smith and Radcliffe, realized early on the importance of committing themselves to reentry women and providing fellowship support, and the Carnegie Foundation underwrote many of these initiatives.[11]

Demography has had another major effect. The increased numbers of the "Baby Boom" generation worked their way through the educational system, stimulating the creation of new programs and institutions. Then, when the boom subsided, many institutions looked around for new customers. The so-called nontraditional student was created by a convergence of the interest of women in returning to school at later ages and the interest of academic institutions in filling their seats.[12] Thus education throughout the life cycle has percolated through the system, starting from institutions that did not have enough new high school graduates clamoring at their gates to fill their freshman classes. State universities are more age-diverse than the Ivy League, and community colleges most diverse of all.[13] Similarly, new ways of packaging and delivering education have been developed partly to help institutions make ends meet.

Only gradually has it become apparent to many privileged institutions that older students, rather than being a new group of consumers to exploit, contribute experience and dedication to the classroom. In the same way, there has been a growing understanding that all students deserve classrooms that are diverse in many ways so that affirmative action is a program that benefits not only the underserved but the entire institution.

Someday soon, it will be necessary to drop the term "nontraditional students." We have clung to the convenience of graduations and age segregation for far too long. At the same time it may be necessary to explore seriously the implications of the common assertion that an education is never completed, and to offer long-term membership in a community of learning alternating with other life experiences.[14] This shift may in turn involve a movement away from deficiency thinking, as if all education were remedial, and a movement away from expecting authority figures to know the answers and giving an excessive respect to "experts" (never trust an expert who is not also a learner!). The life cycle will look rather different as we realize that we live most of our lives in a liminal state. Last, because lifelong learning entails lifelong change, we will need to think about adaptation and flexibility within commitments.

Women have a critical role to play in this process, one that arises both from biology and from recent history. Arguably, women have always had to learn and relearn their roles and their own bodies, moving through stages more sharply distinguished than in the lives of men. But the expectation that women would adapt to these changes and to the changing needs and characters of family members has limited their participation and their access to learning of other kinds. Today we have the huge resource of women who know what it feels like, as an adult, to learn to see the world differently, to have one's whole sense of possibility transformed. Women have approached both education and lifelong learning differently from men, because their path has been different. As we begin to explore the deepest implications of lifelong learning, we will need to draw on the experiences of women — and of the men who have learned to respect them in new ways.

COMMITMENT AS A MOVING TARGET

This piece about marriage and partnership grew out of an op-ed in 2001 commenting on new data about rising divorce rates among the elderly and evolved into an exploration of the nature of commitment and fidelity. It remains a discussion of the values of marriage considered not in the context of youthful romance but from the point of view of midlife or later. But in a broader sense it is an examination of how relationships to partners as well as to children can evolve over time, incorporating both learning and bodily change.

— MCB, 2004

As a people, we continue to value marriage, but divorce rates continue to climb, for both good and bad reasons. Gay or straight, we like to live in pairs, but we insist that our partnerships be freely chosen. We seem unable to understand that loving is different from liking and each is different from being in love — and that it is rare to sustain all three.

It is unrealistic to expect, in a society where individuals who withdraw from an unhappy marriage need not face ostracism or penury, that there will not be many who do choose divorce. That's a freedom to be grateful for. We live longer than our ancestors did, so that new beginnings now seem plausible at fifty or sixty or seventy-five, and divorce rates are rising among older couples. But what is even more important, we continue to learn and grow through the life cycle in ways that were accessible to very few in the past, so that couples not only get bored and fed up but may also outgrow each other. Yet growth and aging proceed for partners at different tempos, in and out of sync, so dissatisfaction may not be permanent.

Every breakup represents pain for one or both partners, at least for a time, and every partnership ended wastes years of building. The hostility generated around divorces is corrosive to society in ways that go beyond the dissolution of households, involving vast numbers of adults in actions they would find unethical in any other context, and we vacillate between piously condemning those whose marital behavior does not match traditional standards and ignoring it completely. It doesn't make sense to have social arrangements that generate so much bitterness and so many lies.

First, we need a new definition of fidelity, one that does not take sexual activity as the defining characteristic of marriage. It's a mistake to expect sex to be enough to hold marriages together when other social supports and constraints are lost, and it's also a mistake to define any and all outside sexual activity as infidelity. However we understand fidelity, it should be a value that continues even when sex comes to an end.

Many societies try to prevent sexual activity, including masturbation, before marriage, but although there are advantages to doing so, the cost is the institutionalization of guilt and secrecy and a poor foundation for later on. Most societies try to limit the sexual activities of women after marriage, especially if women (and sexual access to them) are regarded as property, and many societies, although usually with less severity, try to restrain men, with only partial success. But in addition to these limits, most societies have a concept of commitment that holds regardless of occasional male sexual adventures, and some societies — increasingly our own — offer the same tolerance to women. Everywhere there is some value placed on partnerships that can outlive sexual attraction. Fidelity is about more than sex. A couple is a partnership in child rearing, business, and meeting the wider society. These are common goals that must be honored in spite of wandering erotic or romantic impulses.

Even in sexual activity there are distinctions to be made: there is a kind of fidelity involved in practicing safer sex with all but a single partner — surely bringing home disease or having a child outside the marriage is more serious than a romantic interlude. One can value the respect expressed when the dignity of a partner is protected and humiliation avoided, when two people who are no longer romantic partners cooperate in sustaining a public good name or share in dedication to a cause, when some dimension of an earlier commitment is honored in spite of a new involvement.

Second, we need to rethink who we are making commitments to.

The people we live with are always in many ways strangers, changing as fast as we get to know them. It is not just that spouses get gray hair or wrinkles, spare tires or bald spots. Human beings have always been aware of the need to sustain relationships in spite of aging and disease. No, the problem in our era is that spouses get younger or stronger or smarter, suddenly develop new talents and new aspirations or assert new needs. What do you do when a spouse or partner, rather than preferring someone new, seems to *become* someone new? It used to be common to urge young couples to defer marriage for an extra year or so and really get to know each other — now they may wait a dozen years without tying the knot, and lo and behold, they still discover they don't know each other. The great advantage of an arranged marriage is the freedom, while building a relationship, from the illusion of knowing the other person and the expectation that romance should last forever. Couples in such marriages face an awkward or ambivalent honeymoon period, but they avoid the letdown of falling out of love; similarly, where families broker marriages, couples may have reduced privacy, but they benefit from familial support and interest when times are rough. In societies with arranged marriages, the value is on learning to get along, practicing mutual respect, and building a shared history. Our fascination with romance jump-starts a marriage, but it has made us unobservant of the slow learning that fosters adaptable and resilient love. Commitment is a moving target.

Why not think about marriage as we think about parenthood? Children are forever unfolding into new persons, surprising and sometimes dismaying their parents, but mostly we continue to love them and stand by them — and if we are wise we understand the limited control we have over their becoming in a changing world. We are slowly giving up dictating careers to children and accepting the fact of our children's freedom to experiment and change without repudiating them, just as we are today accepting more and more kinds of youthful sexual activity. But change happens at every stage of the life cycle. Adults today, enjoying their own new freedom, are still frequently shocked by the exploits and initiatives of aging parents who refuse to fit the role definitions offered to them. We are equally slow in learning to allow our elders to continue to grow. So what of partners and spouses? Is growth a form of infidelity? A poem I wrote to my husband for our fifth anniversary was full of the sense of alternatives not chosen:

We are together where so far
Long orphaned bright and many selves have passed . . .
Those are bright spheres that fall away.

There is a certain sadness to the poem, but at the end I used the old metaphor of the potter to speak of what was constant and what could change, to phrase a kind of permission for change that seems to me an essential part of commitment:

We never promised we would stay the same,
But only we would shape our change
From this now single clay.

Significant change in someone you love can often feel like a form of infidelity, even if it is recognizable as growth. It may require a major effort if a relationship is to survive. New ambitions disrupt the lives of whole families. Sometimes they herald changes in economic status or moves to other cities and countries, or changes in the texture of daily life to fit a new religious commitment or a return to school. We expect our partners to accept these, saying, This is who I *really* am. If you love me why don't you accept me? But this expectation is inconsistent with the ethos of lifelong learning, because no stage in the process can be guaranteed as the final, correct outcome. Why not say, I am still discovering who I am and surprising myself too: let's take the time to understand how and whether we can still fit together.

With our new longevity, a marriage can be terribly long. Fortunately there is the possibility of discovering a new partner behind the familiar face at the breakfast table — and the chance to welcome that discovery instead of experiencing it as a betrayal. Fidelity means sharing in change instead of imposing it. The very acceptance of change could be the basis for a deepening relationship, while the burden of living with someone who has ceased to learn and grow, who has no unfolding interests, can destroy a marriage.

There are also physical bonds that go beyond sex, for even with the help of Viagra or estrogen, sexual interest eventually declines. For relationships that last a lifetime we need a renewed affirmation of touch and a new awareness of caregiving as a physical act of love. Women have traditionally been cast as caregivers — one unspoken reason for choosing younger wives is so that a majority of men have the privilege of going first. cared for and spared bereavement, while a majority of women must look forward to widowhood. But while some men run away from caring for a partner in sickness, many now stay close and learn new ways of tenderness, and we can speculate that a generation of fathers who were present in the delivery room and learned to change and burp their babies will find new uses for their skills over time. With adequate support, caring for another can be fulfilling as well as draining, a new dimension of intimacy. The poignant memoirs of gay men who have cared for partners dying of AIDS offer evidence for the skeptical not only of genuine love but of the deep meaning to be found in caring for the beloved. Fifty years or more with one person is a long time, but the changes that take place over the decades can be a source of discovery.

Sometimes creativity bridges deterioration. Sometimes a common history is enough for survival. Alzheimer's is a nightmare both for the patient and for the caregiver, but it does offer food for thought about who we are as individuals and as human beings, what our rights should be and how we might make choices. My thoughts about Alzheimer's begin with the conviction that the ability to recognize another human being with some continuity of personality and emotion is the irreducible condition for genuine humanity. One patient, whom I knew at quite an early stage, was not quite sure who I was, but she was very much herself: her ladylike upbringing stayed with her, and she was entirely considerate and gracious in conversation, even as she repeated the same questions: How was my family? What was I working on now? After I had patiently answered each question more than once, concealing my irritation, it occurred to me that there was a creative challenge to be met in this questioning, one that would eliminate from my answers the exasperation that we all feel on being obliged to repeat ourselves, which she would undoubtedly sense and be hurt by. So I gave myself the assignment of saying something fresh and new in response to each repetition. There are always multiple answers available — who would want to reduce their family or their work to a single sentence? Knowing that she would forget my answers tempted me to abrupt and simplistic answers, but if I forced myself to fresh replies there would be a kind of fidelity in honoring her courtesy and learning something about how I could define and redefine myself.

Another woman gave me a glimpse into the value of a common history. She had been married and divorced before World War II, and as she sank into Alzheimer's, all of her postwar life disappeared and she remembered only her first husband, with whom she had had no children. When the son of her second marriage visited her, she knew he was someone important to her — so she assigned to him the identity of the first husband, whom he had never met, part of a separate history. By contrast, my godmother in old age called me by my mother's name, and my daughter by mine. It was easy for me to be comfortable and indulgent with my godmother's errors, within a shared frame of reference and congruent relationships — but harder for a son to be assigned the role of long departed fiancé.

Alzheimer's is an argument for continuity in the way we live. As the fabric of memory is rolled back, into the distant past, familiar places and friendships survive the loss of foreground. Sometimes immigrants lose their adopted language first, retaining a language from a distant childhood. Styles of valued behavior learned in childhood remain acceptable. Continuity does not come easily today, however. It seems worthwhile to ask, in the twenty-first century, what continuities of commitment are even possible, and what kinds of effort are worthwhile to sustain them. Even though we all know that a whole range of eventualities may necessitate changes, the twenty-first century demands more commitment, not less — things move so fast that unless we take time to build we will never arrive.

We can't expect to sustain relationships alone. Circles of kin and community are needed to survive over the long haul, whether in dealing with new infants or unexpected economic fluctuations. The weakening of other ties makes sustaining marriages much harder, for marriage has not traditionally been a private matter. One of the most important reasons for affirming gay marriages is to give gay couples as well as straight the social support that all couples need to sustain them. Couples of many years' standing cherish common friends, who can urge them to keep trying and can remind them of a common history, wisely refusing to take sides. Couples are set loose, like two passengers in a lifeboat, when they move across the country to retirement communities, leaving the friends and the history they have shared, the landscapes that evoke the best of times and the worst, the support systems that have made a shared life possible.

There will be divorces and breakups at every stage of the life cycle, with harsh words spoken and tears. No one is immune, no relationship endures beyond all risk, and some truly cannot be saved. So let us be clear that not every ending represents failure and that a future with time for growth and friendship is not always bleak. Yet as a society we seem to have lost — deleted from our computers — the reasons that would make sense and satisfaction of staying together.

THE ATRIUM

A Space of Light

In "You Will Know the Future When You Get There" I
compared extended life expectancies to a new room
added on to a house. But as I approached the age of sixty
myself, I felt the need for some more powerful metaphor
for the discovery of opportunities for fresh starts at
midlife, as well as the need to begin to imagine the institutional changes that would be needed. In the context of
anxieties about Social Security and Medicare, a new way
of looking at the later stages of the life cycle is becoming
a priority, for our present methods of funding retirement
and health care seem to be leading us toward either a
betrayal of the elderly or a cynical exploitation of the
young. So I coined the atrium metaphor in *Full Circles*
and began using it in public speaking. I wrote this essay
to begin to apply the idea to institutional change.

—MCB, 2004

One of the main topics around the millennium was the increase in life
expectancy, as news stories pointed out that some twenty years had been
added to life expectancies in the developed world since World War II.
The choice of the verb *added*, however, was an overly simple reading of
the arithmetic. Commentators spoke as if the new years of life were like a
wing tacked on at the back of a building, a mere extension, as if it simply
meant being *old* for a lot longer time. But changes in life expectancy really
have two meanings: One is an increase in survival at earlier stages of the
life cycle, particularly a reduction in infant mortality, potentially leading
to larger numbers of people at every age. The other is an extension of the
years of healthy and productive middle age. This increase is not at the end

of life but mostly in the middle: life is not a building with an extra wing but one in which an atrium has been opened at the center, full of light and air, and passages toward new possibilities.

It is true that other stages of the life cycle have to some degree been lengthened. Childhood has become longer, not as a period of innocence but as a period of dependency to be used for education, postponing full adulthood. And there is some lengthening at the end that many of us would like to skip, when participation is no longer possible but technology prolongs dying. But the real changes fall after fifty, in the years wher it is now widely possible, really for the first time in history, to make new beginnings, new relationships, new careers. Women have been the pioneers in claiming this open space in the midst of life for self-discovery, have almost been forced to it by the reduced time now occupied by child-bearing and child rearing. But men are following along behind. As a nation, however, we are still more concerned about the costs of aging than about celebrating and releasing its potential productivity.

The space I have called the atrium is one that neither men nor women are used to thinking about. We have had a lot of talk about a midlife crisis in the forties, triggered by the urgent sense that time for new choices is running out, as it most certainly was for our ancestors by that age. Today ambitious business school students speak of making a million by the time they are forty and starting a new career, though in the event many may find it easier to walk away from a family than from a lucrative profession. Women who have deferred reproduction while they started careers have a different kind of urgency, having been lured into believing it would be easy to start a family in their forties, often spending years trying to do so and having to reevaluate their commitments in the light of childlessness.

We still apparently think of the forties as the middle of adulthood, with some twenty productive years ahead to be followed by a relatively insignif-icant period of retirement. In reality there is more time for a possible second (or third) start than ever before: the urgency lies in the fact that without an understanding of the possibility for recommitment or refocusing there may be many arid years ahead. Many people now remain employed well into their eighties. If they do not they may find themselves confronted with a retirement far too long for healthy bodies and restless minds.

In the past, women were told that the best part of their lives was over even earlier than men, marked by the end of reproductive possibility and beauty faded. Men often attempt a rerun of their youth with young brides, but precisely because it is hard for a woman of forty or fifty to do this, we see a wide range of creative improvisations and inventions, for the models are few and our expectations still stunted. One of the women I taught at Spelman College described the approach of her fiftieth birthday as coming to "a bridge called cynicism, struggling to cross over treacherous waters of fatigue, indecision, and sorrow . . . the business of aging, negotiating menopause, moving from mother to girlfriend in my daughter's life — a crossing of cultures, transitioning from known to unknown, from futuring to memory."[1] This is a description that combines the negativity associated with menopause in our culture, the assumption that the best is past, with the insight that we live these atrium years in a new and unknown culture where the patterns are not yet defined. Six months later she described herself as having found "the real of me." Fifty is no longer a time for endings and memory, it is a time for new beginnings, some of which will be profoundly disruptive both within families and in the world of work. So is sixty. But in spite of disruption, we can expect new levels of creativity and productivity when a traditional lifetime of experience is brought into play for additional years.

We will need new institutions that support a walk into the atrium. At present many of us do not begin to think about how to use the years ahead productively until we approach a standard retirement age, but as we begin to understand the nature of the atrium years we will be able to make plans and take action earlier. We have been inventive of ways to support young people in higher education and to prepare them for the professions, so that these are understood to be the ordinary stages of career development. Huge strides have been made in protecting older people, but we remain largely trapped both by the entitlements of retirement and the fear of losing them. The American Association of Retired Persons solicits membership at age fifty and is already one of the most significant interest group lobbies in the country, regarding more than half the adult population as its own special constituency and sending an extraneous graveyard chill down the spines of adults many years away from retirement when they receive their form letter invitations to join. More serious, it seems to me, is the distortion of the meaning of retirement, which the AARP could be illuminating rather than obscuring. We should strive for a society of increased satisfaction in work throughout a lifetime, a short period of retirement coinciding with diminished strength and mobility, and options for continuing appropriate activity. Instead of fighting the deferral of "retirement age," organizations like the AARP could serve their younger members by supporting the institutional changes and deepened commitments that will allow satisfying and productive uses of the atrium years.

As a society, we are quaking with fear at the graying of America instead of recognizing that gray hair is not synonymous with feebleness and disability or with prolonged and finally frustrating inactivity. Hidden behind these anxieties is the notion that as people grow older, even with excellent physical health, they become more conservative, less flexible, and less willing to learn and think new thoughts, while at the same time wishing to hold on to the authority and respect traditionally given to age. It is not the increase in the sheer number of elders that has led us to doubt that wisdom comes with age, however, but the rapid rate of change. Regardless of chronological age, we can appropriately question the competence of anyone who is not continuing to learn. When individuals stagnate intellectually they are not only left behind by technology but uninformed by events and unchallenged to grow in ethical understanding. One thinks of senior professors who have stopped reading in their fields and are still hostile to female colleagues but expect, nonetheless, to control future hirings. Wisdom is real and valuable — but it is not automatic.

Similarly, selfishness is not an automatic result of aging, but many older people are drawn into self-concern by a mix of anxiety and isolation, strengthened by political manipulation. Ideally old age should be a time when wisdom and love combine in caring for future generations, for justice and peace and the viability of the planet. Elders can be profoundly political, and not only in their own interests. The environmental movement was largely begun by "little old ladies in tennis shoes." In a society where the fully employed are often overemployed, retirement might be a time to work hard but slightly less hectically for public goals.

One way to go, both for effective planning and for intellectual vitality, is to look at the years of adulthood well before standard retirement age and invent ways to build in a break, like a sabbatical leave, making it the norm rather than an exception. Many people might be willing to defer the beginning of pension or Social Security payments to seventy in exchange for an advance on pensions at around forty-five or fifty, say, to leverage new beginnings, as long as they were protected in case of genuine disability. For some, such a break might become a transition to a different sphere of endeavor, public service, perhaps, or the full-time exploration of an avocation. But for many such a break may be simply a refreshment of mind and spirit, energy and creativity, to be carried back to the existing career. Perhaps this outcome would be common enough so that employers and institutions would see it as worth the risk to grant unpaid or partially paid leaves of a year or two, with the additional benefit that an employee who had come to dislike the job would move on voluntarily. Without such a break, adulthood has simply become too long except in professions with a great deal of built-in learning and diversity. Far too many adults burn out and then plod through their later years, prevented by institutional and financial structures from making new beginnings. We need punctuation, a way to end and begin chapters, to break up the run-on sentences of same-old same-old.

Many problems would require solution beyond the individual: It would become inappropriate to expect parents to mortgage homes for children's college tuition, thus locking themselves into new and immobilizing cash flow demands. They might need loans themselves for a transition that would potentially lead to an extension of their earning years. Savings over a lifetime would be patterned differently and probably some tax-sheltered savings should be made accessible for transitions. Health insurance would need to be thought through. New housing patterns might develop to match new careers begun by parents whose children have grown up, perhaps preferring the stimulation of urban life for an extra decade or two before settling next to a golf course. We would be trying to persuade young couples to focus savings not on survival needs forty years ahead but on the needs for freedom and growth only twenty years ahead. Along the way, we might discover that this positive incentive stimulated more savings and more imaginative daydreams. Dual careers would require consideration, especially where partners were already moving on different rhythms. Today some women go back into the workplace when their husbands retire (if only to avoid providing lunch!), but other women are pulled away from careers that are still unfolding by the expectation of synchrony.

Today even considering a second career looks like throwing away a sure thing, except in professions like sports or the military or child rearing where the first career ends early in any case. Because of the wider social benefits of keeping people in the workforce, it would be wise to reduce the element of danger for those making such a choice. It should not be necessary to burn one's bridges in order to consider a change. We would need to think creatively about volunteer and service opportunities that might be more attractive if they covered some cash needs. And, if the individual wished to return to the same employer, the road back would have to be protected, with the expectation that productivity would probably increase and retirement would no longer be so tempting as an escape from tedium.

One of our most positive associations with later life is the role of grandparent, but the changes that reduce access and contact across generations are already most visible, due to geographical mobility both in the job market and at retirement, are diluting that role. There is a trend among middle-class young people toward deferred marriage and later childbearing, but even with this postponement grandparents don't quite fit the traditional roles. People do not start looking like our stereotypes of grandparents until well after the current retirement age, and they certainly cannot be regarded as pinned to rocking chairs, reliably available for hugs and stories, until they are old enough to be *great*-grandparents, who were rare in the past but are becoming more common. In the past, when society mostly consisted of three generations, members of the adult generation were often simultaneously concerned with child care and elder care. Ironically, one of the threats to the flexibility of the atrium years today is the obligation men and women are now not confronting until they reach their sixties and seventies, to begin caring for their own long-lived parents gradually joining the ranks of the old old. We will need new images of grandparenting and new ways to build strong connections between great-grandparents and their great-grandchildren, as well as ways of connecting children to elders sharing ties of locality rather than of blood.

New beginnings at midlife are often coerced rather than chosen, although a surprising number of people who are forced out of a job or a marriage discover new kinds of satisfaction. We become prisoners of job security and seniority, pension plans and mortgages, expectations and lifestyles. Any reduction in cash flow evokes the specter of penury, and often women, knowing that they are likely to be widowed, fearfully imagine themselves as "bag ladies." All too many adults feel that they have somehow become trapped by youthful decisions of career or marriage and have cut off the possibilities of future growth, or equally trapped by spending habits and accumulated debt. The entire economy would be changed if more people valued flexibility and work satisfaction over income and predictability; if they had the option of taking a time for reflection and retooling they might clarify priorities. In my work I have seen women and some men joyfully discovering the atrium years. Is it a fantasy to suppose that with the progress we have made in health care these years could be freely available and chosen by many?

Step one, it seems to me, is to recognize a new and wondrous opening in the shape of lives, a new and uncharted stage of the life cycle. Lives not only are longer but suddenly offer choices and possibilities that were unavailable to our grandparents, that are still barely emerging in our imaginations, so we are just now becoming able to build and plan.

I like the image of the atrium. I imagine it protected from the cold winds, with a fountain in the center, the sound of running water and banks of flowers and herbs. A place to celebrate the miracle of continuing health, if we are lucky enough to have it, with a renewal of both effort and reflection. A place to look for new kinds of wisdom as our learning years extend.

"AN OAK TREE IN FULL LEAF"

For over a decade, I taught a course called Women's Life Histories, at George Mason University, based on materials from many parts of the world. In 1996, at the invitation of Johnnetta Cole, who was then president, I took the course to Spelman College, a historically black women's college in Atlanta. At Spelman the solution to providing age diversity for the seminar was to make it cross-generational, with a mix of Spelman undergraduates and older women connected in some way with the college, including Johnnetta herself.

This excerpt from *Full Circles, Overlapping Lives,* the book I wrote after that year, gives a glimpse of my teaching and of the way I have written about lives. The Spelman experience gave a new focus to my thinking about how lives are composed and moved it forward to considerations of how different lives resonate across generations. This half chapter includes a sketch of the life of one member of the group who turned seventy during the semester, Marymal Dryden, drawing both on interviews and on an autobiographical essay she wrote for the course as well as a comment from one of the undergraduates. Marymal's story belongs here because of the creative weave of continuity and discontinuity, but it offers only a fragmentary glimpse of the group as a whole and the excitement we shared. When I returned to the Spelman campus for a book party in 2000, Marymal was unable to attend, because she and another member of the seminar were taking a computer course, which gave me one more example of how women adapt and go on learning. But

Iyabo Morrison, the undergraduate who is mentioned at
the end, was there, adult, independent, and blooming.
                                                    —MCB, 2004

⤳

It was Marymal, with her billowing, exotic robes and waved white hair,
who reminded me of an oak tree in full leaf, so "that the birds of the
heaven come and lodge in the branches thereof." Her writing made a
vivid impression not only on me but on the students in the class, who felt
she had given them a glimpse into the lives and times of the elders.

When Marymal spoke about her life, she started by describing a much
protected seedling. "I had some very strict rules and a great deal of
emphasis on being a lady. You represented your family, so how you
behaved was a reflection on your family, and you did not want to do anything to disgrace them. I always had that in mind, and I never got too far
off the beaten path. The kind of fella that asked to kiss or — God forbid
— anything else was not a good man to know, not the kind of fella my
mother described as the kind to listen to. One of the courtship rituals at
Spelman was to walk around the oval, and there was this fella who would
come by very dutifully on courting days and we would walk the circuit. He
made no demands, and he always had this friend with him. Then about
twenty years later I met him again and I said, Aha! He and this fella who
was walking with us all the time were lovers. Well, he'd just seemed like
the epitome of what my mother approved of.

"I'm kinda glad that I lived the way I did, because when I see people I
knew when I was at Spelman they can look at me and say I was always a
lady. Mom's warnings about my virtue, her expressed fears, were always
paramount in my mind: Do Not Get Pregnant! But no advice about the facts
of life was offered. 'Just don't do it!' She literally scared my legs together.
Sexual activity was viewed as fearful, unfulfilling, not very satisfying, and
full of risks. Now I realize that my mom's sexual life must have been filled
with frustration. I wish we could have had more open discussions."

Marymal's first marriage lasted for nine years of social, prosperous
living with her lawyer husband, George. She had graduated from
Spelman and gotten a degree in social work at Atlanta University, following the insistence of her mother and grandmother: "Get your education, and you will always be able to take care of yourself and not be

dependent. You won't have to take any *stuff*!" When she married, no one would have thought her choice inappropriate; within a few years she could say, "My husband is a brilliant, handsome, up-and-coming, successful young attorney at law; I have three adorable sons, all born within a four-year period, a lovely home, and status in our community. Don't I have it all?" But then she had to ask herself, "Why am I miserable?" Like so many other women of that era and since, Marymal woke up to the fact that she had become trapped in the conventional roles of wife and mother and become a stranger to herself.

Marymal's father had gone to Tuskegee when George Washington Carver was there — arguing the appropriateness of practical, vocational education for the Negro — and later he had worked as a railway porter and then as a teacher at a vocational school. Her mother had two years of college and worked as a matron in the county jail. Marymal herself was a catch, educated, beautiful, refined, and her husband often teased her about being a "Spelman woman."

Although they moved in separate circles, women like Marymal followed the patterns of white middle-class society — what black Atlantans sometimes refer to as the "majority culture" — in assuming that marriage and childbearing would be the center of their lives. Often they married right out of college and had children while they were still unformed as adults. Many of my classmates at Radcliffe in the fifties followed the same pattern as Marymal, marrying men who would be expected to provide for them and would, in turn, expect them to reflect credit back on them by entertaining and maintaining a glamorous image. In the black community, however, it was the norm for women to work. "I wasn't marrying to settle down and not have a career," Marymal emphasized to me. "I have met friends from other racial groups for whom marriage *was* their career. That was their goal in life, but they weren't ending up happily ever after. They were so frustrated, but they still had the attitude of being rescued. I never had the attitude of being rescued.

"I tended to do what they expected of me. I finished high school, college, got my master's, got a job, had my children. It was all in a progression. A social work degree in that time was like an MBA, so when I was married to George, wherever we went, I just got a job. But when the children came I didn't work; they came in rapid succession."

As Marymal wrote the story and read it in class, the inspiration she needed to take charge of her life and her future came not from her mother, concerned with what the neighbors might think, or from the friends who surrounded her and her husband, but from a portrait of a woman named Rosalee. Marymal and her husband had begun to build an art collection as part of being among the "beautiful people," but this time their guests rejected her taste: "What do you see in this painting? She looks really depressed, as if she had a really hard life." This set Marymal wondering, "Am I that different, my tastes so different?" With her paper, she included a copy of the portrait, part of the final art school project of the artist Herman "Kofi" Bailey, who described the subject as a black tenant farmer in rural Alabama.

"Once while looking at the picture of Rosalee, I saw something in her expression. It was as if she was speaking to me. As if she was quoting snippets of Langston Hughes's classic poem 'Mother to Son': 'Well, Son, I'll tell you./Life for me ain't been no crystal stair.' In Rosalee I saw determination, hope, a willingness to fight against the odds, working from sunup to sundown, in conditions akin to slavery. Always tired, with few comforts, little money." But Marymal's husband and their friends did not respond to what she saw, so the picture brought into focus not only a neglected part of their reality but Marymal's realization that she was living with strangers.

Against her mother's urging Marymal decided she had to leave. Realizing she could not take her children until she could get her own life together, find a job and housing, she set out for Cleveland with one suitcase and fifty dollars from her housekeeping money, and found a job in child welfare. "George would send postcards and address me as the 'mother of my sons who has abandoned them.' It was just so ludicrous. He wanted the kids, but I knew him well enough to know that wasn't going to last, not three children, three little boys. That's a big responsibility." It was not long before the boys arrived in Cleveland. "Once he realized that I wasn't ever coming back and his ego was massaged enough, we were able to communicate more. He knew I was totally unprepared for taking care of three little boys, 'cause I had just rented a room and I had no furniture, so one weekend he brought the children to visit. He said, 'I really think the boys need to be with you,' so he just left them." Marymal improvised and coped.

Later Marymal told me that after their divorce, she found out George had been having an affair with a woman in his office. "I knew he wouldn't ever marry this woman, but she didn't know that. He was the kind of man who liked trophy wives. . . . I'm glad I found all this stuff out after we were divorced. Anyway, that young lady worked for him, and I did know she would take very good care of the children. A lot of this stuff was so painful I had actually blocked it out and didn't really recall it until I started writing my story for class."

Marymal today has multiple versions of her résumé, one a summary, one focusing on international programs, and another on domestic. Happy in a third marriage, she now has five grandchildren. She said to me, about halfway through the seminar, "I've been thinking over what you've said, and I've decided that I really have had a very successful life." Marymal was one of the students who reported in class on *Blackberry Winter,* the autobiography of my mother, Margaret Mead.[1] Like Marymal, my mother was married three times and had to deal with the cultural bias that suggests that the termination of any marriage is a failure on the woman's part. My mother did not regard her marriages as failures, though I think she grieved for the rest of her life about being rejected by my father, and she prided herself on maintaining a friendship with each of her ex-husbands. Whatever the understanding of divorce, Marymal's life is impressive as a record of decisions taken about what wasn't working and the adaptations she was able to make, not a straight line but a series of chapters, a zigzag development.

Marymal described her encounter with a piece of art as providing the framework for rethinking her life; now she had the task of composing it in a new way in a new place. At first she was very much alone, and it took time to put her life together and make space for her children. Like an artist gradually adding different shapes and colors and bringing them into relationship on a canvas, she found ways to fit together the pieces of her life. Many women today, with greater resources, are similarly preoccupied with the problems of composing lives that include both child rearing and career. The most common way of describing this complex composition is the cliché of juggling, a pernicious metaphor because it suggests a frivolous trifling with what is most precious — and constant anxiety about dropping something, perhaps a baby. The metaphor of composing suggests instead a search for distinctive ways of fitting diverse elements into a unity, combining the familiar and the new, as artists work within their traditions and blend in materials from other cultures in novel ways. One advantage of aesthetic judgment is that we are accustomed to the idea that fashions change and tastes may vary.

Music is composed in a different sense, unfolding through time with interwoven continuities and discontinuities, development and resolution. More and more people today have to find meaning in lives like Marymal's that do not follow a single clear plan. We face interruptions, downsizing and layoffs, returns to school for retraining, time off for childbearing . . . but we want to recognize all the twists and turns as parts of a single life, as expressions of a coherent identity, finding the familiar in the strange. How are the periods between transitions to be understood — as chapters? the movements of a symphony? the verses of a poem? Tastes change. Often we interpret the unexpected as a sign of failure, but we no longer expect each new generation to be an overlapping repetition of the previous one like the lines of a canon or round.

When new works that artists offer seem inharmonious or unsatisfying to a particular generation, as they have again and again, they may prefigure a change in the shapes of lives or in the way lives interconnect. Lives that seem admirable in one setting may be rejected in another, and the most puzzling behavior of a neighbor or family member may express an unfamiliar sense of grace or balance. Yet a comparison with the arts is a reminder that curiosity and respect do not necessarily entail imitation.

Composing suggests a continuing search both for harmony and for dynamic dissonance, the many elements never brought into perfect balance, certainly never completely merged. Within the last generation old metaphors of community, especially the metaphor of the melting pot with its suggestion of homogeneity, have been rejected. As a child I imagined a melting pot as an old-fashioned stewpot and rather liked the image of myself simmering in a wonderful spicy bouillabaisse, not homogeneous at all. In fact the reference is to the melting down of scrap metal, often enough to make bullets. More common today is the metaphor of a salad, in which the different elements remain recognizable, tossed up in a common dressing. But no single dish is an adequate metaphor for a diverse community. Good cooking, in my view, involves composition and often improvisation. The elements that give a meal its distinctive zest are sometimes mixed and sometimes not, sometimes side by side and sometimes in sequence.

There are other metaphors that pervade discussions of human lives, and these too can be expected to change. It has often been useful to think of lives as having a shape, outlined by biology but modified again and again by culture. The image underlying discussions of development or education is often a ladder or flight of stairs: the ascent must be made in sequence, with each step seen as an achievement providing access to the next, a foundation underlying subsequent progress. Today, however, such continuing progress seems uncertain and foundations seem infirm.

The stories our children need most to hear are not the stories of daunting success, achievements so impressive and final that they are hard to identify with, but the repeatable stories of composing and improvisation, in which adaptation is more central than dazzling accomplishment. Learning occurs in stages, but the process never completely ends for the individual even as it is repeated from generation to generation. In a world of accelerating change every graduate needs to understand that much of the shiny new learning is obsolescent, while the authority of elders is contingent on their willingness to continue to learn even as they teach. When society is fluid, young and old alike need to improvise and to teach each other. Wisdom is gradually revealing a whole new meaning, traced out through the life cycle. Today we do well to think of wisdom as depending on the flexibility, playfulness, and willingness to learn that are sometimes lost or denied with age, the kind of intelligence that includes self-criticism and the habit of reflecting on experience.

Narratives focus on dramatic events and transitions. But within our repertoire of ways of thinking about human lives, we need ways of thinking of the plateaus between transitions, long periods of little obvious change or learning, when maintenance and continuity are paramount, even as we remember that all such periods are temporary. We are skilled, in this culture, at talking about change and transformation, not so skilled at thinking about sustaining what follows. We deal with ongoing problems with quick campaigns promising spurious victories: crash diets instead of new habits, urban renewal by bulldozer, or such a flurry of simultaneous experiments in schools that parents and children are simply bewildered. Excitement about change leads all too readily to short-term efforts that are abandoned as quickly as they begin to show results.

Some diagrams of lives move straight across the page while others rise. In most human cultures age has been respected, and often an ascent continues even beyond death, for "now we see through a glass, darkly, but then face to face." "He will go from strength to strength," in the words of the Anglican burial service. In some traditions there is a progression from one life to the next, while in others the authoritative voices of the ancestors weaken slowly over time.

Other traditions see a similarity between the end of life and its beginning, and depict a rising trajectory turning downward into a declivity, just as our accounts of history often deal with an ebb and a flow, a rise and a fall: of a movement, an empire, a fashion. Americans have been all too ready to take the metaphor of ascent only through middle age, and to regard the rest as over the hill. The curve may even be reversed, falling and rising again, tracing the loss and recovery of innocence: for the Balinese, infants and old people are revered as closest to the gods.

When aging is seen as a return to the beginning, the young and the old are brought closer together and everyone is aware of a cyclical repetition from generation to generation. Erik Erikson, perhaps the most insightful recent thinker about the life cycle, used diagrams that seemed to suggest a sequence of *steps* but usually spoke of lives in terms of *cycles,* one of the most common metaphors of pattern through time, although he never drew them. Linear diagrams seem simply to end at the margin of the page; a cycle, by contrast, returns on its path.

The model that I find most comfortable is a spiral, which suggests both development and return. From above it looks like a circle. From the side it looks like a zigzag. A spiral models both a temporal movement and an internal process of reflection, revisiting experience through new eyes. But any of these models plays out differently today because the timing of lives is so changed and because the new timing puts generations out of step with one another.

Marymal had a kind of charisma for the young women in the class, for even though she did not fit their assumptions about successful lives, she had an unmistakable aura of success. If she was like the generous oak tree, firmly planted, then beside her Iyabo Morrison, the tallest of the students, was like a slim, resilient sapling. When Iyabo talked to me about why she valued the cross-generational structure of the group, she was especially grateful to Marymal for telling us about her first marriage because she was not used to hearing older people she admired acknowledging the losses and failures in their lives. "You know," she said, "I guess we expect, when we graduate from Spelman, we're gonna be successful, have a husband. I guess Marymal sharing about her divorce and eventually having three different marriages, that surprised me. That story could take place at any time, in the nineties or whenever it happened to her. The things that were kept quiet might not necessarily be kept quiet now, but our problems seem to be the same, just different time periods that they take place. It's really useful to talk to people who have done a beautiful job with their lives with what they found, and to know they've had to struggle." Stories like Marymal's encourage the younger generation to do some growing up before they commit themselves to marriage.

"A RIDDLE OF TWO WORLDS"

An Interpretation of the Poetry of H. N. Bialik

I came to love the work of the Hebrew poet H. N. Bialik in Israel, where I learned Hebrew and completed my senior year of high school, coming back to college in America with new interests in language and in religion. Reading and writing poetry were important to me at that time, and Bialik's long poem "The Pool" seemed to resonate with my own earlier imagery, while his poetry and his research on Talmudic legends gave me an entry, as a non-Jew, into the many layers of the Jewish tradition and the tensions between the Israeli assertion of strength and the memory of weakness in the diaspora.

Forty years later, the concept of artistic improvisation as a way of adapting to change seems prefigured in my effort to understand how Bialik used his poetry to make meaning from the conflicts and discontinuities in a life bridging from the nineteenth to the twentieth century. Reading this essay in the context of my work on mother-infant exchanges, I am struck by how often the poet refers to the failure of response by Adam, who does not answer God's call in the garden, and by God, who fails to answer prayer. Erik Erikson described the infant's experience of gazing into the mother's eyes, as Bialik gazes at the pool, and receiving a reliable response to cries of need as the basis of adult faith and trust. Bialik also started me thinking about immanent and transcendent concepts of deity.

This essay evolved to this final form over a ten-year period. It was my earliest effort to think about an individual life, connecting childhood experience with adulthood, and individual creativity with cultural tradition and the dilemmas that tradition can pose for the individual. It was first published in a student journal and then, reshaped at Erikson's suggestion after I had gotten my doctorate, appeared in *Daedalus*, in an issue titled *Tradition and Change*. My time in Israel led to an interest in the shades in meaning that seemed to accompany linguistic differences, so I read Benjamin Whorf and Edward Sapir and began to think about the nature of translation and cross-cultural communication. During that interval, my interest in the Middle East had continued and broadened, and I had written a dissertation on the linguistics of Arabic poetry.

Bialik is said to have ceased writing poetry after he immigrated to Palestine during the British mandate, believing that poetry was a distraction from political action. But sometimes poetry contains a depth of insight that is not available to the author elsewhere in his life, and an artist's visions can affect the way others think about the future and the decisions they make. Poetry is anything but a distraction. During my year in Israel, in 1966–67, I found many of my contemporaries were scornful of the traditions and literature of the diaspora and impoverished by that rejection. It seems clear that the issues of grief and assertion and the self-consuming nature of violence with which Bialik struggled remain relevant to Israel's conflicts today. Bialik reframed the sacred in the context of nature and arrived, at least in some of his writing, at an understanding of the relationship of love and power that is sorely needed still.

—MCB, 2004

From time to time a poet or writer may be credited with having "created" a language or a literary tradition, but in most cases this is a statement about the symbolic inventory of the culture rather than about the language as such. There seem to be writers who take up the materials of their language and culture and use them so that forever after they seem more deeply related to the lives of the people than they ever were before, although they were always used in the nursery, the field, the schoolroom, and the place of prayer. Haim Nahman Bialik, the greatest modern Hebrew poet, was one of a generation of intellectuals who prepared the way for a new use of Hebrew in all these places. Hebrew had to be freed from the suffocation associated with its traditional use in schoolroom and synagogue, and Bialik was able to do this by tracing through Hebrew the paths of the open fields of his childhood and the way back to his own nursery and the unresolved conflicts that lay there. He found a language wonderfully rich, which had been shaped by the Hebrew prophets and by the many poets who called themselves David or Solomon, using great names or going nameless, but had since long been impoverished by feeble indoor use. Bialik found the way to use a symbolism uniquely Judaic to express the nostalgia of every Jew for the days before he confronted his heritage and for some escape from it — the longing for some light and fresh air: "At my restoring the destroyed temple of the Lord — I will spread its canopies and cleave in it my window." To save his own soul he had to form a new understanding of his religion, his culture, and his art.

Bialik was born in 1873 in the village of Radi, Volhynia Province, in Southern Russia. When he was six, the family moved to Zhitomir, and a year later his father died, leaving his mother destitute. They went to live with his grandfather, a Talmudic scholar, and from his household Bialik entered the various stages of Jewish education, first the heder and then the yeshiva, where he stayed until his early twenties, so that his entire education consisted of the study of Jewish law and tradition. Later, he began to write both poetry and prose and worked with a group of young, nationalistic Jewish intellectuals who were publishing in the city of Odessa. After World War I, Bialik became increasingly involved in political activity and eventually went to Palestine. He gave up writing because he said he felt that the time had come for action and that poetry would be only a distraction. He may have resolved the problems from which his need for poetry had sprung or he may have been discouraged by the adoption in the Zionist settlements of the Sephardic pronunciation of Hebrew in place of the Ashkenazic (Eastern European) pronunciation on which he had based his meter. Bialik died in 1934.

A great portion of Bialik's writing is autobiographical. In attempting to present his poetry, with its many unfamiliar strands of imagery, I have taken his life as a loom, reweaving the diverse threads of his work within the frame of his life, treating his poetry as "case material" — as evidence of his psychological make-up — although an understanding of that make-up, in turn, may be valuable only as it leads to a new appreciation of his work. Bialik made a conscious effort to speak for the Jewish people as a "national" poet and the fact that he wrote in Hebrew tended to enhance the cultural content of his poetry. Hebrew was a second, a ritual language for him, so that the best worn phrases are not homely scraps of conversation but fragments of prayers; thus, Bialik's command of Hebrew does not reflect the everyday conversation of parents and siblings but the discussions of long-dead rabbis in the schools of Asia Minor. Bialik's symbols, too, are secondary: instead of verbalizing what he has seen and touched, he tends to use previously formulated symbols which draw their dynamic from the printed page and are then associated with the real world. In this way, continually conscious that he speaks as a Jew — or as The Jew — he is able to bridge the gap between two spheres of experience.

But Bialik could not be fully representative of Jewish culture. After all, only a few members of most cultures become poets, and that only by some inner distantiation.

> In the midst of my childhood I was set apart
> And panted all my days for secret places and silence —
> From the body of the world to its light I yearned,
> Something I knew not clamored in me, like wine,
> And I sought out coverts. There I gazed silent
> As if peering out at the eye of the world . . .*
>   "SPLENDOR"

If fantasy represents an area of refuge from the narrowing realities imposed by the society in which one lives, then the very manipulation of fantasy in the arts is in some sense an escape from cultural limitations and

---

*In preparing these translations, I have tried to be as literal as possible, frequently retaining Hebrew gender and the extensive use of conjunctions. Wherever possible, I have tried to make my translations "read like poetry," and I find that this has resulted in a large number of approximately iambic lines; I have encouraged this trend but not made it a requirement.

an appeal for validation to the most personal and, as it were, the precivilized elements of the psyche. Thus, though a poet must work with the tools and materials which his culture affords, he does so obliquely, aiming for a freedom not completely sanctioned by that culture. The paths of reference by which Bialik frees himself present a striking similarity to those which Sigmund Freud described in the precivilized elements of the psyche, and part of this similarity rests on the fact that Freud was himself a Jew, tracing his theories through the same mythology and the same history that Bialik inhabited. Poetry, then, was the only way Bialik could survive the culture to which he was so closely tied; but he escaped only in order to come back, reshaping his own understanding of Jewish traditions and eventually deeply influencing their interpretation by all Jews who adopted Hebrew as a spoken language.

Bialik's life may be seen as a complex variation of a familiar pattern. Born in a sunny village where his childhood was relatively free, he garnered a few years in paradise to carry with him through life, a remembered, day-to-day paradise which was merged not only with the lost paradise of his people but also with that of every child; for every child must lose the unlimited right to his mother's body and presence and learn that he will never possess her but must turn toward the competitive world of the father. In this way, the memory of a lost paradise is for Bialik truly "overdetermined" and he carries within himself a manifold nostalgia for previous happiness: the "milk and honey" of his mother's breasts, of the village of Radi, and of Eden and the Land of Israel. His father's death a year after the move from Radi to Zhitomir, instead of restoring paradise, plunged Bialik into complete dependence on the masculine world of his grandfather, where not even Bialik's mother had the right of intercession, for she was tolerated as a poor relative who had to be taken in. And then the boy was locked in the Hebrew school, where the hours of study were lengthened from year to year until his whole adolescence was worked out — to the extent that it was worked out — in the dark room of the yeshiva at his grandfather's command.

This pattern corresponds to both the myth and the history of the Jewish people and to Freudian theory; it is present in a culturally very specific form in the individual lives of Eastern European Jews, where the image of the mother as warm and sheltering is very highly developed until suddenly the boys are shut up in a rigorous, academic discipline which, for the talented ones, continues into or through manhood. Not only is this study oppressive; it is also fiercely competitive, for it is the only area of distinction, the only area in which a Jew could hope to manipulate reality or even be a good Jew.

> In this house, between these walls,
> Not a day — but six years have passed on his soul;
> Here his childhood bore its first fruits, and his youth ripened,
> And here his eyes were quenched and his features paled.
>   . . . . . .
> All day and half the night, he does not move from his place,
> There he eats his black crust in hunger —
> For who are you, adamant, who are you, flint,
> To a Hebrew boy occupied with the Torah?
>   "THE CONSTANT STUDENT"

Bialik built on his relation to the cultural prototype in his effort to tread a line between the two paths taken by his contemporaries. On the one hand, he would not join those Jews who repudiated their religion and most of the culture of the diaspora and became violently nationalistic and aggressive, because he was aware that a Jew can justify the demand for special consideration for his people only by sharing with them a precious culture or a divine designation: when these are denied, the nationalists are involved in nothing but a banal contest for power.

> So say: Enough for me of satiating hate
> And shame and abasement in place of my love.
> Do I still not see the lifted hand of falsehood?
> Whom have I there? What have I there? I'll return to my rest.
> I'll not soil the true God's wonder in the dust,
> I will not sell my birthright for a mess of pottage,
> My voice won't mingle in the trumpet-blast of falsehood,
> Rather than a whelp among lions' whelps I will perish with sheep.
> I was not endowed with claws and fangs —
> All my strength is God's, and God — life!
>   . . . . . .
> I saw the lions' whelps with golden curls
> Who fell as carrion on grazing ranges of deer.
> All flesh is grass, its strength withers,
> For the spirit of the Lord blows through it — and it is gone.
>   "ON THE THRESHOLD OF THE HOUSE OF STUDY"

Bialik could not accept the substitution of the extrinsic values of nationalism for the intrinsic values of Judaism, that is, the substitution of self-
definition by aggressive confrontation with the outside world for the
unique internal features of Jewish life. Yet, on the other hand, he felt that
those Jews who adhered to the old orthodoxy and remained passive were
on a path of rottenness and surrender which would lead to their destruction. This life is represented either by the yeshiva or the image of the
"wandering Jew": "a staff and a pack and a whispered prayer."

> It's not the staff I fear — not the pack that's terrible!
> But more cruel than they, twice seven times more bitter,
> Are life without hope and eyes without light;
> Life without hope, life of rotten decay,
> Sinking like lead, drowning in dark places;
> The life of a hungry dog, confined by a chain —
> Oh, you are cursed, you life without hope!
>   "REJECTED STAR"

Caught between these two alternatives, Bialik was in the desperate position of the rebel who can rise only in the name of the values he was born
with, yet must repudiate the system in which those values survive. How
can one rise in the name of the Jews when the Jews themselves live a life
that one must disown and deny?

Bialik could resolve this basic ambiguity only by interpreting it in
terms of the cleavage between the periods of his own life and their relation to the choices faced by his contemporaries. He had to divide his view
of his culture, but, as he internalized its contradictions, he was left with a
crippled structure which he struggled to support with all the passion he
could muster. Because he had had so little emotional life outside the
yeshiva, all the energies of his adolescence were bound up in traditional
learning, and the emotional poverty which would result from denying it
completely was only too clear.

> Shrine of the God of my youth — my old house of study —
> Your rotted threshold once again confronts me,
> Once again I see your walls which are crumbled like smoke,
> The muck of your floor, the murk of your ceiling.
> Redoubled ruin you are ruined, without the comers in season;

The weeds have risen in your walks and your paths grassed over,
The spider's weaving shudders on your rafter,
Upon your breached roof sons of ravens cry out;
Stone by stone you are tumbled and battered to fragments,
Your pillars quake, all of you stands by miracles.

In dust of yours an Ark without a Torah writhes,
Green, wilted pages rot in a barrel,
And light rays, brooding in crevices, peer out,
And every corner mourns and every angle weeps.
        . . . . . .
And again, my house of study, head bent like a pauper,
And desolate as you, on your threshold I stand.
Shall I weep for your destruction — do I weep at my destruction —
Or at both of them together shall I weep and mourn?
Hah! Your nest is emptied, your chicks have gone and fled,
They are vanished like a shade among the tall trees.
Many are smashed on the heads of boulders,
And many still stray in other fields.
Will they die the death of the straight? or find rest
In the life of scoundrels and forget you forever?

I have plucked no combs of honey on the paths of rebellion
Since the evil wind separated us;
Eternally lost from the Lord, all my world crumbled,
The waters rose to my soul — but she came not into them.
    "ON THE THRESHOLD OF THE HOUSE OF STUDY"

Bialik's ambivalence toward his culture is expressed in the way in which he uses the division of God into two aspects which developed in relation to the needs and experiences of the Jews during various periods of their history. There is the mighty Lord of the Old Testament and the later Shkhinah. Against the one he rebels, while the other he conserves. The Lord is challenged (but not quite denied) and becomes the focus for the burgeoning rage which the extreme nationalists turned outward, giving the poet an expression of dynamism in a Judaic context. The Shkhinah, the immanent, merciful aspect of God, first becomes important in Jewish writing early in the Christian era, after the destruction of the Second

Temple. The development of the concept, partly the result of Hellenistic influence, coincides with the period when the political situation prevented the Jews from asserting those elements in their culture which would reflect the attributes of the Almighty God, or, at any rate, prevented those Jews to whom the earlier idea of God was congenial from dominating the stage. In the Talmud, when God retires to a secret place to mourn the destruction of His Temple, it is as the Shkhinah that He weeps. When a man feels a sudden wave of pious joy, it is the wing of the Shkhinah which has touched him. The development of Chokhmah, "wisdom" (see especially Proverbs VIII), as a feminine principle in Biblical Judaism, which has been pointed out by Jung, was extended through the concept of the Shkhinah, which later absorbed many attributes both of Chokhmah and of the Rachel who weeps for the sufferings of her children. This feminine aspect of God seems to have no power of intercession with Her masculine aspect, and yet Her sympathetic weeping is a comfort and perhaps more, for the tears of the Shkhinah are precious things to be gathered up and saved. It is the Shkhinah Bialik wishes to save for his people and for himself — the Shkhinah who must be saved, for no action is anticipated from Her.

> The wind has carried them all, the light swept them all away,
> A new song has set the morning of their lives to singing,
> And I, a tender fledgling, was forgotten
> Beneath the Shkhinah's wing.
>
> Alone, alone I remained, and the Shkhinah even She
> Made Her broken right wing to tremble above my head.
> My heart knew Her heart; fearfully She hovered over me,
> Over Her son, over Her only one.
>
> Already She is driven from all the crevices, only one
> Secret place, small and desolate, remains to Her —
> The house of study — and She cowers in the shadow,
> And I am together with Her in sorrow.
>
> And when my heart yearns toward the window, the light,
> When the place is narrow to me, under Her wing —
> Her head falls on my shoulder, and Her tear
> Drops on the page of my Talmud.

Silent She wept above me and clung to me,
As though sheltering me with Her broken wing
"The wind has carried them all, they have all burst out,
And I must do without, all alone."

And like the coda of a very ancient dirge,
And like a prayer, — a petition and tremor in one,
My ear heard that silent weeping of Hers
And that seething tear.
    "Alone"

The Shkhinah is clearly identified with the poet's mother, and is the
main focus of his nostalgia for the lost paradise. This identification is supported not only by the consistent reference to himself as a son in relation to
the Shkhinah, but also in the interweaving of imagery in his religious and
love poetry and all the poetry in which he refers to his mother. In one poem
his mother faces the Sabbath with only enough money for either food or
candles, and chooses to kindle the Sabbath light rather than feed her
family. They stand around the empty table saying the blessing, and the
mother is unable to control her weeping, and a tear falls and extinguishes
one of the two candles:

The Sabbath stood shamed, her one eye blinded —
And the woman trembled:
"Would you scorn, God, the gift of a widow? Has your handmaid
    sinned?
Your Sabbath, how has she transgressed?
Why have you pierced her eye?
    . . . . . .
Still no ear heard her on high, the Throne of Honor did not yet see
This fainting of a soul in her grief.
Then there fell from the cheek of the pious woman a single burning
    tear,
A fragment of a burning flame,
And fell, and dropped to double light, for there was kindled
The candle which had gone out.
My mother barely opened her blurred eyes when I saw
The light of the seven days shining there,

For the Shkhinah had kissed them — may the merit of this saint stand,
For us and for all Israel.
   "MY MOTHER, OF BLESSED MEMORY"

The Shkhinah was the aspect of God his mother turned to; because of
her piety, the Shkhinah lived in her eyes. And the Shkhinah suffered as
his mother suffered, for She too lived with sorrowing love and a feminine
weakness and poverty in a world of masculine strength, taking Her only
joy from Her son and so completely dependent upon his love of Her.
Bialik had to remain oriented toward the Shkhinah or his mother would
have been completely alone. He never tore himself away from this mutually protective relationship which was reflected in his later love affairs.
One love he addresses:

Enter me under your wing,
And be to me a mother and a sister,
And be your breast a shelter for my head,
The nest of my rejected prayers.

And in the hour of mercy, between the suns,
Bend down, and I will show you the secret of my bonds:
They say, there's youth in this world.
Where is my youth?
   "ENTER ME UNDER YOUR WING"

Here we see the one Bialik, the one that delved into the Talmud to
bring out beautiful legends of the Shkhinah and free them from their
imprisonment between the dry legal discussions (the Talmud itself consists of two kinds of material, legend and anecdotal material written in the
colloquial Aramaic, and legalities in purer Hebrew). Bialik was primarily
responsible for making this aspect of Jewish tradition available to his contemporaries in a form they would use, greatly deepening their thinking.
This is the Bialik who wrote poems of nature and childhood, recalling the
lost paradise and comforting himself in the hard world with an image of
his mother who had also been expelled (perhaps because she loved him too
much, as he loved her? — at any rate, too purified now by tears to be considered in any other than a spiritual sense), an immanent feminine deity
whose Temple had been destroyed and Her sons scattered, and could only

protect them with a precious but broken right wing and a tear with something of flame in the midst of it, the consolation of poetry. In the Talmud the question is raised of whether a wise student who has grown senile and lost his learning shall still be honored, and the answer is that when Moses had broken the first tablets of the Law and new ones were given, the broken chips were put in the Ark along with the new. This is what Bialik clings to, the fragments of tablets; and the culture of an exiled and oppressed people permitted him to do so. But this was also the solution of hundreds of Eastern European Jews of Bialik's generation who divided their religion between an abstract fear of God and a love for the Shkhinah, and surrendered completely to the loss of paradise.

Surrender alone is not an appropriate movement for a poet; simple mourning and nostalgia do not make great poetry. There is another aspect of Bialik's childhood which is absent in the cultural prototype — for, after all, his father, the powerful figure who might be blamed for the loss of paradise, had died. Here a question arises which, again, is reminiscent of some of Freud's original findings. Bialik's father died when he was seven, and it may be that the child linked the memory of this drastic event with the death wishes which every boy is said to harbor against his father, not without deep guilt and ambivalent love. However, if he could believe he had "killed" his father, he had been left with another, sterner one, his grandfather, and beyond him an even sterner, an Almighty God, there both to punish him and to serve as a focus for a love with all the ambivalence involved in his love for his father. He had won a victory in a struggle for his mother which showed that such a struggle would remain hopeless and paradise could not be obtained in that way. For him, therefore, violence and aggression could not be tied to the success and acquisition to which Western thought has generally attached them. For Bialik, any chance of salvation, or rather relief, is relegated to the feminine principle, but masculine assertion still retains a certain brilliance, a Pyrrhic victory that did not involve an irremediable loss. Bialik has a memory that, somewhere in the far past, assertion was meaningful. This became closely tied up with the simplified form of Nietzschean thought that was adopted by many Jewish intellectuals and, as the ambiguity posed by his father's death prevented a complete surrender to orthodoxy and drove him into the intellectual arena of his period, he had to come to terms with it.

But here, too, the poet's idiosyncratic fate only gave special meaning to the theme of victory by unsuccessful violence, a continuing theme in

Jewish thought. Violence on the part of man is consistently denied as a means to human success in the Old Testament, although it may be used in the fulfillment of some divine purpose, just as transgression and rebellion are. This is because violence is met by violence on the part of a God who always wins — although by this response He spares the rebel from the ultimate loss of a severed relationship. Rebellion is sanctified in primitive Judaism by the assurance that it will not succeed. This is the theme that Bialik plays on in "The Dead of the Desert." The corpses of the generation of Sinai, those who left Egypt and were denied entrance to the promised land, lie defeated and mighty in the desert.

> Mighty ones have stuck to the ground, fallen asleep — and their
>   weapons are on them.
>   . . . . . .
> Their heads are sunk to the ground, heavy with the growth of hair,
> And their curls grind and scrape together, like the manes of lions;
> Their faces are daring, are darkened, and their eyes tarnished as
>   copper.
> Their brows are hard and strong, set against heaven,
> Their lashes — terrifying; and from their thicket horror lurks in
>   ambush,
> And their chests rise like quarried adamant.
>   . . . . . .
> This is a camp of God, a primeval generation, a race mighty in daring,
>   ancient of days.
> Lo, brave in spirit and hard, as boulders in the desert, was this race:
> They embittered the souls of their prophets and even enraged their
>   God —
> And He sealed them between the mountains, and sent eternal sleep
>   upon them,
> And commanded the desert over them, to guard them to the memory
>   of all generations —
>   . . . . . .

And these, these are the fathers of the People of the Book! And once, in the eternity of the unmoving desert, the waste itself rebels and rises against the Creator in protest at its own desolation. And with it rise again the giant warriors of the desert, to protest once more against the God who has turned the face of His wrath against them. They shout:

"We are heroes!
The last generation of slavery, and first to redemption are we!
Our hand alone, our mighty hand
Has broken the weight of the yoke from the pride of our neck.
We lift our heads to heaven and it dwindles in our eyes —
And we longed for the desert, and said of the waste, 'Our mother!'
      . . . . . .
Who is lord to us?!
Even now, when an avenging God has closed His desert upon us,
Barely does a song of insurrection and revolt sound among us — and
    we rise!"
      . . . . . .
"Here we are, we have come up!
If God has taken away from us His hands,
And His Ark does not move from its place —
Then we rise without Him!"
      . . . . . .
And the desert at that moment was . . .
Something bitter, a tyrant, very terrible.
      . . . . . .
And the storm passed. And the desert silenced itself from its wrath and
    became pure.
And very bright and shining are the skies, and great is the stillness.
    "THE DEAD OF THE DESERT"

God has won, as always. But the corpses remain in the desert, staring up at their tyrant with terrible eyes, and woe befall any man of this weak generation who approaches their mighty secret or violates their armed camp. The fallen Maccabees, the defeated Bar-Kochba, the David whose hands are too soiled to be allowed to build God's Temple — these are the heroes of the past, and He who decreed their defeat remained their God. There are many interpretations of the word *Israel* as it was applied to Jacob and the Jewish people, but Bialik may well have supported the interpretation that it means "one who struggles with God." This aspect of the religion of the Father God was almost dead in the Judaism in which Bialik grew up and for which he had to dig into the past; a metamorphosis of the same theme can be discerned in the victory which followed the death by violence of Jesus of Nazareth.

Given this memory of violence, it was necessary to confront the circumstances of a period when the Jews themselves were on the whole
passive, while the gentiles were violent and unjustly successful. This
produced a crisis, first because it removed the area of violence from that
of justice, and second because the Jews were at any rate too weak to pro-
cure by violence either power or recompense. For Bialik it was the
Kishineff Pogrom of Easter, 1903, which brought the matter to a head.
Almost the whole Jewish population of the town was brutally murdered, probably with the encouragement of the Czarist government,
and Bialik's lines from "In the City of Slaughter" were quoted all over
Jewry; as a result, Kishineff brought on both his most personal crisis and
his sudden emergence to fame: "For the Lord called forth the spring and
the massacre as one. The sun shone, the acacia bloomed, and the slaugh-
terer slaughtered." Bialik describes the town, the dried-out blood and
brains on the sidewalks and walls, the shattered remains of day-to-day
domestic life, all of them in every part of the town bearing witness to

> What was done to the gored belly which they stuffed with feathers,
> What was done with a pair of nostrils and nails, with skulls and
> hammers,
> What was done to men slaughtered and hung from the beams,
> And what was done to an infant found by his riddled mother's side,
> As he slept with the nipple of her cold breast in his mouth;
> What was done to the child ripped in pieces so his breath escaped with,
> "mama!" —
> And here are his eyes too, asking an account of me.
> And more like this and like that the cobweb narrates to you,
> Deeds boring the brain with that in them to kill
> Your spirit and your soul with a total, eternal death —
> And you controlled yourself, and choked your roar in your throat,
> And entombed it in the depths of your heart before its explosion,
> And broke away and went out — and, lo, the earth after her own
> manner
> And the sun like yesterday and the day before spills down its glory to
> the earth.

> So you go down from there and come among dark cellars
> Where they tainted the decent daughters of your kin, among the tools.

A woman — one woman — under seven, seven of the uncircumcized,
The daughter in the eyes of her mother, the mother to her daughter's
    eyes,
Before slaughter and during slaughter and after slaughter:
With your hand touch the soiled featherbed and the bloodied cushion,
The lair of wild swine and rutting of horses of men
With an axe dripping boiling blood in their hands.
See, then, see, in the dark of that same corner,
Under that matzoh-mortar, behind that very barrel,
Husbands lay, grooms, brothers, peering from the holes
At the writhing of holy bodies under the flesh of mules,
Smothered in their desecration, choking down blood from their own
    throats,
As, like a man portioning out tidbits, a loathsome gentile divided their
    flesh —
The men lay in their shame and saw — and did not move or stir,
And did not gouge out their eyes or go out of their minds —
And perhaps each even prayed by himself in his heart:
Lord of the world, work a miracle — may the evil not come to me.

The cowardice and degradation of the survivors are as terrible as the cru-
elty of the butchering gentiles. Bialik tells of a dozen men who crowded
to hide in the bottom of a privy and suffocated themselves and then of
how the survivors rushed to the synagogue to pray for forgiveness and to
ask the law books whether their wives who had survived were permissible
to them after being raped! In this poem, the Shkhinah is unable to weep;
the poem is addressed to the poet himself (as if to Ezekiel, "Son of Man"),
as he is led through the humiliations and horrors of the deserted town. He
too is unable to weep or do more than list what he sees, until finally,

And now, what is there for you here, Son of Man? Rise and flee to the
    desert,
And carry with you there the cup of your despair,
And there you rip your soul in ten shreds,
And your heart you give as fodder for the impotent wrath,
And send your great tear down on the tops of hard boulders,
And send forth your bitter roar of fury — and let it be lost in the storm.
    "IN THE CITY OF SLAUGHTER"

This is violence which cannot be met with violence, nor can it be met with poetry. Violence can only deal with itself and Bialik can only send it on its own evolution. Such are the alternatives within the circle of violence:

If there is Justice — Let Him appear at once!
For if after my destruction from under the sky
Justice should appear —

Let His chair be hurled down forever!
The heavens will rot in the murk of ages,
And you, presumptuous ones, go, in this violent wrath of yours,
Go and be suckled on your blood.

Cursed be the one who says: Revenge!
Such a revenge, revenge for the blood of a small child,
Satan has not yet created —
Let the blood pierce to the depths!
Let the blood pierce to the depths of darkness,
And consume in darkness and mine there
All the rotten foundations of the earth.
    "On the Massacre"

Here is the end of violence. Neither the Shkhinah nor the Almighty, each expressing one set of divine attributes, offers an adequate solution to the conflict which Bialik faced. The extreme contrast between the different periods of Bialik's childhood had allowed him to experiment separately with "masculine" and "feminine" forms of expression in trying to find a personal solution to the historical and cultural conflict in which the Jews of his period found themselves. The fact that Bialik had entertained these two kinds of solutions and had partaken of two trends in the development of Judaism which were not normally combined in a single individual had prevented him from settling for either one and resulted in his use of two almost completely separate poetic modes — songs of anger or heroism, and religious and lyric poetry. If the essential problem of life is the resolution of love and force or aggression (or, formulated on a different dimension, Eros and Thanatos), then Bialik has no more than separated them in the poems discussed so far and stands orphaned — and, finally, mute — in the center.

This conflict seems finally resolved in "The Pool," a long poem written three years after the Kishineff Pogrom; here Bialik deserts the mode of aggression and uses the imagery of nature and the gentle, nostalgic tone associated with the lost paradise, and yet asserts, in an interpenetration of feminine and masculine modes, an eternal source of strength.

> I know a forest and in the forest
> I know a single, humble pool:
> In the depths of the glade, cut off from the world,
> In the shadow of a high oak, blessed by light and taught by storm,
> Alone she dreams for herself a dream of an inverted world
> And spawns for herself in secret the fishes of her gold —
> And none knows what is in her heart.

The pool is buried deep in the forest, while the tall trees above her gather the rays of sunlight in their own branches and compete in a world of strongly masculine symbols. And the pool

> Suckles his roots in silence, and her waters are serene,
> As though she rejoices, silent, in her part,
> That she has merited to be a mirror to the mighty one of the forest
> And who knows, perhaps she dreams in secret
> That not only his image with his suckling is in her —
> But all of him is growing in the midst of her.

The young Bialik, still not deprived of paradise, approaches the pool by a

> Path known only by the wolf and the hero of the hunt,

and sits on the bank meditating on a double world, on the existence of two suns, and waits for a revelation.

> And while my ear is still tuned and hoping,
> And in holy yearning my heart attends and pines and dies —
> The echoed voice of a hidden God
> Breaks suddenly through the silence:
> "Where art thou?"

"Where art thou?" — the words of God who went seeking Adam in the garden when he had sinned and must be driven from paradise and plunged into a competitive world. So the next word is from the masculine trees; they stand amazed and ask, "What is he doing among us?" Now, for the first time, the trees notice the poet and he finds his place among these trees which are strong but are always nourished by paradise and are in paradise through their reflection in the pool. And then the image is reversed again as Bialik suddenly turns to define the language of poetry: this is the language in which the pool has posed to him her eternal riddle.

> And hidden there in the shade, bright, calm and quiet,
> Looking out for everything, and everything reflected in her, and
>   altering with everything,
> It seemed to me as though she were the open eye
> Of the prince of the forest, great with enigma
> And wide in his musing boughs.

Bialik has accepted the reproach of God, and the accompanying demand that he relate himself to the masculine world. He has discovered that it is only the high tree which towers above the pool that can see its reflection in it. He has discovered that ultimately, living in the world, he can have access to his own creativity only if he can approach it by the path of the fearless hunter — by the conscious manipulation of the creatures of fantasy in relation to a real and hard world.

> I have not taught my hand to strike with the fist;
>   · · · · · ·
> I was born to sing the song of the Lord in this world,
>   · · · · · ·
> So the words of our God are established forever
>   "ON THE THRESHOLD OF THE HOUSE OF STUDY"

In "The Pool," we see Bialik formulating a resolution to a conflict which is both individual and cultural. Because historical circumstances had cut the Jews off from any possibility of collective or individual assertion on their own terms vis-à-vis the gentile world in which they lived, they had reacted by shaping their personal and community behavior in terms of a feminine ideal and finding comfort in a feminine concept of

God, the Shkhinah; they had learned to live in the sheltering world of memory and tradition. In the nineteenth century, however, a growing number of Jews sought masculine assertion in nationalism and repudiated this feminine passivity, at the same time rejecting all the nurturing elements of their culture. Bialik could accept neither alternative. On the one hand, he recognized that the nationalists rejected far too much that was precious in Jewish culture while their image of masculinity was, in fact, formed primarily on a gentile model. On the other hand, the events of Bialik's childhood fostered a particular attitude toward aggression, harking back to Old Testament Judaism, so that he could never be content with passivity. Any solution acceptable to Bialik would have to be much more complex than the divergent solutions of his contemporaries; his solution would have to be a synthesis of both.

It was in his poetry that Bialik tried to find this solution. In some ways, this made the task more difficult, for poetry itself is a maternal mode — a feminine form of creativity. It renounces the attempt to manipulate the external environment, shaping instead the forms and fancies of the mind. For a poet, then, a directly paternal mode is impossible, since it involves aggression which, if turned inward, becomes self-consuming. In his religious and lyric poetry, Bialik accepts the limitation of the maternal mode, and these poems are in harmony with the traditional culture.

At the same time, aggression remained attractive, and in the poems on the great pogroms we see the consequences. There is no real outlet for the poet's fury, and it must be internalized, so that he stands mute in the streets of Kishineff.

In "The Pool," finally, Bialik sees poetry itself as a way of relating to the world which need be neither masculine nor feminine. The pool is reflective and receives the strength of the trees around her. But at the same time the masculine trees are nourished by the pool, gaining the strength of their masculinity from her and becoming transfigured as they are reflected in her. Poetry becomes the source and the goal of strength and the only perfect offering, as the poet is able to offer back what he most desires by setting it in the context of the acknowledgment of power. Bialik thus takes the verbal and introspective richness of Judaism and transmutes the passivity which it had seemed to imply into a basis of a new and vigorous kind of national identity. When Bialik is able to imagine a relationship between love and power, he places God in a new position. In this poem God becomes the axis of the relationship between Bialik and his

poetry, and religion becomes the end of that use of poetry which bravely
takes the elusive and fragile and goes quietly and strongly with it in the
world. Bialik once wrote of his soul as coming to one possible terminal
after another, and yet failing to come to rest either in the delights of childhood or in the aridity of Talmudic study where, parched and straitened,
his soul found expression in poetry and then escaped.

> To this day she flies and wanders in the world,
> Wanders at random, and finds no comfort;
> And on the holy nights at the beginnings of each month,
> At the prayers of the world for the dark side of the moon,
> She clings with her wing to the gate of love.
> Clinging, she knocks, and her weeping is in secret,
> And she prays for love.
>   "IF THE ANGEL SHOULD ASK"

Such an estrangement was the special burden of the poet with too vivid an
insight into the extremes of contrasting potential in his culture. But the
pool represents a refuge for such a divided soul and a lens through which
those who followed Bialik, writing in modern Hebrew, could view their
divided tradition. His contribution to the revival of Hebrew consists not
so much in linguistic creation as in a reappraisal of the symbolic inventory
of the culture, interpreting it in such a way that it is wide and deep
enough to live in fully. For all who would be nourished by the Eastern
European Jewish tradition without capitulating to it, Bialik has found in
the pool that statement of the riddle in which two worlds are reconciled,

> . . . the open eye
> Of the prince of the forest, great with enigma,
> And wide in his musing boughs.

INTO THE TREES

I surprised the editor of an anthology dealing with ecological and environmental issues, *Sacred Trusts,* by
choosing to write not about threatened species or wilderness but about death and its continuing but threatened
importance in life. Between 1980, when I wrote about
my father's death, and 1993, when this essay appeared, I
had been present at other deaths and I had had a chance
to move from the specific to the general. No discussion
of learning through the life cycle is complete unless it
poses the question of learning how to die.

— MCB, 2004

∽

Death too is a trust, one that requires us to go beyond individual consciousness and to be aware of natural process.

Walking through the woods, I am reminded that there is as much
death here as there is life. It is a mistake to think the word *forest* refers
only to the living, for equally it refers to the incessant dying. It is a mistake to speak of preserving forests as preventing the death of trees. Forests
live out of the deaths of toppled giants across the decades, as well as the
incessant dying of microscopic beings. Without death, the forest would
die. Ultimately, it is only the removal of trees that can deplete the forest.
Both fallen giants and fallen leaves collaborate with the bacteria of decay
to produce the fertile soil from which new growth comes. By itself, no
single organism can long survive. The forest is its own memorial, the conclusion of its own conversation. You can lift a log, the corpse of a fallen
tree, and find a whole community at the rotting face where it touches the
moist ground.

Within organisms, living means the continual death of cells. Some are replaced; some linger, no longer living but still providing protection or support; some wither and are reabsorbed, part of an organ no longer needed, like the tadpole's tail. Within the human body, death is, from moment to moment and day to day, an essential part of life. Within the ongoing process of healthy functioning of an organism, there is a steady rhythm of cell death and replacement, and this, we now know, is not only a matter of replacing casualties but also, in many cases, a programmed process in which cells themselves switch into an active mode of self-destruction, synthesizing the enzymes that will shut them down. The cells that live on memorialize the others, but these will also die. Only cancerous tissue can be kept alive indefinitely. Death is apparently not a failure of life but a mode of functioning as intrinsic to life as reproduction. To see life without seeing death is like believing that the earth is flat and matter solid — a convenient blindness.

Human communities are unlike the forest, for dying and decay are often concealed, the story distorted. In our society, we treat dying as if it were separable from living, and we surround the process of dying and its aftermath in secrecy and expertise, much as we treated birth until recently. Decay, the same process that in the forest undergirds all new life, is denied. The all-too-perishable bodies of the beloved dead are both beautiful and horrible. They could continue their journey, back into the unity of natural cycles, but instead we struggle to deny this return and bodies are segregated from the cycle of living things, preserved with chemicals and sealed in metal-lined caskets. In many societies the preparation of the dead — washing them, closing the eyes — is a final act of loving intimacy. They are laid out in the home, where both caring and grieving nourish ongoing love and those who live on become familiar with death.

Respect could be expressed in other ways. For years I have had the fantasy of buying a hillside suitable for terracing, where the dead might be buried without coffins and chemicals, and fruit or olive trees be planted above each one. No waste of fertile land, no whispering between rows of statuary; rather, an annual harvest and families coming for laughing picnics. And for the dead, the slow intimacies of groping roots and a merging with organic process rather than protected separation from the earth or the quick, furtive transition to sterile ash and gases in cremation. After a time, especially for the children, it would be easy to believe that the lives ended had passed into the trees.

That is what I believed after my father's death. Every tall tree is my father now, I thought.

Health has a different face in a society where death and aging are denied. We have come a long way in the unwinnable warfare against death. More and more, human beings are products of technological interference with natural process. Whenever I enter a room filled with people, as thickly gathered as underbrush, I am reminded that I am in the presence of an artifact. Not the hall, with its air-conditioning or heating, its loudspeaker system and lighting, but the assembly of human beings. I share the room with others who except for technology would be dead or would never have been born, the creations of public health and immunization programs, of surgery and medication of all sorts, of treatments both heroic and routine. As infants, some were kept alive in incubators; others have had open-heart surgery. More and more of us are started on our way by parenthood consciously chosen, rather than by nature taking its course, and increasing numbers now are brought into life by in vitro fertilization. Any gathering today is likely to include vital "senior citizens" actively enriching their retirement with lectures and seminars into their eighties and beyond. Most of them would not have been alive under the circumstances of human life only half a century ago. It is curious that so many religions that define the prevention of conception as an interference with divine will do not question the prevention of death.

Not only life but also health, youth, and beauty are artificially sustained. Looking around I see skin, hair, and teeth kept healthy and shining; sight and hearing corrected; age camouflaged. Physical pain is anesthetized. Each of our bodies is a declaration that technology can overcome nature, not perfectly, not indefinitely, but to a significant degree. Yet there is a shadow side to this achievement. Almost everyone in the room is dissatisfied with the reality of his or her body, trying to pummel it or squeeze it into a new shape, to mask its natural odors. The consequences include eating disorders, addictive exercising and dieting, and steroid abuse. Huge sums of money are spent on cosmetic surgery, which can itself be addictive, and on the less drastic cover-ups of makeup and clothing. Rejecting death, we reject ourselves. In a society that rejects the beauty of mature bodies, forcing people to strive to be endlessly adolescent, it is also predictable that there will be some who follow this obsession with youthfulness into the sexual exploitation of children.

Finally, after looking around me at others, I look at my own hands. The joints ache sometimes now and will probably get worse. The skin hangs rather loosely, showing the beginning of age spots, and there are new ridges in my fingernails. My culture tells me I too should want to resist these gradual changes. After years of arguing that the desire to dominate nature is leading to its destruction, I am at that moment of transition when for almost everyone, the battle against nature begins to be fought within the boundaries of the body. The rhetoric of longevity is full of references to natural foods, the outdoors, and exercise but not to the natural necessity of return to the earth. Do I then want to defeat old age, to control death? It is the transient body that we hold in trust.

None of us have known our parents as they were as children, so we must invent childhood for ourselves. Usually we have known our parents in maturity and old age, so we might have learned from them something about dying. Yet as a society, we have failed in the duty of teaching to new generations the process of dying, knowledge traditionally passed on through contact with the peaceful courage of the old and the passionate expression of grief that is then allowed to heal. Death, so often taken for granted like the air and often so difficult to accept, will someday again be treasured for the meaning it gives to life. Dying, a natural process too often masked by medical heroics, will someday be embraced as a final stage of maturation.

I knew people in my childhood who died, and I saw their bodies laid out for mourners. I learned something of death from reading the poems of a friend who committed suicide and from the death soon after birth of a premature son. But I did not begin to learn about dying until the death of my father. He had been impatient for years of medical and dental care, so his body was a clear testimony to aging. At the end, his death was expected and accepted, awaited without tubes and monitors, shared as an extraordinary gift. If my own aging brings me closer to him, does it bring me closer to the trees and to the forest?

Every tall tree is my father now.

Some natural processes have been taken for granted, while others have been matters of artifice and effort, concern and prayer. I doubt that any human group has prayed that gravity continue — on the contrary, mythology and technology are full of efforts to outwit it. Even a tepee, after all, is a negotiation with gravity. Gravity is a fact of the natural order so reliable and so pervasive that the entire body is constructed to come to terms with it. We remain, as a species, handicapped by lower back pain — the result of a recent and imperfect defiance of gravity. Only when it became possible to send human beings into space did lack of gravity become recognizable as a problem, complicating the simplest activities, like eating and elimination. Without gravity to work against, bodies deteriorate rapidly. Walk through the forest and notice that "up" and "down" are reflected in the structure and behavior of every visible being. Sunlight above and the downward pull of gravity are mast and unseen keel for every motion. Gravity is a servitude that gives shape to our lives.

Death is like gravity, shaping and balancing our lives. Legends offer immortality as they offer flight, sometimes combining both in the image of an afterlife above the clouds. There are cautionary tales that suggest that immortality would be a burden without eternal youth, innocence, or the companionship of contemporaries — that death might be longed for in the absence of these. But, in general, death has been reliable, and so it is survival that has been longed for and pursued through ritual and technology.

In nature, effort often seems one-sided when you look at a single organism, for the characteristics of the organism are balanced by the characteristics of the environment, with the two together forming the unit of survival. Eating, breeding, even moving, the behavior of every creature takes much for granted and is organized around what is scarce. In the rain forest, species can be sorted by their adaptations to the filtered light; in the desert they can be classified by their strategies for storing moisture. The effort to survive is intrinsic in life, but when we humans gain the capacity to make our desires effective, our one-sided struggles can be disastrous. We are like people who have been walking against a high wind, leaning into it; when the wind drops, we risk falling over.

Where food is plentiful, human beings are slow in learning not to overeat; where almost all infants survive, we have difficulty learning not to overbreed; where death can be staved off by ever more elaborate technologies, we have trouble learning when to let go. We go on struggling against death because this has been a battle impossible to win. Death has been a safe enemy, since we have never had to face the disaster of victory. We have not in the past needed to ensure our own dying, for death has been the one thing we could count on.

All pathologies of immoderation must be one side of the coin of survival, emerging as problems when the coin no longer spins true. Human greed and human hoarding have been adaptive responses to scarcity and tenuous survival, but, backed by the power of technology, these can come to threaten survival. For humankind, aware of struggling for millennia against predictable natural processes, the extent of reliance upon our opponents has been obscured.

The mythology of wish fulfillment underlines the fact that what human beings strive for is not desirable when it disrupts the environment in which they survive. Of all the many stories, the most poignant perhaps is that of King Midas, who wished for and was granted the golden touch and found that he could no longer eat or drink, that his touch caused the death of those he loved. Midas suffered the fate of being cut off from those exchanges necessary for life and happiness; his error was the assumption that he could prosper in separation from the environment. What you want as a single organism is not what you want as a system consisting of an organism in an environment.

Years ago, at a conference on conscious purpose and human adaptation, Tolly Holt said, "It's the idea of the conceivable existence of anything which is independent of process. It's the confusion that what I strive for is what I strive for, which is nonsense . . . . The illusion that if strawberry shortcake is a good thing, then more strawberry shortcake is a better thing."[1] Good and evil are contextual, and even orchids and roses are weeds in the wrong setting. We have believed that prolonging life is always good and always an obligation for family members and medical personnel. This is not true. The individual who wishes too efficiently may disrupt the larger system. The mechanism of wishing may have evolved to push against environmental constraints, but not to succeed in overcoming them. Now, with so much power, we must learn to override our own wishes. Kierkegaard once said, "Purity is to will one thing," but it seems possible that a divided will is the beginning of wisdom.

Struggles and anxieties change and new solutions give birth to new concerns. Infants seem at first to take the mother's breast for granted, as if it were a part of themselves. Fear of loss comes into being when they discover their fundamental separateness. Then, as adults, they learn that the possibility of separation is an essential and poignant element in the understanding of love. At times, human beings have worried about the sun, about whether it would rise the next morning or whether after the winter solstice the days would once again lengthen and warm, and green leaves appear. In other places, the perennial focus of anxiety was the rain or the salmon run or the arrival of migratory flocks of birds. Ceremonies were held that were believed to sustain and regulate the natural order; humans were participants, with a part to play and limitations they were required to accept.

One of the modern nightmares is the loss of those goods that have always been trustworthy in the past. Yet the notions of air as a free good and of the ocean as an unfillable garbage dump have not been universal, even among peoples who lack our modern experience. For these groups, it is often an essential courtesy to avoid certain kinds of pollution. Now we face the awareness that the destruction of the ozone layer will make the very sunshine dangerous, the recognition that rain can be poisoned by airborne wastes. We are preoccupied with failures in parental care, the discovery that the desire and wisdom to bear and nurture children are not reliable universals of human behavior, that parental caring is not a free good that can be drawn on, but rather must be cherished and rewarded, and only flourishes in an appropriate context. The battles about incest and child abuse, about abortion, about family leave and day care all reflect the horrifying discovery that the care needed by the next generation of human beings cannot be taken for granted, any more than it can be taken for granted that running water will always purify itself.

Forest peoples may revere the forest and treat it with respect, but rarely do they imagine that the forest might simply cease to exist. Yet today the great trees are at risk, the forests are at risk, the seas are at risk. Some argue that forests that were protected should be opened up to loggers to preserve jobs, jobs that will disappear soon enough when the trees are cut. Lumber companies claim they restore the forests — sometimes — but what they do is plant young trees for harvesting later. In this system no trees will be allowed to mature like the ancients, and the elders of the forest will not be permitted to die and melt into the ground.

Whenever I hear of ancient forests being cut down in the American Northwest, the tropical rain forests, the Siberian taiga, I know that living graves and cradles are being destroyed. During the memorial service for my father at Big Sur, held on a wide lawn, I looked up at a great tree and thought, there is my father. Every tall tree is my father now.

Waiting by the deathbed of someone we love, we want to salvage every day or hour of life; but looked at from the perspective of the future, unless there are key tasks to be completed, important farewells to say, those extra hours are trivial. Later we learn to ask about the completeness of the life ended, the dignity and surcease granted, the grace afforded to the entire composition by its closure. My father had a book he had begun and wanted to finish, a book I eventually completed for him. When his final illness began, we took him to the hospital and prepared to fight for more time. It's natural when you love someone to want to keep that person alive. Soon, however, my father realized that the medical efforts being made did not correspond to his idea of life and that it was time to die.

One of the ways of affirming death today is the living will. Sometime in the fifties, early in my adolescence, my mother wrote such a document. I doubt that she was the first to do so, but the idea was a new one at that time, with no clear legal standing. Now we are beginning to believe that it is not obligatory to sustain human beings in permanent coma if they have clearly expressed a different preference, and a few believe that human beings have the right to be helped to end their lives if they are confronted with painful terminal illness. The creation of hospices frees patients and staff from the obligation of deferring death when it is no longer preventable. But we still resist any social affirmation that ending life might also be an obligation: Death has been left to take care of itself.

Death is not regarded as natural but as an intrusion on primordial harmony, instituted as a punishment for sin. The act of ending a life is not yet accepted as an act of caring but only as an act of hatred, a crime, a maximum punishment, or a necessity of warfare. Suicide is regarded in many places as a criminal act. People may be medicated to destroy the desire for death, and patients who ask to be allowed to die are often treated against their will, since the desire for death is seen as pathological.

Perhaps we will only progress to the affirmation of death if we no longer use death as a punishment and no longer withhold the prolongation of life on a class basis. At present, in American society, death rates are an index of inequality: African Americans can expect to die some eight years sooner than Caucasians. Death rates of black infants show the same inequality: less education, worse nutrition, more toxic environments, less disease prevention, less conviction that a black individual's life is valuable. To learn to value each person's death, we will need to conserve and value life equally.

Whenever humans gain greater power to affect the course of events, they become responsible for new choices. Ethics follow efficacy. Eventually, just as it will be necessary to bring birthrates into balance with death rates around the world, we will need a new affirmation of the positive value of death. Indeed, we will need to learn to choose and cherish death. We cannot continue to believe that death is always an enemy and extended life always good, a right of the individual to demand and an obligation of the community to provide. Soon we will want, instead, to own our deaths.

The living will that my mother prepared was troubling to me, not because it affirmed the necessity of death but because it contained a criterion of life that I rebelled against. She listed the circumstances under which she wanted medical intervention withheld, and together these added up to a definition of what she valued in her life: intellectual functioning and ability to communicate about ideas. She drew sharp distinctions, asserting that she could learn to function effectively with the loss of one sense or of mobility but not if both these conditions occurred. She also asserted that preserving her life would be inappropriate given any intellectual diminution.

At fifteen this seemed wrong to me. Even though I could reject the evidence of a heartbeat or wavy lines drawn by an electroencephalograph as a meaningful criterion of life, I would not accept as criteria the gifts that made one individual extraordinary — intellect or beauty or athletic skill. I was threatened by the fact that my mother did not define the give-and-take of love as central, but rather the working of intellect. Yet it is not surprising that an individual might say, on the loss of a skill or the death of a loved one, "My life is over." Today, I believe my mother's choice was her right. If we assert the right to make choices in life, we surely must uphold the right to express those values in death. Decisions about dying offer the opportunity to explore basic values: human dignity, recognition and response to others, moral autonomy. Dying has always been a measure of dedication and courage.

Today I believe we must work toward a pattern in which human beings deliberately reverse the struggles that were necessary at one stage of human evolution: to reproduce as many young as possible and to stay alive as long as possible. We have been engaged in a tug-of-war that required that every muscle be strained in one direction. Now, when resistance is overcome, we may collapse through our own unbalanced effort. We have spent millennia struggling against death; now we must find a way to reclaim it. Judging by the conflict surrounding responsibility for reproduction, this new effort will not be easy. The ancient words of poets and religious teachers that preceded modern technology will help, but we need more than resignation as a model for choice.

Each time I am closely involved with a death, I find myself re-thinking these issues: the death of a premature firstborn, the death of my parents and my parents-in-law, the death of elderly friends and of friends in midlife. I have three times been closely involved in caring for someone during the process of dying when they have rejected medical intervention. With each encounter, my understanding spirals back over the same issues and I gain a new level of intimacy.

Several years ago, a friend was dying of metastatic melanoma in an Israeli hospital. He had read things I had written about my parents' deaths and knew I was one of the few people in his circle, perhaps the only one, with whom he could discuss not only the struggle to survive but also the decision to let death take its course. Others pressed on him the obliga-tion to hope for miracles and cling tenaciously to every moment and every treatment. Even after he had decided to discontinue medical intervention, that decision had to be worked through with every family member and every staff member.

All of us were learning. It was clear that friends and family and even hospital personnel were ignorant of death except as a threat to be resisted and were strangers to the capacity to choose to die. I could see how uncomfortable the decision made them, how sharply it undercut their very reason for being. Whatever new patterns emerge, they must be developed without squandering the resources of medical compassion. When the medical team ceased trying to control the course of the illness and were confronted with an unknown process, it was striking that they had little ability to predict its course. In the same way, generations of doc-tors had no idea how to manage childbirth without anesthesia. Medical personnel overemphasize the suffering created by lack of treatment and lose the awareness of how burdensome medical treatment can be. Without this burden, my friend survived longer and with greater clarity than the doctors expected.

We know something now about the process of coming to terms with terminal illness, of maturation in dying, but we know little about how individuals might come to terms with death gradually, throughout the course of a life. Dying may be a choice that needs to be made in health, for pain and medication and impaired awareness throw us back on instinctual responses that are no longer appropriate. We will no doubt continue to use technology to protect and lengthen life, but perhaps someday we will develop the convention of writing and revising living wills at multiple stages in the life cycle and accept these testaments as ways of exploring and constructing meaning, of savoring the treasure of life. It will take time to develop new attitudes toward death, to recognize that we will only learn to hold this living earth in trust when we acknowledge our own dying. No one can know the form this new outlook will take, the debates about legislation and medical ethics and funding that lie ahead.

It is hard to imagine how those who live by the rejection of mortality and fallibility can care for and protect our natural landscapes. Surely they may be tempted to turn them into manicured parklands, to remove the signs of decay — memento mori, the reminder of death. Surely the temptation to cut and clear and destroy, the assertion of power, is a rejection of the inevitability of death. For me, it works the other way: I can accept the fact of death as long as the trees remain, as long as natural cycles continue and lives are reabsorbed into the larger life of the planet.

In the life of the forest, nothing is lost. One day, I too want to be a tree.

~ III ~

Culture and Conviction

INTRODUCTION

Belief systems and the customs derived from them are the most difficult parts of unfamiliar cultures to encounter with full respect and are the sources of some of the most intransigent conflicts in the contemporary world. Whatever we believe today, the old exclusivism that asserted that a particular set of beliefs contained absolute truth is only a generation or a hundred yards or a single kinship link distant. We all have had relatives or friends or neighbors who believed that those who did not accept their convictions were damned — or, in the case of ideologies, doomed by history. These are the parts of other cultures that seem not simply odd or exotic or inferior but wrong and dangerous. For fear of infection by alien ideas, even curiosity about the beliefs of others has repeatedly been condemned or suppressed, although this is less and less possible in the twenty-first century.

The essays in part 3 deal with matters of belief and identity, including religion, along with the possibilities of conflict and coexistence. One of the continuing themes of my life has been an interest in religion, an interest that preceded anthropology and even linguistics. I can trace this interest through the titles of research projects in high school as well as through efforts to engage directly with organized religion. Sometimes it manifested itself as an interest in the range of possible beliefs, at other times it became a personal search for truth and commitment, a longing to find some acceptable orthodoxy. As with revolutions, travel has brought me into contact with beliefs of many kinds: Judaism in Israel, Islam in Iran, Roman Catholicism in the Philippines, and more recently and superficially, varieties of Buddhism, mostly in the United States. I grew up attending the Episcopal Church and spent my senior year of high school in Israel, learning Hebrew and learning about the Jewish tradition, which in turn led me to study Arabic, Islam, and Middle Eastern history. There has been an intellectual and academic side to each of my encounters with the religions derived from Abraham, expressed in reading and study.

In each case I have gradually become aware of the diversity and variability of beliefs within a given tradition, held and experienced differently by different individuals at different stages of their lives, whether that diversity is acknowledged by theologians or not. The psychologist Donald Winnicott was right when he wrote of the "good enough mother" in the face of dogmatic and guilt-inducing expectations laid on women;[1] faith now looks to me like a series of approximations, multiple versions of "good enough" truth that at least provide a context for decisions, sustaining both humility and hope.

Anthropologists have played an important role in opening minds to cultural differences and promoting tolerance. For some, cultural *relativity* is a methodological principle, the suspension of criticism of another culture pending an understanding of where a particular custom or belief fits in. Reaching this understanding may take a very long time, while researchers resist condemning, for instance, the practice of killing the weaker of every pair of twins until they understand its relationship in a particular time and place to subsistence resources, migratory patterns, or customs of land tenure, and understand the positive values it is believed to serve. For others, cultural *relativism* has become an orthodoxy of its own, an ism, that forbids any external criticism or attempt to change the folkways of another people. This is an orthodoxy that is breaking down today, partly in response to new waves of indignation at such customs as genital mutilation. Most anthropologists, however, have always felt that certain customary behaviors, like pogroms or slavery, could

indeed be repudiated, but only after the clear-eyed effort
to understand them in context. Today, as all cultural
groups are exposed to external influences and must,
willy-nilly, interact with the rest of the world, dogmatic
relativism is becoming irrelevant as a defense of the
integrity of cultures against outside pressure.

Neither relativism nor relativity denies the fact that
every community necessarily maintains some norms
internally. Relativity, however, can be a working tool for
life in the twenty-first century, for it continues to promote a degree of tentativeness in one's own beliefs, and
curiosity and respect for those of others.[2]

What anthropologists have not emphasized sufficiently in their teaching and in their communication with
the public is that the notion that members of a community share a single homogeneous, stable, and integrated
culture is something of a myth, since everywhere human
beings sometimes find themselves at cross-purposes and
caught in misunderstandings. Each of the pieces in part 3
deals, in one way or another, with the ways human beings
cope with apparent inconsistency and suggests that the
internal contradictions and ambiguities in a system may
be creative or offer resilience, while a demand for total
consistency may be destructive. Even ambivalence and
doubt may be resources.

Some convictions often held as absolutes are not recognizable as religious, but they have a similar passionate
intensity — political and economic ideologies, for
instance, or nationalisms, beliefs for which people are
ready both to die and to kill. Somehow we need to set
aside the more lethal forms of conviction while conserving
the fealty on which they are built. We need commitment
combined with the capacity to adapt. Local loyalty
remains one of the few ways of conserving distinctive traditions, loyalties to particular styles of art and story, key
elements of personal identity. Many environmentalists
believe that conservation must be built upon a "sense of
place," and that respect for the systemic characteristics of

the biosphere is necessarily grounded in loyalty to a specific biome and landscape. Patriotism is built on the ties to place as well as on the essential ties that sustain family and community, yet these can be amplified into suicidal rivalries. It is not possible to construct a pluralistic global community if there is only a single right answer to every question, so we need to accept both multiple answers and continuing mysteries, the richness of tradition and the riches of continuing improvisation.

Today it is common to reject religion and affirm "spirituality," without any very clear definition of what that term might mean. My own belief is that a commitment to lifelong learning is, for many people, a spiritual stance, requiring both humility and openness.

"THIS FIGURE OF TINSEL"

Themes of Hypocrisy and Pessimism
in Iranian Culture

I lived in Iran with my husband and daughter from early in 1972 until the Iranian revolution, with a one-year break. I went there hoping to do research on the nature of trust, since many social scientists, Iranian and foreign, had remarked on its dearth in Iran, which seems to run deeper than specific political arrangements, for it has recurred under the new regime. One reason for the emphasis on distrust in social science writings on Iran is that this is a society where much of life is lived behind high walls and people are suspicious of someone hanging around and asking questions, so I quickly became convinced that I needed some kind of participation more legitimate than that of observer, and while we were there I taught and became involved in planning and development for graduate education. The other method I found for getting beyond the sense of distance I felt, even while I was living in the middle of the country, was to gather a small group of Iranian social scientists who became our close friends and met regularly to discuss themes in Iranian national culture and valued personal traits and relationships.[1] I also worked to identify and describe the kinds of misunderstandings that developed between Iranians and Western expatriates working in Iran, and between husbands and wives in mixed marriages.

It turned out that I never wrote on trust specifically, but it remained an organizing question for me in exploring Iranian culture. This piece was commissioned shortly after my return from Iran in 1979 for a collection of essays dealing with "hypocrisy, illusion, and evasion" from many points of view. Even the apparently straight-

forward distinction between truth and falsehood is culturally constructed, and very different kinds of honesty
can elicit trust.

— MCB, 2004

Come, Sufi, let us cast off the pious cloak of hypocrisy,
And strike out and cancel this figure of tinsel.

— HAFEZ

Traditionally, the "whited sepulcher" (Matt. 23:27) was the paradigm of
hypocrisy in Western culture: the concealed grave that looks clean and pure
but actually contains corruption, so that it can pollute those who inadvertently come into contact with it. What is concealed by the hypocrite is traditionally uglier, dirtier, and more selfish than what he shows to the world,
and in the Western tradition, the ugliness within is innate to the unregen-
erate personality. In general, then, hypocrisy was preferred to the expression of what it concealed and was condemned only because what society
really demanded was an unrelenting effort by the public and acceptable self
to colonize the secret and reprehensible self. The inside was to harmonize
with the outside, not vice versa, and the civilizing of children involved an
imposition of virtue, starting with externals and working inward.

More recently there has been in this country an increasing assertion of
the fundamental innocence and wholesomeness of the inner self and its
right to expression. Evil lies in the concealment itself, not in what is concealed. If the grave is opened and exposed to the air, the argument runs,
corruption will be dissipated and what was concealed will be seen to be
simple and natural. Harmony is to be achieved by letting the outside
directly express the inside. Thus frankness and outspokenness are
regarded by Americans as good, and honesty is preferred to kindness, tact,
or prudence in the scale of virtues. This shift means, among other things,
that people are less and less encouraged to conform outwardly — which
provides the necessary predictability that makes social life possible — and
that child rearing is a process of providing the tools of self expression.

Thus we have radically changed our view of hypocrisy within this
century, as we have changed our view of the human individual and the
topography of knowledge, learning, and expression, and the possible
dissonances between them.[2] The concept of hypocrisy depends on theories of personality and motivation implicit in a culture, which vary from

place to place and time to time. The intent of this paper is to present a tangle of issues related to hypocrisy and dissimulation as these are seen in Iranian culture, which provides an interesting counterpoint to the Western view, and to highlight some of the moral issues involved and, more topically, the way in which a given theory of the relationship between inner feeling and perceptible expression contributes to the stability or instability of a society.

Iranians care deeply about sincerity. The ideal is someone in whom the exterior expresses the interior, who is not *dowru,* 'two-faced, hypocritical.' At the same time, Iranians believe that much that is good and precious is concealed, and that the mask of conformity is not only used to conceal corruption but also to protect a secret virtue from the corrupting pressures of society. Little is what it seems: gold is likely to turn out to be gilt, and yet precious metal may also be protected under a concealing layer of base. This leads to a view that is more situational and relativistic than the Western one, for dissimulation, while never the ideal, is genuinely ambiguous in its moral value. The negative view is the commonest, for Iranians tend to look at others from the point of view referred to in Persian as *badbini,* literally 'seeing evil, suspicion, pessimism,' but often translated as cynicism, and this increases as the social context widens. Strangers and people with wealth or power are often assumed to be corrupt or hypocritical in their public virtue and this goes with being shrewd, calculating, and opportunistic. Obsequious flattery, ostentatious virtue, and insincerity are the source of undeserved and unearned wealth and influence. Iranians will condemn whole categories of fellow Iranians on all of these counts, so that they combine to form a standardized critique or stereotype.[3] In reference to themselves and to their intimates, however, Iranians imply the belief that virtue and purity may be concealed, awaiting expression, or may be served by dissimulation. This model is in sharp contrast with both the old and the new models in the Western tradition.

Iranian culture explicitly accepts certain types of deception and dissimulation. To begin with, the values of kindness, courtesy, and hospitality stand higher in many contexts than the values of frankness and honesty. Why tell the truth when feelings will be hurt? Why, indeed, linger on painful truths? Even deaths in the family may be concealed when circumstances are not conducive to informing the bereaved tactfully and supportively. It is important to note that this is not a case where honesty is not valued but where, given a certain type of dilemma in which honesty will cause pain, a kind deception is preferred — which would not be regarded as a lie, for real lies are very much condemned.

Further, Shiite Islam stands alone, among major religious traditions that emphasize the truth or falsehood of beliefs (most notably Christianity and Islam), in allowing the believer to conceal his belief for his own self-protection. This tradition of *taqiya* (or *ketman*) developed, of course, in an Islamic context, where it was a question of concealing from fellow Muslims, when the majority was Sunni, that one was a Shiite, not of denying Islam. Interview questions about *taqiya* elicited examples that cut close to issues of general morality, however. The principle of *taqiya,* for instance, might be used to excuse a good man who, upon seeing his colleague accept a bribe, did not comment or denounce him and apparently accepted the standards of the majority. The acceptance of *taqiya* suggests that a pointless martyrdom is not incumbent upon an honest man, although martyrdom in an effective defense of the truth would be.

In all of these cases, dissimulation is a response to external forces, which may be negatively conceived, and goodness lies within — an inversion of the Western situation where hypocrisy conceals something ugly. Indeed, in Iranian folk psychology, although evil may run in families, people are not in general inclined naturally to evil or innately depraved. The main source of evil is in social life; it comes from without, not from within. Children are, on the whole, innocent, and adults interpret their behavior on this basis whenever possible. Thus, when a child knocks over and breaks something or misbehaves in a way that an American would regard as a clear attempt "to get attention," Iranian adults excuse it as accidental. Little boys may accompany their mothers to the baths; or children may listen with avid interest to the conversations of adults who believe that children have neither prurient interest nor understanding. In the words of a popular song, "children have no dissimulation," and this is good, because the single self they express is good.

There are a multitude of contexts in Iranian culture in which what is concealed and covered is purer and finer than what can be seen from outside. Religious texts, for instance, have an exoteric meaning *(zaher)* and an esoteric meaning *(baten),* and the esoteric meaning, which requires seeing through the exterior, is the higher one. (It is interesting to contrast the ways in which a mystic and a psychologically oriented literary critic study a text, each seeking a secret and hidden meaning on the basis of different assumptions about what kind of thing is naturally secret and hidden.)

Again, the goodness and innocence of women are preserved by concealing them. Women, while not intrinsically evil, are corruptible, and therefore must be protected. Seclusion and the veil are not regarded as concealing something ugly and offensive but as concealing something precious that is to be kept unsullied, even though both also secondarily protect men from temptations and distractions. This, incidentally, is a misunderstanding that lies behind many discussions of the veil between Muslims and non-Muslims, who make the assumption that to conceal something is a mark of disesteem. Houses, similarly, traditionally turned drab faces outward, with high concealing walls, while within, the welcome visitor found the green garden and warm hospitality.

For all kinds of reasons, then, the externally visible may differ from what lies within, but passive concealment is only one kind of difference; often a more elaborate mask is necessary. The opinions of others must be considered and substantial effort put into keeping up appearances. Thus a front must be created for acquaintances who pass within the garden wall and yet are not trusted members of an inner circle, and the creation of such a front may require engrossing effort. Within the drab walls there are elaborate reception rooms, which differ from the informal living quarters of the family farther in, and whose maintenance requires coordinated and sustained effort and expense to protect the family's corporate *ab-e ru*, its 'public respectability.' Affluence has tended to increase the elaboration of this semipublic front, and the need to maintain it is seen as a principal source of greed, profiteering, and corruption.

At this point the discussion becomes as complex as an onion. At the center of the personality there is, ideally, a core of goodness, or at least of potential goodness, and this is hidden to conceal it from corrupting social influences, the most important of which perhaps is envy. But social life is a necessity, as are interactions with individuals outside the inner circle, and in fact one of the by-products of modernization is a pressure to interact with more and more people, most of them strangers. This runs very much against traditional preferences and brings out the worst in all parties.

Relationships with nonintimates are governed by conventions of courtesy. The stylized patterns of thanking and deprecating, greeting and offering, and the elegant phrases that accompany them have an aesthetic value that gives to their performance a certain pleasure. Ritual courtesy *(taarof)* affirms basic values and represents a visible claim to virtues such as generosity and humility, and yet there is a certain ambivalence that surrounds it. For one thing, the courtesies are used too publicly and in relation to too many people for the underlying feelings to be always there, and yet they must be used, for social pressures dictate that the courtesies be preserved for the sake of *ab-e ru*. Furthermore, ostentatious humility suggests its opposite, and ostentatious generosity is often palpably aggressive, as the flagging guest is given yet another plateful of sweets. Iranians today often use the word *taarof* almost as a synonym for hypocrisy and enact their ritual courtesies with the disclaimer, "This is not a *taarof*" (I really mean it). An excessive external show may be hypocritical *tazahor*, an acting out of what is absent within.

In spite of this ambivalence, there are ways of achieving a sense of harmony between inner and outer, and these can be illustrated by looking at the circumstances under which the rituals of *taarof* are either experienced as sincere or laid aside.

Some examples may be helpful. Suppose that I am walking down my own street near sundown; I meet a neighbor whom I do not know well standing at her doorway, and we greet each other. Routinely, I will be invited in, and if I do enter, I will be offered food in addition to the obligatory cup of tea and perhaps urged to stay for a meal. Since I know that to accept would be an imposition, I probably will not enter, and if I do, I will refuse the continued urgings to accept more with profuse thanks, and go on my way. Again, if I admire something in a friend's house, he or she may offer it to me, but I will refuse to accept it, although the ritual of offer and refusal with thanks may last many minutes. Similar graceful byplay will surround a quarrel between diners about the paying of a check in a restaurant and even the sequence with which people pass through a doorway. A conversation with the driver while riding in an uncrowded taxicab may cause his sense of being a host to overbalance his sense of performing a commercial service, leading to his saying at fare time, "Be my guest" *(befarmaid)*. The passenger will of course insist on paying, adding a little extra in appreciation of the gift of hospitality, and go on his way cheered.

Iranians deny there is any necessary behavior in such situations. Apparently, this openness is the criterion of sincerity. They concede that usually one should not accept certain invitations or offers, but they insist that one may do so. The actual outcome is not believed to be fully determined by canons of politeness, although observation suggests that in fact it is, in all of these cases. However, it is possible to manipulate the *taarof* situation to eliminate that freedom, and then the *taarof* will be hypocritical and unsatisfying.

Thus the manner of offering may be such that the ordinary pleasure of offering and refusing with thanks is lost. For instance, *taarof-e khoshk,* 'dry *taarof,*' is sterile and unrefreshing, somewhat like the way an Englishman says to his guests, "Do come again," as they leave, according to one Iranian. The invitation or offer is made in a way that makes it clear it is no more than a social formality; there is no possibility of believing it is meant sincerely. Again, the '*taarof* of Shah Abdolazim' is one that cannot be accepted or that would commit the guest in some undesirable way. The person who issues the invitation is looking to his own advantage, perhaps by inviting you in a lavish and exaggerated way when he knows you are committed elsewhere. The term ostensibly refers to a certain shah, but an alternative explanation sometimes given is that in the town of Shah Abdolazim, famous for yoghurt, all the yoghurt sellers urge you to have a taste, but if you do, having thus broken the skin of the yoghurt, you are committed to buy.

The sincerity of *taarof,* then, depends on preserving a certain element of unpredictability. It involves a real exchange, not the exchange expressed by words, but rather an exchange involving a degree of risk and trust. When this is absent, the *taarof* is indeed hypocritical. The paradigm situation is one in which A has offered more than he can conveniently give and B must show restraint in accepting it. In effect, A has given B the opportunity to refrain from injuring him. B will usually give more in return than the negative offering of restraint — for instance, he will give thanks for the gift he has not accepted and was not expected to accept. A sincere *taarof* conveys a measure of trust because it involves a certain risk or the acceptance of vulnerability in relation to the other, who must then show self-restraint.

This paradoxical quality, in which the actual offer is not meant to be accepted but in which the offering conveys a real message about the quality of the relationship, is directly parallel to a type of ritual that has been described for many species by animal ethologists. In these rituals, intraspecific conflict is halted by a display of total vulnerability on the part of the weaker that inhibits aggression on the part of the stronger. Displayed vulnerability is based on the certainty that it will not be exploited: a wolf may bare his throat to a stronger wolf, confirming his dominance but preventing his attack. Much of Iranian social ritual has exactly this paradoxical quality, where one individual ritually displays weakness and humility that obligates the other, or makes an offer that the other acknowledges but cannot accept, and so it is no wonder that this ritual is surrounded by ambivalence. A host may say to a guest *nowkaret am,* 'I am your servant,' but the exact phrase occurs as the equivalent of "crying uncle" in street fighting and in formal wrestling. As in many paradoxes, the messages are not contradictory because they occur at different logical levels. The apparent message "You are welcome to impose on me, injure me, cheat me of my livelihood" is not true, but it carries the metamessage "Because I trust you not to do so, I can say . . ." This is *taarof* at its best, and it is sad when Westerners, not accustomed to thinking of such complex relationships between inner and outer and between layers of meaning, dismiss it as hypocrisy; it is sadder yet when westernized Iranians follow them; for whenever inner and outer differ or are in tension, a resolution of that tension provides an additional dimension of meaning.

There are other ways of resolving the tension between the literal meaning of the external form and the underlying intention. For instance, there is a certain type of person who is often referred to as *darvish,* possessing some of the qualities associated with the traditional Sufi or dervish. This person accepts simply whatever he is given and offers whatever he has without fanfare; his behavior is modest and introverted, and he avoids situations calling for elaborate courtesy or acknowledgment of status. If someone is known to be *darvish,* he is respected rather than regarded as ill-mannered. His external behavior expresses directly his inner attitude. Where the *darvish* person is like this all the time, most people are like this only in their closest relationships, for intimacy is marked by lack of ceremonial, a rather brusque taking for granted of anything the other might offer, combined with restraint in taking it. An encounter in which ceremonial hospitality is waived (I stop at a friend's house to talk briefly and succeed in persuading him that I've just had tea and don't want any) is a step toward intimacy. Thus the existence of a complex ceremonial system creates the possibility of communicating by not observing the ritual. Omitting ritual, which is not itself necessarily insincere, supplies the metamessage of sincerity.

Not surprisingly, just as there are those who achieve sincerity by saying what they mean, there are those who achieve it by meaning what they say — that is, by the literal acting out of the rhetoric of courtesy. The *luti* is apparently the opposite of the *darvish,* flamboyant and extroverted, the traditional chivalrous tough who defends the weak in his territory. He means every word of his *taarof.* He really will sell the coat off his back to entertain an unexpected guest and will insist until the guest gives in. Indeed, such a person may lock the door and pocket the key until his guest agrees to stay. He also takes the *taarof* of others literally, and may show up with his friends at the rich merchant's house and empty his larder and his pocketbook.

Oddly enough, informants readily recognize the similarity between the *luti* and the *darvish* and are quick to associate them in terms of the trait *safa-ye baten,* literally 'internal purity,' but more freely, integrity or sincerity. Both types are respected, but at the same time they are a little pitied, because neither is expected to make a great success of life. They have dealt with the tension of the difference between inner and outer in a way that is less flexible and less nuanced than the usual rich and ambivalent way in which the offer of a meal which is not eaten is sweet and conveys a benison.

The *luti* and the *darvish* as ideal ways of transcending ambiguity recur in Iranian imagery. Individuals seem to believe that, deep within their personalities, there resides the simplicity and purity of the *darvish,* and they express this through references to a diffuse spirituality, by quoting poetry, and by nostalgic statements about the simple life. They also seem to believe that, like the *luti,* they are in some relationships and in some situations completely unstinting and uncalculating, expressing directly what they feel. Thus there is a range of situations in which strong emotion is expected to break through social dissimulation. However, just as formal courtesy is structured to allow for sincerity, so also strong emotion can be ritualized.

Grief for the dead, for instance, is an emotion that is deemed to require full expression, and the suppression of grief is deplored. The bereaved are supposed to be completely carried away, throwing ashes and dirt on their heads, and wailing. The common remark that Westerners do not really feel things as deeply as do Iranians is often supported by some story of a foreigner's stoic behavior when there was a death in his family. Someone who suppresses his grief is not respected — he is less of a person for it. On the other hand, the expression of grief at funerals is inevitably ritualized: at key words and key moments there are fluctuations in the audible weeping, and there is a convention that one should weep a little even if one had not been close to the deceased.

The tension between the kind of sincerity expressed in giving way to strong emotion, where powerful inner feelings simply burst out of the individual, and the socially required simulation of such emotions is complicated by the fact that Iranians have learned how to weep under appropriate ritual arousal. However, one should not explore the sincerity or hypocrisy of ritualized weeping without bearing in mind the partial truth that acting *as if* one has a certain feeling may bring that feeling into being and, on the other hand, the actor's technique of recalling emotion from another context in order to produce a convincing performance. Again, we see a two-way traffic between visible expression and what underlies it.

One of the principal religious activities of Shiite Islam, the form commonest in Iran, is mourning for the death of the Imams, Muhammad's descendants through his daughter Fatimah, who, it is believed, inherited the leadership of the community and were persecuted by the majority Sunnis. Weeping for the death of the Imams gives religious merit and will cause the one for whom you weep to intercede in your favor at the last judgment. Meetings and dramatizations are held at which, interspersed with prayers and singing, the stories of the deaths are retold, and all present weep: they sob or moan and tears flow freely, especially at key evocative points and phrases in the narrative. Sessions of ritual mourning (*rowzeh*) may last several hours, with weeping at varying intensities combined with head and chest beating.

At such meetings, my companions cheerfully expect to weep and half expect me to weep as well, for they feel the stories of the deaths of the Imams, especially the martyrdom of Husayn, are so tragic, that weeping would be a natural (i.e., not necessarily ritual) response. Yet there is a mood of communal effort for greater weeping, with the leader, often a member of the clergy, urging them on. Informants compare the skill of different leaders in eliciting response and sometimes speak of the *rowzeh* as a sort of mental hygiene, like "having a good cry": one described his grandmother, when she felt depressed, as saying, "How I wish I could go to a good *rowzeh* and cry." Tissues may be passed before the ceremony, and at a private women's *rowzeh* in a wealthy house, ornate tissue holders spaced around the room are part of the furnishings; afterward, a maid comes around with a ewer of rosewater. Between sessions, cheerful, unsubdued gossip prevails, but when the session begins anew, weeping takes only five or ten seconds to get going, although it does increase gradually. There are even some happy rituals that involve brief references to sad events,[4] where participants may stop and weep immediately and briefly for a few seconds and then return to the cheerful mood of the occasion.

How sincere is all this strong emotion? Ritual weeping in Iran is apparently "method" weeping: it depends on a skill in emotional arousal, not just on the ability to produce tears, and this in turn depends on arriving at a certain maturity and complexity of emotion, not expected of children. Yet the distinction between real, uncontrollable weeping and ritual weeping is usually clear: for one thing, children are not unduly worried by their mothers' sobs, and indeed play games of *rowzeh,* although they do not themselves weep during the ceremonies. Also, occasionally I have seen a woman who has been recently bereaved carried away by her own grief during a ritual mourning ceremony, and this is disruptive beyond a certain point, although informants agree that all of life's griefs lie behind their ritual weeping.

The connection between ritualized expressions of emotion and the interest in personal emotion overcoming the dividedness of calculation and dissimulation provides a potent political weapon. In effect, the nostalgia for sincerity and the sense that most of life is lived in a state of compromise with a corrupting society can be transformed into a readiness to put lives on the line for idealistic reasons, and this readiness can be organized into public expression. During 1978 and, to a lesser degree, in other periods of protest, the build-up of popular opposition to the regime was almost entirely structured around occasions of public mourning, starting with the funerals of those actually killed in protests — which were then commemorated, as is customary, on the seventh day, the fortieth day, and the anniversary — and later, with the commemorations of the Shiite martyrdoms, especially the martyrdom of Imam Husayn in the month of Muharram. This sequence of mourning ceremonies sets a rhythm, accelerating toward consummation, for each time crowds march through the streets there is the likelihood of new incidents and new deaths. The private grief of people actually bereaved is picked up and made a public matter, and the same clergy who specialize in evoking ritual tears can act as cheerleaders to fan the expression of strong feeling, bringing it into being. Private and therefore sincere emotion gradually extends its authority to the crowd, becoming public property, and the external sharing of shouts and tears becomes internal rage and grief. When people are swept up in popular protest, they feel a certain joy in the strength of their outrage, as if for the first time in their lives they are not divided.

It seems probable that the thematic understanding of the relationship between inner and outer in Iranian culture has interacted throughout history with autocratic forms of government that forced the concealment of individual convictions and the elaboration of external forms; yet the interest in hidden purity, as expressed in these many different areas, seems too basic to be an artifact of a form of government or a tradition of police surveillance. The cultivated consciousness of dissonance between inner and outer, in which influences from society are the source of evil and corruption, seems to transcend political externals, and yet it cannot but influence political developments.

The most obvious effect of the sense of dissonance between inner and outer and the nostalgia for bringing them together is clearly a certain volatility. Both the conformity enforced by political suppression and the conformity that makes a broad social life possible are attended by discomfort, a romantic yearning for the breakthrough of costly and euphoric nonconformity. Iranian autocracy does not conform to the classic European authoritarian model that assumes authoritarian control is necessary to prevent the expression of innate viciousness. Instead, it is based on a pessimistic view of the possibility of maintaining innate innocence in broader society, for as soon as large and complex social units are concerned, Iranian *badbini* reasserts itself.

Thus when a given position becomes fashionable or advantageous, the sincerity of those who hold it becomes suspect: anyone who is successful is probably not sincere but opportunistic, calculating, and hypocritical. Trust is fragile, and the success of any political movement creates the context for cynicism. Where a leader manages to secure trust in his integrity, this trust is so demanding that he may have no room to maneuver at all. The same brittleness can be observed in friendship where high expectations combined with pessimism leave people always vulnerable to disillusionment and betrayal. Alternatively, of course, the leader may be martyred before he meets the nemesis of popular cynicism, for martyrdom is the natural outcome when true virtue is confronted by society, and Shiites emphasize the martyrdom of every single one of the Imams, beginning with Muhammad himself (those who apparently died natural deaths were actually poisoned). So strong is this logic that, whenever a prominent individual who is still trusted and admired dies, he is assumed to have been murdered, an assumption that resonates with other kinds of paranoia.

Thus Iranian concepts of the nature of integrity and the dangers of corruption and hypocrisy produce a tendency toward autocratic government by undermining popular trust and consensus. Any society that attributes evil to social life and expects to find goodness hidden deep within the individual has a proclivity for anarchy. Public virtue and conformity that make social life possible may indeed be based on diverse and inconsistent motivations, and yet any ongoing social order must learn to support virtue as publicly defined, whether it is hypocritical or not. In Iran, the play of inner and outer winds through the enigmas of social life, with generous courtesy and ardent sincerity balancing prudential concealment and dissimulation. At the same time, the elaboration of the difference between inner and outer provides a fundamental and ongoing source of instability, as society is perpetually liable to be turned not upside down but inside out. No public virtues can be stabilized if public approbation immediately evokes the suspicion that these are insincere; yet no complex society can be constructed only on that private virtue that is cultivated in the heart and with one's closest intimates; and no society can be effectively led if the only proof of a leader's sincerity is that he receive no social benefit from his leadership.

LEARNING TO LEARN AND
KNOWING WHAT YOU KNOW

South Africa 1991

Major social change often involves fundamental shifts in identity, including the acceptance of the role of learner struggling to function in a changed world, something which many people feel they left behind in school. I visited South Africa for a conference on leadership shortly after the apartheid laws had been repealed and Nelson Mandela had been released from prison, but democratic elections were still to come. The theme of the conference was what we were beginning to call "the learning society," and it focused on changes in education. It was clear that equality required a reconstructed economic system, and this in turn would require an educated workforce, so massive reeducation of some kind would be needed. Apartheid had depended on separate schools with different goals for different racial groups: "Bantu education" had been designed to provide basic literacy combined with docility, so the great mass of the population (and the teachers trained to teach them) was deliberately maleducated. There were issues both about educating the rising generation and about reeducating adults, adults who had been minimally educated to keep them in inferior positions as well as adults who associated their status as teachers under apartheid with a claim to greater wisdom and higher skills.

The focus of the conference was on repairing the educational deficits of blacks, but my focus in this talk was on the learning disabilities of the whites, primarily white men, that went with having been in positions of power. I was struck by the tiny number of women in the audience, of whatever race, and the small number of brown or black faces. Visiting schools and dispensaries, however, I became vividly aware of the critical role played by strong, determined women, trying to protect their children and make sure they had some education. I have edited the transcript for clarity without changing my approach, designed for that early stage of transition when so much new learning was obviously going to be necessary for every racial group. Most names in the text refer to other speakers.

—MCB, 2004

&

I thought I would open today with a story from my own life. My daughter, Vanni, was in her last year at a very fine secondary school, which in the United States is the time when young people apply competitively to multiple colleges and universities. One of her teachers had told me that they would soon start preparing the students to write the personal essays they would need for their applications, introducing themselves and projecting their talents and interests for admissions officers. Vanni came to me in distress, and said, "I don't know how to write an essay in the first person singular."

She had been disciplined throughout her years of education up to that time not to do what is called "personalizing." Not to give opinions. Not to use school essays as vehicles for self-expression. At that point, I devised a solution that was helpful to her, bypassing the context of a school essay completely and instead replicating a context where her confidence was strongest. Her primary interest is in acting, so I said, "All right, develop a dramatic monologue, expressing who you are. Stand up, speak it, act it out." I tape-recorded it and said, "Now take it and write it down." Instead of leaving her feeling ignorant and helpless, it was important to build on her strengths.

I have told you that story to emphasize that the process of education in modern society is terribly costly to the individual. Peter Schwartz has expressed one side of that, the way in which the emphasis on competition makes some students feel they are inferior. Beyond that, even to enter the education process, you have to concur with the system's premise that you are ignorant and that your parents are ignorant. Those are very expensive agreements to have to make. Of course, what you get in exchange is the implication that at the end of some number of years of submission and self-classification as ignorant, you will be allowed to become one of the pillars of adult society.

I can't imagine why anyone would put themselves through that process. Look, there's a sign outside the door to this auditorium that says, "Declare All Firearms," like we used to have on the outside of pubs in the American west — "Leave your gun at the door." But leave your *self* at the door? Leave your self-esteem at the door? Leave your skills and the confidence accrued from learning to walk, from learning to speak? And do that without the genuine confidence that at the end you will have a share, that being adult in your society is a desirable thing? I can't think why anyone would put up with that, yet this is the situation everyone growing up under segregation or discrimination is in: to arrive at any kind of participation you have to move through contexts that enforce a sense of inferiority. This is also why privileged adults, especially adults who have already achieved a status they value and a sense of competence, hesitate to return to school. I think that if we are going to talk about the learning society, it is very important to talk about the issues of adult learning as these affect all South Africans, black and white. Everyone here will have to leave a lot at the door, not only because of a redistribution of power but because of the inherent cost of learning as it has historically been presented. The willingness to accept this cost affects the capacity to go through a transition, a major change. What in fact are you willing to learn?

An example: I would be very curious as to how many of the white people in this room can carry on a reasonable conversation in an indigenous African language. Hands? Well, I saw two. Now that is not a learning society, but it is easy to understand why it happens. When my husband and I went to the Philippines, he and his group were all professors of management, brought there by the Ford Foundation. They started trying to learn a little Pilipino, the language of the Philippines — phrases and greetings. One day one of them walked into a room of six young Filipina secretaries, and said, "no breasts, no breasts" (he meant to say that he had "no keys" for the car), and the room was reduced to laughter. The story was told for months thereafter, and that was the end of those gentlemen trying to learn to speak the language. They were after all in a situation where their status prohibited them from making fools of themselves. Were you all to undertake to learn one of the — I like to say *other* — African languages, you would make fools of yourselves from time to time. You would have to work with the reversal of status involved in being ignorant and becoming a learner.

Someone referred earlier to the notion that schools are a way of keeping children off the streets, keeping them busy and out of mischief. They are that, but they are instruments of social control in a much more profound sense. You see, you learn skills in school and you learn some subject matter in school, but beyond that you learn how the world is organized. You learn the underlying assumptions of the society: What is authority? What is truth? What kind of creativity am I allowed? Who decides what my ideas are worth? These are the basic communications of school.

You also learn *how* to learn or, all too often, how to *not* learn. To the extent that we have developed societies that do not support adult learning, we have to be skeptical of the deutero-learning (learning to learn, second-order learning) that takes place in school. We need to ask what people learn in school that retards their later learning, often for the most intelligent. There was an article in the *Harvard Business Review* by Chris Argyris in which he talked about the fact that it is the smart, successful people who can't learn.[1] Once they have gotten away from school and gotten themselves established, it's the smart and successful people that are most often unwilling to acknowledge their ignorance, make mistakes, and put themselves in a one-down position.

This morning we were at cross-purposes about the question of "recycling teachers" who had come up through the Bantu education system, asking about their ability and willingness to be retrained. On the one hand, they surely know that Bantu education has enforced inferiority, but as individuals it has given them status and a livelihood and sense of service. Everybody blames teachers, they are in the middle. In all debates on education, we tend to put them down. We blame them in the United States also. When we ask here whether it will be possible to "recycle" the teachers, we're making it clear that we think they are performing in an inferior way and may not be educable. We are speaking of asking them to be learners, yet most of us have come out of school rather pleased not to be put in that one-down position anymore. We can only demand this level of relearning if we make the assumption that adult human beings — of whatever color — are in some significant sense constantly recycling themselves, learning new things and finding a way to balance the pains and joys of learning, instead of the assumption that there is something *wrong* with them. We are also failing to address the fact that the system has put them in a contradictory position that probably over time consistently retards new learning.

I want to compare this kind of "recycling" with another kind of adult learning. I was very interested in something Arie de Geus said yesterday, about the indicators that precede economic takeoff. One of these was an average life expectancy of sixty-eight years. Now that number, of course, sums up a great many other facts of medical care, nutrition, education, public health, all of these things. But right about at a life expectancy of sixty-eight, something very significant and interesting begins to happen in the human life cycle, which is that many adults have significant numbers of healthy, mature years after their youngest child has grown up. Now, there are lots of caveats to build in here, and it's easier to do the calculations for females than for males, because societies have very different rules about age differences between husbands and wives. But if you think of a woman reaching the age of sixty-eight, what you are saying is that her youngest child has grown up and is an adult, so a woman who has been primarily a mother now has the experience as an adult of learning new roles, including the grandparent role, and the in-law role, and the wise elder role. In most places, too, you will find that even a man who has fathered a late child with a younger wife also learns to interact very differently with that child than he did with the children of his youth.

I believe the abolition of apartheid creates a discontinuity for everyone in South Africa. The circumstances within which you live are suddenly changed — what do you do? How do you adapt? You adapt in the fundamental human way, by learning. This is something that I have been studying in relation to women in the United States, in order to understand how people in general deal with discontinuities in their lives. Women are often exposed to quite abrupt discontinuities. They have sharp physical developmental discontinuities, they have to deal with the discontinuities of childbearing and child development, and women's activities are subject to disruption because of the choices made by men. Women have to learn new roles and skills to match the changes made by every member of their households. In many societies, the tasks done by men are substantially more constant through the adult years than those done by women, and many of the discontinuities that occur in men's lives are of their own choosing.

I will give you an example from my own life, from the time that my husband and I went to the Philippines. We adapted in two different ways. I had gotten a Ph.D. in Arabic linguistics, and then my husband decided to go to Manila. How do you survive under those circumstances? What I did was to go back to kindergarten. Going to a new place meant for me learning the language and the culture of the place all at once, like a child, and eventually I got to the point where I could give an informal talk in that language if I had a friendly audience. I can't anymore. But even though I was apparently starting from scratch, I brought with me the knowledge of how to learn a new language and the confidence from having done it before. Now, my husband has taught management in several different countries. He teaches in English, and he's very good at it, and he learns a great deal gradually about the place where he is, about the business climate and how people function. But he doesn't try to learn the system from scratch. Those are two models for new learning.

A more radical model can be studied in Alcoholics Anonymous, which no doubt exists in South Africa as it does around the world. Alcoholics Anonymous teaches that it cannot help you until you hit bottom. This is something I have been thinking about all morning: Does South Africa have to hit bottom? How much distress, how much facing of unpleasant facts is necessary to make the necessary new learning possible? I don't myself feel that hitting bottom is necessary. A great many people are having to face the fact that the way they have been living is wrong, but it seems important to retain much of their accrued skill and confidence for the future.

It's odd, you know. In my study of life histories, I have been struck by the fact that many women in my society are forced by the standard ideas of the shape of a successful life to regard their own lives as unsuccessful, and this undermines their confidence and ability to adapt. Most of you wouldn't hire me if you saw my résumé. It's a mess. I've lived in four countries and had to retool so often I estimate I have had five careers. One of these days I'm going to wake up and discover that I've forgotten more languages than I've learned, and then I'll have to be quiet. Now that is not the kind of résumé that we regard as reflecting a successful life. On the other hand, you might want someone like me if you needed someone who had learned the skills of adapting to a strange situation, a confident and conscious willingness to recycle myself.

The standard idea of a successful life, which is now becoming obsolete, is built on a model that suggests education is something you complete and then you are ready for a job, for real life, building a family and a career. You learn a little bit as you move along, taking in information of familiar kinds, certainly, but you have done the basic learning that equips you for adult life. And so you move up and onward on a continuous curve.

Now, I don't think that this is going to be true for very many people in the world in which people live past sixty-eight. That's why I was so intrigued by that number. We are moving toward a situation where the norm of a successful life involves shifting gears repeatedly, as athletes and military people often do when a first career ends. Where not only will people who become immigrants and refugees, or people who become technologically obsolete, or people whose businesses are destroyed have to retool and learn new skills, but the learning of new skills and sometimes the total shifting of gears from one identity to another will be fundamental to adult development in societies undergoing rapid change. And it will be critical to support that adaptive process without too much waste.

That, you see, is what I think we might mean by a "learning society." Hidden behind the word *recycling* at present is the idea of things or people that are useless in their present form, which you don't quite throw in the trash. A learning society is one in which teachers and everyone else learns new skills but also translates old skills to new contexts. We don't think of this as "recycling," or perhaps the word itself takes on a new and respectful meaning. If we take seriously the notion of learning and teaching as perhaps the most fundamental of human activities, activities that are satisfying for longer than sex, we need to take much more seriously what it is to be a learning society.

So what would happen if every one of you started to learn an additional African language? I know the white folk here had to learn two languages in school, but after all, Afrikaans and English are related, historically similar in so many ways. There's very little intellectual gain from exposure to both of them. But if you were to learn a language belonging to another language family, if you were to learn Japanese, or Iroquois, or Arabic, then you would be stretching your mind. You would probably think some new thoughts. Try it. It might turn out to be good practice.

In the Philippines I was teaching at a Jesuit university. When the Americans went into the Philippines, the Spanish were not very popular, so the Jesuit order decided to remove the Spanish Jesuits who were serving there and send in American Jesuits. In that way, the Philippines became part of the New York province of the Society of Jesus — it's an independent province nowadays. There were quite a few American Jesuits when I was there who had come to the Philippines as young priests and had been there for twenty to thirty years. They were told when they came that they didn't need to learn the language and they hadn't, in spite of their intelligence and dedication. Around the world, it is said, people without shoes learn the language of people with shoes. One of the things I did, with some success, was to persuade the president and vice president, and the dean and the treasurer and one or two others, who were all American Jesuits, that if they could, as their rule provided, devote one hour to meditation every day, they could spend one hour a day learning the language of the people they had to work with. They could do that as something to be proud of, rather than embarrassed by, even when they made mistakes. There is a way to avoid the social bankruptcy of hitting bottom. The key is to make the learning commitment that recognizes that real social change is happening, both practically and symbolically, and that learning is the way to adapt for everyone.

If I went to live in a new country now, because my brain is somewhat atrophied, I would not do so well as I did twenty-five years ago, and I doubt I would become fluent in a new language or languages, which gets harder with the passage of time. But I would work at it, and what I would hope is that, because I've done it before, I've learned how to do it. Learning to learn as an adult, like learning to learn as a child, involves knowing what you know and having your knowledge acknowledged — what a lovely pair of words — having your competence recognized.

It's been said that the most important intellectual achievement of any human being is learning to speak a first language. There's something very powerful and liberating about using language and being understood, and this is something we all do. We all enter school speaking a first language. But when a child goes into a school system where the language of instruction is not the language of the home, some of that early achievement is disallowed, denied recognition. Even if the language of instruction is the same as in the home, the child is at risk. English teachers spend their time teaching correct English and not acknowledging the fact that every child coming from an English-speaking home is able to speak really pretty good English of some sort or other at the entry to school.

Each language is a system with an internal consistency, and one of the things you learn when you learn your first language is how to handle pattern. Learning a second language — which many human beings do —

needs to build on that sense of pattern rather than disrupt it. You also learn to interact with people within the rules of participation in conversation, which will underline other rules of participation, whether politically or in the market, buying and selling, give and take, back and forth. But all too often the emphasis of school is on what you don't know rather than on finding increasingly elegant uses for what you do. This is trouble. You've learned all these complex patterns — then to have those patterns disallowed, to be told in school that you don't even speak one language right! I tell you that this is one of the most profound violations of the mind of another human being.

The critical thing is to think about all of the times in your lives when you have had to do a radical piece of rethinking and relearning. Part of your experience no doubt fits the continuous model of a lifetime: it has education at the beginning and after that you are a grown-up, and you climb up the ladder, you progress, you mature, and you hang on to power. But most of you probably have had some experiences of relearning, zigzagging rather than following a single sequence, yet without necessarily losing ground, and that is the model to reflect on.

Unless you can find ways to relearn and recycle, you are left with the model of hitting bottom and starting over. This is the model where you reach a certain point and you are converted, you are born again and you completely leave your old life behind. There is certainly plenty in the history of South Africa that one might want to leave behind, to purge or erase, but it seems to me very important for South Africa not to become completely drawn into that model. What is important is to use the experience up to now, the skills, the learning, to approach the moment of transition with the memory of what has been learned before, and therefore the knowledge of what new learning felt like. This will be as important for the black majority as it is for the white minority.

As I have studied these patterns with women in the United States, a number of interesting things have turned up. One is that there are very important roles to be played by women in times of transition. I think I am correct in saying that in the traditional cultures of this part of Africa, as in the European cultures of those who have colonized Africa, women are encouraged to accept a subordinate status most of the time. Ironically, this means they are less vulnerable to the discomforts of new learning: I am more willing to make a fool of myself than my husband is. That's very useful. That is a huge strength in life. The downside is that women suffer many problems of self-esteem, and many cultures disadvantage them significantly. But the capacity to lay self-esteem aside or to hold on to it at such an abstract level that it can survive major new learning will serve you well.

I believe that the flexibility needed for new learning is connected to other kinds of flexibility. The traditional definition of women's work included all of those tasks that could be done simultaneously with caring for a child — all fifty of them. And men traditionally do those things that can't be done simultaneously with caring for a child. What this means is that although optimally we would all be able to function in both of these ways, women are socialized to be interruptible and to have their minds on four or five things at one time and men are socialized in the skills requiring focused concentration. The male emphasis on a single focus leads in complex societies to high degrees of specialization, with reduced flexibility. I have been sitting here and listening to discussions of resources, and the thing I keep thinking is that as long as every activity is separated from every other, in the hands of specialists, there will not be enough resources. You have to find a way to enfold them within one another; to have the same institutions do multiple things with the same budget, and the same people thinking about these complex processes.[2]

Peter Schwartz and I met for the second time at a conference that was doing long-range planning on the future of the American army. I expect he remembers that I sat there singing one tune, a tune the military people had great difficulty hearing. From their point of view, the purpose of an army is "warfighting," but I kept pointing out that the army had a great many other functions in American life. One of the most important is education. Just as you can take a second look at the school system and say that one function of this aspect of society is social control, persuading young people to buy into the authority system and allowing them to become adults only on condition that they concur in the basic premises of their society, you can see that your army could be (as the Israeli army is, as hypothetically the South African one might be, were it freed from racial bias) an instrument of education and unification for South Africans serving side by side. In the same way, businesses need to be places of education, schools need to be clinics, and the military and the schools are also businesses. All of these things. Most significant, the division of labor that used to be the greatest economy can lead to rigidity and wasteful duplication.

What we have been hearing for two days, about the need for educational resources, argues for thinking of every organization as potentially a nurturing, teaching organization. Attention to process is absolutely essential to make that possible — and new learning is needed to develop that attention to process. You have to be thinking about several things at the same time, sustaining respect and confidence as well as completing a task. The people who are most able to relearn at a moment of discontinuity in their lives are the people who are in the habit of learning — who remember what it feels like to learn and who value that experience. They are also people who have had multiple interests and curiosities at earlier stages of their lives.

As the transition in South Africa moves forward, if it is solely a transition of power and politics, there are hazards ahead. Instead, you have to have the whole range of emphases: on conserving, on bridging, on nurturing. Women will play a key role, not because these tasks are necessarily female but because in many cultures this is what women are socialized to do, and those energies must be brought into the process.

I take the presence of the people in this room as a hopeful indication. You are not people who will go ahead pursuing a single narrow task without also looking out of the corner of your eye and thinking about how other tasks fit in. All of you have a special kind of "peripheral vision." I suspect that all of you can do what you do superbly well, but just as the smartest people may not be successful learners, so those who do what they do superbly well can be blindsided if they are not watching out for the whole range of what is happening.

There are lots of circumstances in which change is distressing and frightening. On the whole, women have been less likely to seek out change than men, even though they seem to do pretty well, given time, at adapting to it. I have met with rooms full of women who were taken by surprise at midlife when their role, their place in society, changed in some fundamental way — whether simply by their children growing up or by their husbands dying or abandoning them. I'm talking about people starting, very close to scratch, on new careers in their mid-forties, not at all sure they will make it. The extraordinary thing is that, although few of these women would have chosen that degree of change, there is often a surge of energy released by the excitement and satisfaction of new learning. South Africa has the opportunity to become a learning society — not just a society with a good school system but one in which openness to new learning and the energy that it releases are available to every member of this society. Anybody feeling a little middle-aged? My friends, this is your chance!

COMPROMISE AND THE RHETORIC
OF GOOD AND EVIL

This paper was presented in 1984 as part of a panel connecting anthropology to issues of national security. I was struggling to understand the usefulness of generalizations about diverse national populations and used the example of the Iranian revolution, which took so many pundits by surprise. Psychological testing of individuals does not confirm enough uniformity in populations to predict behavior or national policy, and it was the expectation in the study of "national character" that it would, which effectively killed the field. Yet certain themes turn up again and again in national policies and rhetoric — and societies behave very differently under apparently similar circumstances. The Germans were simply unable to imagine the British response to the blitz. No thinking person should expect an Arab population to behave under occupation in the same way as the Japanese.

In this essay I use the phrase "national culture" to emphasize that I am not talking about a statistical summation of individual personalities but about patterns at the societal level. Perhaps the most useful metaphor introduced here is that of *editing*: a work of art or national policy will be more or less related to national culture depending on how much it is subject to review by many individuals and required to be widely intelligible. I am also trying to emphasize that the elaboration of a particular theme in the national culture might have contrary effects, so that for instance Victorian prudery and prurience can be seen as connected by a shared preoccupation, even though they appear to be contradictory, and might be expressed in very different individual traits and behavior.

My own effort to explore the issue was stimulated by the attacks of Derek Freeman on my mother's first book, *Coming of Age in Samoa*, a year before, since Freeman and Mead emphasized opposite aspects of Samoan culture. Groping for clarity, I chanced upon the term *axis*, which has turned out to be a rather troublesome word. I was thinking of the axes on a graph, lines of variation connecting opposite extremes; *axis* also can mean a fulcrum or pivot. American foreign policy rhetoric, in this phrasing, varies along an axis from the pragmatic to the moralistic. But today the term has been revived in political rhetoric in an almost contradictory way, as in "axis of evil," to mean similarity (with an implied but undocumented suggestion of another earlier meaning, of alliance).

Rereading this paper today illuminates the transitions that Iran is going through a generation after the Islamic revolution and suggests the hazards of moralistic political ideologies, including those arising within the United States, that define others as "evil." At another level, this paper can be seen as an effort to understand pluralism and how contradictory views can coexist around common themes in a society.

—MCB, 2004

The attempt to use cultural analysis to improve policy making in the area of international relations has run into repeated frustration, and yet seems intuitively to be promising and valuable. Events occur in the international arena which reflect national decision-making processes and ways of interpreting available data; these become intelligible if they are interpreted in cultural terms. Yet clearly, cultural analysis based on the study of individuals, like historical analysis based on previous foreign policy decisions, is not adequate for prediction, particularly since the stakes in international relations are often too high to make probabilistic forms of prediction useful. We would like our anthropologists to tell us that the people of such and such a nation share a given characteristic and therefore will behave in a given way, expressed in singular and centrally determined policies of immense moment. Unfortunately, culture is not determinative or predictive in any such simple sense. If it were, the world would be a very much duller place.

The problem of prediction may even include the possibility of diametrically opposed styles, a problem anthropologists have become increasingly aware of. My own recent work on the history of cultural anthropology, in the context of a familial memoir,[1] has involved a reconsideration of how anthropologists account for the presence of apparently contradictory possibilities within a culture. Margaret Mead, Ruth Benedict, and Gregory Bateson were among the first anthropologists to attempt to use generalizations about culture to anticipate the policies of nation-states.[2] A few years earlier, they had been among the first to attempt to extend psychological categories appropriate to the description of individuals to whole societies. We will only be able to mobilize an effective use of anthropology in this area if certain problems in the earlier work are confronted, problems more clearly present in that work as it was popularly understood than in its original statements.

In her writing and teaching in the 1920s, Ruth Benedict developed the powerful but flawed concept of a cultural configuration as "personality writ large." This concept is most fully elaborated in *Patterns of Culture* (1934), but was already expressed in "Psychological Types in the Cultures of the Southwest" (1930), which was read by Mead in 1928 before going to Samoa and reflected in *Coming of Age in Samoa* (1928) and *Social Organization of Manua* (1930).[3] This approach, which sought for psychological homogeneity, was, however, rapidly left behind by further theoretical advances. By 1932, Mead and Bateson were already noting that a culture might be organized around contrasting psychological themes rather than around homogeneity, beginning in their consideration of sex roles in two Sepik River cultures, the Iatmul and the Tshambuli (now Chambri).[4] This insight was reflected in wartime work such as Benedict's on the Japanese, in which she expressed the presence of contradictory cultural themes in the evocative title *The Chrysanthemum and the Sword* (1946),[5] and other wartime and postwar efforts to apply anthropological modes of analysis to such complex entities as modern nation-states. The early work has been extensively criticized, most recently by Freeman, who unfortunately replicates the original error by assuming that an accurate account of Samoan culture will describe psychological homogeneity.[6] Freeman differs with Mead, depicting an equally monochrome Samoa, but simply emphasizing his own perception of conflict as pervasive and failing to see that an adequate account of Samoan culture must account both for the harmonious ethos perceived by Mead and for the conflictual ethos emphasized by himself — and for the mechanisms of selection and alternation.[7] A contemporary approach would recognize that cultural systems work with alternatives, many of them discontinuous, often embracing contrasts or complementarities along culturally defined axes.

Thus, theories of psychological homogeneity do not work to account for foreign policy, much less to predict it. The central question remains whether we can express the sense in which policy decisions are framed by cultural rules in a useful way. Even if it is not possible to predict a given outcome or to attach a statistical probability to it, it may be useful to be able to define the set of alternatives from which a selection is being made, and indeed to define the sequence of operations of selection through which a policy is generated.

In this context, the analogy frequently made between language and other cultural forms is useful. Grammar constrains speech, but does not allow the prediction of any single utterance, and indeed the number of possible grammatical utterances that may be generated by a speaker is infinite.[8] Happily, this is a very exclusive infinitude. Linguists look at possible sentences in terms of whether they are "well formed," or "grammatical," acknowledging that many actual utterances are not even well formed, are, for instance, interrupted, or produced by speakers who are drunk or aphasic or deliberately violating grammatical rules — linguists shaping hypothetical examples, for instance. Similarly for actions, an individual at a given moment of time often has a great many alternatives open to him which an observing member of the same culture would find plausible, would regard as "making sense" in relation to a diversity of possible goals and information available to the actor. Some actions may be so likely as to seem almost determined, others may be much less likely but still culturally plausible, and a few occur which simply do not make sense in cultural terms. An example would be the filing of an income tax return: there is no doubt a predictable distribution of filing dates, around the first weeks of April, as well as a series of intelligible reasons for failure to file, ranging from ideological protest to incompetence, and once in a while one may run into a case that simply does not "make sense" in terms of available information.

Yet in this case we are not dealing with convention (say the mailing of a Mother's Day card) but with legislation, an aspect of the cultural system that attempts to be determinative. Cultural rules are not like natural laws; knowledge of the rules will not allow prediction for any single case. Indeed, because some culturally inappropriate instances are always liable to arise, cultural forms of prediction are least likely to be useful where single instances are of high importance. Not surprisingly, cultural analysis seems at first glance to be more useful to advertisers, say, than to secretaries of state.

Cultural forms of prediction are most likely to be useful in relation to behavior that involves large numbers of actors. This is obviously true for multiple actions that allow for statistical prediction, but significantly, it also includes behavior that produces a single outcome but only after undergoing extensive review by many members of a society considering whether it seems to them appropriate, wise, or intelligible — what we might call "editing." Under most circumstances, the actions of governments on matters of international relations and security are very heavily edited.

An example will clarify this: the sentences which I am likely to generate as I sit by my word processor are in general well formed, recognizably English sentences, even when the ideas I put forward have a certain *soupçon* of originality, but I review them before printing them, and they will be further reviewed before they appear in a publication. Anyone who has tried to include an odd or informal turn of phrase, for instance, in an op ed piece for *The New York Times* knows that what e. e. cummings could get away with, they cannot. The foreign policy establishment of a nation is a bit like the copy editing office of a newspaper — sentences don't get through that are not seen as plausible, that do not make sense, except under very special circumstances, for instance, an insane despot, an incompetent or quixotic chief of state, or a private action that gets converted into policy.

A heavily bureaucratic nation, or one in which decision making is clearly collective, is much easier to deal with than one in which decisions reflect individual creativity. Similarly, movies are much more useful for cultural analysis than novels: a movie is a collective project, involving a great many different minds who reshape the materials given to them so that they make sense, and furthermore it is a commercial product, it must have plausibility at the box office, even if that plausibility is based on its shocking character — it cannot seem simply arbitrary or irrelevant. A

Khrushchev or a Sadat may make decisions that disconcert and scandalize their bureaucracies — clearly, if members of their societies are surprised, we cannot assume that their actions were predictable in any simple sense. Truman, recognizing the new state of Israel, is said to have surprised and scandalized the State Department, but the decision worked at the box office. A novel may reflect an idiosyncratic vision, may fail or be ignored for many years and then recognized as great art. No system of anthropological analysis would have predicted *Finnegan's Wake,* and such a work can only be used evidentially with the greatest of care — but formula books, such as Gothic novels, are far more immediately useful to the anthropologist — you have only to see them displayed in a supermarket to know that they fit with some existing concern in the society.

Actions taken by governments, then, are in general heavily edited. Not only are they formulated by one or more individuals, they usually have to pass through a filter of plausibility for a considerable number of others involved in decision making, implementation, or other kinds of concurrence, a filter which in no way precludes disagreement with the wisdom of a given policy, just as the copy editing at *The New York Times* does not signify agreement with content. Just as *The New York Times* is hospitable to contradictory opinions, the culturally plausible foreign policy decisions of a nation-state may contrast sharply.

The purpose of this paper is to examine a situation in which the foreign policy community was taken by surprise by events in a nation-state of some significance to the United States, namely Iran, and in which assumptions about Iranian political styles proved inaccurate. I will examine these events in relation to a research project conducted in Tehran in the years 1973–1976 which suggested that Iranians pose alternatives in terms of two sharply contrasting cultural styles. On the one hand a style that emphasized opportunistic maneuvering under circumstances of moral ambiguity and allowed for practicality, dissimulation, and negotiation, and on the other hand an absolute style, dealing with binary opposites, in which good and evil are contrasted and compromise devalued. We found both styles present in the popular culture and in the accounts given by individuals of the way in which alternatives present themselves in personal life, although they are as dissonant as the harmonious and violent pictures of Samoa presented by Mead and Freeman.

Iranian public policy and public rhetoric, both domestically and internationally, went through an apparent radical change at the time of the

revolution into a style that appeared totally different and therefore unpredictable, but we would argue that the two styles — and more significantly
the tendency to think of them as alternatives facing individuals and societies — were and still are both implicit in Iranian culture. The change
was more like shifting gears in a car, in which the system has built into it
multiple modes of operation, than like the replacement of something old
by something new; the post-revolutionary style was always implicit. Thus,
a second purpose of this paper is to demonstrate the way in which a given
technique for studying popular culture is able to define a given *axis* on
which alternatives may be formulated, although it cannot predict which
pole will be chosen or when. A given initial decision will generally involve
subsequent sequences of choices. The particular shift that occurred in
Iran, from a rhetoric of opportunism accessible to compromise to a binary
rhetoric of good and evil, is of immense importance because of the way it
structures subsequent decisions and alternatives. Then, too, partial analogues can be found in other contexts, including United States policy,
which goes through cycles of being more or less pragmatic or moralistic
in its rhetoric.

Our original work, which included interviewing and the analysis of
popular stories and films, was done by a group consisting of Iranians and
Americans trained in a variety of social science disciplines, including J. W.
Clinton, J. B. M. Kassarjian, Hasan Safavi, and Mehdi Soraya (and several
others for shorter periods), as well as myself.[9] I must take responsibility
for the 1984 formulation in this paper. The research should be regarded
as preliminary, oriented toward the identification of themes and the
development of hypotheses, since historical events have precluded the
kind of follow-up that would have been desirable.

This work was done prior to the Iranian revolution, and was not primarily oriented toward public issues. We were concerned to clarify the
values that motivate individual Iranians in their private lives and inform
their judgments and evaluations of others, whether or not these were
reflected on the larger political scene. In the event, we found that we got
a set of composite images, each of which evoked a certain ambivalence.
On the one hand, there was the image, often devalued, of someone who is
opportunistic and calculating, but disapproval was mixed in this image
with appreciation of cleverness, and it was suggested that only such a
person could be successful. On the other hand, we found several variant
forms of an ideal character type whose absolute integrity precludes
maneuvering and compromise, summed up in the title of one of our

papers, *safa-yi batin,* inner purity. Attitudes toward such a person were ambivalent, since he was seen as unlikely to be successful, and yet informants expressed the sense that at some deep level they longed for and were capable of that kind of integrity, conformed to it in certain relationships, and were nostalgic for a society in which it would be the norm. Thus, we collected many statements of conflict even within private life — narratives of individuals torn between two sets of values — and repeated statements that public values were in contradiction to the more idealized vision that was seen as viable only in a private context. Interestingly enough, whether or not our informants were prepared to say that they repudiated the values represented by the Shah's government *per se* (not a risk we encouraged them to take), we observed a wide-spread agreement that it is of the nature of social life to distort virtue. We were struck by the fact that the basic contrast depicted was not between good and bad but between two ways of approaching situations of choice.

Two different readings of these results are possible. One reading suggests that the true Iranian self-image is that of integrity and the situation of living under a corrupt despotism left many feeling they could not be true to themselves, a temporary distortion during the Pahlavi dynasty. This reading would predict the revolution rather nicely but dismisses the pre-revolutionary situation as an aberration, as unrepresentative. Pro-revolutionary Iranians would of course concur. It is satisfying to find that a study of popular culture identifies the value themes that would predict a social upheaval, but I would argue that the governmental structures and policies during the monarchy involved large numbers of individuals who had considerable scope for what I have called "editing," so that an adequate account of Iranian national culture must account for both the Pahlavi dynasty and the Islamic Republic as representative variants — an example of the need to account for sharp contrast within a tradition. This is not a view that would be popular with any group of Iranians on first hearing it, and yet it allows the pointing out of a number of other continuities. In effect, it requires that partisans recognize that both they and their adversaries are acting within a culturally defined range of possibilities, a potential contrast built into the tradition. This alternative reading, then, is one that recognizes ambivalence as built into the culture, sometimes visible in a public-private contrast, but always present as a dual potentiality. The question to ask in attempting to forecast policy is when and how the pragmatic emphasis will be ascendant and when and how the idealized emphasis will be ascendant, and how these two stylistic preferences will be interwoven in the relationship between rhetoric and implementation.

An example may clarify this. In our work on Iranian popular culture, we observed a number of films in which there is a turning point of decision, when the protagonist rejects a dishonorable course, often one which he has followed in the past or which members of the audience say most people would choose, and takes an honorable course that will be costly to him, perhaps costing him his life. We wrote then,

> Overriding commitment, pushing an individual out of the sphere of calculation, beyond the need to balance one course of action against another, so that what he does is a complete and direct expression of who he is, is profoundly admired. Such an individual cannot be moved by threats or co-opted or bribed, all of which are strongly supported in most people most of the time by the habit of living in ambiguity.[10]

Against this background, the admiration for Ayatollah Khomeini's intransigence and unwillingness to negotiate or compromise four years later becomes intelligible. More complex is the process whereby individuals who had always felt a certain admiration and nostalgia for the stance of unambivalent commitment — combined with a degree of pity for the failure or martyrdom it may imply — shifted gears at a personal level and became identified with the revolution, accepting the risks involved.

Calculation involves recognizing and weighing a multiplicity of alternative courses, each having advantages and disadvantages. Once a decision has been made to conceive of a situation in terms of a binary choice, to focus on only two alternatives, valuing one and devaluing the other, the stakes are set so high that the outcome is predetermined. One thinks of *High Noon*: "Oh to be torn twixt love and duty . . ." or of the old hymn "Once to every man and nation, comes the moment to decide, in the strife of truth with falsehood, for the good or evil side." There are still many members of this society who would limit alternatives to "Live free or die." The choice of the "good" is already committed once the alternatives have been formulated in this way, and the maintenance and consideration of multiple alternatives depends on avoiding the rhetoric of binary choice.

It is not, however, sufficient to say that under certain circumstances Iranians (or Americans) formulate decisions in heavily value laden binary terms, unless one can define when this framework comes into play and how the binary axis is defined. Even binary decisions may contrast on different axes. Some of the most familiar are right versus wrong, fair versus unfair, good versus evil, honorable versus dishonorable. The rhetoric used by representatives of the Iranian government during the hostage crisis, and since, implies that Iran, in the form of the Islamic Republic, is pitted against evil, the Great Satan. The rhetoric of the United States during that same period asserted that Iran, in tolerating and endorsing the hostage taking, was acting wrongly — against the rules of the game. Where they spoke of good versus evil, we spoke, with equal certitude, of right versus wrong — there is more than one variety of self-righteousness.

The posing of binary alternatives is such a radical simplification that it would seem extremely important to know when it comes into play. Will the actor conceptualize a given situation as presenting many alternatives, with a decision to be made pragmatically, or will he conceptualize it as binary? Indeed, as noted above, the binary phrasing may predetermine the subsequent decision: once you label a decision point as offering good or evil, honor or dishonor, have you not committed yourself to choose the good, to seek honor?

To sum up, a study of cultural patterns of decision-making must visualize multiple stages of culturally formulated decision before the formulation of action, in some cases starting from sharply contrasting and discontinuous alternatives that exemplify dissonant themes coexisting in the culture. However, even though multiple decisions follow the basic decision to define a given situation as appropriate for subsequent opportunistic decisions or as appropriate for binary decision — posing an absolute choice — these subsequent decisions are inevitably constrained by the initially established premise: either there is a *RIGHT* (good, true) answer, or there is a *BEST* (most advantageous, most appropriate) answer. The community operating on a rhetoric that asserts that its policies are right, rejecting evil, may be able to mobilize very strong feeling, but it will have limited flexibility and be subject to the dangers that Iranians see for individuals with integrity, including the danger of martyrdom. (Incidentally, the actual dangers may be even greater for societies in which many people believe that rightness leads to success, as they sometimes do in our own, in which the hero may triumph precisely because his heart is pure — unless they believe, as we on the whole do, that he is simultaneously clever. Perhaps only heroes who are both clever and virtuous are likely to prosper.)

Thus, it seems clear that although alternative modes of posing issues for decision exist for both the United States and the Islamic Republic (and may create apparent inconsistencies and unpredictabilities in both cultures), the contexts in which they are evoked differ. However, the tendency to formulate alternatives in absolute terms must represent a dangerous loss of flexibility wherever it arises. Whether the rhetoric concerns the Untied States as the "Great Satan" or the Soviet Union as the "evil empire," it sets up a context that may tend to preclude effective negotiation and needed compromise.

One of the advantages of recognizing that the tendency to define a decision-making context as opportunistic or binary is part of Iranian culture is that we should recognize that the opportunistic mode is present within the Islamic Republic instead of failing to see it, as many observers failed to see the idealism present within the Shah's Iran. Just as there was a reservoir of self-sacrificing idealism present in the Shah's Iran, so there is a reservoir of cynicism in the Ayatollah's Iran. Iranians expect, on the whole, to find that power corrupts and that wealth and success are associated with moral ambiguity — this expectation is referred to as *badbini* — and it is one of the ever-present problems for the state. In order to survive, there must be a certain capacity to compromise, and yet Khomeini's intractable integrity must precisely not be compromised, and so the government was both trapped in the war with Iraq and dependent on it to establish its adamant conviction.

In summary, decision-making in Iran, both public and private, is characterized by the prior adoption of a mode that constrains subsequent decisions, a mode that is either opportunistic or binary/moralistic. Each mode is characterized by a degree of ambivalence. Individuals may shift from one mode to the other, often having been quite clear about the two kinds of alternatives. The state too may shift from one mode to the other, as it ostensibly did at the time of the revolution, and yet both modes continue to be implicitly present. An informed foreign policy would note the opportunistic willingness of the Khomeini government to exclude certain issues from its moralistic fervor, and thus to deal with the Israelis when convenient. Similarly, we should cultivate in our own polity the appreciation of compromise and pragmatism as premises that must be adopted well before a given policy is up for debate. As anthropologists, we may contribute most to thinking about such matters as international relations by analyzing styles of decision-making rather than styles of outcome, attempting to characterize the tensions within a procedure rather than seeking homogeneity.

The idea of world government is very threatening to many people, yet it is clear that the world is in increasing need of some form of global self-regulation that will not evoke old patterns of hierarchy and hegemony, and will not impose or depend upon uniformity. Negative images of government seem especially powerful for some Americans who seem to associate all government with the loss of freedom rather than with more effective cooperation, so there has been a movement to reject existing treaties and the gradual development of international law.

This essay was the second of two written for a group called the World Order Models Project, attempting to explore ways in which a more peaceful and integrated world could emerge without a single world government or loss of local cultural autonomy. Today there would be many new examples and metaphors, for the Internet offers a whole range of possibilities and there has been a great deal of new thinking about the nature and functioning of networks both in the brain and in society. Even computers can handle greater ambiguity today. The issue is a cybernetic one, however, not because some of the solutions involve electronics but in the original meaning of *cybernetics,* by which we can imagine the emergence — already underway — of new patterns of self-regulation including non-centralized governance. The basic approach came from a conference in Moscow in 1988, at the end of the Cold War. I had met members of the group through the Lindisfarne Fellowship, an interdisciplinary group of scholars, activists, and artists that began meeting annually in the early 1980s and has

steadily pushed my thinking into new areas. Writing this
essay was, I believe, the beginning of extending my
thinking about ambiguity beyond the arts.

—MCB, 2004

∽

There are two families of solutions to the problem of world order,
expressing very different premises about how human communities can
best be organized. One type of solution is modelled on the state, and proposes a specific and unambiguous locus of power. This might be achieved
by the establishment of some form of world government with unques-
tioned authority, at least in certain areas, with powers of enforcement
achieved by a degree of voluntary abdication of sovereignty by participating nation-states. Equally, it might be achieved by the dominance of a
single power. This form of organization, depending as it does on the same
kind of power as the nation-state, is necessarily seen as inimical to those
who identify with existing forms of government. Power is not readily
abdicated by those who believe they have it.

The alternative approach suggests that the problem of world order
might be solved by the emergence of what has been termed a "global civilization,"[1] a form of organization not analogous in structure to the governments of nation-states, but that represents instead an additional layer of
civility and commonality rather than an abdication of sovereignty. Such an
emerging pattern of commonality might of course be a predecessor to more
formal structures, as seems to be the case in Europe, where a common civilization is gradually leading to economic and political unification. The use
of the term "civilization" presents certain problems because it has sometimes been used invidiously. At the same time, it does express the notion of
a shared body of ideas transcending political boundaries.

A Global Civilization

The concept of an emerging global civilization, as a replacement for the
notion of a world government, is intended here to suggest a loosely integrated system that might have the following characteristics: (1) It could
develop gradually and is already in the process of development; (2) it

would be characterized by ongoing change, indeed by evolution; (3) it could coexist with rich cultural and political diversity; (4) it would not rely on the centralization of power that has characterized the concept of the state. All of these characteristics are related to another, the focus of this paper: (5) It would make a virtue of ambiguity, in the traditional sense of the term, finding in what might be construed as a flaw or weakness a source of strength *(virtù)*. Change, fluidity, diversity, diffuse focus, these are all characteristics alien to traditional concepts of political power, as is ambiguity, for since the days of the Medes and the Persians or even earlier, rulers have wanted to know how far their writ will run. But if such a loose, flexible form of organization were to develop, it need not present an obvious threat to existing structures.

Such a development is already under way, for arguably the modern world, with its increasing density of communications, is a gradually self-organizing system. The necessary models for understanding such an emergent order come from ecology rather than from traditional political science.

A global civilization is not achieved by negotiation as we know it, where the process of international negotiation has been pervaded by a search for fixed, verifiable, and unambiguous formulations. Rather it is achieved by a dense web of communication of many different kinds, forms of exchange that percolate into the daily lives and imaginations of ordinary people around the world. What is needed is not unambiguous agreement but rather a homely and familiar sense of relationship, a resilient substructure of global community that will allow more flexibility in tackling the vast and urgent issues that we as a species must face together. Trust and a tolerance for ambiguity within some broader framework are built from the ordinary. At the local level, such a substructure is built up from day-to-day, face-to-face interactions; at the global level, it is likely to develop by listening to the radio and walking in a marketplace that draws on worldwide resources, rather than through legislation and formal educational programs.

Thus, in discussing the kind of integration implied by the idea of a global civilization, it is important to include a discussion of the ways in which a multitude of exchanges and borrowings, each one perhaps trivial, create a structure of familiarity. A viable form of world order must be pieced together from only partially shared systems of meaning, crossing over existing cultural diversity. Such systems of meaning will be very different from the systems developed by diplomats or philosophers, for they will be improvisational and ambiguous, with room for both contention and humor.

Assumptions and Models

Models of world government are affected by the existing "commonsense" of ideas carried over from the state system, with its focus on central authority. Beyond this, they gain their appearance of self-evident necessity from the congruence between established conceptualizations in different spheres, such as religion and family life. Yet central control, in the sense of an unambiguous locus of power and of authority as the only possible basis of integration, is by no means universal or necessary. Substantial human communities may be organized acephalously — without central authority. This does not mean they are anarchic, for normative expectations and patterns of influence and authority (not necessarily benign) always emerge in human groups wherever there is direct contact within them, and have been observed consistently in social groups of all primates. The question really is, What, for our species, can serve as direct contact?

The state, as described by Bodin and others,[2] presented central authority as the only solution to the problems of disorder and conflict, to the Hobbesian war of all against all. This was based on a notion that conflict is so embedded in human nature that it can only be resolved from above. Certainly conflict is inescapable, but Hobbes lacked the knowledge of alternative forms of order now available from anthropology. We have many models of communities in which, in the absence of central authority, we do not see all pitted against one another. Indeed, we now know that Hobbes' grim vision is a projection, no more descriptive of human prehistory than the myth of Eden. Total harmony and total anarchy, although the brief illusion of either sometimes appears, are both evanescent. As thought experiments, they are less interesting than the study of limited conflicts and the ways of resolving these, a question of far greater moment in a world where certain familiar expressions of conflict have become unacceptable.

It is of course reasonable to question whether acephalous forms of order can be extended to large areas like nations, much less to the whole planet, because the familiar anthropological examples seem to depend on shared cultural premises and a high level of day-to-day, face-to-face familiarity and communication. The invention of the state provided a solution to a problem that has not disappeared: the problem of coordinating large populations lacking dense links of intercommunication. But it is important to recognize that the populations of France, say, and of Germany, when these states emerged, were far less richly intercommunicating than the entire world is today. The solution then, to inadequate interaction, was the centralization of power. Today, the increase of communication offers an alternative solution to the same problem. The recognition of an emerging world civilization is essentially a recognition of the high density of new forms of communication saturating the ether.

Another kind of solution can be seen in the history of constitutionalism. The United States Constitution was deliberately designed to prevent the concentration of power in any one institution of government. It has demonstrated that deliberate pluralism, permitting substantial conflict, with power at multiple points of the system and strong protection for communication and expression of diverse views, is imperfect but possible. Interestingly enough, it has often been argued that the strength of the U.S. Constitution lies in its ambiguity, its openness to debate and evolving interpretation as times change.

Monotheism

Historically, much of the Western dislike of ambiguity has come from its religions. The idea in Western religion of an unambiguous locus of power seems to have an even more compelling logic than the concept of the state to which it is analogous. But it is not necessary. The ancient Hebrews asserted the presence and power of a single omnipotent deity, and since that time the Western religious tradition has struggled with the belief in one God; any belief in more than one has come to seem absurd. But because so many Western thinkers and scholars today reject all religious forms, they tend to be unaware both of the hints of multiplicity within unity that exist even in monotheistic traditions, and of the subtle difference between their rejections of polytheism and of monotheism, for it is not clear that the superiority of monotheism should be self-evident when theism of any kind is rejected. It is one thing to urge that pluralism requires the mutual tolerance of different religious groups, even when such tolerance is intellectually alien. It is quite another thing to propose an intrinsically pluralistic metaphysic, to deny that the "ground of all being" is necessarily solid underfoot. Yet polytheism was apparently not at all absurd for the ancient Indo-Europeans, including the Greeks and the ancestors of present-day Hindus and most Europeans, and for most other human communities whose sense of the divine has been more ecological, multifaceted, and interdependent.

In fact, it is only habit that makes monotheism, like the idea of the state, so persuasive. The Hebrews found monotheism a difficult belief to sustain, perhaps because it was so dissonant with their tribal social organization, their neighboring peoples' religions, and their dispersal across the notably varied terrain of Palestine. They strayed repeatedly, following multiple deities, perhaps most regularly when central political power was in question. Yet the Hebrew prophets made a fateful analogy, from the invention of monotheism to the unity of belief, for Judaism, Christianity, and Islam in their orthodox forms all assert that not only is deity single, but that religious knowledge is also necessarily single and absolute.

In the Middle Ages, when political power was pluralistic and fragmented, divine absolutism was also ambiguous, multiply delegated to a flock of intercessory beings — angels, saints, and clerics — like a corrupt Byzantine bureaucracy. The Virgin Mary played the supreme intercessory role, and one cannot help but feel that much of her significance lay in her ability sometimes to persuade her son to do something against logic or his better judgment, as appears to have been the case at the wedding at Cana. While not in entire synchrony, the emergence of absolutism as a political form corresponds to the inexorable logic that followed the Counterreformation, with its assertion of clear lines of authority. The religious preference for a single unchanging and transcendent deity leads to the preference for unambiguous doctrine and to the whole history of creeds, orthodoxy, heterodoxy and the persecution of heretics, and the Inquisition. Once formulated, the idea of the singular *and* omnipotent has survived as central in Christianity and Islam to this day, focusing the imagination of a great part of the world's population, and accompanied, logically, by the immensely costly conviction that doctrine is either true or false.

Can one imagine a return to a world in which polytheism would seem at least as persuasive as monotheism? Or at least one in which respect for the beliefs of others is not a superficial patina on the conviction that beliefs are either right or wrong? Must even post-religious societies model family and political life on religious forms they no longer accept? At the same time, in other areas, alternative models have been developing. Scientific knowledge has come to seem less determinate. In cognitive science, there is the developing body of thinking about autopoiesis, the self-organizing capacity of complex systems. In organizational theory, hierarchy is rapidly going out of fashion as too rigid for creativity, and feminists point out its analogy to patriarchy. The theory of a necessary single locus of power, with its metaphorical extensions, begins to seem less and less useful.

Early theorists of the sovereign state asserted that only with a clearly definable locus of power could the rule of law be assured, guaranteeing domestic peace and tranquility. It is interesting today to find these intellectual arguments echoed in fundamentalist tracts about family life: It is necessary and logical, they assert, that there should be one voice able to make a final decision, and therefore any attempt at equality between men and women is necessarily unworkable, as absurd as the idea of multiple gods managing the universe by a system of consultation and compromise. There is no difficulty with delegation and subsidiarity, providing hierarchy is unambiguously defined; every ship, they assert, must have a captain.

In Praise of Muddle

The preference for a single center of authority is both temperamental and aesthetic. The alternative argument would be that, if only conflict can be contained, a certain amount of muddle is both beautiful and creative, both in society and in the family. There need not be a single locus of authority — not in the family, not in society, not in the cosmos. It is not easy to maintain a sense of commonality based on partial and ambiguous sharing, but that may be the only option for world order. If this is the case, then many kinds of contemporary efforts to move toward unequivocal rules, precise language, and verification are misguided. There is little willingness to rely on unarticulated and partially shared understandings, and yet the search for fixed and explicit understanding may prove to be self-defeating. Certainly the insistence on total explicitness and verifiability has crippled arms limitation negotiations. The United States over the last twenty years has in many areas been engaged in a flurry of specification and regulation, trying to define exact procedures for decision-making to make these processes more determinate, to make the functioning of democracy less ambiguous — to eliminate ambiguity in a society where consensus is in doubt. If ambiguity is an essential lubricant for the system, that effort may be self-destructive.

The very flurry of disambiguation that draws us in one direction is a reaction that derives from the pluralism and ambiguity of the U.S. Constitution, which serves us because of its supreme ambiguity, but does not always satisfy us with definitions of exact rights. The writers of the Constitution built in provisions for conflicting types of authority and for disagreement in the form of the balance of powers and the protections of minorities. Yet a certain fluctuation in levels of ambiguity and a variable level of tolerance for ambiguity within the population may be a necessary characteristic of pluralistic systems.

During recent years, most of us have had enough contact with computers to experience the process of reducing ambiguity from another point of view. Most computers to date, unlike human beings, are incapable of dealing with ambiguity, which makes them, as they are sometimes fondly called in the United Kingdom, TOMS: totally obedient morons. If there is even a trace of unclarity in an instruction given to a computer, it will not comply. The human mind can, however, tolerate high levels of ambiguity, finding in it one of the sources of creativity. Even as the average number of words in drafts of new legislation is increased, and each attracts additional volumes of administrative specification, it must be clear that we are engaged in a *reductio ad absurdum* of the attempt to escape ambiguity.

In an emerging world civilization, the forms in which ideas are shared, whatever their sources, will be variable and continually liable to diverge, floating in a sea of pluralism and ambiguity, and kept together not by orthodoxy but by a continual process of rapid interchange and the steady need to address practical problems.

We may indeed need to consider the *purposeful creation* of ambiguity. Yet this idea runs counter to a great many common assumptions. The same kinds of aesthetic preference that wound their way through the development of Western religion may respond with distaste to the compromises of pluralism. Yet any constitution appropriate to such an order would require high degrees of ambiguity.

I do not believe we have at present the capacity to generate a world constitution with a level of fruitful ambiguity comparable to that devised two centuries ago. It is as if the forms of a world order would have to be created by biologists and artists rather than by lawyers. But it is possible that patterns of shared understanding might emerge without any single constitutional document. If such a document were to develop, the first requirement would be that it protect the openness of the system to new ideas.

Conclusion

A viable form of world order must exist in the context of a partial sharing of systems of meaning, crossing over existing cultural diversity, and such a development is already under way and might be referred to as a "global civilization." It is not clear that such systems of meaning need to be explicit and formally agreed upon. Probably they will be very different from the systems developed by diplomats or philosophers, for they will be partial, piecemeal, and ambiguous. In order to recognize and benefit from emerging forms of global commonality at every level, it will be necessary to rethink the notion of civilization and the kind of integration necessary to it. What we can see today, however, is that the process is itself not a singular one but a convergence of many streams of thought and effort.

Since the dawn of human history, visions have been drawn from the ambiguous, as diviners imagined the future in the forms of clouds and swirling waters. Social change and innovation are always stimulated by the awareness of difference, the understanding that there are no fixed dogmas, no fixed answers to the most fundamental questions. This is a disturbing prospect for many, but the very ambiguity of the emerging world civilization promises a massive liberation of the human imagination.

CHANGE IN ISLAM

The Status of Women

This paper was originally drafted for a small conference on women in Islam, but the theme allowed me to explore different ways in which a system that has come to be seen as absolute and unchanging may have the capacity to adapt without the sense of a break with the past. Islam has of course adapted repeatedly to new circumstances: when its original expansion brought it into contact with the old and sophisticated Byzantine and Persian imperial cultures, when it encountered unfamiliar religions, and more recently in encountering Western imperialism, modernism, and division into nation-states. There is currently a revival under way in Islam, which has both regressive and adaptive aspects, though in the West we hear more about reaction than about creative adaptation. Oil wealth is both a resource and a complication. By now there have been several generations of Muslim women who seek increased respect and freedom, which most want to achieve in combination with an affirmation of their own tradition. To do so, they need to find and reemphasize congruent elements — and points of leverage — in that tradition. The issues and alternative approaches discussed here have their parallel elsewhere, not only in other issues related to women, such as plural marriage and genital mutilation, but in other areas where the Muslim community must respond somehow to contemporary circumstances.

Women belonging to groups that have been subject to colonization or discrimination face a special challenge, however, in seeking equality with men who themselves feel oppressed and exploited, especially if the men expect

a revival of historic traditions to be the highway to liberation. Because the subordination of women has been so
widespread — and so traditional — in human society,
women have been doubly oppressed in virtually every
disadvantaged group. They want change, but they do
not want the demand for change to put them outside
their community, perceived as traitors or apostates. It is
easy for outsiders to call for radical change but often critical for women to proceed more gradually. The search
for points of flexibility within an existing system is perhaps analogous to what happens in a discussion when,
instead of saying that a particular approach is mistaken,
we try to show a way to build on what we both know to
arrive at a better answer.

In this 1974 essay I used an architectural analogy,
prefiguring my use of a similar analogy in later discussions of the effects of extended longevity on the shapes of
lives, but the analogy was with a real house, so I have
modified the end of the essay to bring it closer to the
house today.

Several years ago, Stewart Brand titled a book *How
Buildings Learn.*[1] Actually I see us co-learning with our
New Hampshire home, for buildings teach as well as
learn, as buildings and people shape each other and are
shaped by the wider environment. In the same sense,
asking about change in Islam is asking about the co-
learning of a vast community over time, an ongoing
process in which knowledge unfolds and evolves.

—MCB, 2004

Adaptation to change and the ability to maintain continuity are both
essential to the survival of systems of belief, and sometimes surprisingly
difficult to tell apart. With the rise in the West of new wave feminism and
women's studies as an academic discipline, a beginning was made in
describing the status of women in the Islamic world, both their ideal position as prescribed by Islamic jurists and the actual position they occupy,

including beliefs, rituals, and kinds of freedom and influence unanticipated by theologians. At the same time, there has been a growing call for
change, both within the Islamic world and from outsiders, and the literature includes descriptions of change in process and polemics on its pace
and direction, while conservatives have adopted ever more rigid positions.
However, there remains a vacuum of sorts, a vacuum which is more theoretical than descriptive. There is a need to ask how fundamental the traditional status of women really is in Islam and how profound a change its
modification would be, which is part of the larger question of the nature
of continuity and flexibility in Islam.

An analogy may help: I am sitting and writing in a New Hampshire
cottage as repairs are being made on its two-century-old structure. Some
of the repairs concern the sills, on which the entire structure rests, while
others are taking place up near the roof. Clearly, decay, removal, or
replacement in these two different positions have profoundly different
implications. And, while we are with our analogy, there is another similarity to consider, for this old house has over the years reached a certain
accommodation in which nothing is quite straight and what supports
what no longer always follows the logic of the original construction. The
carpenters repairing it now need to be concerned both for the original
logic and for the actual state of affairs of compensation and compromise,
realizing that an adjustment at the level of the roof may even affect the
foundation.

Nowhere does an old and complex religion "stand" entirely by the
logic of orthodox doctrine, for reforms that look reasonable or superficial
from the point of view of orthodoxy may produce profoundly disconcerting results when their true effect on the structure is seen. Never has
this been clearer than in the Roman Catholic Church, where the reforms
initiated by Pope John XXIII have had such profound effects on the faith
of some members that it is clear that all along their premises were different from those of the reformers. The reformers saw the reforms as in
continuity with old premises, but huge numbers left the church because of
what might have seemed to be superficial changes. Just as in my New
Hampshire home, when and if new equilibria are reached, these will
depend as much on spontaneous accommodations in the structure as on
planning — whether on the part of theologians or on the part of the local
carpenters.

These two points of view have existed in feminism as well. Some feminists argue that they are simply concerned to improve the position of women, bringing it more into line with existing understandings of justice and equity. Others, however, both advocating and opposing change, argue that the subordination of women is fundamental to the entire hierarchical organization of society, which puts some in authority over others. In 1852 Elizabeth Oakes Smith argued, "My friends, do we realize for what purpose we are convened? Do we fully understand that we aim at nothing less than an entire subversion of the present order of society, a dissolution of the whole existing social compact?"[1]

There are similar choices that I face as a homeowner. Why not find ways to accomplish my immediate goals (a new closet, say, or a roof that does not leak) without worrying about the coherence and integrity of the overall design? Doing so may be cheaper, and may avoid opening an expensive can of worms. So perhaps change can be formulated in ways that we agree are superficial, even though their long-term structural effect is unknown.

To consider the implications of any change in the position of women in Islam, it is necessary to consider first how belief and practice came to be codified and what tradition teaches about change or reform. In dealing with change it will be necessary further to distinguish between changes (1) that are perceived as bringing practice more closely into line with orthodoxy, which we might call *reform*; and changes (2) that are perceived by large numbers or people as representing a real discontinuity with traditional belief or practice, which we might call *alteration*. In the first case, we are often dealing with changes in practices or beliefs which have never been codified, changes in what may be called folk Islam, while in the second case we are often dealing with changes in areas that have been codified, such that the accepted statement of orthodoxy at some point would now be contradicted.

Reform may include change that could as well come from a fundamentalist as from a modernizing thrust, while *alteration* implies recognizable departure from the fabric of orthodoxy.

In general, reforms are motivated by the conviction that a given change is in the direction of the "true spirit of Islam," while innovations are often motivated by reference to some other ethical principle, often a secular one based on Western models, such as the United Nations Universal Declaration of Human Rights. Note that it is not necessary to argue that there is such a thing as a definable "true spirit of Islam" to suppose that this idea is important in people's thinking. Thus, the notion of "religionless Christianity" is paradoxical to someone looking from a descriptive point of view at a religious system which has had various forms at different times and been expressed in a multitude of texts and institutions, and yet this notion is sometimes put forward as more in conformity with what some believe to be the core of their faith than any of these texts and institutions. The idea of a distinction between letter and spirit can have a very great effect on people's behavior, even though salting the tail of the spirit eludes the historian.

An analysis of writers in this area would certainly show some cases where it was possible to say clearly what the touchstone of argument was, but in many other cases this distinction is only a heuristic one. Some writers may simply not allow for the possibility of a contradiction between ethical fundamentals, while others will argue one position disguised as the other, depending on their strategy and their audience. For instance, here is an example by an Egyptian Muslim writing in Arabic of the opposite strategy from the Elizabeth Oakes Smith quotation: "Yes, I come with an innovation, however, it is not of the essence of Islam, rather it is of customs and methods of interaction in which it is good to seek perfection."[2]

The kinds of flexibility that exist in Islam have been discussed in some detail elsewhere in the literature, and no more than a summary is needed here. The codified orthodox structure is based on (1) the words of the Qur'an, (2) the words and practice of the Prophet, as recorded with various degrees of reliability (*sunnah* and *hadith*), (3) analogy from these (*qiyas*), and (4) decisions made within the community of theologians striving to reach new formulations in conformity with tradition (*ijtihad*), and supported by a consensus of the community (*ijma*). This kind of incremental process has occurred in other scriptural religions and legal systems. By the third Islamic century, however, at a time of controversy and efforts to suppress innovation, the number of decisions made in meeting new situations and cumulatively added to the orthodox core was deemed to have preemptively filled the adaptive space in the system. The "door of *ijtihad*" was declared closed.

There has long been an assumption that Muhammad himself stood for higher ideals in some areas than are reflected in legislation (e.g., with regard to slavery) or, looked at in a different way, that the Prophet's words represented in some cases necessary accommodations to the local culture which made Islam acceptable. Some *hadith* represent a greater divergence from the traditional culture of the Quraysh tribe into which the Prophet was born than does the Qur'an. Thus, Islam is regarded as having improved the status of women over local custom, for instance by setting standards for plural marriage and limiting it to four wives, implying a direction for further progress. But the general logic moves in the opposite direction, reinforcing traditional constraints on women: the layers accumulated through *qiyas*, *ijtihad*, and *ijma* are logically the ones through which the greatest amount of local custom has been incorporated, for at any one of these stages (600–900 in the Western calendar), elements of the local cultural environment could have been sanctified as part of orthodoxy. In time, local custom is simply taken for granted, as self-evidently appropriate. The distinction between custom and orthodoxy has always been a part of Islamic theological awareness, but as always and everywhere, there is a tendency in the Islamic world to assume that particular local practices which seem always to have been are right. A historian of culture, looking at the role of women in Islam, can to some degree disentangle different strands of influence, cultural accretions, and the way in which sometimes local customs and new religious ideas have moderated each other and at other times — apparently this is the case with the seclusion of women — amplified each other. However, this is not an acceptable distinction in terms of traditionalist theology.

Modern arguments for opening the door of *ijtihad* do not always make it explicit that new *ijtihad* might not be simply additive but might *replace* old *ijtihad* — that is, that the original cumulative conception would also have to give way. This would in turn represent a profound shift in the conception not only of the nature of orthodoxy, but of the relationship between the community and the revelation itself. The process of consensus was potentially creative, but it was believed to have a kind of infallibility, which tends to imply immutability as well. In practice, the conceptual change involved in reopening the door of *ijtihad* has been rejected, and change has taken place through quite different channels.

One of these has been the use of legal stratagems (*hilah*), practical adaptations which make a particular behavior conform to the letter of the law while, in some cases, apparently representing a deviation from its intention. These were early and extensively developed to meet the adaptive challenge of coexisting with complex economic systems depending on mechanisms such as credit. An example of a legal stratagem bearing on the status of women is writing conditions for divorce into a marriage contract, to be invoked by the wife under specified circumstances. It is still the

man who is *doing* the divorcing, in accordance with religious law, but he
delegates some of his initiative to the woman. Although these go back
many centuries, it is not clear what the overall impact of the use of legal
stratagems is. They would seem to strengthen an emphasis on the letter
rather than the spirit of the law, a tradition of legalism that may be pervasive. This point relates to the whole unanswered question of how integrated a culture can be expected to be and what the effect on people is of
inconsistency. This kind of incremental process has occurred in other
scriptural religions and legal systems.

Another channel for change has been secular legislation, either side by
side with religious law or in some cases contradicting it and leaving it to
individuals to work out the logic of coexistence. All Muslim countries
today have large bodies of secular law, but in some the effort is made to
harmonize secular and religious law, while in others, such as Turkey, large
bodies of legislation simply override religious law. In spite of resistance,
conformity to secular law proceeds along with other processes of secularization, and the presence of such legislation and its enforcement by authorities other than the clergy are themselves forces toward secularization.

In terms of our earlier analogy of the structure of an old house, we
might ask how people experience these different mechanisms. Thus, it is
possible to imagine a Muslim woman able to initiate divorce against her
husband in the following ways:

1. On the basis of the community acceptance of a new *ijtihad* (which
   might not be labeled as such) arguing that the traditional status of
   women was a temporary phenomenon, due, for instance, to their
   lack of education, and that a right for educated women to initiate
   divorce is in conformity with the fundamental egalitarianism of
   Islam
2. On the basis of a legal stratagem which allows her her divorce and
   at the same time confirms the sole right of the husband to initiate
   divorce
3. Through a civil process by which she can subsequently remarry
   although neither the divorce nor the remarriage is recognized by
   religious law

How can we evaluate these alternatives? What are their long-term effects
on the structure? What is certain is that a religious community will not

want to embrace an interpretation that makes the tradition appear to have been in error. But there is always some degree of flexibility, and these alternative routes can coexist. Some of the same tactics have existed around divorce in various varieties of Christianity. Muslim women working for reform today tend to look for changes that will maintain symbolic continuity with earlier practice or that will discern a deeper implication in the words of revelation, like the argument that polygyny was implicitly forbidden by the impossible requirement that a man treat his wives with perfect equality. Outside critics may prefer radical reform and overt rejection. Islam, however, has a tradition of greatness, and that tradition includes the extraordinary adaptability of its early centuries, which can inspire profound reform, as well as a long era of rigidity and the capacity to adapt piecemeal. The choices will be essentially political.

Living in this farmhouse today, with respect for both past and present, may demand some compromise and improvisation. Preserving the look of the front of the house, for instance, while introducing modern features in the back — a picture window, a deck, or a new dormer that would require reinforcing the foundation — or retrofitting the building with new insulation. Some of the people we talk to advise tearing it down and beginning again. Others advise a new building on a new site. Still others talk of restoration to bring the building back to its original character, but this rather humble farmhouse was never particularly distinguished. The land has returned to forest, and we are not farmers, so we must shape this building for the present, using whatever remains sound from the past. The carpenters working on the foundations here refer to any new structure anchored piecemeal on the old and yet reinforcing it as "scabbing," and their fingers itch for more substantive renovation. But the cellar of the old farmhouse is already a maze of "scabbed" construction going back for generations of families for whom it has been home.

LEARNING IN LAYERS

Over the years I have cooperated on a number of projects with the Institute for Educational Inquiry in Seattle, which has had a long-term interest in the relationship between schooling and the development of democratic character. They have been especially interested in facilitating educational renewal by introducing new ideas at more than one level of systemic organization, for systems, whether nations or schools, tend to revert to familiar patterns in spite of efforts at reform. This piece, published in 2001, addresses the question of how a system can inculcate tolerance for various kinds of diversity, including the pluralism essential to democracy, by helping learners to be aware of different logical levels.

—MCB, 2004

My earliest memory of a lesson in how democracy works was in 1948. This was the year of the first post–World War II election; Harry Truman, who had become president through Franklin Roosevelt's death, was running against Thomas Dewey. Dewey was widely predicted to win, so as an eight-year-old, I assumed that my mother would be voting for him. No, she said, she would not be voting for Dewey, for she was a lifelong Democrat. However, she went on, it would not necessarily be a bad thing if Dewey won. I was puzzled, for I must have assumed that the campaign was about winning and that everyone would want to be on the winning side. You see, she said, the Democratic party had been in power for a very long time (because of FDR's multiple terms), and it is not healthy in a democracy when one party is out of power for so long that its elders forget how to behave in power and its younger members never learn.

The preceding paragraph begins with a deliberately ambiguous phrase: "how democracy works." By the age of eight, from school and the radio and overheard conversation, I clearly knew something about the office of president, about the process of voting, about parties and campaigns, or the conversation with my mother would have been impossible. What I lacked, and what apparently many citizens as well as politicians and journalists lack, was a more abstract knowledge about how democracy works: systemic understanding of the contexts in which these different elements fit together. Indeed, I had already acquired unconscious assumptions about the zero-sum characteristics of rightness, a win-lose approach that is arguably inimical to democracy. I suppose the conversation has stayed with me because it was so disconcerting, challenging abstract assumptions I could not have put into words. On the other hand, one could argue that the self-observation involved in knowing that I had heard something startling — and not immediately exiling it from memory and attention — was itself a valuable framework for questioning future assumptions, a foundation for future learning.

I doubt that I had ever considered the need in a democracy for both minority and majority positions. Unanimity and the search for complete consensus are not necessarily healthy, as demonstrated by the use of referenda in totalitarian regimes. The American system of democracy depends not only on the mechanics of voting and party politics but on a curious mental attitude that functions at two logical levels. On the one level, it is important to be committed to particular policies and directions, to have preferences and alliances, and to express them. On the next, and more inclusive, logical level, it is important to be committed to a process that may well defeat those preferences: to be able to say, when one's own candidate is defeated, that at least this is a victory for democracy. As a Democrat my mother supported Truman; as the citizen of a democracy she supported the process that might lead to Dewey's election, and she would have supported Dewey if that occurred. Her comments on the need to learn how to behave in office suggest empathy with both parties. Interestingly enough, she also recognized that particular decisions belong at particular systemic levels: it is probably not appropriate to decide whom to vote for as a way of tuning the party system, as in casting a protest vote for a candidate one would not want to see in office (there were four candidates in the 1948 election). Thinking about the election turns out to be layered, like an onion.

There is a significant but imperfect formal similarity between the layered quality of logical structures, which Russell and Whitehead described
as "logical types,"[1] the hierarchical structure of many organizations, and
the levels of inclusivity and embeddedness involved in systemic thinking.
Thus, a given party exists at one level of the democratic process, while the
party system is more inclusive and functions at the next level up (the party
system is not a party). Voting for a candidate as a way of criticizing the
process is somewhat like chewing on the menu instead of using it to order,
although voting in the election at all does support the system and the
menu is a useful start in ordering something edible. Only a little reflection
is needed to realize that no more than a fraction of the electorate thinks
this way about voting decisions and that the educational system does not
often encourage this kind of thinking, being all too committed to the
notion of right answers: if Dewey is the right answer, Truman is the
wrong answer, and vice versa.

The focus of this essay is the need to teach citizens to entertain multiple points of view and even to hold two apparently conflicting points of
view at different logical levels. This is increasingly necessary for living in
a world of high diversity and rapid change, which presses us all toward
either confusion or insight.[2] A range of skills is involved, some of them
emphasized in several kinds of social science methodology and areas of
training, but there are also "homely" skills underlying marriage and
family life, where individual interests also have to be seen in the context
of the larger whole. Our concern also includes the questions about the
assumptions supporting such skills, which are not easy to change, for the
institutions of society are in every case classrooms — contexts of learning
in the broadest sense — imparting or reinforcing assumptions, above and
beyond the goals of any specific lesson plan or the function of a given institution. What are the assumptions taught by a hospital, a jail, or the network news, above and beyond the performance of a specific task? How
about schools themselves?

Entertaining multiple points of view is relatively familiar in Western
pedagogy. We are often encouraged to try to imagine what we would feel
or do in someone else's shoes. How would you feel if you were Bobby and
someone spilled your juice? How would you feel if you were a factory
worker and your factory were closed? What must it have felt like to be
captured and carried across the ocean to a life of slavery? What would you
do about Iraq if you were president? Why do you think the fairy god-

mother in the storybook did what she did? How did the ogre feel when he faced the hero?

The ability to imagine oneself into totally changed circumstances is a powerful adaptive and creative force, especially when the imagination goes on to devise a way to get there. Yet this ability to imagine oneself in the shoes of someone whose life situation is totally different is not universal, as researchers on the process of modernization have discovered.[3] When Turkish peasants were asked what they would do if they were the head of the government, they answered, "My God! How can you say such a thing?" They could not know because they had not had the experience.

Empathy is not an altogether comfortable skill. A slave owner is better off unable to empathize with a slave, and a soldier is happier if he does not reflect on the fear and homesickness of another frightened boy like himself across the border. In situations of conflict or differential power, it is often the weaker party who understands how the stronger thinks and feels and is likely to behave: the conquered observe their conquerors acutely, while oppressors are careful not to identify with their victims or to observe their own behavior. True believers in any tradition prefer that alternatives be strictly unthinkable to them. Years ago I taught a course titled "The Peoples and Cultures of the Middle East," and after a section on Islam, a student from a Christian fundamentalist background came to me and said, in distress, "It never occurred to me that Muslims actually believe their religion." Similarly, I was disconcerted when a white student said to me in the 1980s, after reading the autobiography of a black author, "Why, he's really angry at white people." "Wouldn't you be?" was a question she did not know how to deal with. Training in conflict resolution, including the ability to phrase an opponent's point of view in terms acceptable to that opponent, has begun to spread through the public school system. But when that skill is applied to areas of profound conflict, as in the attempt to understand and empathize with the convictions of an opponent in the abortion debate, it can be profoundly disturbing.[4]

We do teach children to put themselves in the shoes of others, but only some others and only in limited ways. After all, the idea underlies a great number of religious traditions in the various forms of the Golden Rule, "Do unto others as you would have others do unto you," or, more pointedly in the Jewish version, "That which you hate, do not do to others." Taken too literally (that is, at the wrong logical level), the advice is bad, for others have different tastes and desires: don't give your daddy a teddy bear, but give him something that cheers his heart as a teddy bear does yours.

Participation in a democracy, however, requires not only an ability to acknowledge the beliefs and preferences of others but also the capacity to recognize that divergence is essential to the health of the larger system that includes both the self and the other. Here, moving up the logical ladder involves the resolution of a sort of paradox, which recalls the use of paradox in such traditions as Zen Buddhism as a possible pathway to enlightenment. Teaching at George Mason University, I often wonder about George Mason, a Virginia gentleman who was one of the framers at the Constitutional Convention but who declined to sign the draft Constitution. He understood that the Constitution was deeply flawed because it lacked a bill of rights and because it accepted slavery. He participated by refusing to participate; his critique and adamant withdrawal no doubt hastened the passage of the Bill of Rights in the form of amendments (although the abolition of slavery took another century, and Mason, like other framers, was caught in the paradox of owning slaves himself). Historically, it was essential that most of those present should compromise and provide a majority, but the minority position did eventually prevail. Was George Mason grateful that his was a minority position — so he could feel free to cleave to it, knowing that the work of the Convention would not be lost? Or did he simply go home with a sense of failure? Often enough in discussions, someone takes a position that is unlikely to prevail — at first — but is important to include in the debate.

Democracy requires the ability to say, in the words attributed to Voltaire, "I disapprove of what you say, but I will defend to the death your right to say it." Put differently, it requires the affirmation that there is more than one way of thinking and acting in a given situation, and that these alternatives can be embraced by individuals who are both reasonable and moral and therefore worthy of debating, so that individuals can make choices among the alternatives — and maybe formulate new ones, thereby increasing the freedom of choice for others. We are not speaking of relativism, however; relativism requires suspending judgment, appropriate in some contexts but not to the role of citizen, because there the willingness to make and defend choices and to commit to particular courses of action remains essential. The contrast here is with the habit of demonizing opponents (as opposed to saying their views represent plausible, though perhaps less desirable, alternatives), which tends to subvert democracy and leads to using the structures of democracy for tactical purposes only. Democracy requires that the victory of the other party, even if its members are sadly mistaken in their policies, not be unthinkable; that an affirmation of and loyalty to the overarching system give recognition and respect to those who disagree. In the United Kingdom, it is common to speak of Her Majesty's loyal opposition, a constant reminder that opposition is intrinsic to the system rather than alien and invasive.

Living in a society structured as a democracy and maintaining continuity and stability through a period of rapid change depends on these attitudes also, for what seems right today may seem wrong tomorrow, but is not thereby culpable. Revolutions, by contrast, require the rejection of a whole set of ideas and, usually, of people, declaring them totally wrong and even perhaps deserving of execution. More gradual change, including educational renewal, involves a steady flow of linked interventions while participants continue to function in an imperfect system. This requires a compassionate awareness of change and diversity as systemic characteristics and at least the partial acceptance of their necessity, recognizing and affirming what exists in the process of building something new. We are all dealing with systems whose survival through time has depended on their capacity to resist environmental pressures or, when forced to change, to limit that change in space and time. For the advocates of change, this entails thinking about themselves and their opponents in the context of loyalty to a system that includes them all. In effect, it goes beyond understanding the viewpoint of the other to thinking at a higher and more complex logical level. It also entails valuing the resistance to change, for purposive cultural change involves modifying self-correcting systems while maintaining their viability. For conservatives, it means accepting the inevitability of change, which is a characteristic of any living system, and struggling to make sure that change is genuinely adaptive.

The capacity to maintain potentially contradictory commitments at different levels of systemic organization, then, is valuable in a democracy, even if it is not realized in every individual. But what is especially relevant here is the fact that, although lesson plans (and their testing) are often conceptualized at a single logical level (characterized by lists), learning in general occurs at several levels simultaneously, whether programs are designed to create commitment and sensitivity at multiple levels or not. Thus, in the example of the Truman-Dewey election, although I had learned many specific details about the democratic form of government, I had also formed unstated assumptions in a variety of contexts about such issues as winning and losing or being right versus being wrong. The way in which learning is linked to context affects the transferability of learning — for instance, the application of a given school lesson outside of school.

Gregory Bateson used the term *deutero-learning* to refer to learning of this kind, where learning at one level, specified in a teacher's explicit goals, carries with it potential learning at the next logical level. Deutero-learning is often paraphrased as "learning to learn." The paraphrase is both accurate and inaccurate and should at least be expanded as "learning to learn in a given context," because the real issue is the development of unarticulated assumptions based on the characteristics of the context, sometimes so broad and so deeply rooted that these assumptions can be regarded as intrinsic to character and are almost impossible to change. Children who do well in school are children who have adapted to the school context. They have "learned to learn" particular kinds of lessons in spelling or history or arithmetic because they have absorbed the contextual assumptions within which these lessons are taught, all too often assumptions inappropriate to democratic society, like "might makes right" or "there is only one acceptable answer" (two alternative versions of "teacher knows best"), or destructive of other kinds of learning, such as learning from experience.

Gregory Bateson puts it this way, using the context of experimental psychology:

> In any learning experiment — e.g., of the Pavlovian or the Instrumental Reward type — there occurs not only the learning in which the experimenter is usually interested, namely the increased frequency of the conditioned response in the experimental context, but also a more abstract or higher level of learning, in which the experimental subject improves his ability to deal with contexts of a given type. For example, the deutero-learning of the animal subjected to a sequence of Pavlovian experiences will presumably be a process of character formation whereby he comes to live as if in a universe where premonitory signs of later reinforcements (or unconditioned stimuli) can be detected but nothing can be done to precipitate or prevent the occurrence of the reinforcements. In a word, the animal will acquire a species of "fatalism." In contrast, we may expect the subject of repeated Instrumental Reward experiments to deutero-

learn a character structure that will enable him to live as if in a universe in which he can control the occurrence of reinforcements.[5]

This suggests that our problem is with what schools teach without knowing it rather than with what they fail to teach.

Behavior can be changed by a variety of external pressures, rewards, or sanctions but may snap back if the underlying cultural system remains unchanged, and this is most visible in the preservation of old values after revolutions. A program for sustainable change must be based on a broad, abstract recognition of the interconnected systems involved, and even so may take several generations to become fully embedded.

All of these issues are relevant to educational renewal and illuminate some of the reasons for failure in the past. Effective change must be pervasive and systemic, becoming part of a new equilibrium but also subject to new processes of adaptation. Even as we explore possible ways of modifying educational programs in order to promote democratic character in the young, it is important to recognize that such a change is subject to all the vicissitudes of the larger system, as well as the logical limitations of most schooling. But the conclusion that leaps off the page is the strategy of introducing change at several systemic levels simultaneously. The Institute for Educational Inquiry (IEI) recognizes this fact by asserting that real changes in education can be achieved through simultaneous renewal in teacher training and in the schools themselves, for change in the one without change in the other is likely to be reversed. This recognition is only a partial solution to the "you can't get there from here" quality of culture change, for it leaves untouched a number of other interconnecting systems: the families and households from which pupils come (with the history of enculturation of all members thereof); the faculties, administrations, and students of schools of education; and the general public and the political systems that fund, accredit, and otherwise support schools and schools of education when these are recognizable to them as fitting previously learned standards. There is no limit to the complexity, but the dual process at IEI and the partnerships it engenders promise to create contexts for genuinely adaptive change and learning.

This is especially true of change in the patterns of cross-generational transmission, which is, after all, what schooling is all about. We are the "time-binding" species, not only in the sense that we can remember the past and plan for the future, but also in the sense that cultural patterns and their transmission from generation to generation are designed to sustain continuity, constraining change over time. "Education for change" is sometimes seen as a necessity, but sometimes the words come too glibly: from the perspective of human history, education for change is an oxymoron, a contradiction in terms.

The commonest strategy for change is to introduce it at the top, but we all know from experience how often this fails. It is clear that new policy that comes down in command form from the top of a hierarchical system will not automatically be expressed through all levels. This works only in highly authoritarian organizations, and even there, policy initiatives coming from the top are subverted and distorted as they work their way down, phenomena familiar from such contexts as the Roman Catholic Church and the U.S. Army. School systems contain both authoritarian and democratic elements, but these seem to combine to make any effective change even more difficult. The approach that the IEI offers suggests change not from the top down but at several points and at different logical levels. Simultaneous renewal proposes addressing several nodes so that the resonance between these nodes becomes a systemic characteristic at the next level up, particularly by training individuals to function at several points of the system and to give each other mutual support. This may not be enough to overcome the necessary conservatism of institutions, for it remains necessary to contend with entire tenured faculties who do not accept the new direction. Still, the impact of two professors teaching a new approach in a school of education is far more than double the impact of one. Two courses in a curriculum, two teachers in a school, even two books in a library can create an effective resonance for the learner by suggesting a metapattern. When the situation offers a contrast with two courses or two teachers, it also suggests moving up to a higher level.

One of the most interesting features of the program of the IEI is that it focuses on the question of education for democratic character in the context of asking how to promote systemic change. Character, in Gregory Bateson's sense, is precisely what is learned from the contexts in which lower-level learning takes place. We want our schools to be the kinds of places where young people develop pervasive assumptions about the world that are compatible with a democratic society. We suspect that teachers must develop such a character in order to transmit it and in order to foster the gradual renewal of the system. And we know that any change that is achieved will be the result of the imperfect processes of a society that is only partly democratic in its functioning. Whether we are discussing kindergarten through twelfth-grade classrooms or the lecture halls and seminar rooms of schools of education, we are faced with the need to look at multiple logical levels in order to make sense of a fluid, confusing, and frequently contradictory world.

Increasingly, learners need to make choices even as they receive incongruent and conflicting messages, and they need to be able to affirm a post-modern world in which such incongruities are part of the basic pattern. The necessary learning is unlikely to occur by precept, for teaching by precept notably ignores logical type differences, presenting "Love your neighbor" and "Sit up straight" as if these were parallel injunctions. We cannot simply specify "the right thing to do," for contexts shift and improvisation is critical.

Just as citizenship, conflict resolution, and psychotherapy pose the need for empathy, other areas of research or study also involve attending to more than one point of view and searching for resolution. The traditional methodology of anthropology (and sometimes of sociology) is participant observation, which involves just such a double awareness of self and the larger system and the possible dissonance between them, and this double focus has been enhanced and deepened by recent emphasis on reflexive methodologies. I believe that in her comment on the 1948 elections, my mother, the anthropologist Margaret Mead, revealed the stance of a lifelong participant observer. It should be possible to teach children to be participant observers, able to think about dissonance between their position and the characteristics of the larger system, in order to prepare them to be citizens, just as it should be possible to teach beginning teachers to be loyal critics of the school systems in which they are immersed.

My interest in discussing participant observation in this context came from asking myself the question, "What would you do if you had the possibility of designing only one course out of, say, sixteen that a given future teacher will take?" If a course directly counters the prevailing doctrine, most students will compensate by keeping it separate and forgetting it when they move to other settings; a few will become disciples of the maverick professor and probably be unemployable, for if they reject everything else, they will be converted but uneducated. If the goal is to use that one course both to introduce new ideas and to ensure that those ideas are integrated with other available ideas, it becomes necessary to introduce a process of thought that will be deutero-learned and follow the student into other contexts. My answer has been to propose teaching the skills of participant observation, including self-observation.

Participant observation involves two levels: I am present in the situation as a participant, and at the next level up I am outside the situation as an observer, so I am potentially aware of my double role and the ongoing situation that involves me in that double role.

A small example could apply to either a graduate student or a ten-year-old. Jan is invited to a meal at a neighboring house where one member of the household is known from school or from the workplace. Jan participates in the family meal, eating, joining the conversation, improvising some way of expressing appreciation. In the United States today, such an invitation may involve exposure to unfamiliar foods, table customs, and patterns of relationship.

At the same time, Jan is an observer, noticing and puzzling through the patterns in the behavior of others. The adaptive value of that observation may be effective conformity, learning to fit in, but Jan may be able to articulate the patterns observed in addition to simply imitating and may be able to make explicit comparisons. Part of our contemporary emphasis is on preparing the child not to reject whatever is new or unfamiliar, but tolerance is not enough without curiosity and respect.

Jan is more likely to be aware of being an observer if he or she comes from elsewhere, say another country or region, and has experienced alternative patterns, or if the neighbors belong to a different class or cultural group. Someone habituated to and trained in participant observation may become aware of several possibilities: discussing those observations with the hosts, making them also participant observers of the familiar pattern; reporting back on returning to familiar territory — perhaps influencing the alternative set of mores; beginning to tamper purposely with the pattern, whether through suggestions or initiatives; or making choices — resolving to practice some consciously chosen pattern in the future. Let us say that Jan is used to a sit-down meal, while the neighbor's household depends on catch-up meals, "grazing," and take-out. Or vice versa. Either pattern may be fascinating to someone accustomed to the other. In either case, the meanings of "home" and "self" may be changed. The differences are not trivial.

We can now explore the meaning of this experience. Let us first assume that Jan is enrolled in a graduate school of education. Participation in class is not usually reflexive — learning what you are told to learn is like eating what is set before you, except that the mores of the classroom require regurgitation. Graduate students do, however, all come from elsewhere in the sense that they have experienced other somewhat different kinds of classrooms and must acquire a slightly differing set of mores in order to conform, but the differences are not as great as forks to chopsticks. Teaching styles may vary also within the program, which can either strengthen it or weaken it.

Imagine now that Jan has been exposed to some experience (and this is the course we might choose to design) that makes him or her enter every classroom as a participant observer in the sense in which I am using the term. Jan notices patterns in the way each professor teaches and in the organization of the material, and questions these, pressing the professor to be increasingly self-observant, making comparisons, and challenging the others as well to consider alternative approaches. An awareness of variability becomes part of his or her work — exams and essays — and subsequent teaching style. Aware of making choices and influencing patterns, Jan begins to discuss this also, with colleagues, pupils, and mentors. Jan knows how to conform — how to play the game and meet a professor's or administrator's expectations — but also how to move up the systemic levels, to play a metagame. Without ever fully articulating what he or she is doing, Jan is able to model it for peers and colleagues and in responding to diverse learning styles as a teacher.

Jan has learned several lessons essential to living in a democracy and to teaching in a way that supports democracy: that there is more than one way of behaving in a given situation, ways of behavior that have their own order and elegance, patterns that can be described; that there are choices among these alternatives — and maybe new ones to invent; and that suggesting alternatives opens the freedom of making choices to others. With luck, Jan will go into practice teaching not as the apostle of a new dogma but as the practitioner of a new way of looking at dogma. Democracy requires all of these understandings.

The experience is no doubt different for a ten-year-old, and I believe it is even more important. Children encounter many profound contradictions: between households, between home and school and religious services, and as consumers of the media. To the extent that these experiences are simply juxtaposed, they may undermine the capacity to make sense of the world or support reactions of rejection or envy or confusion. Similarly, it is not sufficient to expose children to multicultural lists of differing customs, offering new and unresolved contradictions. In these confusing times, children need to learn to observe themselves observing even as they participate (even in the classroom, which in its own way is a foreign country from year to year) and simultaneously to move up logical levels when faced with contradictions.

A very small intervention in teacher training, involving training in participant observation and reflection on that experience, might change the way other parts of the system function. What Jan learns from each class may meet requirements and yet be different in logical structure from what the professor teaches; put simply, the professor may assert absolutes, and Jan may listen with respect but hear them as relative. As a teacher, Jan will also continue to learn, drawing lessons by reflecting on classroom experiences, relishing surprises, empowered by failures as well as successes. If we can design a model for teaching participant observation to both graduate students and ten-year-olds, we may also enable them to make the processes of teaching and learning mutual. Not a bad start in creating a school system that is itself able to learn and supporting in the next generation a necessary aspect of the democratic character.

THE LESSONS OF 9/11

The thinking in this essay originated in the weeks following the September 11, 2001, terrorist attack on the
World Trade Center in New York, as I revised lectures I
had earlier planned to give on four different campuses
and fiddled with the drafts of potential op-ed pieces,
hoping that the tragedy would lead to understanding
rather than intolerance. Unfortunately, trauma works
against learning, and following 9/11, U.S. national
policy moved in the direction of military solutions,
reduced debate, and defensive unilateralism.

— MCB, 2004

∽

"Everything is different"

When attitudes and perceptions shift profoundly, it is sometimes possible
to notice and learn from that shift — to compare what one thought one
knew beforehand with what one believes afterward. In effect, such a shift
provides a context for considering the *relative* nature of one's own knowledge and the appropriate respect to give to the beliefs of others. We always
see the world through a lens of assumptions that are only partially shared
even with those closest to us and are very different from the assumptions of
those more remote. A new recognition of contrasting perceptions can suggest changes in behavior and open up new kinds of curiosity and new potentials for empathy. The memory of having held different views and assumptions can become a reminder to remain flexible — or a reason for rigidity.

One of the things that Americans said repeatedly after September
11 was 'Everything is different." Taken literally, of course, this is an

exaggeration. There was a material change in the New York skyline, two huge buildings subtracted, and other changes in the urban fabric. Lives were lost and relatives and friends bereaved. Jobs disappeared. These are substantial changes that will continue to be felt as very direct and immediate. Most of us, however, if we say that everything is different, are talking about a change in perception — a change in the way we see the world and ourselves in it. This change in perception following 9/11 was not a simple subtraction, because it was pervasive, affecting the whole of experience as if the new present were viewed through a gray or yellow filter. Buildings seemed fragile and untrustworthy; so did corporations and investments. The sky itself seemed just a little different in states as far away from the event as cloudy Washington and cloudless Montana, yet it did not fall.

Part of that difference had to do with a sense of vulnerability: Americans, who had felt safe between broad oceans, felt newly at risk. Realistically, the vulnerability had been there previously, but it had not registered in the national consciousness. Terrorism had been known and written about in the press; Osama bin Laden had already attacked the World Trade Center once and had developed the strategy of multiple simultaneous attacks; the shift from using automobiles as bombs to using airplanes is not conceptually a large one and had been predicted, while the possible use of chemical, biological, or even nuclear weapons by terrorists has been providing plots for thrillers for decades. Yet human beings are notably bad at thinking about disasters that are known to be coming on an unknown date — like the "big one" in California or our individual deaths. Relatively few people would have been able to say that the only question open before the attack was when and in what specific form it would occur, but the inability to answer that question blocked consideration of others. Similarly, investors knew that many stocks were overvalued but found no way to think realistically about the implications. One wonders what else we are ignoring for lack of a specific date.

Arguably, the pervasive change in perceptions was more like removing a rosy filter through which life had been seen softened and eased. Hostility toward the United States is no new phenomenon, though it is one we often conveniently forget. It tends to surprise Americans when they are reminded that there are people who regard them with enmity and anger. It may also be surprising to discover the friends they have around them, all too often ignored or taken for granted. In the before and after of registering these attitudes, we could have remembered how certain policies result in hate, prolonging conflicts so that whole generations grow up knowing only war. The Treaty of Versailles sowed dragon's teeth, leading to decades of enmity. Other policies result in friendship. The Marshall Plan made the friendships of contemporary Europe possible. Immediately after 9/11, we could have noticed how much we suddenly cared about the support of our allies — and so renewed our support for the various treaties and international efforts, from Kyoto to land mines, that had previously seemed expendable.

Another way of using 9/11 to inform foreign policy would have been to compare our reactions to the terrorist attacks with our milder reactions to other kinds of dangers with far larger death tolls, like the steady stream of automobile fatalities or an epidemic like AIDS. Our intense sensitivity to this attack and to missiles in Cuba has something to teach about the special sensitivities of all communities to important symbols, especially the symbolic meaning of incursions and occupations. Reactions are not directly correlated with numbers of casualties or with the scale of material damage. We could consider how much the choice of the World Trade Center and the Pentagon added to our distress — and understand why many Muslims are especially sensitive to foreign troops near the Holy Cities.

It was important not to allow the terrorist attacks to leave us cowed but also important to avoid shifting into a purely reactive mode. The attacks could have made us more thoughtful, stimulating the imagination rather than pushing toward a defensive conformity, but at the national level, only the secretary of state, Colin Powell, seemed to feel that reflection should come before reflex. A narrowed and limited imagination is a common product of trauma, while new learning is itself a victory for the human spirit. So is empathy. "Everything is different" can be embraced as a way of understanding. After 9/11, I began inviting audiences to reflect on their own responses, emotional and intellectual, as a way of learning about themselves and about the nature of perception. It is crucial, even as we act to reduce future risks, to include and examine both subjective and objective responses — to approach these events with an awareness of feelings of anger and outrage, but also to approach them with an urgent curiosity: How do the attackers see the world? What leads them to behave this way? Having noted changes in our own perceptions, we could ask: How changeable is this or any other way of seeing the world?

Another way in which "Everything is different" showed up was in the wave of patriotic display that swept across the country. Suddenly red, white, and blue were appearing everywhere, and many of us failed to notice how mixing them with God talk in a soup of nationalism and religion was uncomfortably similar to the motivation of terrorism. Yet perhaps this resurgence of patriotic symbolism indicated for some not jingoism but a changed appreciation of citizenship. I asked a college student about all the flags, and he said to me, "You know, it never occurred to my friends and I [*sic*] to think about what it meant to be Americans. It was just something we could take for granted." So, for him, something peripheral was suddenly perceived as fundamental, in a way that might affect his participation and possibly even become a reason to vote. "Everything is different," because something taken for granted was noticed. One wonders how many fundamental realities are simply not salient in our thinking — the finitude of the planet, for instance, or the unity of the human species.

A further change in perception had to do with the financial structure of the world. There too "Everything is different" and may remain so for years to come. Money, of course, does not exist except by virtue of the social agreement to believe in its value — those green and gray pieces of paper are intrinsically worthless and useless for most purposes. Although our trust in the actual currency did not waver, our perception of the complicated structure of value associated with business — the people who guard and report on it, and the whole incredible virtual reality of credit we live in the middle of — was shaken, with very real practical implications. For secular people, the power of money and credit offers a way of thinking about the power of symbolism and belief. A friend of mine said to me the other day, when I was talking this way about money, "I see what you mean. We live in one of the great ages of faith." We believe that this incredible mythological construct represents reality, and as long as we believe it, it does. That faith was shaken, and because money is so pervasive in our understanding of the world, "Everything is different." Here too a comparison might suggest policy changes, not only in the functioning of the stock market but in our use of economic pressures in international relations. We could think deeply about the damage done to the U.S. economy by the attacks and understand that just as symbols are not harmless, economic warfare is not either. In affluent countries it leads to unemployment and lost savings, while in third world countries it can lead to famine and epidemic. We could look with new eyes at the weapon of economic sanctions, which affects ordinary people rather than governments.

Human beings live together in communities by virtue of what they can take for granted about each other. When common assumptions are lost, "Everything is different." The implicit assumptions we think of as "common decency" and "common sense" are something like common grazing land or fisheries, air or water, that all members of a community can use and that may cease to be self-renewing if overused or polluted. These "commons" are intangible, however, and the interests we share in them are harder to define. They include the range of reasonably expected behavior from most others most of the time that allows individuals to chart their path through the day in our intricately interconnected society, a weave of habit and helpfulness that we come to rely on.

The ability to walk the streets of a city without fear, for instance, is a resource that is shared by the city's people, a resource essential to their lives and livelihoods. That sense of security can survive occasional aberrations and violations, but when too many crimes occur it becomes depleted, a resource lost. In the same way, the willingness to stop and give directions or help someone in trouble and the readiness to believe that public officials are basically honest and that doctors and policemen will help when needed are part of the fabric of life. The assumption that newspapers and scales are mostly accurate and that flowers planted near the sidewalk will not be gratuitously vandalized — these too are part of the commons that make civilized life possible. When times are bad, a shared belief in light at the end of the tunnel keeps people struggling to survive, and the sense of common purpose allows individuals to face death with the trust that what they died for will continue. After 9/11 the sense of living in a predictable world was shaken, and neighbors were newly perceived as strangers.

These social commons have in fact been eroding for some time, as we have steadily reduced the claims of our traditional versions of common decency and common sense. Violations of common decency have been so highly publicized that they are no longer seen as exceptional. We have come to believe that any president may be a crook and that any adult may commit child abuse. One of the effects of the Holocaust has been to convince us all that what happened in Germany could happen anywhere. Indeed, whenever and wherever the unthinkable occurs, thinking is altered forever. The events of 9/11 damaged the tenuous sense of trust and security very deeply, damage only slightly reduced by efforts at reconstruction ranging from charitable donations and candlelight memorials to celebrations of "America's heroes" in the police and fire departments.

The costs of depleting the sense of trust and security extend from empty flower beds to citizens afraid to walk out their own front doors or to travel or invest abroad, from failures to seek medical help in a timely way to pervasive cynicism about the political process. We may become ready to greet virtually all information with a mixture of disbelief and unreasoning credulity, for lack of a common . . . sense of what is likely to be true. When the twin towers imploded it felt as if the impossible had happened, so who could know what would come next? All efforts to protect the material commons rely on the social commons: the trust that covenants can protect their use and that most users will respect them. As game theorists have demonstrated, cooperative solutions to non-zero-sum games depend on trust: without trust, betrayal is rational. Even as we consider the measures necessary for the protection of material commons like the atmosphere and the oceans, we need to be on the alert for analogies to social commons, above all the gradual international growth of respect for human rights and international law, so that these can be enhanced and protected as well.

Unfortunately, in trying to protect and restore a sense of common safety, we are moving toward institutionalizing mistrust and heightening anxiety with measures that invade privacy and can never be fully effective. It is apparently easy to think that only an enforced uniformity will protect the social commons. Like many human efforts, these measures have unintended consequences, so we can say of our dwindling sense of community and of the rights protected by the Constitution that here too, "Everything is different." In fact, tolerance of ambiguity is a necessary component of common sense. We can do rather well with good but imperfect security and partial agreement, combined with a willingness to debate and try to understand other viewpoints, and this possibility has been enshrined in rights now threatened.

Out of all this difference a valuable new understanding could be salvaged: the discovery that different perceptions are possible, a new awareness that any understanding of the world is relative. Perception depends on experience — who you are and where you come from. Americans experienced, after September 11, a number of painful changes in our perceptions of the world and the way we believe other people perceive us. Many of the actions taken after 9/11, which look like practical responses to the event, were ways of avoiding the new perception by translating the threat into familiar forms and acting in familiar ways, including the outpouring of money for the victims without any particular vision of what needed to be done. Because terrorism proved to be a bewildering enemy, we turned our need for action into a familiar kind of action against nations and found warfare comforting. What we resisted in every way we could was the need to reflect on what it means when, from one day to the next, the world is seen with new eyes. Yet this is an experience to be embraced. It is not surprising that one reaction in American society was a denial of the necessity of different points of view, so that debate became nearly impossible.

Comparison Is Key

There are a range of experiences that may lead you to say, "Last week I saw the world that way, this week I see it this way." The shift in view caused by 9/11 was such an experience, which made it an important opportunity for self-reflection. Comparison is key. The moments when individuals experience a change in perception are moments of opportunity, most especially if we can recall the thoughts and feelings that preceded the shift. Different peoples look at the world differently, and it is difficult — indeed, never fully possible — to see the world through other eyes. What you see and what you think does have some relationship to what others see and think, but there is a relativity there, depending on point of view and experience. This means that noticing one's own changing perceptions is key to understanding others.

When John Kennedy was assassinated, many people suddenly remembered thinking of him — living — as a great president, even if only days before they had been ambivalent. Couples who divorce sometimes describe their marriages as having been uniformly unhappy, but usually there really was a time in the past that seemed good, a time that might be worth remembering — if only for sober consideration when those same hopeful feelings recur. It takes an effort to seize the experience of seeing the same person, situation, or idea in more than one way, since both may be true, or neither. Sometimes yet a third vision may be more useful.

Since World War II, the world has seen radical shifts of opinion and perception, and many of them seem to have been positive. Sixty years ago, friendship between France and Germany was unthinkable, alliance between the United States and Japan impossible, and colonial empires an accepted form of policy. Within a few short years after being an ally, the Soviet Union became the Evil Empire, but now we cooperate with the former Soviet Union on space flights. Fifty years ago, legal segregation was taken for granted throughout the American South; women were widely seen as incapable of doing advanced work in science or making tough decisions; homosexuality was seen as perverse disobedience to God's laws — and as for the environment, it was a trivial issue left to "little old ladies in tennis shoes."

If our perceptions can shift so radically and so rapidly, are so clearly relative to circumstance, can we imagine how other circumstances would forge the perceptions of Palestinian children reared in refugee camps? Can we use our imaginations to understand why terrorists act as they do? Both love and hate have a context and a history. We could learn to question assumptions and policies. We could decide to be more widely loved and respected.

A sudden shift in vision is easiest to focus on, but our view of the world changes steadily through a lifetime, and we are constantly learning new information that subtly shifts the focus. As a society, we are changing what we "know" all the time. Medical advice, for instance, keeps changing, so that ways to lose weight or handle infants are rewritten every decade. Sometimes the changes are trivial or move very slowly, but even then it is useful to pause and notice that one has held a belief, accepting it from the social environment, and has later replaced or discarded it.

Values and ethical standards change also. Because I grew up in an anthropological household, I thought of myself as growing up with a very liberated set of attitudes, without prejudices, but I had to learn that the supportive and tolerant attitude toward physical handicaps with which I had grown up did not stand the test of emerging ethical understandings about the right to access and full participation. Noticing that shift in understanding was an important experience for me, because any prejudice or bias that is outgrown is a signal to look out for others. Attitudes have to keep changing; it would be helpful, in passing on current attitudes to children, to indicate their mutability, so that out of that awareness they might forge a new kind of constancy.

Sometimes I suggest to people, as a way of becoming aware of their own change, that they reread a book that was important to them a long time before. Something read in college and then read again at forty — I've got to tell you, it's not the same book; somebody got in there and erased the ink and rewrote it to say something different. A place that you loved when you were six may suddenly seem smaller at twenty. Someone got in there and shrank it. Going back to a place, a person, or a text is in fact a way of becoming aware of the relativity of perception. The same thing happens, however, in trying to understand motives for past action: How could one have felt so enamored of this person who suddenly appears rather ordinary? How could a particular action have inspired such rage? How could a situation that has come to seem manageable have inspired such panic?

The same thing is true of political causes, so perhaps we should approach them a little more cautiously. There is a great deal I would passionately like to see changed: I worry about social and environmental justice, the rights of women and indigenous peoples, the profound threats that our economic and technological habits pose to the viability of the planet. But I no longer wish for the power to set them right, both because the process of *setting things right* is likely to make them worse and because I understand that my own convictions are subject to revision. Nor do I expect to find candidates to vote for who fully reflect my positions. With the passage of time I am more willing to be content with small gains and less utopian in my hopes and efforts, while I remain convinced of the need to go on working and writing and voting. Above all, I have become aware of the destructiveness of the search for absolutes.

For anthropologists, the awareness that perceptions are relative often comes from fieldwork, as it does for many Americans who go to live in another country, where in order to make sense of experience they must acknowledge a different view of the world. People who work closely with infants, observing behavior and trying to understand what is going on in the mind of a three-year-old, or closely observing another species, trying to understand apes or dolphins or even frogs, have the same opportunity. There is a famous essay called "What the Frog's Eye Tells the Frog's Brain."[1] We think our eyes evolved to tell us what is there, but what they tell us is a rather specialized and highly interpreted version, with various corrections and distortions built in. The frog's eye tells the frog's brain what it needs to know in order to catch a fly. That simple. Information about something moving of about the right size, which is what the frog needs to know to survive. What human eyes tell us is rich and complicated, but we always have to remember that it is only what our brains can process and what the lens of experience allows us to think about.

When Margaret Mead discussed gaining this kind of insight, she used to end by saying, "You could fall in love with an Old Russian." By this, she didn't mean an elderly Russian, she meant a pre-revolutionary Russian — New York used to be full of them — the point being that falling in love with someone from a totally different culture combines the earthshaking experience of falling in love with the experience of cultural difference. My sister lived in Thailand for a time with a Thai boyfriend. She has since described this as a wonderful preparation for marriage, because whenever he did something that upset her, instead of feeling that he was doing it on purpose to hurt her, she would remind herself that he came from a different culture, so his behavior might have a different meaning for him. But she went on to say that after she married an American, she found she "had to keep on the same way."

A more drastic but related path to realizing that a given way of seeing the world is not absolute is having a psychotic episode and recovering from it: you can remember what it was like to live in a universe that felt very different. A lot of young people pursued a similar experience in the 1960s and 1970s by taking LSD. They took psychedelic drugs to see the world anew, because for a period of hours everything — time, colors, space, human faces — became different, even more powerfully than in falling in love. In that era they called such experiences "mind-blowing," which is a pretty accurate term for the impact of seeing the World Trade Center implode. Mind-blowing.

Whatever the path we take to it as individuals or as a society, relativizing perception is a first step in building community in spite of difference, and of buffering the discomforts of contrast. You are not going to give up your own way of seeing the world or throw it away. You will just get it clear in your mind that yours is one of many possible ways of looking at the world, and not the absolute way. The second step is to realize that the people you see every day — not just people in other countries but the people you go home to or work with — also see the world rather differently.

The whole point of the human institution of the family is that a group of people who are different from one another — male, female, old, and young — work together and contribute differently to the household and to the future. Of course men and women, adults and children, have different values, of course they have different priorities and see things differently. The only circumstance under which you might assume that all family members see the world in the same way is if you happen to be in a culture where there is just one person who is allowed to say what the family thinks — and you can guess who that one person usually is. As soon as everybody gets a chance to express her or his view and be listened to, what you discover within a household is a lot of diversity and a lot of change going on, a pluralistic family. Changes move like waves through society, so they are experienced first as differences between individuals, with family members surprising and then learning from one another. A necessary precondition to community building across lines of religious, ethnic, and racial difference is, I believe, to become aware of the diversity of the people under the same roof — and to see one's own views in relation to those of others. How on earth can we deal with people who are profoundly different in their ways of viewing the world unless we honor the most intimate kinds of diversity?

The Rejection of Difference

When someone undergoes a religious conversion, the awareness of a changed belief system does not generally produce tolerance — on the contrary, it may lead to a wholesale rejection not only of the beliefs of others but of the convert's own earlier beliefs and the people with whom they were shared. The terrorists of 9/11 understood, of course, that their perceptions of the world were different from those they associated with America, which they had learned to hate. Although they had grown up as Muslims, they also rejected the perceptions of many Muslims, for joining an organization like Al Qaeda is akin to undergoing a religious conversion. If you experience only one such shift in how you see the world, without understanding that it could go either way, it is easy to say that you were simply wrong before, and to reject the previous way of seeing — in Al Qaeda's case to condemn the beliefs of ordinary Muslims or of Muslim leaders. This is the kind of switch that produces fanaticism. Only if you have been through this kind of transition more than once do you have the chance to see that your own present vision, even as you treasure it, cannot

be taken as fixed and absolute. It is a relativizing experience to undergo a
religious conversion and then step back and withdraw from it or feel it
fade: One day you see life one way, the next day you see it another way,
but then, perhaps years later, the new way of seeing life is also no longer
compelling. It works in the opposite direction as well. A Jesuit friend once
remarked that those who have lost their faith and then returned have the
deepest faith.

However great the effort to maintain orthodoxy, there is variation
and diversity in every community, but there is always a risk, especially in
religious groups, that conviction and advocacy may go tragically wrong
when alternative views are condemned too sharply, putting even pluralistic societies at risk. In the context of 9/11, it is important to distinguish
groups like Al Qaeda from stable Muslim communities as these exist
around the world, but this distinction needs to be made in the context of
an understanding of religious movements in general, for analogues of Al
Qaeda have existed in virtually every significant religious community.
From time to time in each of the universalistic religions, groups have
arisen that are literally and actively inimical to every variation in belief,
whether derived from a different historic source or arising from within
the community. In every religious tradition, groups appear that focus on
a fragment of a larger belief system, pulled out of context and used as a
basis for behavior that more integrated and grounded believers reject.
Outsiders can attempt to understand their dedication, but the members of
the group are unwilling to empathize with anyone outside. Indeed, they
are converts from the beliefs of the broader community to a narrowed
version of those beliefs, from which flexibility and diversity have been
excluded, even to the point of death.

The members of Al Qaeda are such a group within Islam, as are the
Aum Shinrikyo, the group that spread poison gas in the Tokyo subway,
within Buddhism. Christian examples range from fourth-century heretics
who sought heaven by violently provoking martyrdom to the People's
Temple in Jonestown. Jewish examples include the followers of Rabbi
Meir Kahane, some of whom have turned to terrorism. This kind of
metastasis has happened often enough so that many thinkers simply feel
that religious belief is intrinsically destructive.

Although the word *cult* is employed in a variety of ways, it can usefully be reserved for groups that, although they are rooted in larger traditions, falsify those traditions by emphasizing a single element at the

expense of others. Again and again cultists have laid aside the commandments to *live rightly* — that is, with justice or love, compassion or peace — in this life in favor of self-torture, suicide, or murder in the name of the next. When cults arise within a community, those who do not join them are often ambivalent, recognizing elements of a shared tradition and a common longing; it is easy to see the cultists as more committed, more willing to make sacrifices. Yet cultists typically reject the majority understanding and segregate their followers. For cultists, whatever is different is wrong.

The commonest element to be pulled out of context in a cult is the expectation of a future event, the coming of the Messiah or the Mahdi or the end of the world. Judaism, Christianity, and Islam all have strong apocalyptic elements, which have repeatedly inspired violence. It is possible to become obsessed with other elements of belief as well, as some Christians have become so obsessed with their hatred for abortion or homosexuality that they forget the gentler teachings of their faith. Restoration has also been an important theme of cults, especially where warfare or colonialism have disrupted the lives of whole societies, as in the rise of nativistic movements hoping for the resurrection of the ancestors, the elimination of European colonists, or the restoration of a disrupted environment.

Al Qaeda has many of the hallmarks of a cult, emerging from Islam but distorting Islam and rejecting other Muslims. In Afghanistan, Al Qaeda apparently followed a classic pattern in which recruits were separated from friends and family for an intensive period of indoctrination and training. They were taught to give allegiance to a charismatic leader, to regard outsiders as inimical, and to ignore the calming and moderating influences of a wider community. They were told that they were chosen to restore a truth from which others had deviated, and that the leadership of the Muslim world had apostatized and been corrupted. Their vision is not the end of time but the restoration of a victorious Islamic empire, spanning the continents, and their Jihad is a violent mission of purification and preparation.

Each of the world's great religions has needed both the capacity to adapt and the capacity to maintain continuity. Each has changed and has developed substantial internal diversity. Each has had to recognize from time to time that certain customs may be alien to the faith when practiced in a new context. Mature religions blend the fervent vision of the original texts with the wisdom of experience, offering inspiration to both believers and nonbelievers and tolerating a certain degree of ambiguity. They produce art and poetry and even science, and become the basis of civilizations, as Islam has done.

In the contemporary world, however, where there are so many changes to adjust to, requiring so much flexibility, it is a common reaction to try to turn back the clock and escape from ambiguity. There are many movements attempting to reinstate earlier, stricter forms of specific traditions, which are loosely grouped together under the borrowed term *fundamentalism*. Al Qaeda has associated itself with fundamentalist forms of Islam and with Islamist groups demanding the political enforcement of Islamic law, but many Muslims recognize it as a distortion of the Islam they know and treasure. Cults do seem more likely to arise in the context of fundamentalism, taking religious texts literally and rejecting development and any consideration of alternative points of view. Christian Fundamentalist parents, for instance, have gone to court to protect their children from schoolroom discussions of other beliefs, including Greek mythology, for fear that the very notion of alternatives might corrupt, while other Christians vehemently protest their narrowness. Fundamentalists typically try to get governments to enforce ancient codes of law on believers and nonbelievers alike. Cults often seem to arise in the context of fundamentalism, but fundamentalist movements are neither as tightly knit nor as likely to turn to violence as cults, which often focus on a single distorted element taken from a larger system of belief.

Extremist groups may arise repeatedly within any religious tradition, but they are unlikely to survive their founders, for the world they want to save will ultimately reject their narrowed vision of creation. One might argue that cults, in their adherence to narrow and specialized doctrinal positions, represent a kind of belief that has always been destructive and cannot be sustained in the contemporary world, but that tends to be self-reinforcing within the closed cult community. Violent cults tend to escalate their actions and eventually to self-destruct or be destroyed. Sometimes, however, they may broaden and mature, becoming respectable and even modestly pluralistic. Once a cult moves beyond the leadership of a single individual and an obsession with a fragment of a complex tradition, it has a chance of becoming a mainstream denomination or a specialized group (like a religious order), as one piece of a larger moderating mosaic. As different aspects of the tradition become available and different voices can be heard, the former cult may regain the capacity for self-correction and balance and, ultimately, for reform and adaptation. A growing acceptance of internal diversity seems to be critical to this transition.

Cultists believe that the world can be reconstructed along the lines of their vision, on the ashes of the conflicts they trigger. Even in secular contexts, the focus on building a perfect world militates against relativity and breeds authoritarianism. Conversely, relativity is the best immunization against cultlike behavior. Those with eyes fixed on a single vision have no patience with alternative perceptions or hard work for small, thoughtful reforms, and little compassion for those who stand between them and their vision.

My husband and I have followed two revolutionary movements because of periods living where they occurred: the Iranian revolution at the end of the seventies and the overthrow of the Marcos regime in the Philippines in the eighties. I have also followed the many liberation and counterculture movements in the United States in the sixties and seventies and the *aggiornamento* of the Roman Catholic Church in the fifties. I have vivid memories of the joyful hope in the streets of Tehran and the friendliness among people in the crowds after the shah had departed, and it is worth remembering that Afghans welcomed the Taliban for their promise of restoring order. However, in observing revolutions you notice how sometimes the system reverts to old patterns, frequently with a loss of the flexibility that made the old, corrupt ways more bearable. In a confusing world, the call for moral clarity becomes recognizable as a kind of religious quest, an emerging orthodoxy, within which true believers, marked by the fervor of their commitment, are endowed with a sort of charisma, especially when the alternatives seem painful or chaotic. The destructiveness of visionaries and the loss of momentum when reality reasserts itself may only slowly become obvious. Constructive compromise proves to be more important than radical consistency.

The twenty-first century requires a new order of relativity, for the context is now global and the costs of intolerance rise steadily. Today, just as we are concerned with protecting biological diversity, there is increasing concern for cultural diversity. Cultural diversity is a valuable source for the human species of resilience and creativity, both locally and globally, but is increasingly at risk. On the one hand, we face a loss of local diversity as small, isolated, and preindustrial communities are swallowed up in majority national cultures. Here it is important to affirm that every cultural tradition is intrinsically valuable by trying to prevent peoples from being forced to change, particularly when hunting grounds and grazing lands are taken away — and to preserve a record of what was and what new patterns are emerging. Often, however, this is a rearguard action. All such communities are exposed to outsiders, to increasing and accelerating change. At the same time, there are pressures toward conformity of opinion in large nations, driven by market forces, by the media, and often by autocratic governments, that hinder the creation of new kinds of diversity. Internal variety, like the individual experience of fluctuating opinions, is a resource in adapting to change. Because it is not possible to contain or prevent change, the efforts to do so lead to horrors like Pol Pot's Cambodia and Afghanistan under the Taliban.

Most human beings through history have regarded change as intrinsically bad and everything subject to change as already shadowed by corruption. Gold is valued for its "incorruptibility" — it is very nearly inert — and the sacred has been conceptualized as immutable rather than as fluid, growing, and changing, as it surely potentially is in human consciousness. Today we are beginning to regard change as intrinsically good, which presents a new set of dangers. Change is a constant, but it is frightening and even lethal without time for adaptation, as can be seen from the destructive helter-skelter conversion to capitalism after the dissolution of the Soviet bloc. The most appropriate stance may be to try to slow the modern embrace of headlong change, not necessarily to stop it but only to ensure enough time to understand the multiple linkages and effects of a given change and, if necessary, to accommodate to them; those who campaign to prevent change and those who wish to accelerate it may be equally dangerous.

Diversity in change is itself valuable, for both conservatives and pioneers play a useful role. At different times the Scandinavian nations and the Netherlands have acted as pioneers — or laboratories — of social change, consciously adopting new policies and taking care to evaluate them. Where and how will the traps and hazards of biotechnology be worked out before the creation of huge vested interests? And why are many new ideas, like three-strikes law enforcement and high-stakes testing, picked up so rapidly before they are fully evaluated? Within a federal system like the United States, it makes sense for one state to experiment with complex and ambiguous legal innovations, as Oregon has been willing to pioneer the concept of physician-assisted suicide. Members of the right-to-life movement should be reminded of their argument that abortion rights became federal law too quickly, without local decision making and experimentation, and should permit the voters of Oregon to continue their local dialogue, but instead they tried to constrain the direction of change at the national level. Americans laugh sometimes at the speed with which new trends develop in California — but California benefits the nation both by its successes and by its failures.

Are there limits then to the respect and tolerance that should be extended to the beliefs of others? The limiting criterion seems to be the determination to impose those beliefs. Relativity entails a patient effort to understand but not necessarily concurrence. As we become aware of social and personal change, it will be important to differentiate between change that increases diversity and therefore resilience and change that tends toward a potentially brittle homogeneity. Similarly, a respectful memory of one's own earlier opinions and perceptions, instead of rejection and condemnation, is useful ballast in the storm.

Day after day, everything is different. There is a link between the diversity that exists within a group and the group's capacity to adapt. The willingness to entertain new ideas is based on past experiences of learning and sustained curiosity, but trauma works against learning, so when catastrophe strikes, the tendency is to lose flexibility and openness, just at the moment when they are most needed. Al Qaeda could not destroy the United States. The question is whether it will have impaired our hard-won capacity to tolerate divergent views and empathize with and learn from other human beings. To the extent that 9/11 makes us value security over freedom, the terrorists will have made us more like themselves.

~ IV ~

Ways of Knowing

INTRODUCTION

Just as anthropology traditionally dealt with whole cultural systems, from nutrition to poetry, it has spanned the academic divisions of knowledge. Anthropology can be included among the social sciences, the natural sciences, and the humanities, in spite of the different ways of knowing associated with each.

It was my good fortune to grow up in an environment where the lines between disciplines were routinely crossed. My mother had moved from psychology to anthropology for her doctorate and drew on the aspects of psychological theory and method that interested her all her life, while my father grew up with natural history and continued to turn to biology for models, with an emphasis on observation rather than laboratory experiment. He also used natural history as a way of interacting with me, teaching me about ecology before there was an environmental movement.

Today, environmentalism has entered the national and global consciousness and become a familiar part of political debate, but the idea was new in the sixties, often attributed to Rachel Carson's 1962 book, *Silent Spring*. Gregory believed that the human behaviors which threaten the balance and viability of the biosphere must originate in flawed assumptions underlying our patterns of perception, thought, and knowledge, which is to say he thought the problem was epistemological, rooted in mental habits that pervade daily life as well as religion and, often, science. The sharp divisions that are sometimes made between "nature" and "nurture," for instance, are partly an artifact of the way knowledge is organized and valued, with each discipline claiming primary importance and validity for its subject matter. Such turf battles are bound to lead to distortion, for any aspect of the human experience is necessarily undergirded by physical and biological possibility and evoked by cultural potentiality. Parceling "nature" and "nurture" out to separate disciplines generates nonsense and bad social policy. Again, the separation of our species from "nature" (in a different sense) has a similar negative effect, as does the separation of mind and body. Although epistemology seems highly abstract, unconscious epistemological assumptions tend to shape decision and action.

Part 4 deals with ways of knowing, including papers that cross disciplinary lines or question traditional models of research, problem solving, or policy making. The branches of philosophy called epistemology (how we know) and ontology (the nature of existence) sometimes seem to converge, so it is not always clear when we are trying to discuss one and when we are trying to discuss the other. Assertions about what exists are ontological — but how can we know what exists? Every ontological statement rests on an epistemological foundation, and these may vary, so the epistemological underpinnings of assertions about human rights or aesthetics or psychiatry are very different. Epistemologists may also notice the possibility of alternative ways of thinking about and perceiving the *same* phenomena, which might have very different consequences for decisions, and they may point out the implications of unstated cultural assumptions or suggest that new questions need to be asked or new connections noted. Some ways of organizing knowledge might tend toward destructive actions, while others might not.

Humans often think in analogies, so assertions about the human body or the family can affect our way of thinking about the planet, and vice versa. Scientific knowledge is fractionated and incomplete, so other ways of knowing might offer choices in dealing with uncertainty. Thus, there may be a vast range of myths, metaphors, and religious beliefs that allow people to live at peace in and with their world in spite of not having all their scientific descriptions and cybernetic formalisms down pat and explicit. Perhaps some traditional ways of thinking about the cosmos which already command deep loyalties can suggest norms of conduct that are respectful and compassionate to other human beings and to the rest of the natural world, and this is a more modest and accessible goal than complete description and the control it promises. Perhaps some religious answers are more viable than others. Even in science there are alternative ways of organizing information, so we can also hope for emerging formulations that make systemic thinking more accessible.

This essay was written as a chapter for a 1996 book dealing with education for democracy. It ended up affirming the importance of congruity between ecological systems and social systems, and the possibility that the organization and conduct of individual classrooms could implicitly convey an understanding of systemic relationships within complex wholes — an understanding that would be holistic in the original sense of the word.

—MCB, 2004

༄

A father is brushing his teeth, busily moving the brush up and down while water swirls into the sink and down the drain. His six-year-old son appears beside him and pulls at his sleeve. "Dad, you're not saving the earth," he says.

This is a scene played out in hundreds of households in different permutations. "Mom," my daughter said, "don't tell me you're still using paper napkins." My friend's daughter has multiplied the number of recycling bins in their home and examines every piece of packaging. When his mom pulls up to a fast-food restaurant, the little boy in the backseat says, "Ugh, not hamburgers. Don't you know they're ruining the rain forest?" And from another child we hear, "I don't care if you've had that fur coat for ten years, just don't wear it when you come to pick me up." Clearly, the last two decades have seen the accelerating creation of an ecological consciousness in children, both in schools and through television and other media. A number of organizations are focusing on ecological education, and materials and curricula are being widely developed.

Arguably, changes in human treatment of the biosphere, the slowing and reversing of existing patterns of degradation and exploitation, must be rooted in childhood learning. A new attitude toward the living world requires a new kind of common sense, new fundamental assumptions, changed expectations and aspirations. A move to sustainability will require a rethinking of both education and the processes and institutions of democracy.

So far, the process is piecemeal. On the one hand, I suspect that few children are proposing canceling vacation trips because of the consumption of hydrocarbons. On the other hand, many of those who are working on the promotion of ecological consciousness through education manage to leave unacknowledged the fact that the changes involved are deep and profound, not only in patterns of consumption and travel but also in basic philosophy. For a long time, nature programming on television was regarded as essentially innocuous and noncontroversial (unlike, say, ethnographic programming), but this is changing and will change further. Today, every visit to the zoo is likely to include information about which species are threatened and why, which begins to open up the issues of competing interests. Kittens and puppies have always been used to teach gentleness and responsibility; today, whales and pandas are used to translate the infant's need for love in the immediate environment of the home into social concern. It is not possible to deal for very long with environmental issues without addressing fundamental questions of birth and death, ancient beliefs about the nature of the good life, about what human beings want and need and what our rights might be in a complexly interlocked biological system, and about how political systems must be structured to take these wants, needs, and rights into account.

Furthermore, I would argue that if ecological issues are to be addressed at any depth, they must be addressed in the *processes* of education as well as in the content. Many of the traditional habits of education are linked to assumptions that have been marked out as sources of environmental dissonance, including the assumption that knowledge can be separated from participation, the value of competition as a classroom tool, the ideal of objectivity, and the efficacy of rationality.

The ecological component in education is sure to become increasingly hotly contested, for it is by no means neutral. Elementary school children are emerging in this country as an earth lobby. It is entirely appropriate that they should do so, for ecological damage is slow and cumulative and they are the ones who will suffer tomorrow the consequences of today's shortsighted policies. Ecological education may be the front line of values education in this country, partly because of the implicit lessons it carries for thinking about other kinds of community, for identifying goals to strive for, and for critiquing business as usual among people as well as between humans and other species.

New ecological understandings demand genuine change. Sustainability is still a long way from being a shared value, from motherhood and apple pie, for Americans carry the memory of pioneers who could simply move on to new forests and grasslands rather than conserving what they had, and as a nation we have perhaps gone further than any other in our faith in technology. The conservation of natural beauty has been around as a rather specialized concern for some time, but it is not enshrined in our founding documents, and the scriptures of Judaism and Christianity have long been read to license human irresponsibility. Furthermore, even the tradition of conservation that we do have is conceptually different from the emerging emphasis on preserving the systemic integrity of the biosphere. We scramble to find ways to link environmental values with older frames of reference, such as in talk of stewardship. Activists search for constitutional arguments, but the Bill of Rights contains no protection for any life other than human. Still, I believe it may be possible to find a certain congruence between the traditions of democracy, if only we read them more inclusively, and the emerging themes of ecological concern. We may be moving toward an understanding of ecology that brings humanistic values — respect for the integrity of others above all — into the debate and ecological arguments into our attitudes toward human relations.

Ecology has three faces in the classroom. The debate about ecological education can be expected to shift between these different points of view.

The first face, *empirical ecology,* is the most obviously academic and practical, drawing on several fields of biology as well as on geography and meteorology to offer children a knowledge of the world they live in and the ways it is changing. It is worth noting that this is an area in which efforts to make education more concrete and experiential — such as field trips, tests of air and water, experiments with plants, and the keeping of aquariums — are likely to be successful. Ecology in the classroom builds upon earlier traditions of nature study that were more taxonomic. It is one thing to collect and identify different leaves, another thing to discuss the interrelations of the various species in a given biome. Bird-watching becomes ecological when watchers attend to the niches of different species rather than simply accumulating lists of sightings.

The second face of ecology in the classroom is *environmentalism,* which turns the discussion to the decision making and actions of human beings and is political, involving policies affecting a range of interest groups. The environmentalist side of ecology is often reflected in school projects: cleaning up a marsh or a wood, planting trees, organizing recy- cling drives. It seems possible that environmental action will educate a new generation for activism, as the generation of the sixties was educated through the civil rights movement. Projects like boycotting McDonald's for using styrofoam containers might function in the same way as pick- eting Woolworth's for segregating lunch counters did for young people long before they went south to register voters; but different fields of activism no doubt result in different kinds of participation. Action for the environment can be projected out to South American rain forests, but it also affects lifestyles and raises new questions about the cumulative effects of individual actions.

The third face of ecology is *systems theory* and has to do with patterns of thought. A new understanding of the interdependence and diversity of natural systems will not be limited to the natural world, but rather will be folded back onto other kinds of issues. Learning to think ecologically goes beyond the development either of an attitude of loving wonder or of a practical concern with conserving resources. It involves a change in ways of knowing and thinking, attention to the characteristics of wholes rather than to their parts, changed models of causality and therefore of problem solving.[1] It is with these epistemological changes that this chapter will pri- marily be concerned.

Today, there is a significant backlash developing against environmen- talism, which is already beginning to replace communism as the favorite target of the far right. Those who want to harvest old-growth forests, to graze cattle on federal lands, or to develop vulnerable stretches of real estate are gradually recognizing that their antagonist is not the spotted owl but a new way of thinking about the biosphere, and that in many cases this new way of thinking is religious, at least in tone. We can expect court cases protesting the use in schools of the photograph of earth from the moon, on the grounds that it is being used as a religious symbol.

Epistemological Change

The contemporary study of ecology is not the study of plants and animals — these are, after all, the concerns of botany and zoology — but of the relationships between them. These relationships involve exchanges of information as well as energy and materials in elegant and self-sustaining patterns linking large numbers of organisms, like the nitrogen cycle or the food chain. Increasingly we see the biosphere not as a sort of background for separate organisms but as itself a product of life processes that determine the characteristics of the atmosphere, the soil, and even the rocks and the weather. One of the primary shifts needed is a shift in gestalt from "I see a robin" and "Look at that pretty flower" to seeing robin and flower and child as part of a single interacting and interdependent whole — a system, many parts of which are invisible to the naked eye. A second shift makes it possible to see basic similarities in pattern among different systems, among robin and flower and child and the forest that contains them all, "a pattern which connects."[2] Such a recognition makes it possible to feel kinship and empathy not only with a dead robin but with a devastated forest or a broken community.

The discipline that studies such patterns of relationship and organization, including those of ecology, is *cybernetics,* or systems theory. Many people associate cybernetics with mechanistic ways of thinking, because of the engineering and computer science applications of the discipline, yet the most persuasive models for complex systems are biological, and the abstract study of systems opens up a whole new range of metaphorical recognitions. I like to express this potentiality of systems theory by saying that "cybernetics . . . makes poets of us."[3] An awareness of the systemic relationships in the environment demands great discipline, for we have inherited many casual metaphors that deny biological processes or reduce organisms to commodities. Sometimes a return to mythology can be more accurate than simplified versions of science.

Alas, metaphor always carries the possibility of distortion as well as illumination and the poets in us may sometimes dilute the force of cybernetic arguments. Thus, James Lovelock used the name Gaia,[4] the goddess of earth in Greek mythology, to dramatize his argument, already metaphorical, about this planet as "a living organism" — a self-regulating system. The multiple layers of metaphor — cybernetic system, organism, person, goddess — made many people nervous, yet the metaphor allowed a certain swift comprehension. The earth as a living organism represents a very great advance, descriptively and intuitively, over Buckminster Fuller's metaphor of "spaceship earth."

Systemic thinking is often referred to as "holistic." Here, too, there are possibilities for confusion. Properly speaking, a holistic view of education includes an understanding of whole persons embedded in whole systems, a view that separates neither developing mind from body nor school from community. A holistic view of the forest is not limited to the growth of trees for potential human use, but includes the interactions of wind and rain and the bacteria of decay in the soil. By now, however, because the term *holistic* has been appropriated and applied to a congeries of antiestablishment movements in medicine, it often obscures more than it clarifies. Traditional establishment medicine has not been holistic, because it focuses on limited aspects of human health and well-being, failing to use the full healing potential of touch and imagination, of ritual and nutrition. Yet, practitioners who specialize in addressing one or another of these alternative areas often lose track themselves of an inclusive model in the pursuit of a specific use of herbs or form of massage. Systemic or holistic thinking about the human body or about the planet must imply inclusiveness: chemistry and poetry, meditation and technology, complex systems approached through multiple paths of knowing.

Central to the study of ecosystems is the study of circular processes of self-regulation and self-correction. If children grasp the concept of self-regulating systems, they can apply it to systems of all kinds, including the functioning of their own bodies or families, schools or neighborhoods. When an abstract pattern has been recognized in a single memorable example, the possibility of multiple analogy is created. In this sense, ecology offers tools for thinking about why it is unwise to experiment with addictive drugs, about the course of family quarrels, or about the damage done by racism.

Everywhere, cultural views of the world include metaphorical extensions of relations within one area of experience, as a given culture constructs it, onto another. Often, relations within the home are projected out onto a wider world, as in the ethical metaphor of the "brotherhood of man." New metaphors drawn from ecology are the modern version of a familiar process, but they may lead to new conclusions, perhaps to a realization that observation can never be separated from participation. Learning to think about how ecosystems function might provide analogies for respect for difference within a multicultural society, or for understanding the interactions between different players and interest groups in a democracy. Valuing ecological diversity might teach pluralism and the conviction that the goal of the political process is not specific solutions but the maintenance of conversation.

Years ago, I wrote about the experience of caring for an aquarium set up with my father as a way of introducing the concepts of cybernetics: circularity, feedback, self-correction, equilibrium, and the coupling of systems. The aquarium that stands today in so many classrooms can teach the same lessons, but the risk is that the children will think of themselves as outside the system. An aquarium makes a good model for what has been called "first order cybernetics," but I was always taught to include myself, outside the glass sides of the aquarium, as a participant in the process, and to see it as coupled with other systems, a point of view now referred to as "second order cybernetics."[5] To understand what an aquarium in the classroom can teach, and what can then be applied to neighborhood ponds and their surroundings, it seems worthwhile to quote my earlier writing:

> The tropical fish were the first living things for whose care I was responsible. The aquarium, both sheltered and exposed by its glass walls, had a certain elusive self-sufficiency. I sat beside it by the hour and brooded on the relationships between the fish and on the balances that would have to be maintained in order for them to live. Sometimes, indeed, I interfered in ways that disrupted the balance in the tank, adding too many fish, uprooting the plants to rearrange them, or dosing the aquarium with tonic. It was the community I learned to care for, self-contained to a degree, and yet dependent on me and on our household on Perry Street, so that the lives of those fish depended on the peace and continuity of our lives, just as our own peace depended on a wider political peace in those early years of the Cold War. The aquarium was a world within a world, connected to these wider systems through my capacity to understand and respond to its needs.[6]

The aquarium was beautiful but frustrating. In a low-keyed way, it could be both demanding and recalcitrant. What is critical is that it could not educate me about ecology without also posing wider questions.

Aquariums stand in the schoolrooms of thousands of children, alongside the cages of gerbils and guinea pigs, which also require care and teach the lessons of living and dying. Unlike much of what is done in a classroom, mistakes made in caring for an aquarium have real costs. Caring for living creatures requires action in uncertainty, for we can never ask the fish about their needs or fully know what is happening. The frustrations of keeping an aquarium or a garden are a reminder that human observers are not omniscient and that human actors often do harm. Seen through the lens of an aquarium, the world looks different.

Models of human relations may be projected onto the cosmos, and models of the functioning of the natural world spill over into societal arrangements. The Great Chain of Being, ordering relations from God down to the most lowly of creations,[7] matched the hierarchical structure of medieval life, including that of the family. Thus, a change in under-standing of any aspect of life is likely to carry over into other aspects.

In 1986, Christian fundamentalist parents in Tennessee brought a law-suit against the school system, arguing that their children were being taught the "religion of humanism."[8] One exhibit showed an illustration from an elementary school reader in which a little boy is putting bread into a toaster while a little girl reads instructions. One can argue that the problem posed by this picture goes far beyond gender and the family, for traditional gender roles are based on the notion that there is an isomor-phism among God's rule over creation, the rule of humankind over the rest of the natural world, and a man's rule over his wife and family — indeed, an isomorphism with all hierarchical systems in politics and business as well. In each of these systems, an emphasis on authority at the top tends to block awareness of circular paths of information and control. Similarly, the teaching of evolution not only undermines the role of God as creator and ruler, but also other social relations constructed on the same model.

The early appropriation of evolution by Darwin's contemporaries was also a source of error, for they extended its meaning in ways that eco-logical study has shown are not good biology. The discovery of natural selection as the mechanism of biological evolution offered a rationale — the survival of the fittest — for the exploitive practices of colonialism and the early industrial revolution, suggesting that the elimination of the weak was beneficial. Our society is still haunted by the notion that com-petition leads to improvement and that the strong should dominate the weak.

Essentially, the teaching of ecology offers the metaphor of interdependence and symbiosis to replace the metaphor of dominance. It represents a profound shift in thinking that goes far beyond nature study to imply changes in family life and in politics. Neo-Darwinian theory emphasizes populations rather than individuals, the resilience given to populations by genetic diversity, and the frequency of symbiosis. In effect, it suggests metaphors of cooperation rather than competition, the need of the individual for the collective rather than the viability of the autonomous individual.

Such metaphors are not automatically applied to all areas of experience, but spread out in ripples, just as it took a long time to understand that Enlightenment ideas of the rights of man might apply to all human beings. Systemic metaphors run counter to much of what is usually taught in economics and political science. They also pose to children the question of their place in the larger system, a possibility of contribution as well as subordination and dependency.

Ecology in the Conduct of Education

Within the larger structure of culture, different societies have different assumptions about where childhood and schooling fit in. When nature is seen as inchoate and threatening, and natural impulses as dangerous, classrooms are likely to be rigidly disciplined, but when the natural world is seen in terms of emergent patterns of self-organization, we begin to treasure spontaneity. Schools, like gardens, are planned and organized; they reflect the basic understandings of a society or of a community. Just as the gardens of France and Japan and England echo different attitudes toward nature and discipline and pattern, so do their classrooms. Even in democracies, however, schools have not traditionally been particularly democratic, and the day-to-day organization of lessons and classrooms has often been based on assumptions that are implicitly antiecological.[9] Much of contemporary education has replicated the patterns of agribusiness or industry rather than those of natural ecosystems. Thus, we divide up the educational enterprise among a series of time-slot subjects and specialists, who often fail to make connections between the subjects they teach, and we teach children in batches selected for various kinds of uniformity particularly age, having segregated them from the life of the community. All too many classrooms are modeled on a hierarchical cosmos, with a teacher who must always be right and in control, because participation and diversity of opinion make for an unpredictable and sometimes noisy classroom.

Education occupies a slot in the life cycle that is variously conceived, sometimes as a model for the rest of life, sometimes as a necessary preliminary to be escaped as quickly as possible, but in either case, school is contrasted with "real life" and children are not seen as full participants in society. Some educators emphasize competitiveness, while others emphasize adaptability, two alternative evolutionary strategies that play different roles in ecology. In the same way, some systems value specialization while others value breadth, some value diversity while others value uniformity. We are living in a time of both creativity and concern about education, and the decisions that are made for the classroom will feed directly into the way graduates participate in society and the way they impact on the natural systems around them. The decision, for instance, to supply funds for the arts has one kind of implication, and the decision to supply funds for athletic teams has another.

We are only a few decades away from a period when schools were deliberately constructed so that classrooms were without windows. This was based on a rather narrow understanding of the kind of attention appropriate in school children and on a selected style of learning. Children were expected to be immobile and narrowly focused on the words of the teacher, achieving specified goals as uniformly as possible. If one takes a group of children on a walk through the woods, however, they will notice different things and bring back different memories, expressing a variety of different kinds of attention. We need those different kinds of attention in the population if we are to be ecologically sensitive.[10]

Both democracy and ecology argue for diversity. In the search for solutions, it is easy to become focused on a single definition of educational goals, to try to maximize some aspect of education, and to set fixed standards. Yet, perhaps any dogmatic adherence to a single strategy is antiecological. One of the great lessons of the end of the Cold War is that in a society in which decision making is highly centralized and disagreement not allowed, a society with narrowly defined goals, many important issues will be unexpressed. Concern for protecting the natural world was limited for years to a small and eccentric minority, who used to be described as "little old ladies in tennis shoes." These peripheral visionaries were not silenced, however, and their concerns have gradually become part of a shared agenda. There is thus a relationship between the development of a viable environmental movement and democratic institutions. If a classroom is to function as an actual model for either democratic participation or ecological understanding (rather than a source of unilateral authority), schools will have to change.

Children in the Democratic Process

Schools are part of the larger social ecology, affecting the place of children in the democratic process. Within an understanding of circular systems, children can learn to see themselves as teachers as well as learners.

Children carry home to their families what they learn, thus influencing the participation and decision making of their families. Children have played a number of different roles in the education of their parents in the history of this country. The children of immigrants have often coached their parents in how to live here, mediating their contacts with outsiders and forging ahead in language skills. Within native-born populations, higher levels of education in succeeding generations have often been the norm, and this continues to be true even in this era of criticism of public education. Children are often exposed to new technologies, like computers, or to new consumer trends in which they are diligently propagandized by marketers, or to new ethical issues, before their parents.

This education in reverse is not always welcome. It is not new for children to say, in effect, "Walk your talk." The "generation gap" of the sixties was interpreted by some social scientists[11] as a process in which adolescents turned the claims of the older generation back against it, demanding for instance that equality and democracy be made into realities rather than slogans. Some young women are able to rebuke their fathers' — and mothers' — assumptions about gender roles. Some of the anger about "political correctness" may originate in parental irritation at domestic debate about derogatory terms still used "all in the family." Young children often dislike cigarette smoke, and today they have the ammunition to complain. Some of these patterns of speaking out are probably limited to middle-class households, but others are more widespread.

Schools today face new demands for the teaching of "traditional values," those values that parents — or small activist groups of parents —

want to see taught. But changing times demand new emphases and recognitions, a new appreciation of cultural diversity, responsible sexuality replacing chastity, lifelong learning replacing early commitment and security. The teaching of ecology represents a major frontier of values change that may often prove as unwelcome to parents as sex education. How should we understand the propriety of teaching values to children when it leads to their criticizing their parents' behavior, and who has the right to make these decisions?

Furthermore, the particular value changes involved in the teaching of ecology suggest major shifts in intergenerational relationships. Children constitute an interest group, one whose interests may not coincide with those of their parents, but which remains disenfranchised.[12]

Democracy has always had a limited franchise, and our understanding even of human rights has had to be broadened time and again. Decisions about suffrage are always ambiguously poised between the issue of competence and the issue of standing, the right to participate in a decision by which one is affected. At one time, only mature white males who owned property were considered qualified to vote, and the struggle for voting rights (both theoretical and actual) for African Americans and for women's suffrage revolved around both competence and standing. Until the Vietnam War, males between the ages of eighteen and twenty-one were considered old enough to be drafted and sent to die on the battlefield, but not old enough to vote.

Today, several groups of people making their homes in the United States and affected by political decisions are not fully enfranchised, including residents of the District of Columbia and Puerto Rico, native Americans, and, of course, permanent residents of this country who are not yet citizens. Beyond these specific groups, we make decisions affecting the lives of others — citizens of other countries and of the future, and above all, children under eighteen. Children are clearly the outstanding stakeholders in the future, the ones most obviously subject to injury by bad environmental policy.

Some environmentalists would argue that forests and wetlands and threatened species themselves have rights, but that is a position that is not yet politically viable. We are moving, however, toward a situation in which children may become effective as the principal advocates of threatened species and ecosystems, and may have the clearest understanding of and identification with their needs.

As surely as the court of King George putting a tax on tea drunk in the distant American colonies was taxation without representation, when the federal government borrows money to be repaid in the future, it is engaged in setting tax rates and commitments for those still too young to vote; the same is true of the creation of new entitlements, which will affect those who are under eighteen, who are given no voice in the matter. Similarly, when policies are enacted that will reduce available resources or make the environment less salubrious twenty years from now, those who are now underage or still to be born have the greatest stake in opposing shortsighted decisions. The situation is summed up in a bumper sticker I saw recently on a shiny camper far from its home state: "We're spending our children's inheritance."

There are a variety of reasons why parents can no longer be regarded as adequate spokespersons for their children's future interests, if indeed they ever were, which I will not explore here, including the credit-based economy and the emphasis on consumption. Perhaps the most important reasons come from increased longevity leading to new anxiety about economic security in old age and changed patterns of generational overlap. Today, most parents die well past the maturity of their children, passing on property and encountering grandchildren at a different stage in the life cycle, and we live in a society that is in many ways segregated by age.

The environmental awareness of children is increasing and being fostered in the schools in the context of a society in which children do not have a political voice and have few mechanisms to defend their long-term interests. The evolution of a childhood earth lobby is bound to lead to an increasing consciousness on the part of children and young people that an injustice is being done to them — and to their children and grandchildren. As a society, we are often preoccupied by issues of equity in the present or reparations for past damages, but we have few tools for thinking about equity across generations. Environmental issues pose a whole new area of social justice, expressed in a widely used slogan: "We do not inherit the earth from our parents; we borrow it from our children."

The issue of intergenerational equity and its relationship to environmental issues is being taken up in many places. In Boulder, Colorado, in the summer of 1993, a mock hearing on whether it would be possible to sue on behalf of future generations was used as part of the inauguration of the new Walter Orr Roberts Institute at the National Center for Atmospheric Research (NCAR) in Boulder, Colorado.[13] At the same time, extending over several days, there was an intergenerational conference at NCAR on the theme "Inherit the Earth." To make sure the conference was intergenerational, local young people were recruited, as were the residents of a local retirement community. The lead-up to the on-site conference was a computer conference in which all participants were anonymous, individual voices not labeled as "youth" or "age" or, among the middle-aged contingent, "scientific expert." At the end, one of the key proposals was that a forum be created for intergenerational discussion of environmental policies that would be sufficiently broadly based to be quoted by the media, offering a voice through an alternative channel.

Central to the message of the younger participants in the Boulder conference was the awareness that it is their lives and their children's lives that are being bartered away. Many of the older people also seemed to be saying that senior citizens' lobbies such as the American Association for Retired Persons misstate the profound interest of the old in a sense of ongoing continuity with the lives of future generations: it is their immortality that is being bartered away. It seems probable, therefore, that the study of ecology in the educational system will change our understanding of the kind of voice children can and should have, whether through formal voting or through some other mechanism of opinion, as children become more aware of the legitimacy of their interests.

In any debate about extending the franchise, the question of competence carries over into questions about whether a given group speaks for itself or simply parrots the views of some other group. Women, it was said, would simply vote as instructed by their husbands. Blacks, it was said, would be manipulated by unscrupulous outsiders — and for many years, demands for improvement by African Americans were attributed to communist agitators. If the rising wave of environmental concern among children begins to have a real effect on policy, whether through developing and expressing opinions or through boycotts and lobbying, far short of actually gaining the vote, the sinister manipulators blamed for using children like ventriloquist's dummies may be teachers and other educators.

Conclusions

Although the models of organization offered by ecology suggest new ways of teaching about society and about family life that are congruent with democracy, the connection is not automatic. One cannot assume that all environmentalists are "ecological" in their social and political behavior, and one cannot assume that "nature studies" are ecologically sound, for all too often the pictures of natural systems leave out vital elements. Thus, saving the whales is irrelevant without a concern for plankton, and forest ecology requires a recognition of the role of fires. Whales or spotted owls, discussed out of their systemic contexts, are just as misleading as an exclusive focus on any other species, including our own. Children respond most easily and directly to the young of other mammals, warm and fuzzy, but that can be no more than a starting point. Baby seals are easy for children to identify with and defend, even within the context of old systems of values, but activism on behalf of seals is rarely extended to the seals' cold-blooded neighbors. One test of whether the teaching of ecology is systemic is whether the necessity of death is included, for the denial of death distorts understanding of wider natural processes. Teaching about nature that does not embrace death, predation, and decay is no more than a form of sentimentality.

Environmentalists are like the rest of us in their willingness to believe that they are right and others are wrong and in using whatever tools come to hand to achieve a defined goal or to get a job done, and this sometimes leads to actions that distort ecological understanding or disrupt the ecologies of human communication. For instance, environmentalists have used the spotted owls as a political lever for the protection of old-growth forest — a single threatened species as the rationale for preserving a total system Similarly, we have heard much about the possibility that ancient ecosystems might include species like the Pacific yew, invaluable for medicine. Yet, arguments based on a single species or the meeting of a single human need obscure the fact that the struggle is really about preserving the integrity of whole systems that can never be replicated — and about the principle that whole systems are really worth preserving. In the same way, no charity is raising funds for a particular poster child, but for a population of the sick and disabled, and for the principle that a society should be concerned about its most vulnerable members. Lawsuits on behalf of the spotted owl may be useful tactics (and critical to halt plans for immediate cutting), but they run the risk of obscuring what is really at stake — and making environmentalists vulnerable to attack and caricature.

Typically, environmentalists approach debate with a sense that the compromises and delays of the democratic process will offer too little too late, and with the willingness to demonize opponents. Competing with other interests, environmentalists have gotten into the position of seeming to deny other kinds of needs, instead of exploring the place of those needs in a larger system. Concerned with correcting flaws in value systems, environmentalists have tried to *add* environmental values to the national agenda, or argued for the need to set environmental values in place of anthropocentrism, without offering an acceptable context for humanistic values, letting these be someone else's business.

Just as a holistic concept of human well-being must include both meditation and chemistry, a holistic concept of the biosphere must acknowledge the place of human beings. Thinking of the natural world as if human beings were not part of it is just as likely to lead to error as is putting human beings at the center and regarding all other forms of life as expendable. Similarly, it is a source of confusion to regard some vegetables as more organic than others or to regard some human behaviors as "unnatural" or outside of nature. There is a new kind of anthropocentrism emerging that starts from valuing humankind, but that emphasizes that humankind is part of and dependent on a larger system — that the unit of survival is *the species in its environment,* and that the species that destroys its environment destroys itself. Within the context of this new anthropocentrism, it is possible to juxtapose compassion for starving children with concern about desertification and soil depletion, and to emphasize the need for population control within a sustainable model for human quality of life.

It seems important for environmental activism and ecological education that the rhetoric used reflect the real complexity of the situation, including the ecology of political change. The political process in this country, however we phrase democratic ideals, is still based on vertical hierarchy and modeled on crude forms of competition and win-lose games. In the past, after all, the lessons of domination and competition were taught in church and in the home as well as in school. The much more systemic notions of pluralism and the balance of powers built into the Constitution have been at odds with other habits of thought, creating an ambiguity that has been uncomfortable but no doubt productive. It is not surprising that environmentalists approach political conflict with the conviction of having the truth and the determination to win, for this is the American way. It is in fact extraordinarily difficult to shift the vast momentum of a society like our own toward a higher level of responsibility, and it is understandable that those who see a need for change might get trapped into action through adversarial institutions and wish secretly that they could bring it about by fiat. But change by fiat belongs to the old model.

Teaching ecology in the schools — teaching children to think systemically — carries with it the lesson that even as each species goes about surviving in its distinctive way, the other species are also necessary. The effort to affect systemic outcomes takes place from within rather than from without — second order rather than first order cybernetics. This is a lesson to be carried over into the process of political debate, recognizing that the normal sequence of change is not one in which one side wins and the other loses, but a long slow process of compromise. Ecology carries with it a set of ideas about what it is to be part of a larger system.

When I was asked for an essay to go into a 1995 book called *How Things Are: A Science Tool-kit for the Mind,* I chose to write about a pernicious kind of muddle: just as there is no logical opposition between nature and nurture, the actions and artifacts of human beings can never be "unnatural," though they may indeed have unintended consequences. Including this essay here, I notice again how easy it is to slip into thinking some things are natural and others are unnatural, just as it is easy to speak as if our species could be separated from nature, and how my own phrasing in some of my other papers slips into the same trap. The way we speak both betrays and shapes assumptions, often unconscious ones, and can lead to dangerous choices. Looking back, I am amazed that I hoped some of these issues would be resolved in the remaining years of the twentieth century. We are carrying our errors with us into the twenty-first.

— MCB, 2004

↶

Clear thinking about the world we live in is hindered by some very basic muddles, new and old, in the ordinary uses of the words *nature* and *natural.*

We seem to slip easily into thinking that it is possible to be outside of nature — that with a little help from on high, we could rise above the ordinary contingencies, evade the consequences of our actions, and be supernaturally delivered from the all-too-natural realities of illness and death. Some usages seem to suggest that it is possible to be below nature, as in "unnatural acts" (sometimes called "subhuman"), or "unnatural paren-" (which means an unloving parent or one who fails in the obligations of nurture, with no logical connection to a "natural child," one born outside of the culturally sanctioned arrangement of wedlock).

These usages have in common the notion that nature is something it is possible to get away from, to get around. The intellectual problems created by circumscribing the domain of "nature" are probably even more confusing than those created by Cartesian dualism, although they are no doubt related. Descartes was concerned to define a domain for science that would be safe from ecclesiastical interference: *res extensa,* matter, the physical body, divorced from mind or spirit. The effect of this was to create two different kinds of causality and separate spheres of discourse that must someday be brought back together. The folk distinctions that describe the concept of "nature" are messier but equally insidious. As with Cartesian dualism, they tend to slant ethical thinking, to create separation rather than inclusion. In Western culture, nature was once something to be ruled by humankind, as the body was to be ruled by the mind.

Recently, we have complicated the situation by labeling more and more objects and materials preferentially, from foodstuffs to fibers to molecules, as natural or unnatural. This sets up a limited and misshapen domain for the natural, loaded with unstated value judgments: the domain suggested in Bill McKibben's title *The End of Nature* or in William Irwin Thompson's *The American Replacement of Nature.* Yet nature is not something that can end or be replaced, any more than it is possible to get outside of it.

In fact, everything is natural; if it weren't, it wouldn't be. That's *How Things Are:* natural. And interrelated in ways that can (sometimes) be studied to produce those big generalizations we call "laws of nature" and the thousands of small interlocking generalizations that make up science. Somewhere in this confusion there are matters of the greatest importance, matters that need to be clarified so that it is possible to argue (in ways that are not internally contradictory) for the preservation of "nature," for respect for the "natural world," for education in the "natural sciences," and for better scientific understanding of the origins and effects of human actions. But note that the nature in "laws of nature" is not the same as the nature in "natural law," which refers to a system of theological and philosophical inquiry that tends to label the common sense of Western Christendom as "natural."

Ours is a species among others, part of nature, with recognizable relatives and predecessors, shaped by natural selection to a distinctive pattern of adaptation that depends on the survival advantages of flexibility and extensive learning. Over millennia, our ancestors developed the opposable thumbs that support our cleverness with tools, but rudimentary tools have been observed in other primates; neither tools nor the effects of tools are "unnatural." Human beings communicate with each other, passing on the results of their explorations more elaborately than any other species. Theorists sometimes argue that human language is qualitatively or absolutely different from the systems of communication of other species; but this does not make language (or even the possibilities of error and falsehood that language amplifies) "unnatural." Language is made possible by the physical structures of the human nervous system, which also allow us to construct mental images of the world. So do the perceptual systems of bats and frogs and rattlesnakes, each somewhat different, to fit different adaptive needs.

It is often possible to discover the meaning of a term by seeking its antonym. Nature is often opposed to culture or to nurture. Yet human beings, combining large heads and the appropriate bone structure for upright posture and bipedal locomotion, have evolved to require a long period of adult care after birth, time to acquire those variable patterns of adaptation and communication we call "culture." How then could "nurture" be "unnatural"? The characteristics of the human species that set us at odds with our environment and with other species are part of the same larger pattern.

Increasingly, nature is opposed to artifact, yet, human beings must always work within natural possibility to create their artifacts, even in the productions of dream and fantasy. Ironically, in current parlance, many artifacts are called "natural." If what we mean by "natural" is "unaffected by human acts," the natural is very hard to find. Walk in the woods, for instance. Patterns of vegetation in different North American biomes were already changed by human habitation long before the first Europeans arrived, and were changed again by the colonists. Today, there are introduced species of birds and insects and plants all across this country, even in so-called wilderness areas. The migrations of human beings to every continent on the globe have transported human parasites and symbionts since prehistoric times. Human beings, as they learned to use fire, weapons, and agriculture, have exerted selective pressures everywhere they have lived — like every other species. Henry David Thoreau was fully aware that what he could study and reflect on, living beside Walden Pond already bore a human imprint. Still, we are wise to treasure and learn from landscapes in which the human imprint is not obvious. This is perhaps what we usually mean by wilderness (one wonders how much the wilderness into which Jesus or John the Baptist withdrew was a human creation, as so many spreading deserts are today). "Wilderness" turns out to be a relative term but still a valuable one. We need areas with no visible structures and no soft-drink cans to remind us of human activity, but still, they are affected by human acts.

If natural means "unaffected by human acts," it won't be found at the "natural foods" store. Most food products have been produced by selective breeding over millennia, turning wild plants into cultivars dependent on human beings, and multiplying or eliminating their variations. Most are also processed and transported in clever cultural ways; after all, tofu doesn't grow on trees. Organic farmers must work hard and skillfully; nature doesn't do their work for them. Still, the effort to produce foodstuffs without the chemical fertilizers and insecticides that produce toxic residues is an important area of ingenuity and persuasion. It would be nice to find a way of talking about it without nonsensical and self-contradictory uses of terms like "natural" or "organic" (what would a vegetable be if it wasn't "organic"?). Some of the animals and plants cultivated by human beings can survive without human help, like domestic house cats that become feral, foreign to their settings, and disruptive to other species. Living in a more "natural" way, they may be more disruptive. It may be useful to distinguish between what we create "on purpose" and unexpected by-products. In this sense, gardens of any kind should be distinguished from the deserts created by some of the ways in which humans use land.

Human populations today exist because of massive interference with "nature." Without the invention of agriculture and other technologies, human populations would have stayed tiny, and most of our ancestors would never have been born.

Individually, we are probably alive because of medical technologies, public health, and immunizations. Without some kinds of technology, you're dead. When warfare disrupts the artifices of public health, clean water, transport, electricity, and so on, the death rates reflect this new level of "naturalness." Even "natural childbirth" is an invention that depends on modern ideas of hygiene, training, emergency backup — and on the use of a watch to time contractions. Some of us pride ourselves on looking and acting "natural," but try looking in the mirror. Do you use hair conditioner, toothpaste, vitamins? Even the so-called natural ones are human artifacts — and so are a clear complexion, shining hair, straight teeth.

All this will become clearer if we try looking at something really "unnatural": a hydroelectric dam, for instance, or a plastic bag, a nuclear plant, or a polyester suit. All of our artifacts exist only because they fit into natural possibility — sometimes all too well. If they did not, they would not serve our purposes; bridges would collapse. Invention, technology, industry — all of these exist in complete deference to nature, subject to its ordinary tests and sanctions, entropy, decay, extinction. Much that serves our purposes in the short term may work against us and the earth as we know it over time.

Human beings reshape the material world in ways that seem to meet their needs and desires. Needs, of course, are both biologically given and passed on by cultural tradition. The wiles of advertising exploit the fact that at the most ancient level, human needs and desires were shaped by the natural pressures and scarcities with which our ancestors lived. To the extent that the circumstances of human life have changed, through the exercise of human adaptive skills, the attempt to meet some needs may have become maladaptive.

This is the great and awful irony of "doing what comes naturally." The desire to have children is a product of past millennia when bands of human beings could barely keep up their numbers and as many as half of all offspring died too young to reproduce. High rates of infant survival are artifacts, not "natural" in the colloquial sense at all. Some religious groups reject contraception as "unnatural," yet the use of contraception to restore ancient balances is the use of artifact to repair the effects of artifact. The attempt to stave off death through biomedical technology is a similar result of desires that were once adaptive for the species. Because scarcity has been a fact of most of human existence, miserliness, overeating, and conspicuous consumption burden our lives today. Perhaps the delight in swift and powerful automobiles is a translation of the need to be able to run, whether in flight from predators or in pursuit of game. It's "natural" to want to own a gas-guzzling monster. It's "natural" to cling to life and the life of loved ones beyond any meaningful exchange or participation. The population explosion is "natural."

Most serious of all, the habit of seeing the human community as in some sense separate from (and in opposition to) nature is a natural habit, one that has appeared to be adaptive for our species through most of its history and may have ceased to be adaptive. Few cultures emphasize this separation as sharply as the Western tradition has, but even with stone-age technologies and the various mythologies of Earth kinship, the awareness is there.

The steady increase in the impact of the human species on all other species, on the atmosphere and the seas and the earth's surface, requires new patterns of adaptation and new kinds of perception, for the natural course of a species that destroys its environment is extinction. What we need to fashion today is a way of thinking that is both new and artificial — something deliberately dreamed up in the twentieth century and learned by all members of our species to protect the lives of future generations and preserve their options. We need to invent new forms and learn some new things: limits; moderation; fewer progeny; the acceptance of our own dying. We need to look further into the future, using more and better science and learning to think more clearly about our interdependence with other forms of life. In doing so, we will be following our nature as the species that survives by learning.

This paper grew out of a series of conferences in the late 1960s and early 1970s.[1] My father was arguing that dualism, the conceptual separation of mind and body proposed by Descartes, is an epistemological error that might be key to understanding why human beings act as if they were separate from the natural world. Other thinkers had argued that the error was even older and were inclined to blame Christianity or the entire monotheistic tradition derived from Abraham. Warren McCulloch commented in response to Gregory that religions in general are "solutions to the mind-body problem." In this paper I was taking McCulloch up on that suggestion but also responding to comments of Gregory's on the difference between Catholicism and Protestantism by arguing that more than one "solution" might be found within a given tradition. A few years later, when Gregory joked about a god named Eco, who "involuntarily sends the pollution and the radioactive fallout . . . [who] is incorruptible and therefore is not mocked,"[2] he may have been responding to this discussion of whether God is constrained by his attributes.

A transcendent deity, outside of the world we know, suggests the same kind of discontinuity as the separation of mind from body. For Gregory, the needed corrective to epistemological error lay in cybernetic description of mind-body as a single system. But cybernetics is not the sort of language in which cultural premises are stored and transmitted, while myth and religion are, so it is useful to explore the many variations of religious understanding. Here I examine the notion that there is an isomorphism, a formal similarity, between theories of God and creation and theories of mind and body. Even animism and polytheism might offer models for holistic thinking.

This paper was drafted for a conference on these questions held at San Francisco Zen Center's Green Gulch Farm in 1976. Previously unpublished, it has been edited and clarified here but still reflects the conversation at that time. Many Americans who have embraced Zen and other forms of Buddhism feel that its epistemology is closer to systems theory than those of any of the Abrahamic religions, but I brought a different set of preoccupations. I came to the conference from Iran, where I taught for a time at a college founded by Presbyterian missionaries who were barred from proselytizing but offered a reduced version of the Great Books curriculum, slanted toward religious writings, with Islamic and Persian classics added. It was in that context that I became curious about John Calvin and about Max Weber's analysis of the Protestant ethic, which seems closely connected to the industrial civilization that so readily ravages and exploits natural systems. I had also been trying to understand the differences between Shiism, the dominant form of Islam in Iran, and the Sunni Islam I had studied in graduate school. Reading this paper in retrospect, I notice that my knowledge of Sunni Islam, based in the classroom, was more institutional and theological than my knowledge of Shiism, much of which came from conversations with Iranian friends for whom it was simply part of the fabric of life.

This was very definitely an exploratory paper, meant to be provocative. Since it was written, a new emphasis on spirituality has emerged and there has been a search for ecological inspiration in all of the major religions. I believe that change is only likely if we extend justice and compassion even beyond sentient beings to all natural systems, including along with animals and plants the systems of atmosphere and ocean we are now threatening and the nitrogen cycle in the soil. We must embrace the natural order and celebrate its holiness, instead of seeking to rise above it.

—MCB, 2004

∽

At one time, most human beings regarded the material world as intricately intermingled with spirit and the sacred as immanent in daily life. Humans encountered and had conversations and even love affairs with gods. There were deities in trees and springs. The world was unified, at once spiritual and material, and evoked awe and respect.

One of the trends that has been working itself out over the centuries is the progressive separation of the spiritual and the material, the sacred and the secular, so they are no longer thought of as a unity. The indwelling spirits of trees and rivers moved to Olympus, the ghosts that used to live in the rafters migrated to more distant resting places, the "everywhen" of myth has been converted to the "once upon a time" of folklore, and the eschaton has been put on hold. Most of the ground underfoot and the food on the table has ceased to be experienced as holy.

The symbolic actions and rituals that affirmed beliefs about the sacred have also increasingly been compartmentalized and limited to specialized ritual contexts. Beliefs in a world simultaneously material and spiritual have been replaced for many by dualism, a separation between the natural, material world and some version of the *super*natural — something transcendent, beyond or above nature. Traditionally, these moves, from pervasive animism to monotheism and to a more formal dualism, have been regarded as forward steps in intellectual sophistication, yet the separation of spirit and matter created its own intellectual problems — suddenly there were two kinds of existence, nature and supernature, with multiple puzzles about how they might interact, how knowledge and communication can connect the realms of spirit and matter, mind and body. The move to Cartesian dualism was critical to the emergence of science and modernity, ultimately including the separation of church and state. But it may be that something was lost in the process or that the sharpening of the contrast between the spiritual and the material has eliminated certain kinds of awareness. It may be that we will pay dearly for blind spots we have created.[3] If the particular exploitive approach to the material world we live with today is based in questionable epistemo-

logical assumptions, it is important to know it, for epistemology can outlive doctrine.

Not surprisingly, the logical next step after this long process of separation was to follow Occam and question the existence of the supernatural. First separation, then amputation, one way of escaping from dualism
to monism. Ours is probably the first age in which a large number of
people — though not as many as is sometimes assumed — believe that it
is possible to live without reference to spiritual aspects of being.
Materialism, which goes back to Greek philosophy as a speculation, has
become a common way of going about daily life. But short of the denial
of the spiritual, there have been many kinds of complex and uneasy relationships between these aspects of existence, partially separated and in
uneasy balance.

For quite a while, most of the world has been Buddhist, Christian, or
Muslim. These three faiths, arising in different places over the space of a
millennium, are sometimes grouped together as universalistic religions. It
is interesting that, while we tend to classify religions in terms of what they
assert ontologically, the religions that have spread most widely around the
planet have certain epistemological characteristics in common and recurrent patterns of internal variation. Thus, mysticism and dogmatism as
ways of knowing turn up in each, and great as their differences are, all to
some degree devalue "this world" or "this life," putting the highest value
on some sort of transcendent spiritual reality that lies above or beyond or
after. It is interesting, too, that all of them see in the individual the potential for receiving or achieving salvation or enlightenment, some kind of
freedom from material reality or a place in some spiritual world. Thus,
each sees the individual as potentially having a foot in two worlds, as not
fully and finally committed to the natural world.

All three of these faiths, unlike Judaism and Hinduism, with which
they share many characteristics, regard certain human arrangements —
kinship, class, membership in a particular cultural group — as essentially
irrelevant to the matter of salvation. This orientation was part of what
gave the universalistic religions their great missionary thrust, letting them
cross cultural lines, but it does not mean that they entirely reject the laws,
roles, and patterned relationships of everyday life in favor of a radically
different spiritual reality. Ironically, all of these religions have been used
in turn to sanctify particular arrangements of family, class, and ethnicity.
Buddhism, Christianity, and Islam have provided the basic premises for

civilizations in which, while the spiritual and material were contrasted, nevertheless the order of the natural world and of human social life was sanctified and respected.

Such was the Christian civilization of the Middle Ages.[4] Indeed, the material and the spiritual were treated more like a continuum in which humankind was at a sort of midpoint, combining both the spiritual and the material, as far below the spiritual ranks above (powers and principalities, angels and archangels) as it was higher than the invertebrates below. The world was understood through two principal metaphors, one the Great Chain of Being, and the other Organism, in which either the natural or the social world could be seen as like an organism in which every part was essential. There was an analogy between the relationship of the mind to the body and the relationship of the Creator to Creation. If even a single species were to disappear (alas for the dodo!), the perfection of the created world, corresponding to a perfection in the mind of the Creator, would be lost. Well might an environmentalist wish that more people thought that way today. But while people could conceptualize and long for eternal life and infinite bliss, they expected to find such things not in this mortal life but somewhere remote in time and space. The dream of an ultimate, infinite spiritual world was counterpointed by the finiteness of this life and the imminence of death. The separation of spiritual and material categorized ideals and aspirations, but they were linked by the ministrations of an elaborate hierarchy mediating knowledge of the divine, a galaxy of familiar saints, and a system of sacraments.

Over time, perhaps beginning during the Renaissance in the West and still working through to its logical conclusion today, the ideas and aspirations which had been related to the world of the spirit — segregated, so to speak, from the possibilities of everyday material life — were transferred back from the one to the other. Increasing numbers began to believe that there could be a sort of paradise on Earth, with the possibility of infinite growth and improvement in the material conditions of life, and that the resources of this planet, exploited by technology, would provide what their forebears had once hoped to find in God — infinite beneficence. Many have even begun to believe that science can confer personal immortality. The idea of transcending finite limitations had been developed in religious thinking, and this idea, applied to economics and technology taken in isolation from religion, has been appallingly dangerous, for in fact we depend on and are part of the natural world we hope to transcend.

It is probably not fair to blame religious traditions as we know them for developing ideas such as perfection, omnipotence, and immutability as speculative attributes of God. These ideas surely developed as part of a unified worldview in which "religion" was not experienced as a separate realm. Not all cultures elaborate these ideas, but perhaps all cultures above a certain level of complexity do develop them. One of the traditional arguments for the existence of God is that human beings, while never directly experiencing eternity or infinite goodness, are capable of conceptualizing and longing for a being with these attributes. Within the Western tradition, this may be partly Plato's fault, but surely the seed fell on remarkably fertile ground and perhaps is intrinsic to human language. Mathematics, at any rate, is with us still.

To recapitulate: the great world religions conceptually separated the spiritual and the material but also partially united them by sanctifying the order found in the ordinary world, both natural and social. To the extent that the worlds of spirit and matter were felt to be richly interconnected within a single cosmology, the total conception remained unified, but at the same time certain ideas were set apart and associated with the spiritual realm. There were variations in the degree to which spirit and matter were decoupled, no longer experienced as parts of a single system, but the material world was largely drained of spiritual value, and believers looked beyond this world to a transcendent deity, ever more remote from his creation. Today, especially in the West, large numbers of people find the whole subject of religion irrelevant, yet they still act as if the limits of the material world could be transcended. And make decisions on that basis.

In the West, the Reformation probably accelerated the desacralization of nature. Martin Luther posted his theses on a church door in 1517, and John Calvin broke with the Catholic Church some seventeen years later. Max Weber (1864–1920) hypothesized, in his discussions of the rise of capitalism,[5] that the economic order we know today derived from the ideas of the Protestant reformers, epitomized by Calvin, although this was far from their intention. A key notion in Calvin's theology was the combination of predestination and election: God, in his infinite wisdom, has determined the elect, who will be saved, and the damned. Nothing we do can change or earn that determination, which, since it is made by God, is good. However, the lives of the elect, also predetermined, will necessarily be congruent with salvation. Thus, in a curious psychological flip-flop,

Calvinists followed patterns of systematic and ascetic virtue not in order
to be saved but in order to be able to look in the mirror in the morning
and think, Surely such behavior as mine reveals that I am one of the elect.
Success was evidence of divine favor. Thus, supposedly, Calvinists
worked hard, saved their money and reinvested it instead of enjoying it,
were systematic and thrifty, and . . . modern capitalism developed.

There are other parts to the argument of course.[6] Calvin's emphasis
on the Old Testament concept of the covenant contributed to the development of contracts and of corporations and voluntary associations of all
kinds; Calvin, in his theocratic Geneva, legalized the taking of interest,
which medieval Catholicism had forbidden; Calvin's theology tremendously strengthened individualism by setting the individual in direct
relationship with (a very distant) God, sweeping away the mediators,
hierarchy, etcetera, to be found in human society, and allowing individual interpretation of the scriptures (though not when it conflicted
with his own readings). For centuries Protestants have tended to be individually richer than Catholics and Orthodox, and Protestant countries
have been richer and more technologically advanced. Today we still
suffer from the notion that people who become rich are admirable and
the poor are likely to be "undeserving." And we still suffer from the
notion that productivity depends on treating rivers, soil, air, and even
workers as expendable means to that end.

The debates about Weber's thesis have continued. It has been
common to assert that all this was a very good thing and that it was
important to determine the transformative capacity of Calvinism and discover equally transformative ideologies to help in modernizing the rest of
the world.[7] Calvinism puts the believer in a double bind of continuing
uncertainty, and the effort to escape that double bind leads to anxious but
conscientious toil. It has also been argued that modern capitalism arises
not directly from Calvinism but from the failure of Calvinism — that it is
Calvinism reshaped as folk-Calvinism, culture-Calvinism, that helps
people get rich. In effect, you don't get rich in order to know that you are
on the road to heaven: wealth *is* heaven. And somewhere along the way
the connection to morality and the concern about sin gets lost. The
Weberian hypothesis about Calvinism and the rise of capitalism, then,
proposes the possibility of a close relationship between human action and
cultural premises derived from religion, even when formal religion has
been set aside.

Here I am arguing a slightly different kind of connection between Calvin's thinking and the modern capitalist industrial order that involves so much environmental disruption. Calvin was one of the great elaborators of the transcendence of God, the theological term for radical separation between God and the material world. The Calvinist God is more remote, more all powerful and all knowing, than most mainstream conceptions of God elaborated in other outgrowths of historic religion, with the exception of Sunni Islam. These two traditions are built on

1. The absolute transcendence, omnipotence, and omniscience of God;
2. Predestination, which follows from 1; and
3. Lack of mediation. No other type of being, no hieratic figure, and no sacrament bridges the gap between the individual and God.

The perennial problem for predestinationists is, What becomes of the belief in God's mercy if free will is rejected and most people are destined in advance to eternal damnation? One solution, that was tried out by Duns Scotus as a theological speculation in thirteenth-century Catholicism and rejected, and was also rejected in its extreme form by Calvin, but is arguably implicit in the rest of his thinking, is this: God's actions cannot be constrained by his attributes — such an idea would be tantamount to polytheism (i.e., mercy could trump divinity). Therefore, his attributes must be defined by his actions: God does not act in such and such a way because he is good or wise or merciful — his actions are good, wise, and merciful because they are his. If it turns out that many or most people are miserable in this life and damned in the next, this arrangement must, because God wills it, be a good and merciful arrangement.

Such a denial of intelligibility in God's attributes is part of the logic that defines him as wholly other. By contrast, medieval Christianity developed, as a basic strand in piety, the concept of empathy with God through the sufferings of Christ; such a God can grieve and one can empathize with him (as with a parent who insists, "This hurts me more than it hurts you"). Once God has become distant and essentially alien, the logical thing to do might seem to be to stop thinking about him, much less praying, but faith is not constrained by logic, and the irrelevance of such a deity did not begin to be absorbed by ordinary people for generations, and then only after a great deal of theological and philosophical speculation tending toward the same result. In any case, ordinary folk find ways of restoring warmth to theological formulations. It is not to be supposed that anyone except an occasional philosopher is really consistent about such matters.

Islam has wrestled with many of these same questions. On the one hand, Sunni Islam is similar to Calvinism in the austerity of its emphasis on the logically linked concepts of divine omnipotence, predestination, and the rejection of hierarchy.[8] On the whole, however, Muslims have not been in the same kind of double bind as Calvinists, perhaps because of the belief that if you were a member of the Muslim community living within the framework of religious law, this in itself meant you were destined for salvation. Again, although "there is no priesthood in Islam," the community, in a sense, plays this role. Sunni Islam, however, did take the explicit position that God cannot be constrained by his attributes, cutting off the risk of polytheism posed by the importance given to the ninety-nine names of God.

On the other hand, Shiism, the second great branch of Islam, took the opposite route. If many people are miserable in this life and damned in the next, this arrangement must be the result of human choices. God's will is to be merciful in spite of the gift of free will. Therefore, God continues to help believers make the right decisions, so there are Imams, born to Muhammad's lineage through the marriage of his nephew Ali to his daughter Fatimah, to lead the Muslim community. It also makes sense that there should be other kinds of support and guidance in Shiism to help the believer maintain faith, and so there are, including the popular possibility of negotiating with God by promising particular offerings or devotions, reminiscent of indulgences. This is a far cry from the austerity of the extreme Sunni position. Whereas Sunni Islam is similar to Calvinism in this regard, Shiite Islam is more similar to Roman and Eastern Orthodox Catholicism, with their helpful saints and shrines, a system of sacraments, and a hierarchy for continuing divinely guided leadership. As a result, in the Shiite and Catholic models religion pervades everyday life in a very concrete way, is interlocked with everyday life.

What happens to the natural world as God becomes more and more remote? The tradition of looking at the natural world as evidence of God's glory and praising the wonders of creation is of course so strong in both the Bible and the Qur'an that it continues to be a part of all these traditions. Neither Christianity nor Islam has ever been so otherworldly that this world was regarded as an illusion. However, the extreme separation of the Deity from the creation does potentially transform the world from something intrinsically holy into a *means*, something without inherent value. When the Protestant tradition is mined for an ideological basis for conservation, the primary rhetoric developed has been that of stewardship: the world is property, to be used wisely, as Calvinists in the past saved and invested, lived frugally, and became rich. The order of the natural world is objectified, no longer a reflection or expression of the divine nature; and natural science speeds up tremendously. Once people cease to think of God, humanity, and nature in a continuum, part of a single interlocking system, God becomes remote and nature becomes equally alien, so that human beings do not properly empathize with a lake or a forest any more than they empathize with God. There is no "pattern which connects."

Similarly for social life and ethics. The theoretical source of Calvinist ethics is revelation (remember — actions are good because God commanded them, not because they are intrinsically so — good actions done by those who are not saved "partake of the nature of sin" as the Anglican Thirty-nine Articles would have it). By contrast, the theoretical source of Catholic ethics is a combination of revelation and reason resting on observation of what the world is like, natural law. In practice, of course, natural law was derived from culturally constructed observations and so was full of cultural assumptions, the common sense of a particular time and place mixed with a large dose of Aristotle. But in theory it was a way of knowing what *ought to be*, based on an understanding of *what is*. The Calvinist theory is more nearly a theory of revelation and artifact. Thus, in Catholicism marriage is basically a natural relationship — the sacrament sanctifies what is. In Calvinism marriage is a contractual relationship, informed by certain specific commands in scripture. Not treating marriage as part of a sacred natural order, of course, made it easier to allow for divorce. Here, as elsewhere, the Calvinist approach makes change easier: what is not sacred can be changed.

The difference between the Protestant and Catholic approaches to the Eucharist is, again, most clearly represented in Calvin — both Lutheranism and Anglicanism take a sort of middle position. Calvin, in his writings on the Lord's Supper, uses again and again the words *like, analogy, symbol*. He gives great importance to the spiritual effect of the Lord's Supper but sharply separates the material event from the spiritual effect, which is achieved by the Holy Spirit acting on the believer. Material things — bread, wine, the water of baptism — are no more than material things. Such thinking devalues metaphor. Metaphorical relationships become rhetorical rather than ontological, and many of them are rejected — no longer, for instance, can sacred images somehow participate in the divine. And no longer will greed be tempered by the sense that lakes and forests partake of a certain sacredness. As soon as it becomes intellectually necessary to distinguish between metaphor and simile, a semimythic reading of scripture becomes impossible, opening the door to a new kind of literalism. Fundamentalism is a modern pathology, not because the Bible is seen as more important or more true than previously but because it must now be true in a different sense. Every statement, from Genesis to the Words of Institution, must be labeled as literally true or a simile — none can be myth or metaphor. There are no poetic truths. It may be important, nevertheless, to retain forms of expression in ritual and in the arts for our recurrent longings, without taking them too literally.

The different strands of Calvinist thinking hang together. But for a great many people who have rejected or forgotten their teachings, premises such as materialism (and the use of this world, desacralized, as a means), predestination (rewritten as determinism, which effectively weeds out ethical elements), and capitalism also hang together as part of a coherent secular worldview. Some thinkers have attributed these ideas to Descartes, but Calvin was over thirty years dead when Descartes was born. I think Cartesian dualism can be seen as a sort of corollary, rather than as the source of the problem. Once God and spiritual matters have been effectively banished from the material world, the Cartesian separation follows naturally to open the path for empirical inquiry. What Calvinist thinking did was to set up the relationship with the sacred in an essentially nonsystemic manner: religion was meant to dominate life rather than be integrated with it, which eventually made it easier to set aside. Conceptually, once one forgot heaven and hell, it was easier to cut them cleanly away — and then forget the sacred — after a few important aspects of the sacred — infinite growth, felicity, and even eternal life, achieved by technology — had been transferred to the possibilities of earthly life.

The relationships between mind and body and between the sacred and everything else are arguably isomorphic, so a change in concepts of the one seems bound to lead to a change in the other. As we learn more about the brain, identifying more and more of its functions as material, it is easy to lose track of what remains mysterious. As materialistic thinking about mind-body is developing, crudely materialistic thinking about the natural world is bound to increase, which must surely lead to the further loss of a sense of its holiness and an increasing willingness to tamper with it. Finding ourselves able to manipulate the mental life of human beings, we seem determined to do so, and in our thinking of the natural world the equivalent of mind is left out, is simply absent.

Workable language for reaffirming the unity and value of human life as a part of nature may not always be explicitly religious, but religious language is at least a reminder that it is not for human beings to claim the attributes of God. We might be better off with some very old ideas like animism (a tree really is more like a woman than like a concrete pylon) or with ancient solutions to the body-mind problem like the hypostatic union (of the human and the divine in Christ), which at least allow thinking of the human and the sacred together. Empathy may be one of the central keys to identifying with all of life instead of seeking to transcend it. It may be necessary to find new metaphors and new reminders that all is not yet known, for the banishment of the ineffable from our curiosity has led to a dangerous epistemological hubris: believing we can know and control everything, we make decisions whose material consequences are unknown.

MULTIPLE KINDS OF KNOWLEDGE

Societal Decision Making

The University of Georgia at Athens is the host of an annual conference on qualitative methods of research in education. This gathering, attracting young researchers from all over the country, has an elegant design in which the keynote speaker, as I was in 1991, meets with groups of graduate students to discuss their research. Although they had specifically invited me to discuss the research for my book *Composing a Life*, I ended by broadening my focus in response to these conversations and discussed the danger that very narrow concepts of scientific method, when they attend only to what can easily be counted or measured, can create their own forms of ignorance and error. The key issue here is how the selective attention of researchers can be seen as influencing decision making. The relationship between gender and attention is discussed in several other papers in this book, but is retained here for continuity. This piece was originally published as a very rough transcript of an informal presentation and has been only lightly copyedited.

—MCB, 2004

I want to start by thanking all of the people who have come to consultations with me, because the talk I'll be giving will be a weave of things I have wanted to say to one or another of you. Some of them I have already said to some of you, stories that you reminded me of, examples I have used in conversations over lunch or this morning that seemed to belong in the conversation of the entire group. So if you hear a bit of a repeat, hear it with my thanks for the fact that one or another of you was able to trigger in my mind the association that has come into this talk.

I grew up with qualitative research. My parents worked in very different ways, as was pointed out, but both of them were anthropologists and both of them brought anthropology into their style of living. From very early childhood I learned to be a participant observer, to be thinking about the patterns in the behavior of others around me at the same time that I was involved in what was going on. This was really a seamless weave of observation, interpretation, and participation. I also grew up with a lot of stories about other kinds of research. My father especially had a collection of stories about psychologists. Well, one example: He happened to be sitting at a conference next to a "rat runner," which is to say someone who uses the learning of rats as a way of studying learning in the laboratory. And in a pause in the discussions, he turned to his neighbor (incidentally, my father was trained as a field biologist before he went into anthropology) and said, "You know, rats are nocturnal. Have you ever tried doing your learning experiments with the rats at night?" His neighbor said, "Gee, no, they bite." What that amounts to is a mass of profound scientific knowledge on the nature of learning based on sleepy rats.

I'm not going to draw the obvious connection between what you can do research-wise with rats in cages and what you can do with children or college sophomores who are stuck in their classroom — and often sleepy. After all, you know, ethnography depends on doing your research in a way that does not bore or irritate or alienate the person you're trying to understand. It's very, very hard to administer questionnaires or psychological tests to people unless either you have them locked up somewhere in a classroom or a lab or you are paying them, because nobody is much interested.

One of the characteristics of qualitative research is that it cannot be based on boring, coercing, irritating the person you are studying, or you get a kind of a sectioning of what they have to say and of their behavior — the equivalent of sleepy rats. At one time, my father worked at a place called Sea Life Park, where among other things, they were studying dolphins. Now if you want to do quantitative research on dolphins, you have the problem that the number of healthy, accessible dolphins in captivity is small. So the researcher who was doing this work, and presumably had gotten the grant for it, had to travel from place to place to find his sample, and he had people that he had hired to conduct the experiment. He arrived at Sea Life Park and set his assistant up with the research protocol. The experiment involved teaching the dolphin to perform a certain procedure with a ball — throw it through a hoop, or something of that sort. There was an "operational definition" of when the dolphin could be said to have learned what was wanted, and this required a certain number of repeats in order to be sure that the dolphin wasn't just accidentally doing the right thing. The assistant was to put the dolphin through the same procedure a number of times and confirm that the results were the same.

The senior researcher went on his way to the next captive dolphin somewhere else and left this woman sitting by the pool conducting her observations. But she was having a very frustrating time. It turned out the dolphins were consistently failing to "demonstrate learning" as defined by the experimental protocol. They would do a certain number of repeats of throwing the ball through the hoop, and then all of a sudden the ball would go off in the opposite direction and she would have to record a failure to learn. My father stopped by to chat — commiserate. She said, "You know, it is so frustrating. Every time they do that there is a kind of a little noise the dolphin makes. I don't know what it sounds like, but in my interpretation it's a snicker." And my father said, "That's really interesting, are you writing that down?" And she said, "No, there's no place for it on the form."

Now what I want to talk about today is the fact that the kind of research that is done not only structures the attention and the experience of the researcher but feeds into the broader social understanding of the nature of the world we live in. We're all of us, as people who do research on human behavior, aware that when we publish our results, those results feed back on people's behaviors, just as poll results affect opinion. They feed into policy making decisions. They feed into journalism. There's a circular process where research is steadily affecting the society in a variety of ways.

This is not only true of findings. The very fact that research is taking place, and people know it is taking place, affects the behavior of those observed, often in very positive ways, as in the Hawthorne effect. But it also feeds into their understanding, their worldview. What I particularly want to emphasize is that the structuring of attention on the part of researchers has a major effect on the structure of attention of all of us.

Many people at these meetings are concerned with problems of legitimacy. You live in university departments where some of the people on doctoral committees question the validity of certain kinds of research. There are people here who don't know how they are going to get past this or that committee and still do the kind of thing they want to do. There are also people who have programs and activities that they would like to see adopted — by school systems, by state regulatory boards — and they find that only certain kinds of data, only certain kinds of evaluation research carry conviction for those who make the decisions. You face a very difficult dilemma if the only way to demonstrate the effectiveness of what you are doing is to misinterpret it. In one example that came up yesterday, if you want the classroom teacher to be collecting data to be used to persuade a local school board of some policy, you may be asking that teacher to distort her or his behavior by asking her to count certain things, to restructure what she was doing in a quantifiable manner. That's somewhat like inviting people to turn themselves into sleepy rats.

We live in a society which has suffered a rising tide of positivism for several centuries. Back at the time of Descartes, back at the time of Newton, the idea was that there were multiple kinds of knowledge, and that certain forms of scientific inquiry should be protected from the interference of those concerned with theological knowledge, for instance. In effect, however, not only have we privileged scientific knowledge but we have defined scientific knowledge as quantifiable knowledge. We have lost track of the fact that these are techniques that are useful and valuable but limited. We have begun to act as if this were the only kind of knowledge there is, not just the only kind of scientific knowledge — that would be bad enough — but altogether the only kind of knowledge.

We have come to believe that only those things that can be quantified can be known. Incidentally, in our society the supreme quantifiable and quantifier is money. This is something that often happens in a culture-contact situation, for money is a wonderful device for bridging culture difference: I don't know what you care about, I don't know how the world looks to you, I don't know what your meaning system is, what's important to you, and you don't know me. But if we can agree on a price, we can exchange money for goods and both feel we benefit from it, feel that we have established a system of equivalency. Everyone who has to make decisions about money knows that we don't value things in direct proportion to their monetary price. The values are not transitive, which they would have to be to truly be reduced to dollars. People have all sorts of specific and, as an economist would say, irrational attitudes that affect the ways in which they deal with money and the illusions that translation into money creates. For instance, I have a terrible problem with things that cost about thirty dollars. That seems very expensive to me. By the time they get up to three hundred dollars, I lose my perspective. "Economic rationality" simply does not hold up when you compare it with behavior, but they're trying to persuade us to make decisions on that basis.

Any cultural system affects what you are able to see and what you are able to attend to. Cultures have built into them theories of relevance: What is connected with what? What needs to be taken into account in making a given decision? When you as a researcher, or others as researchers, pay attention only to that which is quantifiable, a tremendous additional amount of available information is being shut out. It's a little bit like buying a secondhand book, and you go through it and you see that the previous owner has gone through it with a yellow highlighter. Now it's not easy to read freshly a book that someone has gone through with a yellow highlighter. What you get out of the book is what the previous person thought was important. And just as we are constantly getting fed back to us, through the magazines and through the news, the results of social research, we are getting fed back the selective attention of researchers. The case that I want to make to you is that the problem you face is much greater than the problem of persuading doctoral committees or boards of education to think differently. The structures of attention and the structures of relevance are what determine our decision making as a society. To the extent that you can do qualitative research and per-suade people that this kind of research is valid and convincing and more inclusive than the yellow highlighter stuff, you are changing our habits of attention and decision making. What it really amounts to is, shall I pay attention to things that I cannot quantify or shall I shut them out as irrel-evant? This is a matter with huge implications for this society.

I was at a conference recently where a psychologist was speaking about the confusion that goes with being in a society where a value shift is taking place. And he described an experience that he had in a softball game in which both men and women were participating. Now he did give us a fifteen-minute softball lesson as part of his introduction, which I failed to fully absorb so I won't pass that on to you, but the essence of the story was that his team was in the field, runners were running, he got the ball, and the question was who to throw it to. There were two possible people he could throw it to and it was a situation in which any experienced softball player would know who was the "right" person to throw it to, who had the best chance of making the out. However, in this case the "right" person to throw it to happened to be male, and the "wrong" person to throw it to happened to be female. And he caught the ball and he turned and he thought, Oh, my god, if I throw it to the male, the female may think I'm discriminating or I believe she's a bad catch or she doesn't know softball (which clearly he was thinking). What do I do? With microseconds to make his decision, he threw the ball wildly high in the air over both of their heads. And then he went on to talk about how obviously the point of softball is getting runs and winning, and you have to make a decision on that basis and ignore other issues. But people are making decisions for all sorts of extraneous reasons, like making more money for the team from the alumni. They're not just following the rules.

I sat there and reflected that there is research that suggests that in athletic situations women are routinely attentive to the experience of the players along with the score, while men focus on the score. In fact, I think it's nonsense that the point of softball is only to get runs. That may be the point of commercial baseball. But as far as I can see, at least, the point of softball is a group of people out there in the sun having a good time. There have always been vulnerable individuals, long before teams were mixed genders. On an all-male team, there was perhaps one little boy with glasses and braces who was short and his feelings could be hurt, or there was someone who was Jewish, or there was someone who was Polish. Whatever it was, there were always human feelings. What was new was the psychologist bothering to notice them — and he was apparently incapacitated by the experience.

You can always look at the game and say that what is happening is the making of runs. That's great, you can quantify runs. Or you can say a lot of things are happening at the same time, including people's feelings, and their learnings, and their interactions, and how they understand their presence on the field on that day. The speaker was distressed at the preoccupation of college administrations with the money implications of success in sports. That to him was an invasion of a false value. But listening to him I was distressed at his interpretation of the event, the process, the softball, as involving only one issue, the things that could be counted, rather than a multiplicity of issues having to do with the human relations and experiences of the people on the field. Clearly, your interpretation of what softball is about (or ought to be about) is going to affect your behavior.

I'll give you another example, of another kind of narrowing of attention. Another claim that only one kind of factor in a situation is legitimate to pay attention to. Back in the days when students were picketing academic boards of trustees and demanding divestment of stocks in companies doing business in South Africa, one of the things some trustees said was, If we did that we would lose money. But soon it was demonstrated that they could do it without losing all that much money. The cleverer trustees said, You see we have a fiduciary responsibility. Now what this means is that we have been appointed with the responsibility of maximizing return on investment, and if we even *pay attention* to any other factor in our decisions, we are violating our trust. *Any* other factor, there are plenty of them around. . . . It became fashionable to get out of South Africa, but there are still environmental questions, ecological questions, armaments, lots of investment questions that have social implications. The position of the boards of trustees was that to regard those factors (social injustice, environmental degradation, et cetera) as relevant in their appraisal of the situation was a violation of their trust.

That's what I mean by cultural systems of relevance. When you come in, when anybody comes in, and argues for a different interpretation of relevance, notices connections between things, says look at something that isn't listed on the protocol, finds a way to take account of the dolphin's snicker, what they are asking people to do is change their definition of what is valid and relevant knowledge.

The entire educational community is at risk, chronically at risk, because of theories of knowledge that limit what they can see, never mind the introduction of new programs. There are people (who are not themselves in the classrooms) deciding that they want to control the behaviors of teachers with tests, which are quantifiable, which will find out if the children are learning what they are supposed to learn. I haven't quite finished the dolphin story — the point being that dolphins are very intelligent and get bored easily. They like interacting with human beings, and they're captive. They are very like schoolchildren. Many of the children in the classroom don't give the right answers on tests simply because they are bored. And that fact is not supposed to be described. It's one of those unacknowledged things that an observer notices. If you write down everything you see, you get the snicker. If you take down just the numbers, you lose the snicker.

One of the things that happens, between quantitative and qualitative research, is that when you get rid of the fuzzy edge, and you get rid of vagueness, and you stick only to those things that can be quantified and counted, you very rapidly move into a sense of knowledge as dominion or control, with numbers that can be moved around or manipulated. The real situation is wild and woolly and vague and mysterious, and the longer you look at it, the more profound your sense of incomplete knowledge is. It doesn't support the notion of scientific knowledge as dominion. Furthermore, numbers foster the illusion that it is possible to change them. Take an example: the number of young black males who die by homicide, shall we say, which is a frightening number. If we have that number, we believe we can change that number. It's awfully hard to persuade people that to change that number they have to think about the whole structure of race and class and economic inequity in this society. We think we can just make that number smaller.

We have a large number of fallacies that have to do with risk, and the notion of limiting risk. We shouldn't send up space shuttles without understanding that once in a while one of them is going to blow up. There's no way to eliminate that risk. There's also no way to totally eliminate the risk of an accident in a nuclear plant. It just seems like a number, so we think we'll just make that number smaller, without thinking of the whole process, the nature of the system. Because I've done work on AIDS, I've been at some conferences on risk, people talking about risky behaviors in adolescence. They've got these numbers — how many kids are getting killed in drunk driving accidents, how many teenagers are getting pregnant, who's getting hooked on drugs, who's getting sexually transmitted diseases, what have you. Nasty things that nobody wants happening to their children. And what they want to do is to make those numbers smaller.

Well, you discover those numbers correlate with becoming sexually active and early experimentation with cigarettes, to give you just two examples. And so you say, We'd better stop people from becoming sexually active and experimenting with cigarettes and what have you. There's a problem, however, one of many, which is that often the kids who experiment with such things as sex and cigarettes first are the smartest kids. So simply to make the numbers of the experimenters smaller somehow by persuading them not to experiment is a failure to address the whole process of risk taking and experimentation in development, which in fact affects the brightest and most enterprising kids. Kids who need to learn how to manage and calibrate risk, we try to protect by eliminating risk. Because our numbers, which are simple causal interpretations of numerical correlations, persuade us that that's the point to interfere in the situation. Instead, again, of looking at those children's lives or looking at how they are developing.

Well, I said I would talk about my own work, which I'm a bit bored with but I will talk about a little. I got interested in the fact that women suffer a great many interruptions and discontinuities, and have to start again. I got my Ph.D. in Middle Eastern studies and linguistics, but soon after I got a job teaching in Near Eastern languages at Harvard, my husband took a job in the Philippines. We went to the Philippines, and that was the end of that career, like getting a degree in tropical medicine and going to Siberia. Arabic linguistics just didn't hack it in Manila. This is a very common situation of women who move following their husbands' careers.

Women's lives have discontinuities in them involved with time taken off for child rearing. They're laid off sooner. There are the sheer physical discontinuities of menarche, pregnancy, lactation, menopause. Women know more about discontinuities than men do because they deal with so many of them. They always have. Through history, women have also had to think about more than one thing at a time, whereas men have specialized in thinking hard about one thing at a time. These are both very important skills. One way of looking at this is to notice that the primary definition of women's work is all of those tasks that can be done simultaneously with caring for an infant. The primary definition of men's tasks is all of those things that cannot be done simultaneously with caring for an infant.

In a hunting and gathering society, the men go on long hunting trips, or they go off and make war. Women have a baby or two on their hands all the time, and they have to pay attention to the child care as well as the subsistence activities. Often they have to pay attention to the needs of a husband, and a breast baby, and a lap baby, and that one over there getting into mischief. So this primary division of labor has encouraged men to a very high degree of focus on one thing at a time and encouraged women to a multiple style of attention. My own belief is that it is very important for each individual to learn both, which we all do to some degree. It's only a matter of proportion. It's very important not to be so focused on a particular goal that you have no peripheral vision. It's an advantage to be able to handle interruptions, but sometimes when I'm being responsive to many multiple demands, I feel as if I can't pay attention to anything for more than five minutes at a time. Interruptibility is a strength and a weakness. In any case, what I'm saying in passing is that the problem of dealing with discontinuities and the problem of attention to multiple things at the same time are not only modern demands on women but that this situation has always been there. In fact, the modern situation is one in which increasingly men face these same problems, in which the experience of women in bridging discontinuities is going to be drawn on.

I went up to my room yesterday when you were all eating barbecue, and there were MacNeil and Lehrer on TV talking about the unemployment of white-collar workers, and their model was that of men who had assumed they would stay with a single career path all their lives. When that's disrupted they have to learn to switch, to start doing something else. You don't get tenure in the corporation. So this issue of discontinuities is of relevance to men and women, and has always had extra relevance for the situation of women. When I started my work, I felt that in all the research I had read about how women deal with child-care problems, and how they allocate their time, and what it means to have a career, and who goes back for a second career, I could never find a picture of the constellation. Statistics required breaking up the pieces and looking at them separately. It was a perfect situation for case studies. I wanted to know how individuals put these different things together. What I found looking at it is that in detail they put them together very differently. Themes that carry over from one to another are really rather abstract and simply might not show up in any other kind of study. It took months for me to become sensitive to them.

Very rapidly I came to the conclusion that I would have to write about identified individuals. These are unique solutions, I think of them as artistic solutions really. That's why the title of the book is *Composing a Life*. They are very idiosyncratic, as solutions tend to be in periods of culture change, and there aren't a lot of models available. Because I'm not smart enough to disguise a set of cases of this sort, I felt I would have to have an understanding with the women I wrote on that I could use their names, they would have to be able to trust me. The book is written in such an interwoven way that, if somebody had pulled out halfway and said, No you can't use me, I would have had to start from scratch. I couldn't just throw out a chapter. So they had to trust me to go to press without showing them the text, which meant in turn that they had to be friends of mine. And I was quite sure that there was no way I was going to let this process interfere with my relationships with a group of women whom I respect and like, and who trust me and who are doing good and interesting things with their lives. It had to be, for all of these reasons, a process that was enhancing to them. I had to pick people I could write about in a way that would be enhancing. Mind you, there are some discussions of failures in the book that are not identified, but the people who are identified are people who basically have been successful in putting it together in idiosyncratic ways. Then the next thing I realized was that if it was going to be enhancing, it had to be a process that they'd enjoy. Some of them enjoyed the analytical process. For others it was sort of a therapeutic process, thinking about their lives. We ate a lot of good meals together. We drank quite a lot of wine together at various times. We walked in the woods together. The women I worked with ended up, I believe, with a clarified sense of their own lives.

This is a familiar situation in ethnographic fieldwork, where nobody will talk to you unless they enjoy talking to you. And if you plan to go back, you'd better do your research in a way that feeds into their own understanding of who they are, where they're going, and of the meaning in their lives.

I did some work on cross-cultural misunderstandings between Americans and Iranians. I didn't distribute it widely enough, but maybe it helped out in a few cases. An Iranian who had spent time in the United States said to me, "You know, reading this book makes me feel that my culture makes sense. It's not just arbitrary, it's coherent." That's the purpose.

What I'm trying to say by the example of my work is that the research strategy you choose shapes the world of the people you do research on. If I had had a different research strategy, the experience of the women I worked with would have been a different experience, and my world and their world and the world of our friendship would have been affected by that. There is a discussion in the book of what to call these women, who are not subjects. Are they informants, are they collaborators, are they colleagues? What are we to each other? What are we becoming to each other? Basically the format of a great deal of the research that is regarded as valid, rigorous, persuasive is such that the doing of that research creates alienation in the subjects. It also creates alienation in the researcher, who puts on blinders, learns not to notice things. And it propagates alienation in the society.

I'm going to end with one more anecdote. I told you I grew up with qualitative research going on all the time. And in my book about my parents I talk about that. I didn't do a vast amount of archival research so I called it a memoir — because someone else can work on the archives. I decided to do that part which only I could do. And so I did only the archival work that I felt the impulse to do at that moment in my personal understanding of the relationship. But still I learned a great deal about them simply by thinking back as an adult over decisions and behavior that I hadn't thought of since I grew up. So there is a sense in which my understanding of them and their presence for me became a great deal richer out of the process.

But I also discovered something fairly interesting. You know what I remember about my parents now? The things that went into the book. I made a selection, and in making that selection I committed myself to a version of reality. Now I have to make a big effort to recall stories and images that I didn't have or that I did not incorporate in the book at that time. And anyone who has brought up children knows that as time goes on your mental picture of your children as infants looks an awful lot like the photographs you have in your album. We don't remember them as they were. We have a crystallization, a selection of memories. And that is what I have for my parents. That's another example of how recording, interviewing, the variety of techniques we use in our research construct a reality. They constrain and filter and bound reality in various ways.

When the book came out it was reviewed in *Newsweek* by a man who reacted very violently to my description of the fact that my mother and my father systematically photographed and recorded my behavior as an infant. By that time, they had done research on patterns of child care in several different cultures, most particularly Bali and New Guinea. My mother came back with strong, unconventional ideas of what she wanted to do as a parent, and the feeling that if she was going to do unconventional things, they should be recorded. They had the house set up so there were floodlights in every room. (I have to admit that I've sometimes been grateful to World War II, which distracted them from this project. There are two sides to this story.)

Now the man who wrote the review in *Newsweek* was absolutely appalled. He felt that this was a perfectly horrible thing for a mother to do to a child. Well, you know, my grandmother did it to my mother. My mother did it to me. I did it to my daughter, in the context of some research on mother-infant communication and child language development. I mean published research, the real thing. Some of it's even quantitative. But here was this male reviewer, saying that this pattern of behavior that has existed in my family for three generations is horrifying to him. That it is a violation of the fundamental bond between mothers and children. That was something that I had to think about. Because, you see, that is the other side of the problem we're talking about.

He had an image in his mind of scientific knowledge as cold and manipulative, nonintuitive and nonresponsive and uninvolved. That's what science meant to him, and that's not what he wants from a mother. So the other side for him is to say that if you are caring, loving, involved, attentive, responsive, *stop thinking*. You cannot be analytical and maintain those attitudes. You've got to choose. And given that choice, who would want a mother who chose to be a researcher in that sense? But that wasn't the choice my mother saw. Because for her the process of knowledge was not alienating and inattentive, blinkered and limited to the quantifiable. The process of knowledge and the process of caring attention were identical, with this difference, that she kept records and she thought about those records again and again and had them available for helping other people to think about the same issues.

So the point is that if knowledge is constructed positivistically, particularly if it's constructed in relation to the quantifiable, we'll be making bad decisions based on limited attention and limited information. Not only that, we will be separating modes and styles of consciousness and attention, and in a sense draining the caring attention out of those activities that are engaged in to generate knowledge and — heaven help us — draining intelligence out of the situations where emotion is important. One would like mothers, teachers, lovers to have their brains turned on at the same time they're making love, taking care, being bonded, all of those things.

This is essentially what I have brought out of my conversations with all of you over two or three days: that beyond the necessary preoccupation with the legitimacy of what you do and with finding ways to insert it in the political process of school committees, schools of education, therapeutic systems, so on and so forth, we must deal with the issue of how we construct our theory of knowledge and our theory of social systems to include all these forms of knowledge and attention. Each piece that you do that carries conviction becomes part of giving people permission to see their worlds in a richer way. Thank you.

_____ *Question and Answer Session* _____

I'm happy to take questions, and as you know I'm going to hang out outside for a while and sign books and talk with people. People who want to raise questions now, please feel welcome.

When you're talking about male and female ways of knowing the world, I was really struck with the parallel between quantitative ways of knowing and male ways of knowing, female ways of knowing and qualitative research. Is that a valid association in your mind?

I would say yes and no. I do think that the entry of many women into research in these fields does relate to a change in emphasis and that it's helpful. But what has happened in the division of labor in our society has been not just a division of labor but a division of attention, a division in the full spectrum of individual potential of both sexes. Maybe there are some biological differences involved, but I'm not convinced. What you do is push males in this direction a little bit, accentuate part of their potential, and accentuate a different part of the female potential, increasing the differences, and they're both incomplete. Then you say this is the right point of view and this is the deviant point of view, and that's how you construct your society. It doesn't seem like a very good idea.

When you begin to get a recombining of these different experiences, then you have a possibility of broadening that base. Our scientific knowledge of human behavior is largely based on observations of males. Right? Of males and by males, and that's true in anthropology as much as it is in medicine. We simply know much, much less still about females. We know much less about human beings, therefore, and we have to complete it both by doing more research of all kinds on females and by having both males and females do research on both males and females to fill out that picture. But clearly the inclusion of qualitative methods and the participation of more women in research has had a great deal to do with it. Starting with the fact that of all the social sciences, anthropology, which is the least quantitative, has been the most hospitable to women and now we're just sort of infiltrating everything else.

Can you talk about the relative value of qualitative research?

The first thing that I would say is that almost all quantitative research is premature. I think it is very important to work toward getting qualitative research included in the process whereby the quantifiable methods are developed. I see much of what I do that's qualitative as contributing to hypothesis formation. After all that interviewing I do and looking at themes, somebody can design better instruments to study these issues quantitatively. I don't want to do it. I don't like doing it. I don't like doing it to my friends. But it can be done. You can take *Composing a Life,* and you can pull things out of it and test them quantitatively. The man who set up the experimental protocol for the dolphin learning just hadn't spent enough time with dolphins to know that they get bored the same way human beings do. He didn't know that his experimental design underestimated the intelligence and wit of the dolphins. A sense of humor helps. So that particular piece of quantitative research needed someone to do the ethnography first, the fieldwork, the observations, the looking, the listening, before the quantitative instrument or procedure was designed. This is one of the things that we can do with our qualitative work. We can point out where it opens the door to quantitative work.

We also have to realize that people are very much affected by qualitative data if they stop to read it. They don't think they're supposed to be, but they are. Qualitative work does open people's eyes to stuff, I think, and stretches their premises, changes their assumptions.

I think the whole history of research on black families, on the problems of the ghetto, done by outsiders coming in, has suffered from people going in to find pathology with instruments designed with that in mind, instead of looking for what are the strengths that are there. This has been recurrent and is perhaps a prime example that I should have used of how a certain set of research approaches have changed the way society functions. We have been deeply influenced by that work, and the possibility of future work and research has been poisoned. So I think what is critical is to have the ethnography as the starting point and to critique quantitative work in terms of the fact that the person doing it so often has not looked, listened, and thought before designing the instruments. The instruments may be superb methodologically, statistically, and still may not get at the internal issues of the situation.

From that point of view, I think with much better design and with better qualitative input on design, we could work toward a situation where better quantitative data would become available. Small samples, because the actual doing of the work is often so distorted. But you know, policy makers, it's funny, they read reports that are stuffed full of numbers and then they see the evening news and there's a picture of a child crying in India and they respond to that just as much. We have to cut in somewhere in between. Have the same immediacy that journalism has. But at the same time with discipline and not simply tear jerking.

Can whites do research on blacks?

Here is what I feel. You cannot ever truly understand another, even another of the same race, gender, ethnic background, and religion. Right? You can't. Consciousness is private. All right, having said that I would point out that you cannot understand potatoes, laboratory rats, sunbeams, biochemistry. That is, all our knowledge is mediated and constructed. That's our situation. All of our interactions with other human beings are based on constructed internal images which are not the same as anyone else's, all our interactions with the natural environment as well. We try to improve those images so they don't lead us into actions that are disruptive and destructive. To say that this is a problem that is limited to currently salient political categories is simply nonsense. This is a fact of the human condition. It's a fact of all efforts of knowledge.

It's also a fact of all efforts to teach and to transmit experience. I know that you all are not getting what I'm saying. You're getting, constructing, some internal idea of what you think I said as it struck you. It may be, you know, that there's a set of mistakes the males are making that the females aren't, but I've had plenty of experience of being misunderstood by feminists. So the reality is, I am trying to get some ideas across to you, and I know that what you end up with is not what I start with, but I hope it's useful and contributes to what you are constructing internally. It would be nice if it had some vague resemblance, because I've read press stories about things I've said. But anybody who would think that the only person who can teach is someone who is identical to the student is in cloud-cuckoo-land. The point of teaching is that you teach across difference. That's why grown-ups do it with children.

I want to add something to that, because there is something peculiar that we do in our society. It's efficient, but we've got to understand that it's peculiar. We put children together with those from whom they can learn the least. Now I don't mean just that we used to segregate racially or that we send them to boys' schools or girls' schools, parochial schools, et cetera. No, we put them together with children of the same developmental stage. But if their ages are different, they have more to learn across that gap, both of them. So I think that's what people go to school for, to be exposed to difference. That's what it's about.

[*About an earlier reference to letting the interviewees talk to each other.*]

Well I didn't quite say that. See, goes to show, goes to show. Let's be careful, because some of you have bought copies of *Angels Fear,* and that's full of imaginary dialogues between me and my father that I wrote after his death because the only way I could find to write a collaborative book with somebody who was dead was to have "imaginary séances."

That's not what I did with *Composing a Life.* I had separate interviews with four different women, and in a sense I interviewed myself. I wrote long sections that represented what I would have said had somebody asked me the questions that I asked the other people, that I then could excerpt from. I could get stuff off my chest and then be selective, as I was with other people. And what I did was to move back and forth between the responses of different people and weave them together. To many readers it seems as if actual conversations are happening among the women, but the book is quite clear that they are not. None of them had met each other, though all of them had met me. Some readers imagine themselves into this conversation, making a sixth person with the other five. Their words, their phrases, their formulations, their themes were bouncing off each other and echoing in my head so that each juxtaposition allowed me to notice these different kinds of relationships. And in that sense I set them in internal conversation with each other. I set their words bouncing off of each other as a way of thinking about them. Otherwise I would have thought about them one by one.

One of the things that I noticed as I worked along was that every one of the women in the book had an early experience of cultural difference, and of being different from other people. And that's quite an abstract statement. What I had to do was read, say, Johnnetta talking about growing up black in Florida, but not just growing up black but growing up black middle class in Florida and what that meant to her and what she could observe around her, and beginning to think about that. And then saying to myself, Well, do I see this in somebody else's experience? And I would look at Alice as an immigrant to the United States having lived several years in France, who came to the United States and saw a cultural difference, and Ellen going and working in Africa. Johnnetta later in Africa. My own experiences of cultural differences as a child. So having noticed that about one person, I'd look at the others and say, Well, is there anything that seems to me equivalent in their experience, so that having seen and noticed difference in childhood opened their imagination as an adult to further differences? Okay, that's what I mean by making the interviews "talk to each other." That's what I planned to talk about today, but I didn't.

What grounds are there for optimism?

That takes an awfully long answer. I don't know how to do that on the fingers of one hand. I think an interesting example of directions of cultural change has come up again and again in discussions here in relation to support groups, where people are learning to construct elective groups that pick up some of the functions of the family. I see the reemergence of some of the capacities we have emphasized in females and in some of those we have emphasized in males, and the possibilities of getting to a richer and more balanced view coming out of that.

Will we still be around in ten years? That I can't tell you. But I guess I go in and out of despair. One of the things that I have come to feel very strongly in the last couple of years is that again and again I will believe that something should happen and that it's right, and I will argue for it. And it won't happen. Now, I'm not going to stop doing that. It would be wrong to stop doing that. But at the same time I've moved toward a much more ecological vision of the political process, which says that if we can just get things like the environment on the agenda, if we can just get them to be part of the discussion, that's more than half the battle. We're going to be tearing our hair, and weeping and wailing and saying everything's being done wrong, but to get issues onto the agenda, to get points of view expressed is critical, however disappointed one is when that point of view doesn't carry. That makes me feel more optimistic. So the world isn't going to conform to any of my visions of how it ought to be. But if I can just keep circulating those visions, they'll have some effect.

Is it important to be a good writer if you are qualitative researcher?

I think it's important to try to write well and communicatively and intelligibly. I think most academic writing reeks of insecurity. For me writing well is a survival issue. I have a confession to make to you all. When I decided I was going to write *Composing a Life,* I thought, There's no way the National Science Foundation is going to give me the money do to this, or the National Institutes of Health or any other granting agency. There's no way I can describe this project that's going to get by the review committees. And I looked at my savings and thought, Well, maybe I can get a book contract. Then I applied to the Guggenheim Foundation as a writer. I didn't apply as a scientific researcher. What I have done now is that I have a joint appointment in anthropology and English. I have set up a world in which if the kind of scientific work that I do is misunderstood, I'm going to have the hat of the artist, the humanist, available, and that has worked for me, but that's a personal strategy. In a sense that's kind of a sellout, right, because I deeply believe that a book like *Composing a Life* is a part of the scientific enterprise and that the divisions we make between social science, humanities, and science may blind us.

So write well, care about writing well. Not purple prose, mind you. You've got to cut the purple prose out and go for the crystal prose. Thank you all.

IN PRAISE OF AMBIGUITY

Does everything need to be precise and explicit — cut and dried? Or are both learning and creativity supported by a certain degree of vagueness and continuing puzzlement? This essay, first given as a lecture in Keene, New Hampshire, was designed to be published in a 1999 collection for teachers, a reminder that there is more to learning than being able to produce correct answers. Our computers become more powerful year by year, but error and ambiguity remain a part of the human condition and sometimes stimulate learning and creativity. We need to design technologies and policies that take this fact into account and never undertake anything in which we cannot afford, from time to time, to fail.

—MCB, 2004

⌒

Ah, what a dusty answer gets the soul
When hot for certainties in this our life.
GEORGE MEREDITH,
Modern Love[1]

If education is to prepare for life rather than mislead, it is important not to project the expectation of certainty or to promise unambiguous answers. or even the notion that the most important communication between human beings, whether in the classroom or elsewhere, is the transmission of objective information. Preparation for life is preparation for a long meander through uncertainty, for working with partial clues and rough approximations, for skillful guessing and zestful improvisation. Even those facts that seem clear and unambiguous unfold into unexpected implications — and are sometimes contradicted by new findings.

The human capacity to draw pattern from confusion underlies both empirical investigation and imaginative creation. It allows us to find our way, day by day, through an environment in which there is both constancy and variation, and over time has given us both astronomy and astrology, different ways of seeking pattern in the stars. It is fundamental to the ability to perceive and learn and underlies ongoing adaptation most effectively if the discovery of regularity goes with flexibility about conclusions. This is especially true in a time of rapid change and cultural diversity. Patterns that once seemed clear may be blurred or reversed or overlaid with complexity; yet it is still necessary to make decisions and act upon them despite uncertainty and ambiguity.

As an anthropologist, I find that the experience of crossing from one culture into another throws me into situations where I must act on ambiguous cues,[2] just as children must, just as adults must often. In the field, you feel much like a small child. You have to be willing to be incompetent, to make absurd mistakes on matters that are obvious to everyone around you. More generally, you have to tolerate a great deal of ambiguity, responding to and using words and gestures whose meanings are unclear, when the responses of others seem highly unpredictable. Much of the literature on culture contact emphasizes ways to minimize the stress this involves and to avoid dangerous or offensive errors; but there is a positive side as well to learning to live with the ambiguity.

I want to approach the issue of ambiguity through a story about the first year of my marriage, itself a cross-cultural learning experience. My husband was born in Syria and is ethnically Armenian. When I first met him, I looked up *Armenia* in an encyclopedia because the only association I had with Armenia at that time was the phrase "poor starving Armenians." Later, after reading Armenian history and studying the language (and the cuisine), I still had a lot to learn when we got married. As a new bride moving into an unfamiliar culture, I was in many ways facing it as a child must, trying to figure it out as I went along. We went to visit my husband's parents in Beirut on our honeymoon. It was the custom in this Protestant household to say grace in unison before meals, and although it is not easy to pry the words apart when everyone is speaking together and mumbling, I listened carefully and joined in. After our honeymoon, when we came back to Cambridge and set up in an apartment, this became a ritual for us as well, saying grace together in Armenian before dinner.

After a full year, I discovered that I had misconstrued the words we said every day. I had thought that the words of one line of this little prayer were "Give us your love," when in fact the words said "Give us contented hearts." I had been saying it wrong for a year, but the difference in pronunciation was small and nobody had noticed. When we had dinner guests, I would translate, but my husband never listened because he believed he knew what I was saying. The important thing is that my incomplete understanding was adequate for functioning, just as Ptolemaic astronomy is a pretty adequate basis for navigation.

Notice that my analysis of the words of the prayer was plausible because, as a literate adult who had grown up in a related religious culture, I know the kind of thing people are likely to pray for. If the gap of ignorance had been greater, my analysis might have been more remote. As someone pointed out, if I had thought that the words of the grace were "Give us your wheelbarrow," I might have turned to my husband and asked a question. We all share the human tendency to make sense of jumbled or incomplete information, and it is precisely when we think we understand that we *stop* asking questions.

Perhaps it was this confusion that drew my attention to that line of prayer because, for some thirty-five years since then, I have been trying to figure out what it would mean to have a "contented heart." The phrase has meant different things to me at different times, both a hopeless aspiration and an easy familiarity. Sometimes it means something religious; sometimes it invokes family or cultural continuity. An Armenian woman told me that as a child she had asked her mother what it meant to have a "contented heart" and had been told, "That's when your liver isn't on fire (with envy)." In fact, this little prayer keeps changing its meaning on me, no longer because of a mishearing, but because of layers of ambiguity about the nature and shared basis of contentment that I have not resolved.

Children will accept a great deal of weirdness from grown-ups, so almost anything may be plausible. Consider the example of that totem animal of all children taken to Protestant evangelical services, Gladly, a bear who happens to be cross-eyed. The child doesn't turn to the mother and say, "Why are you singing about a bear?" Indeed, the notion of happily carrying a cross constructed for death by torture is at least equally puzzling. From a child's point of view, grown-ups are quite capable of asking God for a wheelbarrow, and following that model, children feel free to ask God for tricycles and pocketknives, which is theologically equally problematic.

Once I was with Iranian friends in the holy city of Qom, when they decided to visit the shrine of Maasume, the sister of Imam Reza, which has made Qom a major pilgrimage center, exporting mullahs from its theological schools and importing the bodies of those who wish to be buried there. Although I am not a Muslim, I was veiled, so I dared to enter the shrine with my friends and sat on the carpet with my veil pulled forward while they prayed. A shabby old woman came over to me, tapping on my shoulder and mumbling, but I ignored her, and my friends tried not to giggle. After they had finished their prayers, one of them turned to me and said, in Persian, "You should ask the lady for whatever you want." I was ready to follow instructions, but for a moment I floundered in confusion: Was the old woman not a beggar as I had concluded? Or, even as a beggar, were her prayers believed to be especially efficacious? In fact, the "lady" *(hanom)* in question was Maasume. But to ask a deeper question, would it be appropriate to ask Maasume for a tricycle or a pocketknife?

A relationship exists between two kinds of incomplete understanding. First, we have what seems a rather simple kind of error: I listened to the Armenian prayer and interpreted it incorrectly. The child does the same for the evangelical hymn "Gladly the Cross I'd Bear." But then we have examples, not of error in a simple sense, but of words that have a potential depth of meaning that is bound to change through the life cycle. Even when I knew who the "lady" was, even when the child grasps that a cross is to be borne, understanding remains incomplete, leaving room for growth through the ambiguity.

How often do we speak or read words that will change their meaning over time? Consider the words of wedding vows. You don't know what you're doing when you get into it, right? More important, the whole system depends on that incomplete understanding. "I do" is necessarily a dusty answer.

What is important for educators here is that the experience of participation in spite of the first kind of incomplete understanding may be supportive in the encounter with the second kind. Avoiding the first level of ambiguity with careful lesson plans may subvert a later potential for growth. What did I do with that prayer? I did what human beings always do: I was getting a muddled input that I analyzed and made sense of in a plausible kind of way that allowed me to participate and left an opening for later reflection. The capacity to participate is more important than, and often prior to, understanding.

In general, I believe, participation precedes learning, not vice versa, and ambiguity potentiates learning. This is one of the great areas where our educational systems need to be reshaped, because they tend to be based on the premise that all problems have solutions and all questions have answers, generally a single answer, that can be marked right or wrong on an exam, and that school prepares the child for participation by teaching those answers. Whereas you can look at infants having conversations before they can speak a recognizable word of adult language and see that it works the other way around.[3] The participation precedes the knowledge.

We live in a technologically advanced mass society where numbers are more and more important. As weapons become more powerful, populations denser, and information more available, the demand for specificity and predictability increases. Nevertheless, in the back of our minds we all recognize that the imagination is nourished by vagueness and ambiguity and that human emotions do not work by the numbers. Approaching marriage with a prenuptial agreement about property has many advantages, but negotiating such an agreement does not build the relationship and may damage it. Civilization depends not only on precise technology but also on play and poetry and humor, all of them shot through with ambiguity.

At an institutional level, the effort to make behavior more and more predictable by specification and decontextualization is pervasive. Education is only one of many areas in our society that undermine the capacity to work with and tolerate ambiguity. Accountants, time and motion experts, lawyers . . . these are all devotees of disambiguation.

Sometimes, when perfect precision is not possible, choices between different kinds of ambiguity are possible. Different ways of coding measurements — digital and analog — open the door to different kinds of imprecision. With any analog instrument, a ruler, a traditional watch, a mercury thermometer, the reading of any measurement is imprecise.[4] Potentially, another decimal place of further precision could always be added, if the instrument were finer, but notice that the errors tend to be at the right end of the readings you record. Your error is going to be by, let us say, 1/100 of an inch rather than by 100 inches. The errors cluster where they matter least.

If you glance at an analog dial on a watch, which uses distances to represent the passage of time, your errors will be of that same order — "Just about quarter of eight" — not precise. If you tell time by the sun, your errors may be greater but they are of the same kind; they are "more-or-less" mistakes, the difference, say, between two and three in the afternoon, but you do know, accurately, that it is early afternoon. Similarly, a slide rule is an extraordinarily elegant analog computer that allows you to compute by adding and subtracting real lengths, always with an element of approximation. One key in using a slide rule is deciding how many places (toward the right) you can be accurate to and legitimately cite.

By contrast, in totting up a column of expenses on a calculator, if your finger does not slip, your answer is precise, but alas, you are just as likely to slip in the thousands as in the pennies. This is a characteristic of many digital processes: that errors are not sorted in terms of significance. Answers are either correct or incorrect. Thus, it is reasonable and usually sufficient to say that it is roughly half past six, but it is not reasonable to say that your checkbook almost balances: Either it does or it doesn't, and several errors can mask each other. Error can occur in any digit on a display, as many people have discovered when they received erroneous bills off by a factor of ten or a hundred.

A significant personality difference may exist between those who go digital and those who prefer the old analog watches or even stay with the sun or with the sundial, which all have a certain congruence. The kind of information that comes from a digital dial is different, and the kinds of errors you are liable to encounter are different. You always have some variation with analog readings, and you learn to accept it and take it into account. You live with an open mind about whether you and others have things exactly right. The digital reading offers the possibility of precision, but when the precision fails, you may be unprepared. Interestingly enough, the habit of reaching ballpark approximations is an important protection — for instance, in restaurants. Those who depend on digital processes tend to take numbers literally, with no sense of approximate plausibility even when they are cited by politicians.

Once upon a time, all engineers had slide rules. Now they have calculators, and so does everyone else, so few acquire the skill of managing approximations. As the world becomes more digital, the properties of digital calculations require that things be gotten right, rather than letting us, without having gotten it perfectly, ease up on precision and work with plausible approximations. This is an important and dangerous change because, in the brave new digital world, with its premium on precision, the costs of carelessness tend to be very high.

The English, rather endearingly, sometimes call computers TOMS, which stands for Totally Obedient Morons — totally obedient, but without judgment or imagination and demanding totally unambiguous commands. In conversation with human beings, especially familiar and beloved human beings, a lot of ambiguity is tolerable. I used to have conversations with my mother wherein I would say, "Look, what was the name of that woman, I remember something about sunshine and morning glories?" And she'd say to me, "Oh, yes, that was Georgianna, and she had a morning glory pattern on the curtains in her guest room when we stayed there." That is really a very effective piece of communication — the kind of communication that family members have with each other, that just gets you nowhere with a computer. It requires, besides a great deal of trust and shared experience, a pattern of heuristics, a shared pattern of search and discovery.

Human beings tend to find things because they know where to look. Well into the 1990s, the best human chess players were still able to defeat the most powerful computers. When a computer is programmed to play chess, it checks and compares vast numbers of alternative moves, far more than any human chess master could explore. A master chess player only thinks through a subset of the possible sequences, knowing, however, what kind of move is likely to be helpful. Skill lies in knowing which sequences to check, by a process that Herbert Simon called "selective heuristics."[5]

Oddly enough, one advantage of not being able to check all the alternatives is that chess is endlessly fascinating and continues to be a form of play. Chess would be trivial if the players could process enough alternative sequences to make it determinate, which is why grown-ups lose interest in tic-tac-toe. Just as there is a lot of ambiguity in religion, there is also a lot of ambiguity in play.

During the campaign for the 1996 GOP presidential nomination, Steve Forbes used a television ad in which he held up a copy of the Constitution, then a copy of the Bible, and then the Federal Tax Code — a great fat manual, much longer than the Bible, whereas the Constitution is just a few pages. Forbes attributed the length of the tax code to the presence of deliberate loopholes, granted as political favors, yet all legislation today is accompanied by massive and detailed regulations designed to be fully specific and unambiguous.

The strength of the Constitution, however, is that it is, in many ways, ambiguous. We know perfectly well that we see meanings there today of which the framers were unaware. The Declaration of Independence spoke of equality, but all that the signers meant was white men over twenty-one. Today, we mean all citizens, of whatever race or sex. Until after the Vietnam War, young men were drafted at eighteen but could not vote until they were twenty-one. They could be sent overseas to die in warfare and yet had no right to express a view. At a certain point, it dawned on the people of this country that this was out of line with the underlying wisdom of the framers, a particularly pernicious kind of taxation without representation. An evolving understanding is, in some sense, implicit in the words of the Constitution even if the people who wrote those words did not themselves fully understand them.

What would happen if we tried to draft a new Constitution today? Today's style would be to strive for something watertight, fully explicit, leaving nothing to the imagination, something that could be understood in only one way, covering every contingency. This would be an inert and tedious document, one that would not grow, one that would not encourage understanding to deepen. The words that are the most powerful for human beings are words like "Give us contented hearts," that set you wondering over decades what they might mean. In the famous Serenity Prayer used by Alcoholics Anonymous, the difference between what can be changed and what cannot is never defined, so the prayer offers, not a decision rule, but a challenge to discover new ways to adapt.

If we wanted to write a Constitution today, I very much doubt that it could be done except perhaps by a mixture of poets and biologists who understood the fact that as long as an organism is alive, the process of development and adaptation is ongoing. Similarly, we are unlikely to progress to any kind of definitive world order by legislation, by formal decision making and voting.[6] If you consider what it takes to reach a disarmament treaty, limiting just a single type of weapon, and the preoccupation with checking and double-checking and triple-checking, it becomes clear that global confederation or cooperation cannot be achieved by negotiations. This is not to say that we should not chip away at it or that it is not particularly important in some areas of trade or disarmament. Yet in such negotiations, the major casualty is trust, and every step reveals the lack of trust.

Ping-Pong, in contrast, and artistic exchange and tourism provide ways to work implicitly toward trust. Trust was generated when I sat at the table with my new in-laws, missaying a prayer but participating. Often what matters is the establishment of areas of vague agreement and nonspecific relationship that can be used as the context — the channel — for transmitting other kinds of things. Another way of saying this is that the communication that establishes relationships is, for mammals like us rather than computers, analog communication. One characteristic of the peace process in the Middle East or in the Balkans has been that whereas a few items are very clearly specified, others, such as the long-term status of Jerusalem, are left vague. This means that the process may break down at a later stage, but it allows joint participation in early stages, working side by side, rubbing along and dealing with frictions and misunderstandings, which may engender trust.

We increasingly tend to think that speech exists for the purpose of conveying unambiguous and verifiable information about some set of facts or circumstances, that speech is primarily referential. Not true. This referential function is secondary to the establishment of relationship. If we are walking down the road outside and we both simultaneously feel large drops of water on our heads and I turn to the person next to me and say, "It's raining," and she says, "Yeah, I guess it is!" am I informing her of the fact that it has begun to rain? And is she confirming this information I gave her? No! Something quite different is taking place. Our words appear to be about the rain, but they actually mean something like the following: "You and I are in the same place and are in communication with each other." I can convey an even stronger connection by rolling my eyes and saying, "Great weather!"

Vast sums are spent to increase the technical capacity to predict the weather. Whether or not it rains on a given day can affect election results and sales, power consumption and transport. But most talk about the weather is not meteorological and would be far less useful in human relations if every statement came equipped with a statistical probability. If I say, "How are you today?" am I seeking medical information? Usually not, even though precise reporting and diagnosis are important in clinical practice. Even in a hospital, a patient may reply with, "Pretty good, Doc," not because he is healthy but because he likes the doctor.

I recently heard of an ethnographic paper by a Japanese graduate student asserting that when Americans ask "How are you?" they don't want the details of health and disease. Correct. But of course they do want information, usually of quite a different kind: Are you glad to see me? Are we still friends? Even, sometimes, How are you?

Well, but these are the trivial cases. The fact is that a very large proportion of our conversation has a small element of reference and verifiable fact and a large element of creating relationship, of establishing communion. When that is achieved, the rest can be vague or erroneous or self-contradictory. This kind of communication, that says, "The channel is open," is called *phatic*.[7] As soon as you start looking for it, you see it everywhere. A pilot who is coming in for a landing has her radio open to the tower, and very often the conversation seems empty for many minutes — "Ah, do you read me?" "Roger, yes, I read you, yes, I hear you . . . all clear, keep on coming . . ." Why bother with that stuff? Because without it, you would not know that the radio channel was open and available for an emergency. At that point, precise information might become important.

We do all this back-and-forthing as a way of indicating that we are in touch, and it is an essential skill. If I tell you I happen to know that the mayor is having an affair with the newspaper editor, am I really giving you information about the mayor? Or am I conveying something about my willingness to gossip with you? We may share disapproval, or we may share glee, and we share the satisfaction of having inside dope. You may well have heard that piece of gossip already, but there's still a gain in sharing it. Even software designers program computers to say Hello, to make the user feel comfortable, not because the computer needs it.

A great deal of discussion today asserts the loss of very basic social patterns. We wonder about the fate of the family, about community, about friendship and loyalty. Perhaps the key loss is a sense of what communication is for or about. Relationships are built through touch and tone of voice and the satisfactions of maintaining a rhythm of low-key conversation, of small talk and chitchat. We live with the vast potential of language and with a framework of science and technology that allows us to convey massive amounts of highly precise information. But all of that depends on establishing a state of connection, of context and relationship, and these are even more important for learning. The sense of connection is much more likely to be created by shared participation than by precision. The sense of being "in touch" is created by actual touch, by eye contact and tone of voice, often by reiteration of the known and familiar rather than new information. My experience with the Armenian grace taught me (or perhaps retaught me) that interaction is more important than precise translation or vocabulary. You make what sense you can out of what you hear, but communion is what matters. And when communion is important, the insistence on precision may preclude it; when lawyers get involved, goodwill erodes.

We live in a period when we find ourselves forced into distrusting others and being distrusted, into feeling that we have to document everything, make everything checkable, accurate, referential, and unambiguous. We are preoccupied in this society with disambiguation, with overspecification of all the details.

Another loss is involved in the cultural shift away from a tolerance for ambiguity, and that is the loss of imagination, a loss of potentials for development and new understanding. What if a given question has no "correct answer" but only the vague intimation of one? Playing with the question and imagining possible answers is still valuable. If you consider the value of reading a newspaper or listening to radio, as opposed to watching television, the older media required more imagination because so much less detail was provided. The process of listening or reading is much more active than the process of watching television. In the same way, educators have long advocated simple toys rather than highly specialized ones: A slightly shaped wooden block with wheels can be a racing car or a police car; a vaguely human figure can be a princess or a soldier or an infant.

It is interesting to sort out the relationship between specificity and ambiguity in the worlds of commerce. Plenty of ambiguity does appear on television, particularly in commercials that might be accused of false claims if they were too explicit, but the ambiguity is designed to lead to predictable conclusions. Many of the best creative minds in the media design commercials to be stimulating to the imagination. Perfume commercials, for instance, cannot be explicit about scent, but hint instead at possible romance, and others suggest agonies of loss and loneliness for lack of the right deodorant or detergent. At the same time, sales often depend on specification: Just as children are urged to demand specialized and detailed dolls and models, there are now as many different deodorants as there are body parts with possible odors, five or six substances to be used in sequence in hair washing, and different cleansers for every part of the bathroom or kitchen.

Religion has a curious fluctuation as well. Various examples in this chapter are drawn from religious contexts, but religious teachers are not known for tolerance of ambiguity. Consider the blood spilled and the effort poured into making religious language "unambiguous" — to be sure that all the people are thinking and believing the same thing when they say the same words. Theologians labor and bicker to put together creeds and catechisms to be absolutely unambiguous and specific and to exclude heresy. But every congregation is full of people trying to give these words their own meanings, and maybe, maybe, the words are more powerful that way, more reliable guidelines for living in a changing world.

It is important to realize that neither analog nor digital coding and neither ambiguity nor disambiguation can be separated out as reflecting a "higher" capacity. Both occur in all cultures and throughout the biological world, in different proportions. It is true that the great majority of communication systems between animals other than humans are iconic and analogic rather than digital, but if we include genetic, neurological, and hormonal communication within the organism, both kinds occur and are essential to life. In a sense, the human use of symbols, including words, that are ambiguous because they have multiple meanings, is unique, but many other organisms have some capacity to respond to ambiguous information. Huston Smith, a scholar of comparative religion, quotes Lewis Thomas, a biologist, as saying, "Ambiguity seems to be an essential, indispensable element for the transfer of information from one place to another by words, where matters of real importance are concerned."[8] Smith goes on to connect this to the need for a sense of wonder and for the willingness to accept incomplete control in order to make commitments that are necessarily open-ended.

The effort to avoid ambiguity affects education in a whole variety of ways. For years, it has been standard to design reading primers using only words that children of a given age could be expected to already know, yet the most beloved children's books are full of totally strange, unintelligible words that demand new meanings and new imaginings: "O frabjous day!" The incomplete and shifting understanding makes reading (and rereading) books of that sort an adventure, with different mental pictures for children of different ages and adults as well. Should a lesson always be unambiguous, or should there be gaps that call for imagination? Should children ever be allowed to believe that they have fully understood a poem or a Shakespeare play or that they know the "causes of the Civil War"?

How often, when a piece of poetry is read in school, are children told, "This is what it means." They may even be told, implicitly or explicitly, "Now you have read *Hamlet,* and this is what it means." Yet no one knows what *Hamlet* means after a high school reading; it will go on unfolding into new layers of meaning as it is read or seen on stage again and again.

This is not just a matter of Great Works from the literary canon. Nursery rhymes, proverbs, and lines from popular songs acquire meaning at every hearing. Why not play with it? We do want, I think, children to have imagination; we do want them to have a capacity to trust; we do want them to discover new meanings that we have not yet seen . . . or do we just want them to be able to reproduce what we tell them? We want them to be free to make original discoveries and to make mistakes. When people try to construct their world so that there is no ambiguity in it, whether they are theologians and inquisitors or arms control negotiators or IRS regulation writers, they are choosing an arid, rigid way of being.[9]

We are suffering today from several related pathologies. What is most worrying about contemporary forms of fundamentalism is the declaration that ancient religious texts — most of which were written as poetry, story, or speculation — should be read (selectively) as if they were explicit and literally true. We are running into a related pathology in debates about the interpretation of the Constitution, with "strict constructionism" emerging as a political form of fundamentalism.

All too often, major enterprises are undertaken on the premise that perfect accuracy is possible, so any error or ambiguity is culpable and opens the door to lawsuits. Yet all of measurement is subject to limitations on accuracy and diagnosis, and treatment must always contain guesswork. A shift in how we handle information phases over into a change in fundamental human relationships, in ethics, and in how we organize all of our common ventures.

Anyone who wants to be an astronaut needs to realize that, at that level of complexity, casualties are going to occur. The *Challenger* disaster was followed by an investigation to find out where the mistake was so that it could be eliminated and blame meted out. That's fine — as far as it goes — provided we don't have the illusion it will never happen again. Other disasters will occur if human beings go up in space or build nuclear reactors. Human beings are not infallible, so we should not engage in activities where error is intolerable. Yet increasingly, we are demanding absolute perfection in performances under pressure of extreme stress and complexity.

The daily papers offer multiple examples of an emerging pattern of assumptions that deny the human necessity of ambiguity. When White House Counsel Vincent Foster committed suicide (in 1993), it seems clear that there was a lot of dither, grief, and confusion, that his colleagues were upset and did not do everything by the book, but the confusion seems to have been human rather than malicious. If every piece of evidence brought to a court in this country were scrutinized the way the evidence in the O. J. Simpson case was, we would stop believing that any police procedure can be trusted because it is impossible to be 100 percent accurate. There are going to be chinks in the chain of evidence, misunderstandings, and misreportings, arising from inefficiency rather than conspiracy. Of course, police procedures need to be criticized and improved, but they will never be perfect, so we must build procedures that allow for human fallibility and still allow us to move ahead — to, as they used to say, muddle through.

One cannot defer decisions until one has found the absolutely correct answer. One must act, get involved, commit. More and more Americans fail to realize that they have to support candidates with whom they do not entirely agree, who are only partially right, and who will learn in office and change their minds. We have to vote for people who are imperfect, people with whom we disagree less than with their rivals. Indeed, any politician with whom I agreed fully would probably be a disaster for this country, and that is probably true for most of us. All our politicians are compromise figures of one sort or another. But those who stay home and do not vote are evading the moral ambiguity of having to act in the world and take positions that are not black-and-white positions.

Children need to be trained to *work with* ambiguous materials, not just reject them: to watch something, to critique it, to puzzle it out. In dealing with the media, children need to begin to be able to sort out layers of news and fantasy and to seek out the purposes and contexts, because at present we are sitting ducks for effectively ambiguous messages! We should regard responding to ambiguity and living with it as a skill. A kind of literacy, for which we need a new word.

These are not easy concepts to express to parents, administrators, and school systems caught up in the current pathologies. In town after town, the model for improving education is writing more rules — and developing detailed curricula that will specify every minute in the student's day and every point that goes into a grade and establish clear and specific objectives for every lesson. Here the effort at disambiguation creates distrust of teachers and undermines the possibility of responding creatively in the classroom.

On the other hand, a teacher can embrace the fact that the members of a class bring with them multiple levels of understanding and will leave with multiple levels of understanding. When I was teaching in Iran, to a class in which the knowledge of English was very unequal, it occurred to me that I faced a choice. One could teach to the brightest and most competent students, making the others miserable and embarrassed, or one could teach to the weakest, making the brightest ones bored and frustrated. Or one could teach in such a way that students at different stages of their own learning each attended to something rather different and emerged with varying understandings. I think this is true of the best teaching and the best writing — that it uses ambiguity — and often one of the slower students absorbs some part of the more complex message that begins to make sense over time. This can only work, however, in situations where alternative understandings or partial understandings are valued and respected, where not all answers are classified as right or wrong. The kinds of differences I encountered in my Iranian classroom are characteristic of any human community; in fact, my six-year-old daughter sometimes sat drawing in the back of the classroom and would occasionally raise her hand. Especially in situations of change or culture contact, gradients of learning run through the entire population, in addition to the differences of gender and age that guarantee different systems of meaning within families.

To prepare people to deal with cultural, religious, and racial differences, it is important to use the experience of multiple levels of understanding by such simple devices as mixing ages, instead of letting the society become increasingly age-segregated. It has struck me as one of the great ironies that we think children will learn best when they are with other children who are the same in as many ways as possible. The tolerances for ambiguity and for difference run together.

All of the different pathologies relating to intolerance of ambiguity add up to a pervasive epistemological hubris in our society. The fundamental question for education, it seems to me, is how to avoid contributing to the problem. We need to swim against this stream of disambiguation and keep a certain balance that embraces ambiguity. Ambiguity can be uncomfortable, but children must be able to function and grow in situations where they do not know the answers, where they cannot help making some mistakes, where they must meet strangers with whom their understanding is incomplete. We need to avoid sending the message that whenever knowledge or understanding is incomplete, someone is at fault.

Above all, children need to see the world and other people, as well as works of art and ideas, as not finite in their meaning. Children need the freedom to reach the kind of misunderstanding I had of that Armenian grace originally, which permitted participation, and to move on, knowing that it is natural to go through life changing your understanding of relationships and of the world and maintaining a playful sense that it's all very serious, very positive, very beautiful.

PURPOSE, GENDER, AND EVOLUTION

In 1970, when relevance was all the rage, I wrote a paper for a conference on anthropology and relevance, but instead of presenting our papers, we were together to hear the news about student demonstrators gunned down at Kent State and the bombing of Cambodia, and we bypassed the papers — mine has since been lost — to talk about the crisis. But the notion of an anthropology of relevance, studying the cultural shaping of attention and the way factors are linked together in life-and-death decisions, has stayed with me and reemerged later in this paper. It was written for yet another conference, this one on evolution and ethics, asking several related questions: How did the human ethical capacity evolve? Is ethics timeless or its evolution continue? And last, does our knowledge of evolution provide a model for ethical thinking? At that time, sociobiology was riding high, suggesting that we would be unable to modify certain behaviors, including male domination, rooted in human evolution. Today sociobiology has been renamed evolutionary psychology, but it continues the fashionable argument for accepting more and more of human behavior as based on innate patterns. My argument was that ethics depends on the connections we are able to see between events and on what our technology allows us to affect or change, both of these being culturally constructed.

—MCB, 2004

355

It is hard to think of areas where comparisons between humans and non-humans have created more interesting and confusing comparisons than in ethics and evolution.

It has been traditional for writers exhorting human beings to virtuous behavior to use imagery from the animal world: be as industrious as the bee, as courageous as the lion, as foresighted as the squirrel, as faithful as the stork. The pelican, traditionally believed to feed its young from its own blood, serves in iconography as a symbol of self-sacrifice and of the Christ.

Social Darwinism built on a new perception of the factors determining and determined by interactions in nonhuman species to propose an alternative rhetoric for the validation of particular patterns of human behavior by natural history. With changes in evolutionary understanding, we see this set of analogies as just as inadequate as those of medieval moralists, but only after they were also condemned as omitting central ethical issues of human behavior and as being destructive of human communities to boot. The writings of sociobiologists represent another stage of this debate. Moving beyond the notion of behavior as oriented to individual survival, they have proposed, for instance, that altruistic behaviors in humans and in other animals (in prophets and in pelicans) can be regarded as maximizing the survival of a shared genetic inheritance.

Ethical Discourse

All of these analogies, however, deal with behavior and its evolution. In this discussion I will work on the assumption that ethics is not a characteristic of behavior, but a domain of human discourse dealing with the act of choice between real alternatives. At the same time, I will assume that making choices is a part of the overall pattern of human adaptation, and that the capacity to discuss and make choices has evolved because it has, so far, been adaptive.[1] Characteristics resulting in the destruction of a species' environment so that it can no longer survive or flourish in that environment would not be regarded (in retrospect, at least) as adaptive.

To the best of my knowledge, there is no evidence that bees are tempted to sloth, or inclined to hoard their honey and withhold it from the common store, or that there exists a domain of discourse to assist individual bees in these decisions. For human beings, whether or not one concedes individual free will in human decision making, such a domain exists. It has changed over time, increasing in complexity and (slowly) adjusting to new realities in the human situation, and it appears to have some relationship to actual decisions made, although not in a uniform way. These decisions, in turn, may have implications for survival of individuals, or of populations, or even of the biosphere.

Ethics consists not only in what we conclude but in what we are able to discuss, and where and how (and involving whom) the discussion takes place. Ethics in this sense is a part of human culture and is variable from one human community to another. It has frequently been argued that for *Homo sapiens* cultural evolution has largely replaced biological evolution, allowing human communities to adjust their adaptive patterns far more rapidly and to transmit new patterns through symbolic communications that do not need to wait on the turnover of many generations for the dissemination of new possibilities. Human behavior also suggests a preoccupation with the survival of cultural information — creeds, dogmas, traditions, and indeed ethical systems — passed from generation to generation symbolically as well as through genetic descent. We die for dogmas as well as for DNA, living, for example, in celibacy to produce spiritual offspring through propagation of a faith, rather than producing biological offspring.

Ethics follows efficacy, but prior to efficacy there is an issue of awareness. The cultural domain of ethics involves those areas where choice is possible, and the ways and criteria whereby choices are discussed and made. This domain is changed by knowledge, by technical capability, and by factors which structure the understanding of these possibilities, particularly attention. The fact that some human beings carry the genetic trait for Tay-Sachs disease or for sickle-cell anemia only becomes a matter for decision making when the nature of these traits is understood, when it becomes possible to test for them, and when there are several alternative courses of action available. The context of such choices varies; at one time, they are seen as matters of individual concern, and at another as matters of community concern.

Some of these issues are raised very sharply by the AIDS story.[2] Human immunodeficiency virus (HIV — the virus that leads to AIDS) represents an apparently new element of human ecology; thus, when we look at efforts to respond to AIDS, a little reflection can remind us that we are watching evolutionarily derived patterns of adaptation in action. The virus is a product of evolution and itself continues to evolve. Its emergence has already had an impact on human culture, including the evolution of biomedical knowledge. In this crisis, there is also a pressure for evolution in the ethical domain.

The potential direct selective pressure of HIV is already being modified by two different kinds of cultural adaptation: individual behavior changes produced by education, and biomedical technology. It is important to notice that these forms of adaptation are not different in kind, for both depend on human capacities to learn and to teach. Adaptation to the existence of the new virus involves a wide range of decisions by individuals and institutions. Individuals must make new kinds of decisions about sexual choices and about whom to inform about infection. Institutions must reexamine funding priorities and modes of functioning. The kinds of information going into these decisions have changed in the course of the epidemic.

The identification of the AIDS virus itself and of its modes of transmission is an interesting example of the way in which knowledge alters ethical discourse. With that scientific step, we moved from an era of amorphous threat (a "gay plague" whose causes were unknown) to one in which effective communication could make the difference between life and death. This created new ethical dilemmas, as did the development of an antibody test and the development of drugs that retard the disease. All of these ethical issues are complicated by the association of the disease with patterns of discrimination and economic inequity and by contemporary sensitivity to ethical issues of privacy and human rights, factors that are regarded as relevant to policy by some and not by others. As with population growth, these ethical sensibilities may be challenged and altered by biological facts.

In the same way, the human capacity to act with ever-increasing impact on the natural environment has led to whole new areas of ethical concern. Interestingly enough, however, once an issue is defined as ethical it becomes important to deal with it symbolically as well as practically. Thus, many environmentally deleterious behaviors are destructive only if performed by large numbers of people, yet bringing these behaviors into the domain of ethical discussion involves a condemnation of their performance by individuals. An environmental ethic is perhaps best expressed in terms of the Kantian Categorical Imperative to act as if one's behav_or were to become a rule for the whole society. Thus, preservation of the ozone layer does not depend directly on my decision or yours not to use aerosol products, but bringing such behavior into the realm of ethics does lead to a focus on individual decisions that proposes changes in patterns of human attention and in the formulation of purposes. People of good will are often highly inconsistent in their efforts to evolve standards, proposing that some decisions should be regarded as completely private while others involve not only the community but the entire planet.

Knowledge and attention are by no means synonymous. A theory of what is relevant to that process is implicit in any decision-making process — what factors shall be taken into account, ranging from commandments attributed (in some sense) to revelation, to an assessment (never complete) of possible effects of a given action. Some systems decontextualize as much as possible; others are sensitive to situational differences.[3]

Several factors of attention affected human response to the AIDS threat. First, the disease was identified because of the institutionalization of epidemiological attention in health monitoring organizations, especially the Centers for Disease Control. Second, mobilization to meet the disease was inhibited by attitudes toward homosexuality and unwillingness to discuss sexual practice, attitudes that mandate inattention. Third, public and media attention has fluctuated between sensation and boredom, suggesting the existence of a cultural pattern of thresholds of attention. Attention has been fragmentary and erratic, rarely including the entire social context of the disease. Finally, narrow problem-solving orientations that ignore broader issues have shown the potential for worsening the situation ("driving the disease underground").

Conscious Purpose and Human Adaptation

Working on this essay has provided an opportunity to reassess a hypothesis put forward twenty years ago by Gregory Bateson and discussed at length at a Wenner-Gren conference,[4] namely, that the human capacity for conscious purpose involves a distortion such that, in the service of conscious purpose, decisions are made based on a biased selection of information. The original proposal was open as to whether this problem was a biological problem based on species-specific neurological limitations, or a cultural one based on learning.

A question of great scientific interest and perhaps grave importance is whether the information processed through consciousness is adequate and appropriate for the task of human adaptation. . . . It may well be that consciousness contains systematic distortions of view which, when implemented by modern technology, become destructive of the balances between man, his society, and his ecosystem . . . It is suggested that the specific nature of this distortion is such that the cybernetic nature of self and the world tends to be imperceptible to consciousness insofar as the contents of the "screen" of consciousness are determined by considerations of purpose . . . Our conscious sampling of data will not disclose whole circuits but only arcs of circuits, cut off from their matrix by our selective attention.[5]

From a perspective of two decades, this hypothesis remains provocative but must be modified in a number of ways.

1. The availability of some portion of mental process for conscious inspection and reflexivity is apparently a precondition for the elaborate capacities for learning and teaching that underlie human adaptation. Similarly, however, the fact that only a fraction of mental process is so available means the existence of some form of partitioning or selection, and the exclusion from consciousness of the great majority of events must also be essential, if only for reasons of economy.[6]

2. Humans resemble all other animals in having the natural sensory capacity to receive and process only a fraction of potentially available information. We must assume that these limitations were at one time appropriate to an early human adaptive pattern. In general, however, as with so many human capacities, the human sensory pattern is wide ranging and not highly specialized, but is subject to substantial learning, including the learning of what to omit. Some of that learning may involve something like Freudian repression, but most of it is a matter of attention, concentration, and focus.

   Among the !Kung (Bushmen) of the Kalahari,[7] a great part of hunting consists in tracking an individual animal that has been wounded with poisoned arrows until the poison is effective. The men in a hunting band no doubt have a slightly better sense of smell than an urban American, but their capacity to track game depends primarily on trained attention to visual cues like tracks or crushed grass that are visible to an outsider when they are pointed out. The outsider can "see" the clues to the animal's worsening condition and the signs of its passage, but he doesn't "notice" them. The training of his attention is related to but not identical with the existence of an interpretive system defining the relevance of the various cues. The !Kung are aware, of course, that there are individual differences of skill and talent that benefit the group. At the same time that they focus on particular kinds of information, they must, of course, exclude others — attention is selective.

3. Technology, broadly conceived to include everything from telescopes to the use of dogs — a symbiont with a range of sensitivity to sounds and smell that has been used for millennia to supplement our own — allows an extension of this range. The question of what information shall be deemed relevant to a decision is not today dependent on sensory capacities — it is, however, dependent on cultural decisions about where and how to attribute relevance.

4. Just as survival is not a characteristic of individuals but of populations, so also attention should be considered in relation to whole societies or communities, which include potentially complementary kinds of sensory capacities and attention. In his original discussion, G. Bateson suggested that decisions by various corporate bodies consisting of "part-persons" might be more biased than individual decisions, but the discussions of his hypothesis led to the proposal that the solution also lay in the construction of groups able to incorporate individuals with different kinds of knowledge and sensitivity.

5. In this context, the function of various kinds of division of labor in human adaptation becomes important, for these carry over to patterns of attention and decision making. Of all forms of division of labor, the most ancient and universal is the division of labor between the sexes. Starting from biologically different roles in reproduction and infant care, human communities assign males and females to socially constructed roles which involve extensive learning of contrastive patterns of activity and attention. The roles assigned to women typically involve attention to more than one thing at a time (one or more children still dependent on constant care as well as some subsistence activity).

While the !Kung man is tracking game, with a very highly focused kind of attention, the !Kung woman is likely to be on a gathering expedition with a group of other women, each one accompanied by one or more children, carried or walking. !Kung adaptation depends on women for 60–80 percent of the food supply, as well as firewood and water. However, the kind of attention needed for gathering is apparently different from that needed for hunting. In both cases a minute knowledge of the natural environment is needed, but the women will be engaged in a broad scanning pattern, rather than in a narrow focus on following a set of tracks, as they look out for signs of the presence of a variety of food sources and keep track of the children as well. The !Kung example then stands here both for culturally shaped patterns of attention and for culturally constructed complementary divisions of labor in patterns of attention, contributing to the overall adaptation of the community. It serves all the better because such a gathering-hunting society exemplifies a very ancient pattern that prevailed for many millennia in the history of our species.

6. We must assume that human divisions of labor are pervasively built on different patterns of attention and inattention, and that these partially carry over outside of working hours. Thus, farmers and factory workers notice different things. Here it is interesting to notice that farmers are less likely to be bird watchers than are urban people, perhaps because of what farmers learn not to notice as they go about their daily work, and, in fact, many ranchers seem to view wildlife only in relation to their own economic purposes, i.e., as varmints. On the other hand, visitors to cities, unlike residents, look up (much of the architectural ornament in cities is at the top of buildings). The "part-persons" that G. Bateson describes as in charge of corporate (or national) decision making are persons following a pattern of attention believed to be appropriate to doing their job. Until recently, members of boards of trustees argued that attention to social policy issues (i.e., apartheid in South Africa) was actually illegitimate when they were acting in a fiduciary capacity.

7. It is still not clear whether recurrent patterns of difference between men and women are biological or cultural, because of the cross-cultural prevalence of learned differences geared directly to biological differences. Interestingly, however, some male-female

differences that have been observed in our culture seem to be related to patterns of attention and to be congruent with the differences described above for the !Kung. For instance, research has suggested that women make ethical decisions differently from men.[8] Women are less interested in fixed rules or principles of right and wrong, and more interested in looking broadly at the context and at the welfare of those affected — in effect, their attention is differently structured. There is evidence that women in the sciences publish less frequently than men but may include more in each paper, and that women's performance on various kinds of tests is more "context dependent" on the average than is men's. Women in management situations tend to combine a concern for corporate goals with a concern for the persons they affect and for the feelings of those participating in the discussion. In my own work on contemporary American women,[9] I have increasingly been seeing the women's style of action as *responsive* and men's as more generally *purposive*. Where men's purposive focus may lead them to ignore peripheral factors and side effects, women's broader responsiveness makes them vulnerable to distraction and ambivalence. Clearly, both men and women are capable of both kinds of attention, but practice them to different degrees. Clearly, too, a broader, more contextualized pattern of attention offers a potential for including full cybernetic circuits but does not guarantee it.

The multiplex attention of the San woman is similar to the situation in which many women involved in careers find themselves: stirring the soup, holding the baby, and negotiating complex transactions over the telephone, all at the same time, or concentrating on one thing but available and responsive to other needs.

8. In general, as societies become larger and more complex and control greater technological possibilities, the division of labor also increases. The progressive division of communities into groups of specialists with noncompeting separate niches provides one of the commoner metaphors relating social and biological evolution. Interestingly enough, one common usage of the term "ethics" is to associate it with particular professions within society (e.g., medical ethics). Specific knowledge, specific patterns of attention, and specific modes of action do indeed require different specialized codes of ethics. Arguably, however, just as peace and war are too

important to be left to politicians, so also, health is too important to be left to physicians, and the health of the biosphere is too important to be left to engineers and economists. The Waddington argument that ethical discourse can be expected to embody some degree of adaptive wisdom does not apply to specialized ethical codes of groups of professionals, for these are adapted to professional solidarity and to competition within human society.

9. When G. Bateson formulated his hypothesis, he used the gender-biased language of the time, discussing a human problem in terms of "man." But it is possible that he was inadvertently accurate, for today we can consider the possibility of erroneous human decisions resulting from reliance on only a part of the human capacity, because of various kinds of division of labor. Since all human beings, within the range of species-specific capacities, learn patterns of attention and inattention, fully human decisions on ethical matters may require engaging a wide range of possible participants. This becomes an argument for deliberately seeking cultural, vocational, and, above all, gender diversity in decision making in order to evoke a variety of sensitivities. Within the species, increasing division of labor may weaken, rather than increase, the human ethical capacity.

10. Of all the complementary patterns which have characterized human divisions of labor, gender differences may be the most promising in looking for ways of correcting deleterious human misperceptions of the natural world. The !Kung hunter on the track of game, with his highly honed attention to particular cues, does not embody the whole of an ancient human pattern of adaptation, for his kind of attention and his contribution to subsistence are not viable by themselves, but must be complemented by the patterns involved in gathering, most highly developed by the women. A !Kung band, in spite of its division of labor, is relatively egalitarian; furthermore, decision making about issues affecting the whole band in relation to its environment (most typically migration decisions) are not made in a segregated setting of exclusively male discussion.

It remains to be determined whether patterns of attention and ethical decision making characteristic of women might correct for "man's" maladaptive behavior. A similar question might be asked about adaptive or maladaptive attitudes to time. The recognition that women are context sensitive, allow attention to more factors at the same time, and are responsive to issues often regarded as peripheral by male decision makers is suggestive but by no means conclusive. Do women conceive of causation in more cybernetic terms than men, and do they only do so as long as they are locked into traditional roles or can they bring these capacities into other decision-making settings? (This cannot be tested by looking at the contributions of token women only, but requires looking at some degree of balanced participation.) Will changes in the social construction of gender roles free men to develop new patterns of attention?

Conclusion

It remains to bring this discussion back to some of the issues raised at the beginning. If ethical discourse is a form of discourse that is important to human adaptation, then it becomes very important to determine who participates in that discourse, how that discourse is linked with practical decision making, and what kinds of awareness are brought into that discourse. Increasing division of labor is typically regarded as progressive in human evolution, yet if it leads to the exclusion of relevant insight from ethical discourse it may represent a form of devolution. The assumption that the human ethical capacity has been a product of human evolution and has been adaptive over millennia does not make it proof against social arrangements that bring only a portion of potential thought and sensitivity into play. The dawning realization of ecological disaster in Eastern Europe, where decision making was highly centralized, is an argument for pluralistic decision making. This paper proposes the need for a different and even more ancient kind of adaptive pluralism.

THINKING AIDS

In 2003, SARS (severe acute respiratory syndrome) burst into our consciousness. By the time this volume appears there will probably be yet another newly identified or emergent hazard, as there has been every two years or so for two decades. Each inspires new journalistic anxiety and is met by new research and new health measures. HIV/AIDS (the more recent convention for referring to it), inspired the greatest awe and horror for a variety of reasons. (Ebola is scarier but more remote.) By now it is widely understood that human actions have linked the human populations of the planet in vulnerability and disrupted stable ancient systems, with unpredictable results. It seems important to get beyond the specificity of particular diseases and the trickle of good news from biomedical research to think about what this all tells us about who we are.

In 1986 Richard Goldsby, a close friend and colleague, suggested that we collaborate on a book on the AIDS epidemic and on the newly identified virus, HIV, that causes it; he would bring his expertise as a biologist and immunologist, and I would bring the understanding of a social scientist. The book appeared in 1988 under the title *Thinking AIDS*. The title reflected our belief that the epidemic posed a challenge to rethink many aspects of the relationship between biology and culture, as well as issues of social justice and the nature of human interdependence. I have included an extensive and internally abridged excerpt from my portion of the book because we believe that such rethinking is still needed.

Writing that book was an education for both of us.

Goldsby was the principal author of chapters dealing with biomedical issues, while I was the principal author of chapters dealing with social, ecological, and ethical issues, but each of us read and revised the other's work, discussing the issues backwards and forwards. Inevitably, HIV/AIDS produced a flood of publications and research that continues to grow, and any book attempting to give a global picture of the issue, particularly a book not written by members of the emerging group of specialists in the field, was bound quickly to seem out of date. But Goldsby and I continue to feel that dealing with the issue narrowly omits important questions. He has agreed that some of the sections written primarily by me might usefully be included here, side by side with other essays with which they resonate in interesting ways. I am immensely grateful to my coauthor for leading me into a sustained attention to the medical and scientific details of a historic epidemic in ways that continue to inform my thinking.

First, an update on the situation.* Worldwide, over 30 million people have died of AIDS, and over 40 million are now infected. The numbers are highest in Africa and rising rapidly in Asia. Transmission of the virus has slowed in the United States, but there are still some 40,000 new infections a year, and over 900,000 Americans are living with the infection, half of them undiagnosed and untreated. Whether in Africa or elsewhere in the world, the disease takes the heaviest toll on people of color and on the poor, and especially on those whose risky behavior is stigmatized. Huge sums have been spent on research, but there is still no vaccine that protects against the AIDS virus and no cure. The first useful AIDS drug, AZT, became available in 1987, and now combinations of anti-retrovirals (the "AIDS cocktail") have improved to the point where infected persons can

---

* Lawrence K. Altman, "AIDS Study Finds Many Unaware They Have Virus," *New York Times*, July 8, 2002, 1, 13. The latest regional and global HIV/AIDS estimates are published annually in December and available at http:www.unaids.org/. The figures used here were posted in 2003. Information on the international effort to provide medication is available at http://www.iavi.org.

survive and maintain good health for more than three times as long as in 1988. The cost of patented drugs was running as high as ten to twelve thousand dollars per patient per year, until recent efforts began to make generics available in the developing world for under two hundred dollars. Even that sum has been beyond the reach of many. At present in the United States, high-risk behaviors are increasing again among young people who continue their own risky activities with others without bothering to be tested for the virus, at least partly because of the belief that the problem of AIDS has been solved. It has not. Some portions of this discussion may seem dated to some Americans, but the same tragic scenarios of discrimination and abandonment are still being played out among the poor on every continent, and we are still withholding from gays and gay couples the respect and social recognition that would support responsible behavior.

It makes you think. This was our point, that it is time for a change in consciousness. Different ways of knowing must be combined beyond the glamorous search for a magic bullet. Inequality has medical implications. Life expectancy is everywhere correlated with economic status and skin color — and so is anger. Developments in medication have triggered a new stage of debate about the responsibilities of affluent nations — but we believe that more than medication is needed. During these fifteen years, *globalization* has become a popular term, and we have understood that globalization, the darling of the economists, has human and environmental implications for which we must take responsibility. We have become increasingly aware of terrorism, which like the spread of disease is facilitated by globalization. The struggle against epidemics raises many issues similar to the struggle against terrorism, for societies are likely to sacrifice openness and equity to the search for safety.

Goldsby and I argued that individuals could make

the choices that gave them a large measure of behavioral immunity to the virus, and that, with international help where needed, societies could make choices that offered the possibility of "zero AIDS growth," but these shifts would entail thinking about the coupling of a wide variety of issues and systems. We applaud the medical research, but actually delivering medical progress would in any case depend on societal changes — and a "technological fix" could easily prove delusory. We argued that the situation could be helped by global improvements in education and public health, the provision of trustworthy information on health and on family planning, individual human rights, peace and prosperity — all goals we should in any case be pursuing, and all changes that will make it simpler to deal with other dangers as they appear. The pandemic rides the clouds of warfare, migrant labor, ignorance, bigotry, and sexual coercion. Although there is still mystery about the origins of HIV/AIDS, it is clear that many new hazards arise from the ways in which we interact with other species and disrupt the biosphere. Thus, the pandemic offers a moment of renewed commitment to a range of social and ecological goals contributing to the well-being of the entire human species — because "no man is an Island." We cannot leave this one to the experts.

—MCB, 2004

A previously unknown life form, the virus that causes AIDS, is now making its way through the human population, spreading around the world with devastating and accelerating effects. That virus has become a part of the biological context of our lives, one of the many life forms that actually live inside of human beings rather than around them. All of these can potentially be known and at least partially controlled but the needed thinking about AIDS has just begun, and it is already clear that it raises the most basic questions about the human condition, about human biology, and about the mechanisms of social life.

The AIDS epidemic, as it moves around the planet, is posing new questions about justice and teaching us new ways of thinking about human learning and human suffering. It throws certain characteristics of society into sharp relief, just as radioisotopes, moving through the body, can be used to highlight physiological processes for diagnosis. At one level the movement of the epidemic reflects communication and travel. At another it belies our habitual self-deceptions, tracing activities that would otherwise be secret: drug addiction and sexual practices that most people have preferred not to know about — extramarital sex, homosexuality, prostitution. AIDS has made us newly aware of human diversity. In our own society it forces us to acknowledge bisexuality, a pattern of sexual preference that most Americans, who like their distinctions clear, have tended to ignore, and is making us more aware of middle-class intravenous drug use. It will probably increase awareness of the sexual use of children, of sex in prisons, of sex and drugs in the peacetime army.

AIDS highlights processes of social change: urbanization and monetary economies in Africa that send men to the cities for cash earnings while their wives stay in the villages to farm; changed sexual mores for heterosexuals as well as homosexuals; the economic dislocations and prejudice that are increasingly turning some minority communities in America into an underclass. The history of failure to heed the early warnings of the epidemic is a statement of our priorities as a society. Now that we know how to prevent the disease from spreading, its continued spread must advertise the ways in which, in this interconnected and interdependent world, we fail to communicate to individuals the very knowledge they need to survive. AIDS moves along the fault lines of our society and becomes a metaphor for understanding that society.

The process of learning how to think about and control AIDS is a step in human evolution, for the application of knowledge is the distinctive evolutionary mechanism of our species. Human beings adapt to their environments not primarily through biological evolution, which works rather slowly, but through cultural evolution, changes in shared knowledge expressed in changes in behavior. We know the history of many of these changes and know that culture makes human beings more rapidly and flexibly adaptable than any other species. We know too that the AIDS epidemic is not the first occasion when the biological context of human life has changed dangerously, nor will it be the last. Still, as the AIDS epidemic tests our understanding of social and cultural mechanisms, it reveals in us a curious kind of helplessness in moving from information to changes in behavior. It is not easy to think about AIDS. Most of us react with a mixture of sympathy and horror to the personal tragedies we read about or encounter, yet in order to think about AIDS we need to illuminate the emotions that the disease inspires with a new kind of cross-section of human knowledge.

AIDS proposes questions of the highest human and intellectual importance. The biology of AIDS lies right at the cutting edge of research. We live in an age when the biological sciences are reaching for the kind of power and clarity that has characterized physics; like physics, this new thrust of knowledge presents both possibilities and dangers. Some of humankind's greatest achievements have involved the effort to control biological phenomena, often only half knowing what we were doing and why. Many of the greatest of these achievements lie in the ancient past: the abilities to shape life forms to our purposes by domesticating plants and animals and even microorganisms like yeast, as well as the ability to defend ourselves against others. The potential of modern biology arises from the development of techniques that permit inspection of the finest grain of physical and biological processes so that the properties and behavior of living things begin to be explicable in terms of the physical structure of molecules. At the same time, questions remain about how these intricate processes are integrated in living wholes.

Viruses are the smallest forms to which we attribute life, and indeed can barely be called living, so whoever would understand the nature of life must be interested in the viruses, right at that crucial threshold. Viruses are not autonomously capable of many of the functions of cells, but they do carry genetic information. To fulfill these missing functions, they must gain admission to cells and inhabit them. Because the AIDS virus selectively invades the cells of the immune system, virology opens into immunology, the science that studies the maintenance of identity within the organism and its internal interactions with other forms of life.

Immunology focuses on the relationship between what happens at levels smaller than the cell — at the molecular level — and the fate of the whole organism. It may eventually provide the intellectual bridge between these different visions. But AIDS also challenges a look at populations and at ecological interactions. Questions about how a biological process like the spread of an epidemic affects a population take us right into contemporary understandings of evolution, where we now know that we have to look at populations in environments rather than at single organisms.

An understanding of the AIDS epidemic and how it can be controlled requires understanding of the development of shared knowledge and behavior patterns, particularly at the interface between biology and the learned characteristics of human communities, like language or purposeful invention or the effort to find meaning in natural events. These are anthropological issues, but AIDS forces us to pose questions in every one of the social sciences and reveals the limitations of our applicable knowledge at every turn. It drives us to psychology, with questions about how individuals learn and change their behavior; to sociology, to understand change and the processes of inclusion and exclusion in large groups and institutions; to economics, to understand the effect of such changes on the use of resources; and to political science and ethics, to understand the processes of decision making when the needs and desires of individuals are weighed against those of the larger society. In order to think about the AIDS epidemic and how it affects the future of our species, all of these different ways of looking at the lives of individuals and communities must be woven together, at one moment emphasizing their commonalities, at another the distinctive features of each.

Human attention is profoundly shaped by love and danger and early death. Diseases and the social responses to them have been critical in human history, and have been explored by artists and philosophers as well as scientists, wondering about issues of good and evil and how these are connected to the mysteries of death and suffering. We have been speaking here of understanding as if it were an analytical process, but analysis is only one step toward understanding. Every generation must integrate knowledge and experience, finding them meaningful or absurd, tempted by distortions and self-deception when they seem to make our world more coherent. Many who have written about the AIDS epidemic have written out of an urgent need to convey the depth of suffering involved and to evoke compassion from a society that appeared unfeeling. We have chosen here to put less emphasis on the horrors of full-blown AIDS and more emphasis on social adaptations to controlling the virus that causes it, for we write out of the conviction that horror is not the best place to begin in constructing individual and social change. Horror creates the impulse to denial. Instead, we are concerned with presenting the AIDS epidemic as a fact of the world in which we now live and with demonstrating that, by responding generously and wisely, we can make our society a better one, enriching our living and our dying.

Of all the literature of illness, the work that most poignantly evokes the tension between cultural meaning and individual suffering is the biblical Book of Job. Job has always been virtuous, public-spirited, and wealthy, when suddenly everything begins to go wrong. His children are killed, his money is lost, and his skin breaks out in boils from head to toe. He longs for death and wishes he had never been born. He gets scant comfort from his friends, who gather to argue that he must have deserved his sufferings at the hand of God, that divine justice must be apparent in the events of this life. Job adamantly denies that he has done anything to deserve his afflictions and longs to argue his case with God: "Though he slay me, yet will I trust in him: but I will maintain my own ways before him" (13:15).

After many chapters of self-righteous sermonizing by Job's "friends," God himself speaks from a whirlwind in chapters 38–41 and says, with a wealth of examples from natural history, it is all much more complicated than you know, you cannot claim to understand my ways. A vision of the intricacy of the natural world is offered that is not organized around human needs but that frames the lives and interlocking needs of all the wild creatures of the forests and mountains, eagles and lions and mountain goats, and the leviathan in the depths of the sea.

Job is silenced, saying, "I have uttered that I understood not, things too wonderful for me, which I knew not" (42:3). His concern with his own affairs and with human definitions of virtue is put into a wider perspective. The gift of wonder assuages his loss.

We know today a great deal about the interlocking lives of different species. We know that to begin to understand the survival of any species requires painstaking observation and detailed knowledge of its environment, and we have learned, at least to some degree, the poet's concern for what goes on invisible to us, in sea or wilderness or on a scale too small for our vision. But we still slip into seeing these matters from the human point of view, turning knowledge of the natural world into parables of divine justice and human mastery. The equivalent today of the lesson in natural history that God gave to Job might be the depiction of the extraordinary elegance and complexity of the finest grain of natural phenomena, the microscopic dramas and adaptations of other organisms, including the AIDS virus that makes its nest and brings forth its young within the human immune system itself. The widened perspective that Job is given might today include other human ways in other times and places, ways of surviving and finding pleasure far outside the Hebrew imagination of right and wrong. But of course Job's comforters are engaged in "saving God," which means hanging on to a way of thinking about the universe that makes sense to them.

The habits of thought that made Job's comforters so ready to condemn him are still with us. Persons afflicted with AIDS lose first their health, then many of their friends and family and resources, then their lives. Unlike Job, many people with AIDS were poor or rejected before they became ill, but the illness will affect rich and poor alike. Many must acknowledge that they have behaved in ways that their neighbors regard as immoral, and may concur in that blame. Many people with AIDS suffer an additional burden of guilt for probably having passed the disease to others.

Nevertheless, the spread of AIDS to the newborn and the horrors of its clinical course are for many sufficient refutation of the argument that it could represent divine justice. The proportion of AIDS patients who are like Job in living highly conventional lives is increasing steadily. More and more people who are neither drug-addicted nor promiscuous are contracting AIDS from their partners, more and more infants are being born carrying their deaths within them. Until the mid-1980s, the AIDS virus was being sown through American and European populations with blood products, and medical transmission is still significant in third world countries. Furthermore, many behaviors that transmit AIDS, even if they might have been condemned in terms of conventional moralities, are now widely shared: not only are almost half of all American teenagers sexually active by the end of high school, but the candidates for the U.S. presidential nomination for 1988 included two ministers whose children were conceived well before marriage.

Almost everyone can find something to disapprove of in the behavior of some AIDS patients. Job's comforters argue that all humans share in guilt, so perhaps from that perspective even Job's children deserved their deaths. But disapproval quickly becomes an obstacle to understanding. The most dangerous thing about self-righteousness is the inference made by those who regard themselves as virtuous that they are different and therefore safe, and that if the disease progresses unchecked, society will be purged while they remain untouched. Not us — them. This attitude was a major block to organizing and funding the medical research needed to deal with the emergency, and continues to hinder efforts to protect and care for those threatened by the disease.

The alternative position is one of empathy and the acknowledgment by the society at large that those who are suffering from AIDS are very much like themselves. Indeed, dealing with the epidemic requires looking at themselves and at the epidemic with new eyes. This understanding requires the insight that people of color are like white people, that rich people are like poor, and that the destinies of people on every continent are woven together. We are defined as a single species by the capacity for interbreeding, and human beings everywhere cross lines of class and race in the search for sexual partners, sometimes in tenderness and other times in exploitation. Epidemiologists must speak in terms of risk groups to explain the development of epidemics, but unlike some diseases whose risk groups are clearly bounded by genetics or geography, the ultimate risk group for AIDS includes every human being.

The appropriate responses to the AIDS epidemic are both social and personal. They are late in coming and it is already clear that the costs of delay will be heavy. It takes genuine emotional involvement to decide to change one's lifestyle and take precautions against AIDS, real concern for oneself or loved ones. It also takes informed understanding and information. When the threat still seems to be at a distance, such changes require deeply felt imaginative identification, and it is the lack of this act of the imagination that keeps people with a full intellectual understanding of the danger from taking action. Unfortunately, infection has tended to spread faster than either empathic emotional involvement or understanding. Fear has proved sufficient to trigger prejudice more quickly than behavioral change, because prejudice creates emotional distance, putting the danger at arm's length.

The AIDS epidemic will cost us dearly. Perhaps we will gain wisdom from it, not only in the fields of virology and biochemistry but also in an understanding of the social costs of exclusion and despair. From a concern for the immune systems of individuals we will have to move to an understanding of the immune systems of societies, the patterns of vigilance and caring that protect their continuing health. The same forces that make it hard to use the biology-culture relationship to address AIDS face every effort to discover distinctively human solutions — the solutions of intelligence and choice, of discipline and imagination — to the problems of the modern world.

In the years ahead, the awareness of AIDS will resonate in visions as well as nightmares, providing the stuff of art and the echoes of revelation, as well as opening new doors of scientific understanding. The AIDS crisis represents an immense tragedy for many persons and a danger for many more. It also represents an opportunity for changes in our understanding of human biology and social life and the ways in which we use knowledge. From this point of view, the epidemic is a moment of opportunity for discovering the full potential of humanness. If we can use the impetus of AIDS to expand and apply knowledge cooperatively and humanely, we may also learn to control the dangers of the arms race and of world hunger and environmental degradation, for the imagination of AIDS is the imagination of human unity, intimately held in the interdependent web of life.

The Ecology of the Virus

Life on this planet involves interactions among a very large and diverse range of organisms which depend on one another in a great many different ways. When we think of human dependence on other life forms, the tendency is to think first of the plants and animals we use for food or fiber. It takes a moment to remember that the atmosphere of the planet — the air we breathe — is the joint product of the life processes of plants, animals, and microorganisms; that the soil from which plants grow is necessarily teeming with organic life; and that the human body itself supports an ongoing population of microorganisms. The environment in which any given organism flourishes is always a community of interacting life forms. This is equally true of the bacteria living in the intestines and of the squirrels in an oak forest.

One of the central concepts of modern ecology is that of the *niche*. A niche involves not only location but also behavior; it is a behavioral space in which an organism moves and competes for resources. Many species coexist in a forest, but each one can be seen to have a slightly different niche. Woodpeckers drilling into trees to find insects boring inside are usually not in competition with squirrels gathering acorns or even with the many other birds species gathering seeds or capturing other kinds of insects. The system of niches orchestrates the encounters and separations of the myriad species in the forest.

Human beings living in a city are similar, for just as a bird or a beetle interacts selectively with different parts of the life of a forest, so different people live differently in a city. For one person — call her Ms. Parker — New York is a gigantic parking problem, but she may never use public transport; for another, whom we recognize as Mr. Rider, the subways are essential to day-to-day life, and he experiences the street grid in terms of the location of stations, reads subway ads, and worries about being mugged. Some individuals encounter each other for help and harm as they move between home and work and recreation; others, even in a small geographical space, might almost be on different planets. You can think of these different individuals as living in different behavioral niches within the city: the way you use and interact with your environment *is* your environment. In the example given here, it is easy to imagine changes that affect the behavioral space of our two individuals, Parker and Rider, bringing them into competition for the same resources or forcing one of them to leave the city. The parking regulations may change and Parker may ride. The public transport workers may go on strike and Rider may buy a car. They may meet each other on foot or get jobs in the same office. Technology may offer a new option — a splendid new form of moped — that both of them want, and they may be in competition for service.

Since the appearance of *Homo sapiens,* the way humans use and affect their environment has changed steadily, altering the niches of all other forms of life, sometimes drastically enough to cause extinction. Human behavioral changes are particularly important for understanding diseases that involve interactions between humans and other life forms, those diseases in which the human body is the natural habitat for some other organism during all or part of its life cycle. Many pathogens live in a stable relationship with a human population, but that relationship may be disrupted by advances in public health or medicine. Worldwide vaccination programs denied to the smallpox virus the only environment in which it could live and reproduce, so it is believed to be extinct. Sometimes a pathogen will suddenly multiply when some environmental change, caused by custom or technology, gives it the chance radically to expand its niche. On the other hand, species that destroy their own environments cannot themselves survive. This has implications for human behavior as well as for understanding the mechanisms of diseases in which one organism lives in the body of another.

It is possible for an epidemic to arise rapidly from a random genetic change or mutation, but that mutation must occur in an environment in which the new form has a selective advantage. Otherwise, new genetic variations may survive but be practically invisible. Any wild species has a great deal of naturally occurring genetic variation. The reservoir of genetic variation is what allows a species to survive when some environmental circumstance wipes out most of its members. What is important to notice here is that epidemics are created by a combination of genetic potential and environmental opportunity.

It will be helpful, in thinking about the AIDS epidemic, to remember that pathogens — life forms that inhabit other life forms and in doing so cause disease — face the same problems of adaptation and survival as other kinds of organisms. There is no way to locate with certainty the original genetic events that bring a disease into being. It may eventually be shown that the pathogen has existed for a long time in a different niche, for example, in another species, like one of our primate relatives; but if it arose from a recent mutation or a series of relatively recent genetic changes, whether in a human being or in some other species, it may prove extremely difficult to establish the exact time and place of those events. In any case, the important question about any newly recognized disease is the niche in which it now propagates. Is this niche one that we have created? Is it one that we have the capacity to control and reshape? Why is this particular life form proving successful enough to reproduce and spread widely? How does the survival strategy of a particular pathogen resemble other diseases? These are the ecological questions we should be asking about the AIDS virus.

In any discussion of disease propagation, numbers are important, for the ecological strategies of many pathogens involve rapid population growth. Pathogens typically enter the body in small numbers, reproducing there to large numbers and causing sickness. Epidemics are created when pathogens are passed rapidly from host to host, multiplying the numbers of carriers.

In the biological world, the question of the control of growth is quite as important as the question of growth itself. Uncontrolled growth of cells in the body is called cancer. Uncontrolled growth of a stable population of bacteria may poison an area of the body where they otherwise live innocuously, and uncontrolled growth of any species in a complex ecosystem may lead to environmental degradation, like overgrazing leading to erosion

and the loss of topsoil. Locusts become a scourge when their rate of reproduction suddenly soars.

Species vary in their reproductive strategies. Human population has
been rising slowly and steadily since the beginning of the Common Era,
but the reason it is increasing so rapidly now is that our species was able
to survive with a much higher death rate than we have today. Reduce
deaths, and births begin to look cancerous. In general, the larger species
(whales, bears, humans) maintain population balances with relatively few
offspring, many of which survive, while smaller species often produce
vast numbers of offspring very quickly, most of which die off. The many
offspring/many deaths strategy seems wasteful, but it allows for quick
evolution.

Behavioral differences within the species mean that the niche in
which the disease is expanding is not uniform, and it is already changing.
Even bubonic plague ceased its exponential spread after killing more than
a quarter of the population of Europe. But the exponential spread of a disease can proceed to the point of disabling a nation or an economic system.
Waiting for the epidemic to establish a natural equilibrium was the only
response available in the Middle Ages to epidemic diseases, but today too
many other equilibria are threatened. Today too we have the possibility of
deliberately changing the population dynamics of the pathogen by
altering its environment — most immediately, the external environment,
in which human behavior determines its transmission from host to host.
At the same time, medical research is gradually moving toward ways of
altering by medication the internal environment of the human body
where the virus multiplies and destroys.

The niche in which the AIDS virus is spreading with such dramatic speed
does not include any organisms, like snails or fleas, other than human
beings nor does it include spaces like air-conditioning systems or pools,
where it could live and reproduce independently. With a few exceptions,
it lives all of its life cycle within the human body and depends on interactions between human beings to travel from host to host, from bloodstream
to bloodstream. Thus, its niche is heavily dependent on behavior and
custom. Because human cultural development has linked the entire population of this planet in a single intercommunicating system, AIDS has the
potential for transmission throughout that entire system. All of the documented modes of transmission of AIDS, except through the placenta, are

based on voluntary behavior, shaped by learning and influenced by culture. The most common form of transmission of the AIDS virus is through sexual intimacy, with the multiple use of intravenous needles and syringes increasing in importance.

The niche in which AIDS is transmitted depends on the occurrence of certain acts within this huge interlocking net of interactions, and is affected by any factor that changes events of transmission, ranging from the cost of air travel to the use of condoms, and including the vast diversity of attitudes and practices concerning sex, medical care, and the use of drugs. Sexual intimacy and needle sharing differ in many ways, but both involve learning and therefore the texture of the network of transmission is by no means uniform, as different biological possibilities are expressed in different cultural contexts.

Although we share much of the mechanics of reproduction with other species, our sexuality is not particularly animal-like but rather is distinctively human, contrasting in important ways with the mechanisms of fertilization in other species. If you compare human sexuality to that of most other mammals (we can leave the birds and bees out of this discussion), you immediately encounter a major contrast: most mammalian sexuality is locked into the estrus cycle, whereby the female is receptive to copulation only during brief periods of high fertility, which are indicated to the male by odor or other cues. It is characteristic of human beings that sex is no longer directly attached to reproduction. Instead, sexuality has evolved to have a potential for enjoyment regardless of fertility, and the pleasure associated with sex underlies other kinds of intimacy and attachment.

Setting sex free from the fertility cycle may have been very important in human evolution, strengthening the bonds between males and females to allow the development of the protective family as childhood dependency became longer. The original separation of sexuality and fertility happened far back in human evolution, so the invention of modern contraception can be seen as the logical development of a process long under way: sex as intimacy, pleasure, and release of tension, as a characteristically human development. This is part of the emergence of humanness, the shift from highly specific and programmed behaviors to much more general ones that can be reshaped in dozens of different ways.

Since Freud, we can see the sources of adult sexuality in very early infant behavior: the infant sucking passionately at breast or thumb; the toddler learning the satisfactions of controlling elimination, holding on and letting go, fullness and release; the nursery schooler avidly exploring genitals and wondering who has what. The pleasures of touching and being touched also start in infancy, and it is possible to recognize a sexual component in all sensory satisfactions: stroking a cat, swaying to rhythmic music, tasting a delicious meal. As a result, all of the senses — sight, sound, smell, and taste, as well as touch — play a role in sexual arousal and response. Similarly, all of the body's surfaces and orifices, particularly the mouth and the anus, have roles along with the genitals in giving and receiving pleasure. Limiting eroticism to unadorned vaginal intercourse, because it is the only expression of sexuality leading directly to reproduction, narrows the human potential drastically and, particularly for women, may exclude real fulfillment.

Sexual behavior is extremely variable from person to person and from culture to culture, but there are some continuities to be discovered behind the diversity. These are essential keys to understanding how human sexuality provides a niche for disease and how human sexuality can be altered. All human cultures seem to work from clues offered by biology, but then they go on to select and elaborate. Thus, there is no human culture, even where body covering is not needed for warmth, that does not ornament the human body in some way, whether with fabric or paint or scarification. Similarly, there is no culture that lacks a concept of modesty about some body parts or functions, though the choices contrast a great deal. When outsiders first arrived in many areas of New Guinea, native women seemed to them naked and therefore shameless, because they did not realize that the net bags the women wore draped across their backs were serving the purposes of decorum. In Bali, urination was traditionally not a matter for concealment, but eating solid food in public was highly embarrassing. The Old Testament suggests that a man's head uncovered before God is like an uncircumcised penis. Americans traveling in Iran often scandalized their hosts by the indecency of blowing their noses audibly in public.

Cultures also vary greatly in when and where and with whom they permit the expression of sexuality, but there are always some prohibitions. A man may be forbidden to sleep with his sister but allowed to have sex with virtually anyone else, or he may be forbidden even to look at most of the females in the community. He may be instructed, as an important part of his initiation into manhood, to have sex with young boys — or he may be risking his life if he does so.

This diversity might suggest that since no particular rule is fully shared by all human beings and humans seem to succeed in living together and reproducing with an incredible variety of rules, perhaps all rules should be discarded, or perhaps only a minimal form of the incest taboo (which does occur almost everywhere) should be retained. But this conclusion misses the essential common element of selection and elaboration: The rules may vary but there are always rules, rules that have to be learned by each child born into the society. *The expression of human sexuality is never just natural.* It is always shaped in some way.

Another cross-cultural similarity that is important is the metaphorical relationship that often exists between sex and other kinds of behavior. It is almost impossible to deal with one behavioral domain in isolation from others and from other cultural styles and values. Human beings use sex to express their feelings, feelings of anger as well as tenderness. Eroticism can express a cultural value placed on risk or on achievement, can convey defiance or comfort, can be an assertion of identity or an expression of dominance — and the same kinds of issues arise in relation to drug use. If in one culture, sex or drugs is linked to courage and risk taking, the risk of death from AIDS may be seen as an additional challenge to manhood; and if the defiance of authority is a key motivation behind sex or drug use, authoritative advice on precautions will not be accepted. If self-sacrifice is romanticized, the risk of disease may be embraced as an alternative route to self-sacrifice.

In recent years we have been changing the rules and meanings associated with sex. Superficially it looks as if all the changes involve a loosening of repression. As a society we have become much more tolerant of sex outside marriage or before marriage and of homosexuality and masturbation, and we read books that suggest new and exotic positions and recommend oral sex. But we have also accepted new sets of limits and expectations: a woman may wear the tiniest of bikinis but she must "cover up" the natural odors of her body; a man may bulge in the crotch but agonize to conceal a bulge a few inches higher up. We have stronger prohibitions on coercive sex than ever before — in many states, although a man may sleep with someone he is not married to, he may not insist on sex with his wife if she declines. We are making real efforts to prevent rape and child molestation, instead of simply covering up areas of sexual violence that must have been routine in the past. And we expect individuals to be sexually active and skilled: college girls worry if they are still virgins at twenty, men worry about losing their potency, and men are increasingly expected to be concerned for the sexual satisfaction of female partners. People used to worry about "impure thoughts," but now they worry about insufficient ingenuity.

Nature does not just take its course. It cannot be a simple shift to permissiveness that decrees that in America today, sexual acts that would have been condoned (by collusive concealment) twenty years ago can destroy political candidates. Teenagers may be newly sexually active, but they still have clear ideas about what kinds of behavior fit their own standards. In other words, although the "sexual revolution" does involve a wider range of sexual activity, with greater possibilities for disease transmission, it does not represent a replacement of regulated by unregulated sexuality. The rules have been changing and they can change again. The invention of new limitations and elaborations is what has made our sexual behavior human. It is important to see sexual expression as variable in many different ways, not as varying on a single dimension between permissiveness and repression. It is similarly essential to understand that even illegal activities like drug use or prostitution are not without rules, for every human group surrounds activities important to it with customs and expectations.

You don't need a great many explicit rules to establish a principle of lawfulness that permits a workable human environment. It is entirely possible to shape biological sexuality into a vast range of pleasurable elaborations, and also to limit it to protect the weak from exploitation and to control the transmission of disease. Possible, but by no means automatic; easier across generations than within a single generation whose habits are already shaped.

Ironically, the particular attitudes toward sex that have historically characterized Western culture now represent a handicap in understanding the human characteristics of sexuality. Christianity has been more negative and secretive about sex than virtually any other tradition, for while all high cultures limit sexuality and elaborate on some forms of asceticism and self-control, Christianity has in many periods suggested that all sexual activity and all erotic pleasure are deplorable. Islamic cultures, which seem extreme to Westerners in the limitations they put even on the imagination of possible partners, are still entirely clear that sex is to be enjoyed.

Americans entered the twentieth century largely as a band of sexual illiterates, like a tribe whose experience of music is limited to a six-toned whistle and a drum. We are still liable to lapse into repression — or reaction to repression — and to be haunted by the imagination of sex as a shapeless and uncontrollable force, hidden by darkness but knocking down all restraints in its way. There have been times when the speculative intellect was treated in much the same manner.

By a coincidence of timing, the early spread of the AIDS epidemic was associated in the United States with homosexuality, to a degree that became one more line of defense against realistic discussion, since there are still those who believe that AIDS is a "gay plague." Gay sex needs to be seen in the context of human sexual diversity and elaboration, rather than set off as a separate phenomenon.

There is still a great deal that is unknown about the forms that gay sex might take in a society where it was not proscribed, since virtually the entire gay community grew up with guilt and self-rejection and secrecy, and the reactions to these have been factors in emerging sexual styles. Some characteristics, however, can be predicted for male-male sexuality for a long time to come. It appears that females are more concerned on the average with sex as an aspect of sustained and caring relationships, while males are on the average more interested in the pleasures of transient encounters. Given an evolutionary pattern in which females with children became increasingly dependent on the presence of the father, this makes good evolutionary sense.

Whether or not these tendencies are biologically given, our cultural expectation is that the woman will look for stable monogamy and the man for freedom. While many gay men do form long-term partnerships, it sometimes seemed as if 1970s-style gay sex was an enactment of a male fantasy common to heterosexuals as well, regardless of preference or partner: uncommitted, impersonal, profligate sex. Another way of looking at this is to notice that heterosexual sex, if it is to be satisfying to both partners, always involves a degree of compromise between different tempos and rhythms, a certain lack of comprehension of the other's body which has to be bridged; this kind of compromise sets constraints of a kind that may be reduced for gays.

Looking at male homosexuality cross-culturally does suggest a predictably lower emphasis on permanent pairing, but it also makes clear that the sexual style of gay communities in the 1970s and early 1980s was a specific historic phenomenon that might not have endured in a society tolerant of homosexual preferences over time. The lid was taken off, that which had been forbidden was permitted, and the explosion lasted for a decade. Sex became an expression of unity and solidarity in the gay community, linking hundreds of men to each other, much as it links couples in happy marriages. Gay liberation meant release from loneliness and exclusion, becoming members not of a family but of a movement which rapidly became international.

The styles of gay sex that developed in the 1970s did have a number of characteristics that quite inevitably accelerated the spread of many diseases, including AIDS. However, from the first appearance of AIDS in Africa and in African patients in Europe, it has been a heterosexual disease. It now seems clear that AIDS will spread among heterosexuals somewhat more slowly than it did among homosexuals, but equally inexorably.

Although AIDS has become a global problem, the picture of the niche of AIDS and its transmission outside the body is not a picture of the planet itself but of a network of human interactions that embrace it, only a tiny fraction of all possible interactions. The disease, like the postal and telephone systems, spans the globe, but just as many individuals do not own telephones and never receive mail, so many individuals are only potentially involved in the interactions that transmit AIDS while others are involved in dense and overlapping interchanges. The behaviors that transmit AIDS actually create multiple patterns in different places, so that it is possible to speak of three or four different AIDS epidemics focused in different "risk groups," but together they constitute the niche of AIDS. Like separate oil spills, each is gradually diffused and the boundaries fade in the current, for no risk group is self-contained.

Individual Choices

One of the first significant developments that followed the discovery of HIV was the development of a blood test for HIV-1, the most common member of the HIV family. The test for the AIDS virus, like the virus itself, is becoming a fact of life, one that is potentially pathological unless we find appropriate ways to manage it, and one that can be expected to cause recurrent debates between those who advocate coercive testing, testing "hawks," and testing "doves," who believe all diagnostic testing should be elective.

We have the test now, and, as with any technological possibility, we must decide what to do with it and what to say to individuals who see in testing a technological "quick fix" and who bring steady pressure for legislation. The hope for a solution through testing is reminiscent of other situations in which it has been tempting to try to resolve problems of social policy with tests or scores whose meanings are not fully understood. The effort to administer schools on the basis of IQ scores, which has the same aura of science and objectivity, is equally ambiguous in the information it provides, and likely to lead to unfairness. Test results are a poor and partial approximation to self-knowledge. The differences in possible outcomes of the testing debate are momentous. At one extreme, there is the possibility of enforced universal testing, used as the criterion for quarantine. At the other extreme, there is the possibility that individual testing can be integrated into a set of policies promoting voluntary responsible behavior.

The situation at the moment is one in which test results can be dangerous — dangerous to the individual because of the discrimination they may trigger, and dangerous to the society because of their ambiguity. Testing may not turn out to be the centerpiece of policy. It may eventually prove easier to persuade most people to practice safer sex and to avoid needle sharing without testing, and this is probably the only way to move in third world countries where testing is clearly a misuse of resources except as a population-monitoring device to advise policy.

Knowledge always has a cost, is always liable to misuse, always brings a burden of responsibility. The person who knows that he or she is seropositive (infected with AIDS) carries not only the burden of the fear of early death but the burden of protecting others, the knowledge that his or her body can cause death. Testing promises to eliminate ignorant transmission, creating culpability, but it is not clear that those who know they are seropositive will behave more responsibly than those who, uncertain of their antibody status, face a double challenge to protect themselves and to protect others. Above all, we must learn to think of the individuals who live the seropositive life with grace and maturity, learning of their own infection and taking steps not to pass it on with all the realism and self-discipline that this entails, as heroes in this encounter with disease, fighting at the barricades while others move to safety. Many in this group will provide the leadership both in prevention of the epidemic's spread and in care for the afflicted. Learning to value them in their difficult role is part of learning to live with AIDS.

~

It's a new world, with new risks and new responsibilities. Some of the inventions to be made will be shared by the entire society in the form of new laws and institutions or technological capabilities. Others will be worked out by individuals, piecing together old conventions and new imperatives, trying to hold on to a sense of self and a measure of delight. Scientific progress and political change take time, but it is already time for individuals, sick or well, seropositive or seronegative, to arrive at a personal understanding of the situation and to begin to make the behavioral changes appropriate to living their lives in the new environment. Not everyone has the capacity to make choices, whether because of a lack of knowledge or a lack of resources or a lack of freedom. Those who do have that capacity will struggle to preserve it by avoiding the servitude of addiction and to increase it by thought and discussion.

The first step is to look around and see who inhabits this new world. Not risk groups and safe groups, for such boundaries are evanescent. Not saints who are uninfected and sinners with AIDS. There are people who know that their behavior puts them at risk and others who know of no present danger. Some are tightly locked into dangerous patterns like intravenous drug use which are almost impossible to escape without help. Others have drifted into habits of casual sex. Some people are already sick, facing a slow and painful death, and yet there are still choices they can make. Others are neighbors or lovers or caretakers of those who are sick. Some people have had the antibody status of their blood tested, with all the uncertainties that implies.

Most of those reading this book can make a reasonable estimate of the extent to which they are at risk at this moment, without knowing absolutely whether they are infected. But the logic of the disease and of the uncertainty in which we live is that every individual should act on the possibility that others around them are infected with AIDS — and on the parallel possibility that they themselves carry the virus and have the obligation to protect others. In the context of these two possibilities, the sensible thing is to take realistic precautions, to acquire a high level of behavioral immunity, and to get on with living a rewarding and constructive life. This is a two-sided ethic that depends on both caring for others and caring for oneself. People will often act responsibly for others even when they will not do so for themselves, but at the same time people need to feel good about themselves to care for their own health.

Living with AIDS is a little like applying Kant's categorical imperative
— acting as if your behavior were to become a rule for the whole society,
affecting you as well as others. It's also somewhat like a version of the
Golden Rule worked out to apply to the many situations, like marriage,
in which the parties are necessarily different.

In working out how to behave in a world that includes the AIDS virus,
driving is a useful analogy. Automobile accidents account for many more
deaths in this country every year than AIDS is likely to do unless the epidemic continues unchecked for some time, and yet most people continue
to drive. The vast majority of drivers have learned to be concerned for
their own safety and for the safety of others as well — in fact, they come
to realize that these are inseparable. Most drivers do not follow the rules
they have been taught exactly but they do work out their own calibration
of risks, going a little over the speed limit sometimes and under it when
bad weather increases the danger, putting together a personal style that
draws on the example of others and on the public rules and is still an
expression of personality. On the road excessive caution can sometimes
cause accidents. Increased knowledge, increased control, and uncompro-
mised mental capacity all make driving safer, and most people find positive pleasure in their own competence behind the wheel, for even with the
need for careful attention and a life-saving seat belt carefully fastened,
driving is an experience of freedom. But to complete the analogy, we have
to compare the arrival of the AIDS virus to a change in road conditions sufficient to require a whole new calibration.

The first decision that presents itself to every individual living in this
new world is *to behave in such a way as to neither contract nor transmit AIDS*.
The behaviors are almost the same, though they can be expressed in elaborate and skillful precautions or by monogamy or total abstinence. The
message to individuals must be: "You care about yourself and about other
people. You like a good time and you plan ahead to have the good time
safely." The difficulty is not so much in defining what is needed as in
reshaping one's own behavior patterns. The evidence is in, however, that
it can be done. While rates of syphilis continue to rise among heterosexual
Americans, they are dropping among homosexuals, and educational programs have begun to affect behavior among such groups as European
drug users and Kenyan prostitutes.

Traditional moral values are helpful but insufficient. Traditional
moralism, however, is not helpful. We live in a society in which, tradition-

ally, sexual activity has been supposed to be limited to marriage, and marriage was believed to be monogamous, permanent, and exclusive. Strenuous efforts were made to enforce the traditional ideals — among other things, by threats of eternal damnation. It's important to notice, as we try to adopt new kinds of guidelines for sexual behavior, that the old system never worked as it was publicly proclaimed. Adolescents have always masturbated (although they have sometimes been wracked by guilt); there has always been prostitution and illegitimacy and incest. This is discouraging, because it suggests that sexuality is so wild and powerful that even intense fear cannot control it, for our ancestors truly feared the fires of hell. Infection with AIDS is frightening, but surely not as frightening as eternal damnation. Both sickness and damnation may be long deferred, but hell goes on forever. Unlike divine justice, infection is not certain: some individuals may continue with risky behavior indefinitely without becoming infected. And yet fear of hell did not persuade the entire society to obey the rules on sex, even though fear did shape and limit their behavior and burden their consciences. This means that a lot of people have always lived by standards that diverge from those they were brought up with.

Attitudes toward the way in which behavior can be shaped have been changing. Even in many of the same denominations that once tried to motivate morality by fear, the emphasis has increasingly come to be on the love of God and the value of caring for others. Lasting changes in behavior are more readily achieved by rewards than by punishment, and sexual appetites can be channeled more easily than they can be repressed. The best way of channeling behavior toward safer sex is to find ways to make it at least as appealing as risky sex. Having a set of ideal rules about sex which are often broken is not the route to safety; it is the *reality* of sex one needs to think about.

There are always some common rules and conventions about sex that are followed by almost everyone in any group. Then on top of them there is likely to be a superstructure of ideal expectations about behavior, with a system of built-in loopholes so that not everyone follows the ideal rules. There is not just one double standard in our tradition, suggesting that women are expected to follow the rules about sexual behavior while men are allowed to violate them; there are many mechanisms for repairing the damage done by breaking rules or by ignoring what has happened so that marriages can remain intact as a means of economic and social organization in spite of violated rules. Theologically this works; medically it doesn't. Divine forgiveness — and human forgiveness — are both valuable in the lives of individuals and of the community. We could use a stronger sense of both. But it is a mistake to believe that forgiveness makes an event "as if it never happened." From the medical point of view, if it happened it happened. The antibodies remember.

Similarly, hypocrisy can be very useful socially. Politicians can base proposed policy for the high schools on the ideal of abstinence from sex even while almost half the students are becoming sexually active. They do this not because they are stupid but because they are smart — and more concerned about ideological advantage than about adolescent health. This is a socially effective way of acting that has been with us for a very long time, and probably does provide a degree of protection and support to those who want to live by traditional rules. Hypocrisy is socially effective but not medically effective. Myths sometimes influence behavior, which gives them a kind of truth. Myths do not influence viruses.

We are having great difficulty working out new ways of modulating sexual expression because we have spent centuries lying to ourselves about our own sexual activity and the activity going on around us. It's worth remembering how often in our cultural tradition we have solved the problem of incest by punishing children for complaining about it. Rules will be broken — but it is possible to have a set of rules about rule breaking that are medically sound. Thus, even as we continue to value monogamy, we need to understand that some departures are more dangerous or destructive than others, just as some divorces are more caring and responsible. True lifetime monogamy is not common, since many women and most men trip up occasionally and can usually do so without destroying their marriages. We need a standard that values a particular relationship as semimonogamous and suggests that, beyond that, precautions be taken. Straying spouses could find an expression of fidelity in using condoms and not let the sense of being sinful lead to self-destructive carelessness.

The relatively late cultural elaboration of sexuality in America has had a number of costs. First, you cannot purposefully regulate or reshape an area of behavior you are determined to ignore. Neither can you enhance or enrich it. Rapid change depends on articulation. You cannot introduce conscious choice, caution, and discrimination into behavior you believe you cannot control. Gluttony emphasizes impulse, while gourmet eating emphasizes moderation and selection, for subtle flavors are lost in excess; if moderation ceased to be associated with repression, a sexual aesthetic might emerge based on subtlety and careful timing, for sometimes waiting increases pleasure. Sex for the gourmet rather than the gourmand. Safer sex suggests a range of options, with the need to discover one's own personal style.

In the United States, we are inclined to confuse quantity with quality. The big watery strawberries in the supermarket are tasteless compared to the fragrant smaller strawberries Europeans prefer. We are only just beginning to achieve a nuanced appreciation of sexuality comparable, say, to the Kama Sutra, and many explorations of sexuality are still tainted with lingering rage at earlier repression. As an alternative to repression and the reaction to repression, we have tended to medicalize discussions of sexuality, like so many other topics, as if an activity must be a little distasteful to be good for you — but who wants strawberries flavored with peroxide? It is now essential that individuals learn to practice and enjoy safer sex. Sex researchers are experimenting with ways to eroticize condom use and so are sophisticated men and women. Condoms are beginning to appear in porn videos as a part of foreplay rather than an interruption, and to be available in colors. The Japanese have treated condoms as sex toys for years.

When people first began discussing the dangers of AIDS it was common to refer to "safe sex," but there has been a growing awareness that safety is relative rather than absolute. It's enough to be as safe in bed with a lover as you are when riding your office elevator or flying cross-country or doing hundreds of other everyday things that carry small amounts of risk. It is a mistake to hope for a risk-free world, or to think that AIDS will soon be eliminated. But if a few individuals do contract AIDS while taking reasonable precautions, that falls in the category of being hit by a falling piano — tragic, but not a possibility you organize your life around or permit to interfere with your relationships to other people.

Panic is not the emotion that reminds you to fasten your seat belt before starting the car, or not to turn on a radio or a hair dryer on the shelf next to the bathtub, and yet in each case there are risks of death or severe injury involved. Preventing AIDS is like keeping the landscape free of trash: it depends on everyone who passes through remembering never to drop a beer can or even a gum wrapper.

The guidelines that a physician would give to an individual known to be seropositive but still healthy and eager to continue an active life are the same precautions that all members of the society should be adopting in interactions with those they do not know well: a man who is infected should wear a condom during sex to prevent transmitting infection; a man who is uninfected should wear a condom to avoid contracting it; a woman should insist on male partners using condoms for one of the same two reasons. Doctors and dentists are being advised to take precautions appropriate to AIDS patients with all of their patients. Sharing hypodermic needles is always dangerous.

In some ways the situation in which one person is known to be seropositive is more difficult than the situation in which either might be. The asymmetry sets up a tension in relationships with one infected partner about the appropriate expression of love. For instance, in many couples where the husband is a hemophiliac infected by transfusions, unprotected sex continues. The wives may feel that taking precautions would be a rejection of the relationship; the husbands may feel that they are innocent casualties for whom taking precautions is an unfair penalty: "If you really loved me . . ." These are the operative words, but who says them? The infected partner cajoling the other into risk? Or the uninfected partner remaining loyally in the relationship and preparing for a possible future of caretaking and bereavement — but not ready to convert it to a suicide pact? In such couples progression toward full-blown AIDS and infection of the spouse may not occur for years, but year by year the increments of bad news continue. People infected with the AIDS virus need to be loved and cared for — and they need to love and be careful.

Oddly enough, safer sex may mean better and more imaginative sex. Certainly it means more caring and conscious sex. In the process of discovering alternatives to penetration, there are new skills to be learned, including talking about sex with a partner and the cultivation of fantasy. Safer sex involves choice and planning ahead and a reasonable level of sobriety, lovemaking following from a thoughtful and unfuddled choice of partner — the kind one would still be glad of by daylight.

The best way to encourage responsibility is to support informed choice and to set a value on conscious decision in all actions, including conscious decisions on having children so that abortions become rare and there are no unwanted children. Planning ahead has to be associated with other desirable traits, especially for women choosing their personal styles of autonomy. Traditionally, one reason for unwanted pregnancies has been the unwillingness to admit planning for a sexual encounter — the Pill was popular because it didn't seem as specifically calculated. Couples will learn to negotiate both condom use and the trust needed for the transition to unprotected sex, often after testing or comparing histories, when a relationship begins to seem permanent or children are desired. The best stance is still the symmetrical one: both partners able to admit the possibility of exposure in the last ten years, both ready to obtain and carry condoms, and both aware that men and women often lie in the search for intimacy.

The fear felt by others is one of the most terrible burdens of AIDS infection. Everyone needs the support of other people and the nourishment of a vast number of day-to-day interactions. Studies of homelessness suggest that those who lack social networks are vulnerable to all sorts of problems, mental, legal, physical. But AIDS patients and those who carry the virus often find when they need the support of others that their social networks are severely compromised by the rejection or even terror displayed by friends and associates. Fears based on misunderstandings of how the AIDS virus is transmitted can lead to dismissal from a job or eviction from an apartment for an infected person who does not know, or is not able to fight for, his or her rights. Frequently even parents and siblings refuse their love and support, particularly if they reject the lifestyle that led to illness.

For all these reasons, the decision of who to confide in and when about the infection is a difficult one. Someone who takes all the recommended precautions to avoid transmitting the disease is leaning over backward to avoid endangering others, so beyond these precautions there is no moral responsibility to inform them of the infection. Research shows that families live with infected individuals for many years without the disease being transmitted, even under quite primitive conditions, and infected hemophiliac children have lived in dormitories for long periods without infecting others. It is safe to drink from the same cup as an AIDS patient, to sleep in the same bed, and even to have sex with appropriate precautions. Above all, it is safe and even essential to cradle and to comfort, to protect a lover or a child or a friend from the sense of abandonment.

Secrecy is an understandable adaptation to the disease in reaction to the risks of discrimination. The burdens of HIV infection are great enough without adding on the results of ignorance. Bad enough to discover that one's own body is freighted with death that can be transmitted to others under carefully defined circumstances, but worse by far if others mistakenly believe they can be infected by casual contact, by working together or sharing food or sitting in the same room. Secrecy brings its own kind of loneliness. It is one of the most poignant burdens on infected persons that even when they are behaving with the greatest and most responsible care, they cannot always trust others to respond rationally.

One of the most important reasons for dealing generously with AIDS victims is so that the inevitable anger that is one of the typical reactions to the knowledge of impending death will not be turned against society. Society needs the cooperation and responsible participation of those who carry the virus, which cannot be evoked by rejection and abandonment. A supportive and caring attitude toward afflicted individuals, whatever their lifestyle or personal history, in no way conflicts with a clear condemnation of continuing irresponsibility.

When a friend tells you he or she has AIDS, the appropriate first reaction is an embrace, not a shudder. If healthy people respond with compassion to those who have AIDS, protecting them from destitution and loneliness, those who have AIDS will be more likely to respond with the effort to protect society from the further spread of the disease.

People can make responsible decisions that make them behaviorally immune to AIDS or behaviorally noncontagious. These decisions involve personal safety, the safety of partners and loved ones, and the well-being of society, for the AIDS epidemic alters forever the line between public and private morality. The precautions necessary are the same in New York and in Zaire, in Amsterdam and in Brazil, but the arguments for these decisions will have to be made again and again to fit different cultural contexts.

Not everyone has the information, the resources, or the autonomy to make such decisions. Providing these and the freedom they represent, both in our own society and internationally, is the key to social policy in the epidemic. The proposals laid out here have multiple goals. Safer sex can control most sexual transmission of disease and provide an effective option of family planning to whole populations. A genuine effort to improve conditions for minorities can bring all the benefits of full social participation, flowing in both directions. AIDS is a powerful reminder that ignorance and injustice are themselves insidious diseases that endanger the entire world community.

Societal Decisions

As long as AIDS was a mysterious and unexplained plague, it could be seen as something separate from human society, an act of God or of random chance or of uncaring nature. But now that we understand its mechanisms — not a mysterious plague but an intelligible epidemic — it has become subject to human decision and social policy. Important as it is to work for medical breakthroughs, the epidemic could be halted entirely by social means, either by means appropriate to a pluralistic society or by means that are coercive and draconian. Either could be effective; either would affect the character of those who used them. When the time comes to count the cost of the epidemic, it will be counted not only in lives lost and dollars spent but in the effect it has had on our institutions and on our understanding of the human condition. This is a way of saying that the threat to society has to do with politics and value systems as well as demographics and economics. At the same time, society might benefit in many ways from lessons learned in these areas.

The basic approach here has been an exploration of what it means to be a species shaped by both biology and culture. On the one hand, we are the product of genetic information and the influence of natural environments. On the other hand, we pass information from one person to another and from one generation to another, learning to shape our environments. In the control of the AIDS virus, we can hope that the transmission of knowledge will prove to be more effective than the transmission of infection.

It would be a mistake, given the diversity of ethical conclusions reached by different human groups, to claim to derive ethics directly from biology. Experience suggests that human beings tend to perceive the natural world in terms of their social experiences rather than vice versa, rewriting natural history to justify capitalism or communism, hierarchy and male dominance or cooperation, imperialism or pluralism. Nevertheless, it is still useful to look, at times of choice, for possible congruence. It is our conviction that an exploration of the distinctive adaptations of our species can suggest ways of looking at the epidemic, and that a metaphorical movement between biology and culture is one way of seeking consistency.

The social experience that the West brings to meet the biological threat of disease is one of democratic pluralism inconsistently maintained and called into question again and again by what are presented as imperatives of biology. It is our conviction that the appropriate responses to the epidemic are in fact congruent with democratic traditions, and that there is guidance to be found in the consistent application of pluralism and democracy. In effect, we are arguing that concern for individuals and open communication are good biology.

In the historic crisis created by the AIDS epidemic, we are dealing with a confrontation between life forms with diametrically different evolutionary strategies. The AIDS virus is an example of minimum structure, rudimentary functioning, and rapid variation. Each individual virion is utterly expendable, for at the microbial end of the evolutionary scale, adaptation is served by heavy and rapid selection in organisms sufficiently simple so that random mutation is relatively likely to propose viable possibilities. Microbes, insects, and most invertebrates are spendthrift of progeny, counting success in the survival of a tiny fraction of the offspring produced. Many are born, and most are wasted.

Human beings are at the opposite end of the scale. Our ethical intuitions of the value of the individual are congruent with our biology, for each human individual, and above all each individual reaching maturity, represents a very great investment for the species. The entire immune system can be read as a parable of commitment to individual survival, for except among a relatively few vertebrate species, safety is in numbers and each individual is undefended against infection. Even in preindustrial societies, over a third of the infants born alive survive to reproduce. The rearing of those infants requires not one or two years of care, which are relatively common periods in other large mammals, but ten to fifteen years, for humans are born almost totally helpless and achieve true viability only after years of learning and loving care. Few are born, and few are wasted.

Paradoxically, we have become so successful that the planet is overburdened with these precious progeny, but this does not change the human capacity to value individuals. We still respond to individual tragedy in the face of vast numbers, and understand increasingly that the path of wisdom is to limit births and dedicate ourselves to optimizing the chances of each individual born. The value of the human individual is a fact of evolutionary strategy; the capacity to care for individuals — at least for our own children — is essential to species survival. Even when all actual child care is done by the mother, she depends on the support of

others and on a community. Human survival has depended on cooperation rather than simple competition.

Why has a concern for individual human lives emerged as so important for human society that it outweighs the benefits of natural selection?
Perhaps because a concern for individuals and for the development of
diverse individual potentials has been a necessary theme in the shift from
biological to cultural evolution. Now that we depend on cultural evolution, we have to ask what kinds of societies provide maximum scope for
the emergence of original thinking. What kind of society can muster the
skill and intelligence and teamwork to unravel the mysteries of the
immune system? Only one in which individual talent and diversity are
valued and brought into interaction.

A similar set of arguments can be made for the congruence between
certain kinds of communication and basic human patterns of adaptation.
Because we survive by knowledge, we flourish in a knowledge-rich environment. We are only just beginning to know how to run societies so that
the talents and capabilities of all members can be tapped. It is clear that a
strategy for dealing with the AIDS epidemic through knowledge and communication highlights problems in our present communications environment. Too many people do not believe what they are told — perhaps with
reason. Too many in fact cannot read. Here, too, there are implications for
contemporary society.

These issues converge in yet another important fact about human
adaptation: the continuing value for human communities of those individuals who do not or cannot reproduce but can communicate. Human
beings tend to outlive their reproductive capacities, but the oldest members of any community are often treasured for their wisdom, for what
they have to say. Similarly, societies have flourished in which large numbers of those who were most talented had no physical progeny but
became, for reasons of asceticism or sexual preference, artists and thinkers
and conservers of the general good, sustainers and builders of civilization.

Just as the values of communication and concern for individuals are
congruent with the human pattern of adaptation, so also is a recognition
of the unity of our species and the interdependence of different species in
the environment. Willingness to care for individuals within the family or
community has not always been extended to other groups, even to those
close at hand. When the poet John Donne wrote that he was diminished
by each single human death, there were still multiple human populations

on this planet unknown to each other and unlinked for millennia. Today that is no longer true. We have all heard the terrifying remark that when we make love, we are intimately linked to every partner our lover has slept with in a ten-year period and to those partners' partners, linked back in a ramifying network of shared passion. We may know our partner and our partner's partners, but two or three links away in the chain there are intimacies in different worlds of experience, down streets we would never walk or even on other continents. Indeed, the AIDS epidemic is the shadow image of the multiple networks of interaction that now unite our species. The hyperbole of infection, even though it is an imagery of horror rather than beauty, is reminiscent of the blue-green image of the earth seen from the moon, defying all borders and divisions projected upon her, united by atmosphere and oceans into a single living community. The most serious dangers that threaten her, including the dangers of overpopulation and pollution, are far more difficult to address than the AIDS epidemic.

We are obliged to act from the sense of being a part of a larger whole: in the words of the microbiologist René Dubos, who projected an ethical vision derived from his knowledge of living systems, we can address the crisis only by "thinking globally and acting locally," choosing patterns of responsible behavior and struggling to offer freedom to make the same choices to those who are constrained by ignorance or poverty or addiction. We can protect ourselves only by protecting others and sharing what we know.

AFTERWORD

To Wander and Wonder

We have always shared, we human beings, some portion of the nomadic pattern. We evolved in Africa, standing upright and foraging for food, moving on as resources dictated. Mobility demands continuing learning, since the survival of migrants depends on the capacity of adults to cope with the unfamiliar. Mobility also engages one of our most basic characteristics, curiosity. We developed the capacity to learn and the skill to teach that made it possible to travel from continent to continent, adopting new behaviors adapted to every kind of environment. Over time, humans made the inventions that allowed them to settle and to support ever larger numbers. Yet movement — and the idea of movement — have remained part of the human repertoire even among the most adamantly settled of peasants. Few groups have been so profoundly isolated that the notion of learning from strangers is entirely absent — even when the last outsiders are so obscured by time that they are remembered as visiting gods.

We learn from difference, but difference often triggers hostility. A pattern of interdependent adaptations, linked by exchange and trade, recurs on every continent and often alternates with conflict. The nomadic tribes of Arabia, for instance, moved to find water and grazing for their animals — camels, sheep, or horses — but maintained a symbiotic relationship with settled farmers with whom they traded animal products for grain. When populations have exceeded carrying capacity, large numbers have spilled out into surrounding areas, often arriving as invaders but gradually learning to live with new neighbors and blending cultural traditions. The planet is now effectively peopled and interconnected, but surges of migration continue. The search for living space and resources for our elaborate forms of subsistence results in conflict of many kinds as well as learning. And as always, we make war with elaborate rhetoric and refer to different beliefs to underline our separations.

We are a single species with a common origin, but we are not notably good at putting it all back together. In the course of their migrations, local populations of human beings lived for millennia largely cut off from one another, developing the variations in physical characteristics that are referred to as race and building up complex learned systems of language and culture and belief. We remain very much attached to the distinctive traditions that continue to keep us apart, yet we are attracted by both novelty and the idea of uniformity, while curiosity is often at odds with loyalty. So people ask, sometimes in hope and sometimes in horror: Will all human beings eventually speak the same language? Will everyone accept a single religion? Will there be so much intermarriage that everyone will look the same? Probably none of the above.

Today we are nomads of the imagination, increasingly familiar with other cultures. In huge numbers, we travel the globe for recreation as often as for survival. And we are nomads in another sense, constantly moving on in our lives and adjusting to new circumstances even in the place called home, abandoning familiar constancies. Ruth Benedict, an anthropologist who often felt like an outsider in her own culture, imagined that for every temperament there might somewhere be a society that would be hospitable in a distinctive way. Even so, her vision was based on homogeneity within a given society and on the expectation of continuity and consistency over a lifetime. Today, we can begin to live in a world where individuals are able to sojourn with the cultures or religious expressions that most nearly match their deepest longings. That match might vary at particular stages of the life cycle, however, guiding choices that need not be irreversible, just as we are finding time in extended lives for changes in careers and marriages and sexual orientations. Perhaps we will learn to live in a shifting and multicultural world by building on the ancient human patterns and skills of nomads.

A European joke about heaven and hell was making the rounds. "Hell," it goes, "is a place where the policemen are German, the cooks are English, the lovers ..." Trying to recall the joke in an airport waiting area, I bogged down halfway through and phoned my husband, who had encountered it at a business school in Lausanne. "Look," I said, "I've got the Germans, the English, the French, and the Italians, but I can't fit it together." "You forgot the Swiss," he said, "it won't work without the Swiss." "In hell," the joke continues, "the Swiss are the lovers, the French are the mechanics, and the Italians are the managers. In heaven, the policemen are English, the Italians are the lovers, the French are the cooks, the Germans are the mechanics, and the Swiss are the managers."

It's a transitional joke. One foot stands in a world of stereotypes and prejudices (a world in which only Europeans matter and only male Europeans at that). The other foot is in a slowly emerging world in which every local negative is matched by a positive distinctiveness and the real question is how to put it all together in a way that works and maintains diversity — as a sponsor from landlocked Switzerland did in assembling fourteen nationalities on the crew that won the Americas Cup in 2003. When we bring out the worst in each other, multiculturalism and globalization both become versions of hell, yet both are good ideas that have become caricatures of what they could be.

There are not enough Italian lovers to go around, and it's not possible to ship every malfunctioning engine to Germany. So today, as throughout human history, ideas move as well as people, and models are passed rapidly from place to place. Every community needs a wide range of skills and personality types. English cooking has become cosmopolitan, Swiss schools train future managers from every country, German policing is firmly informed today by international concepts of human rights. The question is how to promote the free flow of ideas without allowing prejudices to clog or block that flow. However much we borrow, national styles survive, and there is pleasure to be found both in visiting distant places and in returning home.

In such a world, the primary question for any nation would not be competitiveness, for competition tends to promote similarity, but how to be distinctive, how indeed to be indispensable to the others, as a few nations like Switzerland and Costa Rica have made themselves indispensable to the international community by refusing — in very different ways — to take sides or to compete militarily. This would be a world in which we would recognize the value of differentiation in preference to homogeneity, preserving an affirmation of every culture. The emphasis on competition is often bolstered by references to Darwin, but thinking about evolution has moved beyond simple competition. Two very similar species may sometimes survive in the same environment by developing more specialized and distinct niches, like Catholic saints with their specialities and the Greco-Roman deities that proceeded them. Today more and more commercial strategy is focused on offering a distinctive, often customized product or service. Yet even if we recognize that uniformity does not equal progress, we continue to think of ideologies and religions as competing with each other, and we want to think of our own values as universal.

Many values, however, are basically universal but still highly specific. It is possible and perhaps necessary to appreciate the ties of others to unfamiliar places without giving up our own specific loyalties. We share love of place as we share love of family with others whose family members we have never met. We do not often proselytize for our homes or our favorite relatives — so why should we do so for systems of belief? Specific loyalties to different homes are not for export but can be combined with hospitality. Local loyalty remains one of the few ways of conserving distinctive traditions, particular styles of art and story, key elements of personal identity. Many environmentalists believe that conservation must be built upon a "sense of place," and that respect for the systemic characteristics of the biosphere is necessarily grounded in loyalty to a specific biome and landscape. Yet human beings convert the sense of place into patriotism and reshape it as a form of competition; often enough, we go to war to defend ancient convictions about the ownership of territory while casually degrading its distinctive beauty. Why do monotheists applaud the affection of sons and daughters each for their own biological parents while pressing all human being to accept a single father in heaven?

Recently I have been thinking back to the excitement in the late fifties that surrounded the work of the French Jesuit priest Pierre Teilhard de Chardin. He was a distinguished paleontologist who connected his thinking about evolution to his theology and was forbidden to publish or teach by the Catholic Church. He believed that life evolved on this planet, the geosphere, covering and surrounding it and forming the biosphere, and that the same evolutionary process that had led to vast and ramifying diversity around the planet had been thrusting toward consciousness. But he went further, to see a common consciousness or web of intercommunication, which he called the "noosphere," evolving to enfold the planet. His work can be described as a premonition of the Internet, but the Internet is only a recent and particularly vivid expression of a many-layered process that goes much further back. Teilhard expected this emerging shared consciousness to be united, however, in a single spiritual understanding, and this was the Omega point to which he believed evolution finally tends. As a Catholic, Teilhard thought in terms of a single truth, a global convergence on a system of ideas that have been central to the Western tradition.

In this he was untrue to his biological metaphor. Why should not the noosphere be even more multiple and diverse than the biosphere? And why does uniformity appear superior to multiplicity? Following from that, why should not the protection of diverse human languages and cultures — and beliefs — be as urgent as the protection of species? To the Church, however, Teilhard's speculative thinking suggested all sorts of unwanted diversity — heretical ideas, including the possible coevolution of God and creation, and the ethical dilemmas of a merged consciousness. Today we might want to ask not which truth we will arrive at but whether any truth can be either single or unchanging.

Uniformity is alluring and convenient for many purposes, but it is a bad idea. Certain kinds of difference are indispensable to life. Even though societies have again and again attempted sexual and age segregation, reproduction depends on sexual difference and on the interaction of different age-groups. However much we invent ideal types of body or mind, it is essential for any society that individuals have different talents to respond to unexpected circumstances and that they bond with partners and children who are not identical and are perhaps most lovable for their idiosyncrasies. Yet when humans interest themselves in a plant as a potential cultivar, they often work toward a uniform strain that seems optimal for production and consumption, then cultivate it over wide acres as exclusively as possible, controlling developmental timing and fertilization. The dangers of monocultures are not limited to disease and pests, for monocultures degrade ecosystems and limit the choices of the people who cultivate them, making them newly vulnerable to external pressures.

We have long established patterns of thought which suggest that for one answer to be valid, all other answers must be incorrect, and that where there is difference it consists in superiority and inferiority. For centuries, the ideal in many places has been a religious monoculture or at least one in which a single faith (or political ideology or national identity) will be unquestionably dominant. Perhaps there is an interesting analogy between the potato blight that caused famine in Ireland and some of the pathologies that arise in communities closed to new ideas. The ninth-century Golden Age of Islamic science was ended by the theologians, just as the Inquisition attempted to suppress Galileo's discoveries.

Not all organized religious bodies call for a fixed body of doctrine, however, and its achievement is elusive. Except in eras of high inquisitorial fervor, there is a good deal of diversity of belief in the Catholic Church, much of it excused or disparaged as ignorance rather than suppressed — but to dismiss divergent beliefs as ignorant rather than heretical can be part of the bad old habit of translating difference into a kind of inferiority. The Episcopal Church often functions as a living, breathing compromise of different beliefs that at certain times has seemed to me scandalous and at others deeply wise. And I have encountered other ways of holding dogma lightly: in children, in the very old, in mystics — and even in theologians who had transformed their commitment into an elitist sense that dogma was no more than an approximation. Surely equivalent kinds of diversity exist uncelebrated in all faiths. It is an illusion of the recitation of creeds (or pledges of allegiance) that they have the same meaning to everyone present.

The same variations appear in other kinds of conviction, ranging from politics to educational reform. We are having considerable debate in the United States today about national standards of education and whether we should in some way make sure everyone knows (believes?) the same thing at the end of school, yet surely the most important task of schooling is to initiate an open-ended process of ongoing learning that inevitably increases diversity in the society rather than uniformity. Recently, in a discussion of schools of psychotherapy, it occurred to me that it is important for a psychotherapist to have a theoretical base but to hold to it lightly, as a metaphor rather than a doctrine, with a certain poetic relationship to the improvisations of responding to clients. In the care of patients, as in the cure of souls, too much orthodoxy can be toxic. In a post-dogmatic world we need not be bereft of a sense of the sacred and the enrichment of shared ritual, but we do need new ways of valuing and moderating the growth of our own convictions, flexibility without cynicism, and the ability to make commitments even as we realize that these may change.

Anthropology, of course, requires a certain suspension of both belief and disbelief. In order to recognize how a belief in ghosts, say, fits into a culture, it is necessary at least to entertain that belief, for ghosts are real at least in the sense that a belief in ghosts can cause illness or healing in individuals and peace or war between communities. Sometimes, too, beliefs restrain, for apparently irrational reasons, behaviors that would be destructive to health or to the environment. Exposure to multiple systems of belief has made many, but by no means all, anthropologists into casual atheists. Researchers with strong personal religious convictions, like Victor Turner or Monica Wilson, must suspend their beliefs when they work in the context of other traditions in order not to be blinded by them, but frequently they are among the most curious and insightful about the beliefs of others. They may offer a model for living in a world of diverse beliefs, a way beyond referring to the beliefs of others as superstition. Cultural relativity as a methodological principle continues to promote a degree of tentativeness in one's own beliefs and curiosity about and respect for those of others, suspending judgment in favor of understanding in context.

As far as religions are concerned, I have come to believe that each contains some truth not readily expressed in secular contexts and each is riddled with nonsense. I suspect that this is a necessary condition, for the value of religion in human life depends on generous doses of ambiguity and redundancy. I do not believe it possible to remedy this mix of sense and nonsense either through purging — by eliminating apparent error and internal contradiction — or through syncretism — by selecting fragments of apparent truth and putting them together to make something new. There is no single right answer, but perhaps there is truth in multiplicity if only we can sustain it with less bloodshed. At times it may be helpful to accept a corrective dose of some other tradition, as young Americans in recent decades have believed (I think rightly) that they deepened their understanding through encounters with Native American or Far Eastern traditions. Many African Americans have been inspired by Islam, finding at least personal answers to what troubles them in the traditions they were raised in. The offer of a personal answer for a period of time, while respecting the right of others to the same kind of search, may be an invaluable function for the different religious traditions, contributing something not offered by agnosticism or casual atheism.

Each religion is both sacred vision and caricature. Each religion is a partial way of understanding something larger than human consciousness, but each is necessarily built of human experiences that vary from time to time and place to place. Doctrines and institutions are elaborated by human beings. Thus, biological parenthood is universal, but concepts of parenthood vary from place to place and many of us would like to change some of their practical expressions. Nevertheless, motherhood and fatherhood may be essential metaphors to extend to the cosmos in order to believe that our actions matter, to ground essential patterns of lawfulness and respect.

Perhaps as human beings we can sustain such values only in concert with familiar rituals, chants, pilgrimages, texts, all the paraphernalia of organized religion, all the familiarity of shrines and holy days. Because I know that forms and symbols feed the spirit, the forms and symbols of my childhood will do very well, but I no longer want them to have absolute value. They are good enough to comfort and inspire, to mourn the dead and celebrate the spring, to frame new learning and provide the symbols of identity and community in a limited sphere. Especially if, in their details, they are held lightly. They are dangerous, however, if they are infused with the conviction of absolute and exclusive truth, and valued beyond the good of the knowable world. It is no accident that young people with no experience of religion are often drawn into the narrowest kinds of religious movements, but it would be interesting to know why fundamentalisms and absolutist cults emerge even within the context of diverse and sophisticated religious communities.

Systems of religious belief offer both integration and grounding to those broad understandings of life that have been called worldviews and take individuals beyond the self. I believe we do need such a grounding. Ethical convictions survive the abandonment of formal religion for a generation and occasionally for two, but all too often they seem eventually to fade. Religious communities have developed the patterns for transmitting such abstract notions, primarily through stories, and without them we risk constructing orthodoxies of self-interest or dealing piecemeal with a systemic world.

Arguably, the strength and resilience of a tradition lies precisely in something that theologians are constantly trying to root out — in its inconsistencies and ambiguities, its receptiveness to different styles of personality and stages of the life cycle, its mechanisms for change. One can compare the natural genetic diversity of any wild population to the ideas available in a community hospitable to multiple voices. Like a system of agriculture based on monocrops, rigid orthodoxy, whether of belief or of disbelief, is subject to a variety of pathologies ranging from cults to inquisitions, while an awareness of alternative traditions can sometimes make it possible to seek out the elements within a given tradition that will make adaptation possible. Today there are Christian and Jewish writers mining the scriptures for arguments leading to environmental awareness and Muslim feminists making the same kinds of arguments for increased respect and freedom for women. Change is painful, but small changes of emphasis can make it possible to carry a traditional belief into a new cultural adaptation.

There still are groups that plan to extend a single system of ideas to the whole planet, but today it is not only Baptists or Mormons or Shiite Muslims who imagine their teachings spreading and replacing all others. Today the triumphalists of dogma are less likely than in the past to be theologians and more likely to be free market economists. Even a very good idea like democracy can be degraded when we attempt to make it universal or to introduce it too quickly, for democracy takes more than a generation to take root and flourish, developing distinctive local forms. One of the traditional ways of spreading ideas is warfare, but warfare perhaps always leads to a distortion of ideas when they are imposed by force.

Perhaps the right question to ask about an idea is not how to persuade others to accept it but how to get it into the conversation, into the mix. The growth of environmental consciousness over the last fifty years is an interesting example of how ideas spread gradually, finding a niche and a pattern of interaction with other ongoing conversations. On the one hand, we could be tearing our hair out and bemoaning the slowness of the process, the lack of consensus on the urgency of conservation; on the other hand, we could notice that the environment has become an inescapable element in the global conversation. One way to confirm this is by watching the rise of hypocrisy about the environment — it has at least become something that corporations and politicians find worth lying about. When Company X promotes its image by claiming that it is environmentally responsible, it is at the same time reinforcing the notion that this is a good thing; eventually the company's own advocacy may catch up with it. The same thing is true of human rights and issues of war and peace. In 2003, as the United States came closer to a preemptive attack on Iraq, crowds protested on every continent. The protest did not prevent the war, but it offered for the first time the possibility of a global conversation about peace — one that will continue and strengthen.

I use the word *conversation* rather than *debate* advisedly, because these processes are most productive if we can avoid framing them in terms of winning. Often the introduction of a new phrasing or metaphor is as significant as new information. Bad metaphors corrupt both thought and information. In this sense, debate, as a form of conflict, is a bad metaphor for processes that must be sustained by shared and mutual effort. We need to know a great deal more about the movement and development of conversations, even where there is no initial agreement except to go on talking. It might be useful to ask about the sustainability of ideas, just as we have begun to ask about human activities, for sustainability carries with it the notions of resilience and variation over time.

Yet we also need to know more about what it takes to get a new idea integrated into an existing system of ideas or values and how this process differs from the prior step of bringing it into conversation; it is this quality of integration that really gives an idea staying power. Environmentalists in the past, for example, have tried to *add* environmental values, without asking how they fit in. It would perhaps be safer always to speak of value *systems*. As in mathematics, it is possible to memorize rules, but thinking mathematically requires an integrated understanding.

People accept new ideas when they feel a sense of recognition of the new as a translation of or extrapolation from or analogy to something familiar. A pattern developed in early childhood in relation to self and body image and primary family relations may provide a model that is projected onto society and ecosystem. Efforts to teach or change attitudes in these broader contexts are then very difficult. It is relatively easy to use existing domestic values to influence some external ones, like compassion for a starving child in Africa or a baby seal evoked by protective attitudes toward helpless infants, but harder to stimulate concern about soil depletion. An existing pattern of male domination in the family easily plays into oligarchy, colonialism, and environmental exploitation. The denial of sexuality or death distorts understanding of wider natural processes.

In the environmental area, there is a new formulation of anthropocentrism emerging which starts from the familiar base of valuing humankind but which emphasizes that humankind is part of and dependent on a larger system — that the unit of survival is the species in its environment. This approach suggests not a repudiation or replacement of anthropocentrism but a reinterpretation of humankind's best interest. Another strategy that assumes the need to work within an existing system is to take a familiar value and give it a new emphasis. Thus we find new phrasings of stewardship in many forms of Christian environmentalism and new ways of putting dollar values on environmental damage. It is not yet clear which of these changes will be constructive or mutually compatible.

When values are looked at in terms of their place in a system of values, rather than as if they are separate and discrete, many paradoxes of value change become clear. Under certain kinds of pressure, value systems may collapse in ways that are partly predictable and related to the way they are integrated, perhaps by some kind of regression down a need hierarchy. There seems to be a kind of Gresham's law that can operate in the sphere of values. We are all affected by pressures to accept the short-term version of a given good. We are all likely to accept substitutes as better than nothing. Thus, it is common to press for higher wages rather than more satisfying work, to mistake sex for love, to strive for more possessions rather than for quality of life more broadly understood. Sometimes, however, the encounter with other values can move toward higher levels of abstraction, toward a synthesis rather than toward compromise.

We are perhaps becoming nomads in what we care about, so that change and novelty have come to seem more important than continuity and tradition. If values once learned are to be kept flexible and adaptable, there is a need to learn to modify, question, and reintegrate existing values, not simply to discard them. The experience of learning some new value could be used to provide models for integrating new understandings into existing ones in other new situations. Many Americans can remember that the handicapped were invisible to them until they learned to include them in their thinking; can that memory help them to listen and respond differently to some newly recognized excluded group, and how far can the concept of access be generalized? Is there then deutero-learning (learning to learn) in the area of values? Something that is good in a given context can be a danger when the context changes. Today in particular, we live in a world of change, so that our values or the way they are configured or the way we interpret and implement them must be flexible and changeable.

Everyone has some skills for dealing with the kinds of differences that always exist, even in so-called homogeneous societies, like the interaction across difference that obviously happens between adults and children and leads to learning, but often the adults do not recognize that they too are learning and changing.

Thinking about multicultural societies or societies in the process of change would be less threatening if we would reexamine the assumptions we make about continuity in ourselves. I have argued that we need to reflect on the most intimate kinds of diversity and strangeness — strangeness in the self and strangeness in those we love most. We need to question assumptions about the degree of uniformity needed for society to function also. Honing the skills of dealing with diversity means listening and learning as well as making do. There is a whole history of inventions that make limited mutual understanding tolerable, lingua francas and

pidgins for dealing with practical needs, forms of translation like monetization, or seeing everything in zero-sum terms. Sometimes working
alliances based on different goals and crude approximations fall apart, but
sometimes they mature and deepen.

A multicultural society does require some metavalues, such as those
that are embedded in the American Constitution, which has allowed for
growth and adaptation. One of these metavalues is what we call "pluralism." Pluralism essentially means that, whatever I believe at a moment
in time, it is valuable — not just tolerable — to me that there are people
around me whose beliefs are different. The concept of a democracy, in
which you understand that you benefit from the presence and often success of people with whom you disagree, is analogous to the concept of an
ecosystem. Different species, after their order, sometimes compete, sometimes cooperate, and sometimes live right past and hardly encounter each
other. Still, they are present and in the broadest sense interdependent, not
each on each but throughout the system. There are interior or spiritual
aspects of pluralism. Empathy makes it possible to bridge differences, but
one is changed in that process. In fact, if we visualize a continual diverse
interaction of points of view and a habit of trying to understand the ideas
of others, this becomes a definition of lifelong learning and changing in
which the teacher is necessarily a learner, because there is no fixed truth
in this fluid world, and the learner is necessarily a teacher, as of course
newborn infants are teachers who train their mothers and fathers in the
art of being parents.

It's confusing, but *we have a right to be confused*. Perhaps even a need.
The trick is to enjoy it: to savor complexity and resist the easy answers; to
let diversity flower into creativity. Politicians again and again try to wean
people from the effort to understand complexity. They know, for
instance, that war is the great simplification that makes it possible to
silence dissonant opinions and to decide once and for all that guns are
more important than butter instead of seeking a more complex balance.

Working on this volume, deciding what to include and what linkages to
create by discussion or juxtaposition, has brought back many earlier interests and given me new ways of understanding themes that I thought I had
abandoned. Reflecting on all this, I have found myself thinking back to a
group of pre-Islamic Arabic odes, with their conventionalized forms and
language, that I fell in love with as an undergraduate and that still held

me so I eventually wrote my dissertation on them. Following tradition, each cde begins with the poet standing at an abandoned campsite in the desert. He notes the traces of habitation — eroded trenches, old tent pegs, the blackened stones of campfires — and he mourns their slow obliteration by winds and time. He is reminded of a woman of the tribe who camped there, or sometimes several, and speaks of her beauty and her departure. Then after demonstrating his poetic skills and evoking the nostalgia of his audience, he admonishes himself to resist grief and show his courage and resilience by his own departure, which gives him the opportunity for another professional tour de force, describing his horse or camel in loving detail. Traveling on, he passes from the past into the present and the timeless. Only after this double obeisance to tradition does he move to the variable third section, the main business of the poem.

I began this collection with a poem I wrote in high school that reflected anxiety about encountering adulthood and a world of strangeness and at the same time a certain readiness for moving beyond the symmetries of childhood. Some of the other early writings included here, the study of the poet Bialik begun in college, and the essays on my parents, now both dead, also reflect those transitions, though most of this volume was written later. I have wandered through files of published and unpublished work, like the poet "weeping over traces." Mine has been an unconventional career, often wasteful because I have been forced to learn new skills and begin again repeatedly, but this wandering showed me the emerging pattern of lives that must in our era be composed and recomposed, tuned and improvised. It has also led me to wonder at the willingness to learn in a new time and a new place, so basic to human evolution, that is the best protection against the anxieties of change and estrangement. Inevitably such a retrospective as this has been an opportunity to discover the patterns of thought that give unity to a nomadic life. It is these that can carry me into new landscapes and might usefully be passed along.

A CHRONOLOGY

1939–1956 New York City

I was born on December 8, 1939, in New York City. At the beginning of World War II, my parents moved downtown to a brownstone on Perry Street in Greenwich Village, merging our household with that of Lawrence K. Frank while both were absent for long periods of war work. My father lived with us for a year after the war and then moved out in 1947, and my parents divorced in 1951. My mother moved us to another shared household on Waverly Place in 1955. I went to the Bank Street Nursery School, the Downtown Community School, and the Brearley School.

In 1956 I went to Israel, where I completed my senior year of high school in Hebrew in a suburb of Jerusalem.

1957–1966 Cambridge, Massachusetts

In 1957 I entered Radcliffe College as a freshman and met my husband to be that fall. I graduated in 1960 with a B.A. in Semitic languages and married J. Barkev Kassarjian a week later. That fall I began work toward a Ph.D. in linguistics and Middle Eastern studies at Harvard. My 1963 dissertation was on Arabic poetry. In 1962 my husband and I bought a farmhouse in Hancock, New Hampshire.

In 1963 I became an instructor in Arabic in the Department of Near Eastern Languages at Harvard. During that three-year appointment, I also participated in the teaching group of Erik H. Erikson's course on the human life cycle and worked on my *Handbook of Arabic*.

1966–1968 Manila, Republic of the Philippines

When my husband finished his doctorate at Harvard Business School, he took a position in Manila, and I became assistant and later associate professor of anthropology at Ateneo de Manila University, teaching anthropology and linguistics, developing materials for the teaching of Pilipino, and conducting fieldwork in a village on the outskirts of the city. I began to consider myself primarily an anthropologist and secondarily a linguist.

In 1968 I became pregnant, but our son, Martin Krikor Kassarijian, was born prematurely and died.

1968–1972 Cambridge, Massachusetts

For the first year after our return from the Philippines, I had a senior research fellowship in psychology and philosophy at Brandeis University in Waltham, Massachusetts. I worked on *Our Own Metaphor,* increased my background in communication, and developed the beginnings of a theory of performance coding that carried over to later work on mother-infant communication and on ritualization.

In the fall of 1969 we moved into the Cambridge apartment we have owned ever since, and our daughter, Sevanne Margaret Kassarjian, was born less than a month later.

From 1969 to 1971 I was associate professor of anthropology at Northeastern University in Boston, and research staff member of the Speech and Communications Group of the Research Laboratory of Electronics at MIT, doing intensive analyses of filmed and recorded interactions between mothers and infants during the first year of life. My teaching in this period included introductory anthropology and graduate and undergraduate courses in culture and personality, language and culture, peoples and cultures of the Middle East, and anthropology of religion.

1972–1979 Tehran, Iran

During our first two years in Iran, where my husband was teaching at a newly established graduate school of management, I did research on values in modern Iranian culture and organized an Iranian national character study group in Tehran. I taught (in Persian) as a visiting faculty member in anthropology at the University of Tehran and acted as consultant to the

Institute of Research and Planning in Science and Higher Education, working on the plan for Bou Ali Sina University in Hamadan, an institution to train students for development work in their own region.

In 1974 we returned to Cambridge for a year, and I resumed teaching at Northeastern.

In 1975 we went back to Tehran, where I joined the faculty at Damavand College, a private English-language women's institution. My activities included teaching, leading a major curriculum revision, and developing master's degree programs. In 1977 I moved to Reza Shah Kabir University (later renamed the University of Northern Iran) as dean of social sciences and humanities for a newly envisioned graduate-level institution, which involved curriculum planning, recruiting, and budgeting. A handful of faculty were recruited, and the small first group of students admitted, and a research program undertaken.

In January 1979, as the Islamic revolution reached climax, the whole project was indefinitely suspended, and pressures from outside the university caused all the non-Iranian and most of the Iranian faculty to leave. I returned with Sevanne to the United States, to be joined by Barkev a year later.

1979–1980 Cambridge, Massachusetts

Back in the United States and unemployed, I reclaimed our apartment and dealt with the issues created by my mother's death the previous November and her intellectual legacy. I became president of the Institute for Intercultural Studies in New York, which she had founded in 1947, and began work on a memoir of both my parents (*With a Daughter's Eye,* 1984). The Center for Middle Eastern Studies at Harvard gave me an office and arranged a visiting scholar appointment in anthropology while I wrote articles and op-eds on Iran and looked for jobs.

My father had developed cancer in 1978 and died in the summer of 1980. I had returned to the United States to help him finish *Mind and Nature* when he first got sick, and before his death he had passed on the task of completing *Angels Fear.*

1980–1987 Amherst College, Amherst, Massachusetts

In 1980 I was appointed dean of the faculty at Amherst College. This involved the ongoing administration of academic programs and faculty personnel policy, planning and budgeting, working closely with the president and other senior administrators in policy making and appeals for funding, and participating in the coordination of the Five College consortium. In 1983 I was forced out of the deanship after the sudden death of the president, and I spent 1983–84 as a fellow of the Bunting Institute of Radcliffe College, where I completed my memoir. Since I was still professor of anthropology, I taught at Amherst for a year before taking an extended leave, during which I completed *Angels Fear* (1987), the book my father was writing when he died, and *Composing a Life* (1989).

1987–2000 Fairfax, Virginia, and Hancock, New Hampshire

In 1987 I was appointed Clarence J. Robinson Professor in Anthropology and English at George Mason University, with an agreement that allowed me to take multiple unpaid leaves and complete *Thinking AIDS* and *Peripheral Visions*. I was a Guggenheim fellow in 1987–88, did fieldwork in Israel in 1989, and spent the spring semester of 1996 at Spelman College, a historically black women's college in Atlanta, Georgia, as distinguished visiting scholar. I generally taught only the spring semester at Mason, where I developed a course on women's life histories and combined this with an ecology of culture course in some years and freshman seminars in others.

In 1997 I developed chronic fatigue syndrome and took a two-year leave, returning to teach in 2000, then after an additional leave formally retired from Mason in 2001. *Full Circles, Overlapping Lives,* drawing on my teaching on women's life histories at Spelman and at Mason, was completed in 1999.

Our daughter, Sevanne, was married to Paul Griffin in 1999 in the meadow of our Hancock house.

2000–present Cambridge, Massachusetts, and Hancock, New Hampshire

In 2000–2001 I was scholar in residence at the Radcliffe Institute for Advanced Studies (the former Bunting Institute, now absorbed by

Harvard), where I began work on this collection, and in 2001 I was appointed to a three-year term as visiting professor of education at the Harvard Graduate School of Education, where I taught a seminar entitled Narratives of Learning and Discovery.

Our first grandchild, Cyrus James Griffin, was born in 2002.

A BIBLIOGRAPHY OF WORKS BY
MARY CATHERINE BATESON

N.B.   Translations, book reviews, short opinion pieces and columns in newspapers and magazines, papers presented at professional associations, and addresses in a variety of academic and nonacademic settings are not included.

1961   "A Brief Study of the Armenian Language." *The Armenian Review* 14, no. 3-55, (Autumn): 23–45.

1964   Edited with T. A. Sebeck and A. S. Hayes. *Approaches to Semiotics: Anthropology, Education, Linguistics, Psychiatry, Psychology.* Proceedings of the Indiana University Conference on Paralanguage and Kinesics, May 1962 The Hague: Mouton. 294 pp. 2nd ed., 1972.

1966   "'A Riddle of Two Worlds': An Interpretation of the Poetry of H. N. Bialik." *Daedalus* issue entitled "Tradition and Change" (Proceedings of the American Academy of Arts and Sciences) 95, no. 3 (Summer): 740–62.

1967   *Arabic Language Handbook.* Washington, DC: Center for Applied Linguistics. 125 pp. 2nd edition. Georgetown University Press, 2003.

1968   "Linguistics in the Semiotic Frame." *Linguistics* 39 (May 1968): 5–17.

    "Insight in a Bicultural Context." *Philippine Studies* 16, no. 4: 605–21. Reprinted in several anthologies in the Philippines.

1970   *Structural Continuity in Poetry: A Linguistic Study of Five Early Arabic Odes.* Paris: Ecole des Hautes Etudes. 168 pp.

1971   "The Interpersonal Context of Infant Vocalization." *Quarterly Progress Report, Research Laboratory of Electronics,* no. 100, 170–76. Cambridge, MA: MIT Press.

1972   *Our Own Metaphor: A Personal Account of a Conference on Conscious Purpose and Human Adaptation.* New York: Alfred A. Knopf. 356 pp. Paper editions by Smithsonian Institution Press and Hampton Press (forthcoming).

1973   *At Home in Iran.* Tehran: St. Paul's Church. 43 pp. 2nd ed., 1976.

1975   "Ritualization: A Study in Texture and Texture Change." In *Religious Movements in Contemporary America,* edited by Irving Zaretsky and Mark P. Leone, 150–65. Princeton: Princeton University Press.

        "Mother-Infant Exchanges: The Epigenesis of Conversational Interaction." In *Developmental Psycholinguistics and Communication Disorders,* edited by Doris Aaronson and R. W. Rieber, 101–13. Annals of the New York Academy of Sciences, 263.

        "Linguistic Models in the Study of Joint Performances." In *Linguistics and Anthropology: In Honor of C. F. Voegelin,* edited by M. Dale Kinkade, K. L. Hale, and Oswald Werner, 53–66. Lisse, The Netherlands: Peter de Ridder Press.

1977   With J. W. Clinton, J. B. M. Kassarjian, Hasan Safavi, and Mehdi Soraya. "Ṣafā-yi Bāṭin: A Study of the Interrelations of a Set of Iranian Ideal Character Types." In *Psychological Dimensions of Near Eastern Studies,* edited by L. Carl Brown and Norman Itzkowitz, 257–74. Princeton: Darwin Press.

        "'Daddy, Can a Scientist Be Wise?'" In *About Bateson,* edited by John Brockman, 55–74. New York: E. P. Dutton.

1978   "Marrying into Iran." Mimeographed. Publication canceled at the time of the revolution. 200 pp.

        "Anthropology as Transitive and Reflexive Knowledge." In *Anthropology for the Future,* edited by Dimitri Shimkin, Sol Tax, and J. Morrison, 228–30. Urbana, IL: University of Illinois Press.

1979   "'The Epigenesis of Conversational Interaction': A Personal Account of Research Development." In *Before Speech: The Beginning of Interpersonal Communication,* edited by Margaret Bullowa, 63–77. Cambridge: Cambridge University Press.

        "'This Figure of Tinsel': A Study of Themes of Hypocrisy and Pessimism in Iranian Culture." *Daedalus* issue entitled "Hypocrisy, Illusion, and Evasion" (Proceedings of the American Academy of Arts and Sciences) 108, no. 3, (Summer): 125–34.

1980   "Continuities in Insight and Innovation: Toward a Biography of Margaret Mead." *American Anthropologist* 82, no. 2 (June): 270–77.

        "Caring for Children, Caring for the Earth." *Christianity and Crisis* 40, no. 5 (March 31): 67–70.

"Six Days of Dying." *The Co-Evolution Quarterly,* (Winter, 4–11). Reprinted in *News That Stayed News,* edited by Art Kleiner and Stewart Brand. San Francisco: NorthPoint Press, 1986.

1983   "Formal and Informal Systems of Knowledge." In *The Optimum Utilization of Knowledge,* edited by Kenneth Boulding and Lawrence Senesh. Boulder, CO: Westview Press.

1984   *With a Daughter's Eye: A Memoir of Margaret Mead and Gregory Bateson.* New York: William Morrow. 242 pp. Paper editions by Pocket Books and HarperPerennial.

1985   "The Search for Absolutes: Iran." In *High Technology and Human Freedom,* edited by Lewis H. Lapham, 127–33. Washington DC: Smithsonian Institution Press.

1986   "Earth Kinship." In *Is the Earth a Living Organism?* Sharon, CT: National Audubon Society Expedition Institute. Section 4. 11 pp.

1987   With Gregory Bateson. *Angels Fear: Towards an Epistemology of the Sacred.* New York: Macmillan. 224 pp. Paper editions by Bantam Books and Hampton Press (forthcoming).

        "The Revenge of the Good Fairy." *Whole Earth Review.* (Summer) 34–8.

1988   With Richard Goldsby. *Thinking AIDS.* New York: Addison-Wesley. 153 pp. Hardcover and paper editions.

        "Compromise and the Rhetoric of Good and Evil." In *Social Dynamics of Peace and Conflict: Culture in International Security,* edited by Robert Rubenstein and Mary L. Foster, 35–46. Boulder, CO: Westview Press.

1989   *Composing a Life.* New York: Atlantic Monthly Press. 241 pp. Paper editions by New American Library/Plume and Grove Press.

        "Language, Languages, and Song: The Experience of Systems" (1968). In *The Individual, Communication, and Society: Essays in Memory of Gregory Bateson,* edited by Robert Rieber, 129–46. Cambridge: Cambridge University Press.

1990   "Beyond Sovereignty: An Emerging Global Civilization." In *Contending Sovereignties: Redefining Political Community,* edited by R. B. J. Walker and Saul H. Mendlovitz, 196–220. Boulder, CO: Lynne Rienner.

1991   "Reflections on Risk and Calibration." In *Self Regulatory Behavior and Risk Taking: Causes and Consequences,* edited by Lewis P. Lipsett and Leonard L. Mitnick, Norwood, NJ: Ablex Publishing.

"Multiple Kinds of Knowledge: Societal Decision Making." *Diversity and Design: Studying Culture and the Individual* Proceedings from the fourth annual Qualitative Research in Education Conference, edited by Mary Jo McGee Brown. Athens, GA: Georgia Center for Continuing Education. 1–21.

1992   "The Construction of Continuity." In *Executive and Organizational Continuity: Managing the Paradoxes of Stability and Change,* edited by Suresh Srivastva and Ronald E. Fry, 27–39. San Francisco: Jossey-Bass.

1993   "Joint Performance Across Cultures: Improvisation in a Persian Garden." Address, Western States Communication Association convention, February 1992. *Text and Performance Quarterly* 13, no. 2 (April): 113–21.

"Into the Trees." In *Sacred Trusts,* edited by Michael Katakis, 1–11. San Francisco: Mercury House.

"Purpose, Gender, and Evolution." In *Evolutionary Ethics*, edited by Matthew Nitecki, Proceedings of the Field Museum Spring Systematics Symposium, 1990. Albany: State University of New York Press.

"Toward an Ambiguous World Order." In *Constitutionalism and World Order,* edited by Richard A. Falk, Robert C. Johanson, and Samuel S. Kim, 245–52. Albany: State University of New York Press.

"Composing a Life." In *Sacred Stories: A Celebration of the Power of Stories to Transform and Heal,* edited by Charles Simpkinson and Anne Simpkinson, 39–52. San Francisco: Harper.

1994   *Peripheral Visions: Learning Along the Way.* New York: HarperCollins. 243 pp. Hardcover and paper editions.

Foreword. *Media Anthropology: Informing Global Citizens,* edited by Susan L. Allen. Westport, CT: Bergen & Garvey.

1995   "Democracy, Ecology, and Participation." In *Democracy, Education, and the Schools,* edited by Roger Soder, 69–86. San Francisco: Jossey-Bass.

"On the Naturalness of Things." In *How Things Are: A Science Tool-Kit for the Mind,* edited by John Brockman and Katinka Matson, 9–16. New York: William Morrow.

"Commitment in a Time of Change." Keynote address, first international conference of the Armenian International Women's

Association. In *Armenian Women in a Changing World.* 4–10. Belmont, MA: AIWA Press.

"Holding Up the Sky Together." *Civilization,* May–June. 29–31.

"'A Spade with Which to Dig': Valuing Human Occupations." *Dalhousie Review,* (Summer–Fall). 172–79.

1996 "Enfolded Activity and the Concept of Occupation." In *Occupational Science: The Evolving Discipline,* edited by Ruth Zemke and Florence Clark, 5–12. Philadelphia: F. A. Davis.

Foreword. *A Mythic Life: Learning to Live Our Greater Story,* by Jean Houston. New York: HarperCollins.

"The Earth Our Kin." In *Crisis and the Renewal of Creation,* edited by Jeffrey Golliher and William Bryant Logan, 37–40. New York: Continuum.

1998 "Stories in the Learning of Values." In *Vivitur Ingenio: Essays in Honor of Thelma Z. Levine,* 35–42. Fairfax, VA: George Mason University. Originally published in Dutch in 1964.

1999 "In Praise of Ambiguity." In *Education, Information and Transformation: Essays on Learning and Thinking,* edited by Jeffrey Kane, 133–46. NJ: Merrill-Prentice/Hall.

"Ordinary Creativity." In *Social Creativity,* vol. 1, edited by Alfonso Montuori and Ronald E. Purser, 153–71. Cresskill, NJ: Hampton Press.

2000 *Full Circles, Overlapping Lives: Culture and Generation in Transition.* New York: Random House. Paper edition by Ballantine.

2001 "Learning in Layers." In *Developing Democratic Character in the Young,* edited by Roger Soder et al., 114–25. San Francisco: Jossey-Bass.

"The Wisdom of Recognition." Paper presented at the meeting of the American Society for Cybernetics, Vancouver, May 2001. In *Cybernetics & Human Knowing* 8, no. 4 2000: 87–90.

2003 Foreword. *A Place to Stand: Essays for Educators in Troubled Times,* edited by Mark A. Clark. Ann Arbor, MI: University of Michigan Press.

"Lives of Learning." *Chronicle of Higher Education,* July 25.

Preface. *Gifts and Nation: The Obligations to Give, Receive, and Repay,* by William Dillon. New Brunswick, N.J: Transaction Publishers.

ACKNOWLEDGMENTS

As will be clear to any reader of this book, I am indebted for parts of it to many individuals and institutions that have had a part in shaping my thought over a forty-year period. The institutions are mentioned in one way or another in the chronology, but in every case there have been multiple colleagues, teachers, and students from whom I have learned. The most recent hospitality to acknowledge, however, is for part of the period when I was putting this particular manuscript together, while I was at the Radcliffe Institute of Harvard University and then at the Harvard Graduate School of Education. Every move has helped, for new ideas have grown from participation in new conversations and from living in unfamiliar places, but in many cases I have lost touch with individuals who played key roles. Many, like my parents, are no longer living, but other family members have joined that cast, my husband, who has read all of the pieces in this volume in various guises, my daughter, her husband, and their son, Cyrus, to whom the book is dedicated. It is important to remember how many people have helped, how many voices are echoed here. I had to choose between an expression of appreciation that would be very brief, as this one is, or very lengthy.

A second group has played a part in getting my words onto paper or urging me to turn to a particular topic. I need especially to acknowledge the generosity of those who have allowed me to reprint pieces originally written to be used elsewhere. These permissions are acknowledged in the notes. John Brockman, my agent since 1979, has dealt primarily with books, but every book project has spawned a series of articles or lectures. My editors at various publishing houses have urged me in different directions (and have migrated themselves from one house to another). Richard Goldsby proposed a collaboration on AIDS and others have proposed anthologies or organized conferences that allowed me to explore new territories. Often what appears here is my half of an extended conversation. This particular volume is the first I have done with Steerforth Press; it owes its origin to one of the founders of Steerforth, Alan Lelchuk, who proposed the project. I owe thanks to the people at the press and to Susan Brown, who has now copyedited three of my books for different publishers.

NOTES

Introduction: Thinking Back

1. William Blake, *Jerusalem*, ch. 3, plate 55, l. 60 (London: 1818–20).
2. Mary Catherine Bateson, *Our Own Metaphor: A Personal Account of a Conference on the Effects of Conscious Purpose on Human Adaptation* (New York: Alfred A. Knopf, 1972).
3. Mary Catherine Bateson, *With a Daughter's Eye: A Memoir of Margaret Mead and Gregory Bateson* (New York: William Morrow, 1984), 117.
4. Ibid., 186.
5. Ibid., 16.

Ghosts to Believe In

This article first appeared in the November 15, 1987, issue of *The New York Times Book Review,* and is reprinted with the permission of *The New York Times.*

Continuities in Insight and Innovation

This paper first appeared in the June 1980 issue of the *American Anthropologist* (volume 82, number 2).

1. Margaret Mead, *Coming of Age in Samoa: A Psychological Study of Primitive Youth for Western Civilization* (New York: William Morrow, 1928), 234–48.
2. Margaret Mead and Rhoda Métraux, eds. *The Study of Culture at a Distance* (Chicago: University of Chicago Press, 1953).
3. Unpublished draft material for Margaret Mead, *Blackberry Winter: My Earlier Years* (New York: William Morrow, 1972).
4. Morris Freilich, *Marginal Natives: Anthropologists at Work* (New York: Harper & Row, 1970).
5. Pertti Pelto and Gretel H. Pelto, "Ethnography: The Fieldwork Enterprise," in *Handbook of Social and Cultural Anthropology,* ed. John Honigmann (Chicago: Rand McNally, 1973).

6. Frank A. Salamone, "Epistemological Implications of Fieldwork and Their Consequences," *American Anthropologist* 81 (1979): 46–60.

7. Mary Catherine Bateson, "Insight in a Bicultural Context," *Philippine Studies* 16, no. 4 (1968): 605–21; Mary Catherine Bateson, "'The Epigenesis of Conversational Interaction': A Personal Account of Research Development," (1979) in this volume, page 92.

8. Peggy Golde, "Odyssey of Encounter," in *Women in the Field: Anthropological Experiences,* ed. Peggy Golde (Chicago: Aldine, 1970), 57–96.

9. Margaret Mead, *Letters from the Field,* 1925–1975 (New York: Harper & Row, 1977), 12.

10. Margaret Mead, "Marriage in Two Steps," *Redbook* 127, no. 3:48–49, 84, 86.

11. Margaret Mead and Dana Raphael, "Of Mothers and Mothering," *Lactation Review* 4 (1979): 1, 5–19.

12 Mead and Métraux, *Study of Culture;* Margaret Mead, *Continuities in Cultural Evolution,* The Dwight Harrington Terry Foundation Lectures on Religion in the Light of Science and Philosophy (New Haven: Yale University Press, 1964); Paul Byers and Margaret Mead, *The Small Conference: An Innovation in Communication,* Publications of the International Social Science Council 9 (The Hague: Mouton, 1968).

13. Mead and Métraux, *Study of Culture.*

14. Norman E. Whitten, Jr., and Alvin W. Wolfe, "Network Analysis," in *Handbook of Social and Cultural Anthropology.*

15. Ruth Benedict, *Patterns of Culture* (Boston: Houghton Mifflin, 1934) 21–22.

16. Margaret Mead, *Culture and Commitment: A Study of the Generation Gap* (Garden City, NY: Natural History Press/Doubleday, 1970).

17. Gregory Bateson and Margaret Mead, *Balinese Character,* Special Publications 2 (New York: New York Academy of Sciences, 1942).

"Daddy, Can a Scientist Be Wise?"

This piece was written for *About Bateson,* ed. John Brockman (New York: E. P. Dutton, 1977).

1. Gregory Bateson, *Steps to an Ecology of Mind* (New York: Chandler, 1972), 47–48.

2. Ibid., xxi.

3. Ibid., xix.

4. Ibid., 372.

5. Ibid., 140.

6. Mary Catherine Bateson, *Our Own Metaphor: A Personal Account of a Conference on the Effects of Conscious Purpose on Human Adaptation* (New York: Alfred A. Knopf, 1972), 279–80.

7. Ibid., 253–54. (Gregory's slightly different listing of key properties occurs in *Steps to an Ecology of the Mind,* page 490.)
8. G. Bateson, *Steps,* 439.
9. Ibid., 146.
10. Ibid., 444.
11. Gregory Bateson, "Ecology of Mind: The Sacred," in *Loka: A Journal from Naropa Institute,* ed. Rick Fields (New York: Doubleday, 1975), 25.
12. Henricus Denziger, ed., *Enchiridion Symbolorum: Definitionum et rationum de rebus civii et morum,* 33rd ed. (Freiberg, Germany: Herder, 1965), nos. 1606, 1639.
13. G. Bateson, *Steps,* 462.
14. This term was developed by Margaret Mead during the Adolescent Study directed by Caroline Zachary in 1934–35.
15. G. Bateson, *Steps,* 48.
16. Archibald MacLeish, "Ars Poetica," in *Modern American and Modern British Poetry,* ed. Louis Untermeyer (New York: Harcourt, Brace, 1955), 272.

The Wisdom of Recognition

An abridged version of this talk was published in 2001 in *The Journal of Cybernetics and Human Knowing* (vol. 8, no. 4), and is reprinted with the permission of the publisher.

1. Mary Catherine Bateson, *With a Daughter's Eye: A Memoir of Margaret Mead and Gregory Bateson* (New York: William Morrow, 1984), 185.
2. William Bateson to Gregory Bateson, April 23, 1922, in David Lipset, *Gregory Bateson: The Legacy of a Scientist* (Englewood Cliffs, NJ: Prentice-Hall, 1980), 96.
3. Margaret Mead, *Blackberry Winter: My Earlier Years* (New York: William Morrow, 1972), 116–17.
4. Margaret Mead, *And Keep Your Powder Dry: An Anthropologist Looks at America* (New York: William Morrow, 1942), 20.
5. See Mary Catherine Bateson, *Our Own Metaphor: A Personal Account of a Conference on the Effects of Conscious Purpose on Human Adaptation* (New York: Alfred A. Knopf, 1972).
6. Gregory Bateson, "The Moral and Aesthetic Structure of Human Adaptation," in *Sacred Unity: Further Steps to an Ecology of the Mind,* ed. Rodney Donaldson (New York: HarperCollins, 1991), 253–57.
7. Ibid., 225.
8. Gregory Bateson and Mary Catherine Bateson, *Angels Fear: Towards an Epistemology of the Sacred* (New York: Macmillan, 1987), 49.
9. Ibid., 73.
10. Angelica Nuzzo "Constructing the World of Experience: The 'Enigma' of Beauty and Life" (draft, 2001).
11. Bateson, *Our Own Metaphor,* 304.

12. Margaret Mead, *Continuities in Cultural Evolution* (New Haven: Yale University Press, 1964), 299–302.

13. Richard J. Herrnstein and Charles Murray, *The Bell Curve: Intelligence and Class Structure in American Life* (New York: Free Press, 1994).

14. Derek Freeman, *Margaret Mead and Samoa: The Making and Unmaking of an Anthropological Myth* (Cambridge, MA: Harvard University Press, 1983); and Freeman, *The Fateful Hoaxing of Margaret Mead: A Historical Analysis of Her Samoan Research* (Boulder, CO: Westview Press, 1998).

Six Days of Dying

This article first appeared in the Winter 1980 issue of *The CoEvolution Quarterly,* and is reprinted with the permission of the publisher.

Composing a Life Story

This essay first appeared in *Sacred Stories: A Celebration of the Power of Stories to Transform and Heal.*

You Will Know the Future When You Get There

This talk was published in the Fall-Winter 1996–97 *Alumnae Bulletin* of the Santa Catalina School and is reprinted with the permission of the school.

1. Marjorie Shostak, *Nisa: The Life and Words of a !Kung Woman* (New York: Vintage Books, 1983).

"The Epigenesis of Conversational Interaction"

This essay appeared in *Before Speech: The Beginning of Interpersonal Communication,* ed. Margaret Bullowa (Cambridge: Cambridge University Press, 1979), and is reprinted here with the permission of Cambridge University Press. This research was conducted at the Research Laboratory of Electronics at the Massachusetts Institute of Technology and supported by the National Institutes of Health (Grant 2 RO1 NB-04322). Preliminary versions of parts of the research were reported in M. C. Bateson 1971 and presented at the 1971 meetings of the Society for Research in Child Development. A complete summary of its empirical aspects may be found in Bateson 1975b.

1. A. E. Scheflen, *The Stream and Structure of Conversational Behavior* (Bloomington: University of Indiana Press, 1972); R. L. Birdwhistell, *Kinesics and Context: Essays on Body Motion Communication* (Philadelphia: University of Pennsylvania Press, 1970); and Mary

Catherine Bateson, *Structural Continuity in Poetry: A Linguistic Study of Five Early Arabic Odes* (Paris: Ecole des Hautes Etudes, 1970).

2. R. E. Pittenger, C. F. Hickett, and J. J. Denahy, *The First Five Minutes: A Sample of Microscopic Interview Analysis* (Ithaca, NY: P. Martineau, 1960); Birdwhistell, *Kinesics and Context;* and N. E. McQuown, Gregory Bateson, R. L. Birdwhistell, H. W. Brosin, and C. F. Hockett, *The Natural History of an Interview,* Microfilm Collection of Manuscripts in Cultural Anthropology, ser. 15, nos. 95–98 (Chicago: University of Chicago Library, 1971).

3. Mary Catherine Bateson, "The Interpersonal Context of Infant Vocalization," *Quarterly Progress Report of the Research Laboratory of Electronics,* 100 (1971): 170–76. (Cambridge, MA: Massachusetts Institute of Technology); and Mary Catherine Bateson, "Mother-Infant Exchanges: The Epigenesis of Conversational Interaction" in *Developmental Psycholinguistics and Communication Disorders,* ed. Doris Aaronson and R. W. Rieber, Annals of the New York Academy of Sciences 263 (1975): 101–13.

4. Konrad Lorenz, *Studies in Animal and Human Behavior,* vols. 1 and 2, trans. Robert Martin (Cambridge, MA: Harvard University Press, 1970–71).

5. Noam Chomsky, review of *Verbal Behavior* by B. F. Skinner, *Language* 35 (1959): 26–58; reprinted in *The Structure of Language: Readings in the Philosophy of Language,* ed. J. A. Fodor and J. J. Katz (Englewood Cliffs, NJ: Prentice-Hall, 1964), 547–78.

6. Noam Chomsky, "The Formal Nature of Language," in *Biological Foundations of Language,* ed. Eric H. Lenneberg, (New York: John Wiley, 1967), 397–442.

7. Gregory Bateson, *Steps to an Ecology of Mind* (San Francisco: Chandler, 1972), 306.

8. Lorenz, *Studies,* xv.

9. Margaret Bullowa, "Infants as Conversational Partners," in *The Development of Conversation and Discourse,* ed. Terry Myers (Edinburgh: Edinburgh University Press, 1979).

10. J. Jaffe, D. N. Stern, and J. C. Peery, "'Conversational' Coupling of Gaze Behavior in Prelinguistic Human Development," *Journal of Psycholinguistic Research* 2 (1973): 321–29.

11. C. F. Hockett, "The Origin of Speech," *Scientific American* 203, no. 3 (1960): 87–97.

12. Birdwhistell, *Kinesics and Context.*

13. W. S. Condon, "Neonatal Entrainment and Enculturation," in *Before Speech,* ed. Margaret Bullowa (Cambridge: Cambridge University Press, 1979), 131–48.

14. P. H. Wolff, "The Causes, Controls and Organization of Behavior in the Neonate," *Psychological Issues* 5 (1966): 1–99 (monograph).

15. Mary Catherine Bateson, "Ritualization: A Study in Texture and Texture Change," in *Religious Movements in Contemporary America,* ed. Irving Zaretsky and Mark P. Leone (Princeton: Princeton University Press, 1975), 150–65.

16. Further references on the structure of glossolalia may be found in ibid. and in other papers in the same volume.

17. Mary Catherine Bateson, "Linguistics in the Semiotic Frame," *Linguistics* 39 (1968): 5–17; Bateson, "Linguistic Models in the Study of Joint Performances," in *Linguistics and Anthropology: In Honor of C. F. Voegelin,* ed. M. Dale Kinkade, K. L. Hale, and Oswald Werner (Lisse, The Netherlands: Peter de Ridder Press, 1975), 53–66; and Dell Hymes, "Towards Ethnographies of Communication," in *The Ethnography of Communication,* ed. John Gumperz and Dell Hymes (American Anthropologist Special Publication 66, no. 6, pt. 2, 1–34).

Holding Up the Sky Together

This article first appeared in the May–June 1995 issue of *Civilization.*

Caring for Children, Caring for the Earth

This homily was published in *Cathedral,* the newsletter of the Cathedral of St. John the Divine, New York, in fall 1979 and appeared in abridged form in the March 31, 1980, issue of *Christianity and Crisis* (volume 40, number 5). It is reprinted with the permission of the Cathedral.

"A Spade with Which to Dig"

This article first appeared in the summer–fall 1995 issue of the *Dalhousie Review,* and is reprinted with the permission of the publisher.

The Unending Threshold

1. Arnold van Gennep, *The Rites of Passage,* trans. Monika B. Vizedom and Gabrielle L. Caffee (Chicago: University of Chicago Press, 1960).

2. Jerome D. Frank, *Persuasion and Healing: A Comparative Study of Psychotherapy* (Baltimore: Johns Hopkins University Press, 1961).

3. Gregory Bateson, *Steps to an Ecology of Mind* (New York: Chandler, 1972) 279–308.

4. Jack Mezirow, *Education for Perspective Transformation: Women's Re-entry Programs in Community Colleges* (New York: Center for Adult Education, Teacher's College, Columbia University, 1978).

5. van Gennep, *Rites of Passage.*
6. Victor Turner, *The Forest of Symbols: Aspects of Ndembu Ritual* (Ithaca, NY: Cornell University Press, 1967).
7. Mary Catherine Bateson, *Peripheral Visions: Learning Along the Way* (New York: HarperCollins, 1994).
8. Jack Mezirow, Gordon G. Darkenwald, and Alan B. Knox, *Last Gamble on Education: Dynamics of Adult Basic Education* (Washington, DC: Adult Education Association of the U.S.A., 1976).
9. For changes in longevity and fertility, see *National Vital Statistics Reports,* vol 52 (13), February 11, 2004, and vol 51 (12), August 4, 2003; both are available at www.cdc.gov/nchs.
10. Mezirow, Darkenwald, and Knox, *Last Gamble.*
11. Carnegie Commission on Higher Education, *Less Time, More Options: Education Beyond the High School, A Special Report and Recommendations* (New York: McGraw-Hill, 1971).
12. Mezirow, Darkenwald, and Knox, *Last Gamble.*
13. Ibid.
14. Etienne Bourgeois, Chris Duke, Jean-Luc Guyot, and Barbara Merrill, *The Adult University* (London: Society for Research into Higher Education and Open University Press, 1999).

Commitment as a Moving Target

A portion of this essay appeared in an op-ed piece for the *San Francisco Chronicle* on February 11, 2001, under the title "Rethinking Fidelity."

The Atrium

1. Mary Catherine Bateson, *Full Circles, Overlapping Lives: Culture and Generation in Transition* (New York: Random House, 2000), 100.

"An Oak Tree in Full Leaf"

This excerpt first appeared in Chapter 2 of Mary Catherine Bateson *Full Circles, Overlapping Lives: Culture and Generation in Transition* (New York: Random House, 2000), and is reprinted with the permission of the publisher.

1. Margaret Mead, *Blackberry Winter* (New York: William Morrow, 1974).

"A Riddle of Two Worlds"

This essay first appeared in the Summer 1966 issue of *Daedalus,* Journal of the American Academy of Arts and Sciences in the issue entitled "Tradition and

Change," volume 95, number 3, and is reprinted with the permission of *Daedalus*. The poetry quoted here was translated from the Hebrew text of *All the Poems of H. N. Bialik* (Tel-Aviv: Dvir Company, 1950) for this study. I should like to acknowledge the help of Rabbi Ben-Zion Gold, who was kind enough to go over the translations for me when a previous article, much of which has been incorporated into this one, was published in *Mosaic* 3, no. 2 (Spring 1962).

Into the Trees

This essay was written for *Sacred Trusts,* edited by Michael Katakis (San Francisco: Mercury House, 1993), and is reprinted with the permission of the publisher (www.mercuryhouse.org).

1. Mary Catherine Bateson, *Our Own Metaphor: A Personal Account of a Conference on Conscious Purpose and Human Adaptation* (New York: Alfred A. Knopf, 1972), 90.

Introduction to Part III

1. Donald W. Winnicott, *Mother and Child: A Primer of First Relationships* (New York: Basic Books, 1957).
2. Many writers use the terms *relativity* and *relativism* almost interchangeably, depending on adjectives to draw the contrasts. But see Melvin Herskovits, *Cultural Relativism: Perspectives in Cultural Pluralism* (New York: Vintage Books, 1973), and Elvin Hatch, *Culture and Morality: The Relativity of Values in Anthropology* (New York: Columbia University Press, 1983).

"This Figure of Tinsel"

This essay first appeared in the Summer 1979 issue of *Daedalus,* Journal of the American Academy of Arts and Sciences, in the issue entitled "Hypocrisy, Illusion, and Evasion," volume 108, number 3), and is reprinted with the permission of *Daedalus*.

1. The only joint publication of the research group was an article, "Ṣafā-yi Bāṭin: A Study of the Interrelations of a Set of Iranian Ideal Character Types," by M. C. Bateson, J. W. Clinton, J. B. M. Kassarjian, Hasah Safavi, and Mehdi Soraya, in *Psychological Dimensions of Near Eastern Studies,* ed. L. Carl Brown and Norman Itzkowitz (Princeton, NJ: Darwin Press, 1977), 257–74. I would like to acknowledge the contributions of this group to this article as well as to my other papers and publications on Iranian national character without, however, holding them responsible for the errors.
2. See Margaret Mead and Martha Wolfenstein, eds., *Childhood in*

Contemporary Cultures (Chicago: University of Chicago Press, 1955).

3. This negative stereotype occurs in Western writing also, as argued by Ali Banuazizi in "Iranian National Character: A Critique of Some Western Perspectives," in *Psychological Dimensions,* 210–39. However, Western observers have sometimes regarded this stereotype as true, whereas here it is presented as a stylized area of cultural concern. See also Marvin Zonis, *The Political Elite of Iran* (Princeton: Princeton University Press, 1971).

5. "The marriage of the daughter of Qoreysh."

Learning to Learn and Knowing What You Know
South Africa 1991

This essay is based on a transcript of a talk I gave at a June 1991 conference sponsored by the Centre for Innovative Leadership in Rivonia, South America, and is published with the permission of the centre.

1. Chris Argyris, "Teaching Smart People How to Learn," Harvard Business Review, May 1991; *Harvard Business Review, On Point Enhanced Edition,* no. 4304 (February 1, 2000).

2. Mary Catherine Bateson, "Enfolded Activity and the Concept of Occupation," in *Occupational Science: The Evolving Discipline,* ed. Ruth Zemke and Florence Clark (Philadelphia: F. A. Davis, 1996), 5–12.

Compromise and the Rhetoric of Good and Evil

"Compromise and the Rhetoric of Good and Evil" in *The Social Dynamics of Peace and Conflict: Culture in International Security,* ed. Robert A. Rubinstein and Mary L. Foster. Boulder, CO: Westview Press, 1988, 35–46, and is reprinted with the permission of the editors.

1. Mary Catherine Bateson, *With a Daughter's Eye: A Memoir of Margaret Mead and Gregory Bateson* (New York: William Morrow, 1984).

2. Margaret Mead and Rhoda Métraux, eds. *The Study of Culture at a Distance* (Chicago: University of Chicago Press, 1953).

3. Ruth Benedict, *Patterns of Culture* (Boston: Houghton Mifflin, 1934); and "Psychological Types in the Cultures of the Southwest," *Proceedings of the 23rd International Congress of Americanists,* September, 1928 (New York [reprint, Lancaster, PA: The Science Press Printing Co., 1930]) 572–81. Margaret Mead, *Coming of Age in Samoa: A Psychological Study of Primitive Youth for Western Civilization* (New York: William Morrow, 1928); and *Social Organization of Manua,* Bulletin 76 (Honolulu: Bernice P. Bishop Museum, 1930).

4. Margaret Mead, *Sex and Temperament in Three Primitive Societies* (New York: William Morrow, 1935); Gregory Bateson, *Naven* (Cambridge: Cambridge University Press, 1936).

5. Ruth Benedict, *The Chrysanthemum and the Sword: Patterns of Japanese*

Culture (Boston: Houghton Mifflin, 1946).

6. Derek Freeman, *Margaret Mead and Samoa: The Making and Unmaking of an Anthropological Myth* (Cambridge, MA: Harvard University Press, 1983).

7. These mechanisms are described in a more modern mode in Bradd Shore, *Sala'ilua: A Samoan Mystery* (New York: Columbia University Press, 1982).

8. Noam Chomsky, *Syntactic Structures* (The Hague: Mouton, 1957).

9. Mary Catherine Bateson, J. W. Clinton, J. B. M. Kassarjian, Hasan Safavi, and Mehdi Soraya, "Safā-yi Bāṭin: A Study of a Set of Iranian Ideal Character Types," in *Psychological Dimensions of Near Eastern Studies,* ed. L. Carl Brown and Norman Itzkowitz (Princeton, NJ: Darwin Press, 1977), 257–74.

10. Ibid., 271.

Toward an Ambiguous World Order

This essay first appeared in *The Constitutional Foundations of World Peace,* edited by Richard A. Falk, Robert C. Johansen, and Samuel S. Kim (Albany: State University of New York Press), and is used by permission of the publisher.

1. Although *civilization* is a somewhat problematic term, it was proposed at the conference for which the ideas in this paper were first developed, "The Coming Global Civilization," sponsored by the World Order Models Project and the Soviet Political Science Association, Moscow, October 10–16, 1988, and published as *Contending Sovereignties: Redefining Political Community,* ed. R. B. J. Walker and Saul H. Mendlovitz (Boulder, CO: Lynne Rienner, 1990). See my paper in that volume, "Beyond Sovereignty: An Emerging Global Civilization," 196–220, for a further discussion of the use of the term *civilization* in this context. Portions of this essay are drawn from that earlier publication.

2. John W. Allen (1928), *A History of Political Thought in the Sixteenth Century* (London: Methuen, 1957).

Change in Islam: The Status of Women

1. Stewart Brand, *How Buildings Learn: What Happens after They're Built* (New York: Viking Penguin, 1994).

2. Quoted in Mary Daly, *Beyond God the Father: Towards a Philosophy of Women's Liberation* (Boston: Beacon Press, 1973).

3. Qasim Amin, *The Emancipation of Woman* (originally published as *Tahrir al-Mar'ah,* 1899; Misr: Dar al-Ma'arif, 1970), 31.

Learning in Layers

This essay first appeared in *Developing Democratic Character in the Young,* edited by Roger Soder *et al.* (San Francisco: Jossey-Bass, 2001), and is used by permission of John Wiley & Sons, Inc.

1. Alfred North Whitehead and Bertrand Russell, *Principia Mathematica,* 2nd ed. (Cambridge: Cambridge University Press, 1925).
2. Robert Kegan, *In over Our Heads: The Mental Demands of Modern Life* (Cambridge, MA: Harvard University Press, 1994).
3. Daniel Lerner, *The Passing of Traditional Society: Modernizing the Middle East* (Glencoe, IL: Free Press, 1958).
4. Adrienne Kaufmann, "The Pro-choice/Pro-life Conflict: An Exploratory Study to Understand the Nature of the Conflict and to Develop Constructive Conflict Intervention Designs" (doctoral dissertation, George Mason University, 1999).
5. Gregory Bateson, "Naven: Epilogue 1958," in Gregory Bateson, *A Sacred Unity: Further Steps to an Ecology of Mind,* ed. Rodney E. Donaldson (New York: HarperCollins, 1991), 53–54.

The Lessons of 9/11

This unpublished essay incorporates adaptations of two short pieces published in *Whole Earth:* "Trust & Security: Can the Commons Exist without Common Sense and Common Decency?" (Fall 1998, p 14) and "Compassion Is Key" (Winter 2001), as well as an adaptation of a lecture given at the University of Virginia in fall 2001.

1. J. Y. Lettvin, H. R. Maturana, W. S. McCulloch, and Walter Pitts, "What the Frog's Eye Tells the Frog's Brain," *Proceedings of the Institute of Radio Engineers,* 47 (New York: Institute of Radio Engineers, 1959): 1940–52.

Democracy, Ecology, and Participation

This essay was written for *Democracy, Education, and the Schools,* edited by Roger Soder (San Francisco: Jossey-Bass, 1996), and is used by permission of John Wiley & Sons, Inc..

1. Mary Catherine Bateson, *Our Own Metaphor: A Personal Account of a Conference on Conscious Purpose and Human Adaptation* (New York: Alfred A.Knopf, 1972).
2. Gregory Bateson, *Mind and Nature: A Necessary Unity* (New York: E. P. Dutton, 1979).
3. Mary Catherine Bateson, *With a Daughter's Eye: A Memoir of Margaret Mead and Gregory Bateson* (New York: William Morrow, 1984; New York: HarperPerennial, 1994).

4. James E. Lovelock, *Gaia: A New Look at Life on Earth* (Oxford: Oxford University Press, 1979).
5. Heinz von Foerster, *Observing Systems* (Salinas, CA: Intersystems, 1982).
6. Mary Catherine Bateson, *Our Own Metaphor*, 6–7.
7. Arthur O. Lovejoy, *The Great Chain of Being: A Study of the History of an Idea* (Cambridge, MA: Harvard University Press, 1936).
8. Alan Sanford, "Tilting at 'Secular Humanism,'" *Time,* July 28, 1986, 68.
9. C. A. Bowers, *Education, Cultural Myths, and the Ecological Crisis: Toward Deep Changes* (Albany: State University of New York Press, 1993).
10. Mary Catherine Bateson, *Peripheral Visions: Learning Along the Way* (New York: HarperCollins, 1994).
11. Ken Keniston, *Youth and Dissent: The Rise of a New Opposition* (New York: Harcourt, Brace, Jovanovich, 1971).
12. Richard Farson, *Birthrights* (New York: Macmillan, 1974).
13. National Center for Atmospheric Research, Inherit the Earth: An Intergenerational Symposium on the Environment, Boulder, CO, July 14–17, 1993.

On the Naturalness of Things

This essay was first published in 1995 in *How Things Are: A Science Tool-kit for the Mind,* edited by John Brockman and Katinka Matson (New York: William Morrow).

Visions of Transcendence

1. Mary Catherine Bateson, *Our Own Metaphor: A Personal Account of a Conference on Conscious Purpose and Human Adaptation* (New York: Alfred A. Knopf, 1972).
2. Gregory Bateson and Mary Catherine Bateson, *Angels Fear: Towards an Epistemology of the Sacred* (New York: Macmillan, 1987), 142–43.
3. Bateson, *Metaphor.*
4. C. S. Lewis, *The Surging of Love: A Study in Medieval Tradition* (Oxford: Oxford University Press, 1936); and Arthur O. Lovejoy, *The Great Chain of Being: A Study of the History of an Idea* (1936; New York: Harper, 1960).
5. Max Weber, *The Protestant Ethic and the Spirit of Capitalism* (1904–5; London: Unwin, 1930); and James Peacock and A. T. Kirsch, *The Human Direction* (1970; New York: Appleton-Century-Crofts, 1973).
6. François Wendel, *Calvin: The Origins and Development of His Religious Thought,* trans. Philip Mairet (1950; London: William Collins Sons, 1963).
7. David McClelland, *The Achieving Society* (New York: Free Press, 1967).
8. John Alden Williams, ed. *Islam* (New York: George Braziller, 1961).

Multiple Kinds of Knowledge

This piece was originally published in *Diversity and Design: Studying the Culture and the Individual,* Proceedings from the Fourth Qualitative Research in Education Conference, edited by Mary Jo McGee-Brown (Athens, GA: Georgia Center for Continuing Education, 1991).

In Praise of Ambiguity

This piece was first published in 1998 in *Education, Information, and Transformation: Essays on Learning and Thinking,* edited by Jeffrey Kane (Columbus, OH: Prentice Hall), and is used with the permission of the publisher.

1. George Meredith, *Modern Love* (London: Campbell, Thompson, and McLauflin, 1862), l. 50.
2. Mary Catherine Bateson, *Peripheral Visions: Learning Along the Way* (New York: HarperCollins, 1994).
3. Mary Catherine Bateson, "Mother-Infant Exchanges: The Epigenesis of Conversational Interaction," in *Developmental Psycholinguistics and Communication Disorders,* ed. Doris Aaronson and R. W. Rieber, Annals of the New York Academy of Sciences 263 (1975), 101–13.
4. Gregory Bateson, "Redundancy and Coding," in G. Bateson, *Steps to an Ecology of Mind* (San Francisco: Chandler, 1972), 417–32; and T. A. Sebeok, "Coding in the Evolution of Signaling Behavior," *Behavioral Science* 7 (1962): 430–42.
5. H. A. Simon, *Sciences of the Artificial* (Cambridge, MA: MIT Press, 1969); and H. A. Simon and L. Siklossy, eds., *Representation and Meaning: Experiments with Information Processing Systems* (Upper Saddle River, NJ: Prentice-Hall, 1972).
6. Mary Catherine Bateson, "Toward an Ambiguous World Order," in this volume, page 233.
7. Karl Buhler, *Sprachtheorie* (Jena, Germany: Fischer, 1934); and Sebeok, "Coding."
8. Lewis Thomas, *Lives of a Cell: Notes of a Biology Watcher* (Toronto: Bantam Books, 1974), 111, cited by Huston Smith in *Excluded Knowledge: Beyond the Western Mind-set* (Wheaton, IL: Theosophical Publications, 1989), 186–89.
9. Alliance of Artists' Communities, *American Creativity at Risk: Restoring Creativity as a Priority in Public Policy, Cultural Philanthropy, and Education.* Report on a symposium held November 8–10, 1996.

Purpose, Gender, and Evolution

This essay was first published in 1993 in *Evolutionary Ethics,* Proceedings of the 1990 Field Museum Spring Systematics Symposium, edited by Matthew Nitecki (Albany, NY: State University of New York Press) and is used by permission of the publisher.

1. C. H. Waddington, *The Ethical Animal* (New York: Atheneum, 1961).
2. Mary Catherine Bateson and Richard Goldsby, *Thinking AIDS* (Reading, MA: Addison-Wesley, 1988); see excerpts in this volume, page 366.
3. Joseph F. Fletcher, *Situation Ethics: The New Morality* (Philadelphia: Westminster Press, 1966).
4. Mary Catherine Bateson, *Our Own Metaphor: A Personal Account of a Conference on Conscious Purpose and Human Adaptation* (New York: Alfred A. Knopf, 1972).
5. Gregory Bateson in ibid., 13–16.
6. Gregory Bateson and Mary Catherine Bateson, *Angels Fear: Towards an Epistemology of the Sacred* (New York: Macmillan, 1987).
7. See Richard Lee, *The !Kung San : Men, Women, and Work in a Foraging Society* (Cambridge: Cambridge University Press, 1979); for gender differences, see Marjorie Shostak, *Nisa: The Life and Words of a !Kung Woman* (Cambridge, MA: Harvard University Press, 1981).
8. Carol Gilligan, *In a Different Voice: Psychological Theory and Women's Development* (Cambridge, MA: Harvard University Press, 1982).
9. Mary Catherine Bateson, *Composing a Life* (New York: Atlantic Monthly Press, 1989).

Thinking AIDS

These excerpts first appeared in Mary Catherine Bateson and Richard Goldsby *Thinking AIDS* (Reading, MA: Addison-Wesley, 1988).

INDEX

A Note for Users of This Index

This is primarily a thematic index. Thus, under the entry for "couples" you will find an essay on marriage and divorce referenced in its entirety, although the word does not appear on every page. This kind of entry is sometimes conventionally indicated by the word "passim." Some references to couples elsewhere may not be included, while others are — not because they are substantive but to underline connections and associations. Some themes are pervasive. The theme of learning, for instance, runs through the entire volume, but is indexed only in sections where it is referred to in some specific way. The index does include the kinds of items that conventionally appear in indexes, especially proper names, but sparingly. Proper names mentioned only in passing are not included, and unless the names appear somewhere in full, they are grouped under more general rubrics. Titles and names of institutions mentioned in the chronology or in my bibliography are only indexed if they are also mentioned in the text. Only authors are indexed for the notes. Memories are quirky, however, so I have included some items that would normally not be included, because I suspect they may offer a mnemonic clue that sticks in the mind. My sister, Nora Bateson, put a bagel in our father's coffin, referring to a quip of his about reincarnation. So you will find "bagel" in the index, just in case you are looking for that particular story.